The First 1(

by

Martin Paul Roche

www.martinpaulroche.com

For Jan, who puts up with me and I still can't figure why.
For the late Geoffrey Holme who taught me so much about theatre without either of us realising it.
For Brian Seymour, whose passion, positivity and kindness inspired me to stick at it 20 years ago.
For David Waters of Stagescripts Ltd for his confidence, friendship and wine.
And last but my no means least, for Mum and Dad ... which needs no further explanation.

Contents

		Pages	Cast	Type
1.	*Where is the life?	3 – 62	7m, 3f	2 act comedy
2.	*Soul Without End	63 – 105	6m, 2f	2 act drama
3.	*Is there anybody there?	106 – 152	3f	2 act dark comedy
4.	*The King's Orphan	153 – 199	2m, 2f	2 act drama
5.	Changing #1	200 – 226	3f	1 act comedy
6.	Changing #2	227 – 253	3m	1 act comedy
7.	Changing #3	254 – 265	1m, 1f	1 act comedy
8.	Last Bus to Whitby	266 – 276	1m	1 act monologue
9.	Gymnopédies	277 – 320	3f	2 act drama
10.	Ancient & Modern	321 – 334	1f	1 act monologue

Also available from the same writer are the musical play *'To Be Frank'* and the full stage musical, *'Witchfinder'* co-written with Ian Crabtree, details of which may be obtained from their publisher, Stagescripts Ltd.

© **Martin Paul Roche, 2020. All Rights Reserved**

The scripts within this book may not be copied or transcribed by any means electronic, optical or mechanical without the prior permission of the copyright owner or their agent. Unauthorised alterations to the plot, to the characters, or to the dialogue, are strictly prohibited.

These plays are works of fiction. The characters are entirely the product of the authors' imagination and any resemblance to actual persons, living or dead, is entirely coincidental. In the case of *'The King's Orphan'*, the nature of this is fully explained within the notes..

This collection is fully protected under the international laws of copyright which are enacted in the UK as the Copyright, Designs and Patents Act 1988. Martin Paul Roche hereby asserts his right to be identified as the intellectual owner of the work in accordance with the above Act.

While every precaution has been taken in the preparation of this collection, the author assumes no responsibility for errors or omissions, or for damages resulting from the use of the material contained herein.

At time of going to print, the published works (as indicated above*) and worldwide rights are managed by: Stagescripts Ltd, Lantern House, 84 Littlehaven Lane, Horsham, West Sussex, RH12 4JB, UK.

> Telephone: 0345 686 0611
> International: +44 700 581 0581
> sales@stagescripts.com
> www. stagescripts.com
> Stagescripts Ltd
> Registered in England and Wales No. 06155216

ROYALTY FEES

A royalty fee is payable every time any of these works are performed in front of an audience irrespective of whether that audience pays for attending or not. Producing Organisations MUST obtain a 'Licence To Perform' from Stagescripts Ltd* or the writer prior to starting rehearsals. Producing Organisations are prohibited from making video recordings of rehearsals or performances without the prior permission of Stagescripts Ltd or their agent. NOTE : The act of preparing material in quantities sufficient to rehearse a performance of any of these works will be taken as intent to stage such a performance should litigation be necessary in the event of non-payment of Royalty Fees later found to be due.

ISBN: 978-1-5272-6787-9

Enquiries concerning the remaining works or any other matters should be directed to the author by visiting: **www.martinpaulroche.com** or emailing **enquiries@martinpaulroche.com**.

'Where is the life?'

Synopsis

The Beeches is a residential home for retired gentlemen of the stage. It is run by Julie, the officious owner who is married to Tony, a letch who is nice but a little dim. Tom, Colin, Alan and Don are residents who have spent their lives in theatre and equally, working together. Despite their ups and downs they have created their own family in The Beeches to replace the families they no longer seem to be a part of.

They have come from a bygone world and have now created a new world in The Beeches which is bound together by images, reflections, memories, longings of the past but equally, yearnings for a future.

Tom is a camp old hoofer who could not be more affected. Alan is a neurotic and frustrated gay man who will not speak of his sexuality. Don is everybody's granddad, warm caring and gentle.

Colin is, well, Colin. He is angry, acerbic, cutting and sarcastic: a past master in schadenfreude. He is the old queen of this castle and resents everything and everybody for reasons that even he no longer understands. His time is spent finding new prey and when Kelly, the new care assistant arrives, he focuses in on her straight away with resentment, anger and jealousy and all because she has the things he can no longer have: youth... and time.

Despite the challenges created by them, Kelly soon comes to appreciate that the men have become part of a family of their own making and moreover, she finds in them a family she has never really known. And in doing so she sheds light into their forgotten world – a world where relatives are just a word and true family is four old men whose lives are inextricably bound together and in time, a young girl who realises that some jobs have the facility to teach you more than you think. She may have years of her life left, but she gives them a priceless gift... by helping them come to terms with the life in their remaining years.

Characters (7m, 3f)

Kelly   Newly appointed Care Assistant at The Beeches. Her age depends on how the director wants to play it. Innocence/naivety is not necessarily a function of age so it is reasonable for her to be as young as 20 and as old as 40. What clearly matters above all is characterisation, sincerity and believability. She is naïve yet street hardened. Her dress and demeanour indicate a rawness which is not necessarily 'common' but more 'modern' and therefore at odds with the residents of The Beeches. She is painfully honest, easily affected by emotions and a complete stranger to the truth of old age and bereavement. She has a passion which emphasises her rawness. Accent is northern (she is from Oldham after all). Early script notes mention outrageous makeup and clothes at the interview. Although subsequently toned down, this should not altogether disappear until her reappearance in the final scene. The best description of her is early on in the script notes: an innocent abroad.

Julie   40/50. The manager of The Beeches. Married to Tony. A larger woman. Officious, dominant. Smart in appearance and business like in manner. She despairs at times of the residents and their attitudes/behaviour but in the main does not 'get' them. She is dismissive of her husband, Tony, and there is no love/affection/respect ever displayed towards him. At times, the story displays her being ill at ease with the residents or anything 'touchy – feely'. There are also times when she clearly demonstrates an inability to deal with conflict: she is not as hard as she makes out.

Characters *(cont'd)*

Mary 30/40 or even slightly older. Don's daughter and married to Kevin. Very plain, cold, dismissive, disrespectful to her father. Neutral local accent. She clearly has no time for him and wants to spend as little time with him as possible. The reasons for this only become clear after his death at the wake. She is an angry and bitter woman and very pointed in her delivery.

Colin 60/70. Resident. Retired actor. Gay, but the character is not fully explored in that respect. Well spoken, articulate. He is cold, a loner but craves company. The notes on the piece sum him up: Colin is Colin. He is angry, acerbic, condescending, aloof, cutting and sarcastic. He resents everything and everybody but when with his lifelong friends (the other residents) he sometimes mellows, although at any time he can treat them badly. He enjoys his status as the 'matriarch'. His bitterness is vented at Kelly and her like and he revels in demeaning her at every opportunity. A complex and challenging character who eventually respects Kelly and what she represents, revealing his demons and how they have hidden humanity.

Tom 60/70. An affected voice/accent, but well spoken. Resident. Retired actor. Tom is a camp old theatre luvvie who could not be more affected. He hits the bell of many theatre stereotypes but at his core is a warm, genuine, funny, full-of-life, fiercely loyal, affectionate man. He is the great rescuer of the piece and of the characters in it. He is sensitive but can pack a punch when challenged, using his humour and sexuality to good effect. He needs to be a man of mannerisms, of poses, of facial expressions. However, he is not a clown and this is not a pantomime. There is a need for boundaries in his playing which prevent it from being over the top and constantly playing for the laugh. An intelligent and sensitive characterisation is essential.

Don 60/70. Resident. Retired stage manager. Father to Mary. Dies halfway through Act 2. Articulate and gently spoken. He is a gentleman; warm, caring, intelligent, open, uncomplicated, understanding, thoughtful, honest, respectful, fair. He is a granddad figure who provides the normality to this group, the grounding for them.

Alan 60/70. Resident. Retired actor. Well spoken. A complex character. There is discussion about his sexuality but it is never actually demonstrated; but the fallout is evidenced. He is at times nervous, insular, vulnerable but in Act 1 he is clearly part of the family and the spirit of its unique humour and attitudes – its pack mentality! In Act 2 his age and condition become apparent, some of which is illustrated by what other characters initially say. Tom in particular is very protective of him. He dramatically 'melts down' in Act 2 due to age related dementia which is a demanding ask of the actor in such a relatively short sequence.

Gordon 50/70. Gardener, maintenance, odd job man at The Beeches. He is very hard of hearing and most of the time, he struggles to articulate anything. When he does say something, it counts! He is very much the victim of circumstance. In the first act in particular, the residents use him as a foil for their humour. He begins very ill at ease with them, around them. But circumstances bring him into the fold as by default, he becomes part of the family. A true character role. Achieves so much by doing very little. Animated, understated, naturally funny without ever trying.

Characters *(cont'd)*

Tony — 40/50. Similar in age to Julie, his wife. Co-owner of The Beeches. Very well spoken, nice but dim type. A little far back so to speak. Always derided by everybody as they appear to see him as a non-entity in the set up and somebody to insult. Julie in particular is very demeaning towards him; there is certainly no hint of affection. He is clearly a supporting role to the piece so therefore needs to be a strong 'off the page' actor who can hold his own outside of delivering dialogue and maintain a presence when not the focus of attention.

Kevin — 30/40, but similar in age to Mary. Husband of Mary, son-in-law to Don. Neutral local accent. Boorish, ignorant, uninterested, rude, ill mannered. A man with a bad attitude who has no respect for anybody, especially Don and then the other residents. He is not difficult to dislike.

Setting

The Beeches Residential home, in present day Northern England.

Scenes

Act One

- Scene 1: a late autumn morning, before 8am
- Scene 2: the following day
- Scene 3: continuation from Scene 2
- Scene 4: continuation from Scene 3
- Scene 5: a couple of days later
- Scene 6: continuation from Scene 5
- Scene 7: Sunday

Act Two

- Scene 1: one month later
- Scene 2: the following day
- Scene 3: continuation from Scene 2
- Scene 4: later the same day
- Scene 5: some weeks later
- Scene 6: a week later
- Scene 7: eighteen months later

Direction/Production Notes

The piece is set in the present day and it is intended to be set in the north of England, but this is left open ended for directorial ease. Although the script is (intended?!) to be at times funny, there are times when it is equalled by tragedy, irony, anger, bitterness, tenderness. With all such pieces of theatre, I feel the last thing any of the characters should be doing is playing for the joke, labouring 'the gag', trying to be funny. I think the less the humour is pursued, the greater the impact of the characters and their situation. In addition, I have often used a device whereby at moments of despair, a safety valve of humour seems to appear. This is not intentionally to relieve tension but more to provide an interesting challenge for the audience: to take the easy option and laugh or to go with the juxtaposition created.

Many of the characters have an opportunity to bare their soul in the first act with pieces to audience. The detail they provide and the use of silence, 'the pause', is vital. The style of the writing will hopefully give a flavour of my intention concerning style and structure. I like the idea of interrupted dialogue as it reflects the nature of the people. There is also a planned for facility of quite marked variations in pace which it is hoped are apparent and do not need to be laboured here with explanation.

I have intentionally avoided stage left/stage right. Rather, there is more an emphasis on illustrating intent, sentiment, objective which is in the notes provided throughout the script and should, therefore, naturally suggest stage directions. Similarly, I have tried to avoid where/when characters sit, move their positions etc. and have opted more to simply highlight when they enter/exit the scene. However, if there is a convincing dramatic reason to do something different, that is the director's decision.

Direction/Production Notes *(cont'd)*

The music to cover the scene changes is clearly not needed with a single-set piece such as this, but I do feel it adds to the context, which is illustrated by the suggested choice of music. I am not precious about those particular pieces being used, but they at least provide good examples of what I am intent on them achieving.

Costume is contemporary but must be dictated in style by characterisation.

From a technical perspective, reference has already been made to this being a single-set piece. The only changes in location take place during the funeral services in Act 2 and are achieved simply by the use of a lectern and lighting effects to close down the playing area and focus the attention of the audience.

The pieces to audience are managed by lighting, focussing the attention.

The lounge of The Beeches will need to comprise at least two armchairs, preferably wing back, and a sofa, appropriate furniture, stocked bookcase/s, tables, side/standard lamps, a stereo. There needs to be at least one window the positioning of which will be dictated by the director's preferences for staging. I have indicated it to be at the side for obvious reasons. There is also a need for a TV. For technical and dramatic reasons, the screen should not be viewable to the audience. It would be more than acceptable for the TV to be alternatively inferred to be on the auditorium side and the company, therefore, delivering out front as they 'watch' it (with appropriate lighting effects?).

The requirement for props is indicated in the direction notes as they occur/are used, such as drinks, food, books, newspapers etc. See end for costume plot.

PS: As a point of clarity the line, "Where is the life", was not in isolation used by Shakespeare. The full quote, "Where is the life that late I led", was used in 'The Taming of the Shrew' in Act IV by Petruchio and subsequently borrowed for the Cole Porter musical 'Kiss Me Kate', although utilised in a different context and subsequently, the title of a song of the same name in the musical. To add to the fun, Shakespeare reused the line in Henry IV part 2 when it is delivered by Pistol to Falstaff in Act 5 Scene 3.

Martin P Roche, 2015

Running Time

With a 7.30pm start and a 20-minute interval, estimated curtain is 10.00pm.

First Produced

'Where Is The Life?' was first produced at Guide Bridge Theatre, Manchester between 29th June and 4th July 2015, directed by Martin Paul Roche, with the following cast:

Kelly	Tracey Rontree	
Julie	Lisa Kay	"... fantastic, hilarious comedy ... stellar show"
Tom	Paul Firth	**(*Tameside Advertiser* 2015 premiere)**
Alan	Jon Comyn-Platt	"Truly amazing ... one of the best plays I have ever
Don	Roger Boardman	seen ... very funny and yet, very thought
Colin	Paul Gledhill	provoking ... a superb piece of theatre ... I cried,
Gordon	John Hankin	but how I laughed! ... wonderfully written ... had
Tony	Brian Ganderton	us in laughter and tears"
Mary	Jill Ratcliffe	**Audience Feedback via social media for the 2018**
Kevin	David Brobbin	**production.**

ACT ONE
Scene 1

The Beeches Residential home, Northern England. It is a late autumn morning, before 8am. Music: 'Anything Goes'. Kelly and Julie are stood centre stage well down front, back to back but angled towards the audience in a stark, focussed white light but as if sat opposite each other. Julie is interviewing Kelly. They are actually on the set, but it is clearly obscured by the lack of lighting. It is the main lounge of the home and the only set for the piece. Kelly is ill at ease with the interview - and Julie. Kelly is not what you might say 'appropriately' dressed for an interview; scant and revealing is the kind description with 'Goth' type makeup. She could not be more inappropriate for the occasion or the environment if she had tried.

Julie	And what experience have you of work in a retirement home?
Kelly	Well, my grandparents were very old. I spent a lot of time with them. Oh, and I like old people. I find them very interesting; their stories, their lives, so I thought that having got on so well with my grandparents...
Julie	... so having spent time around people the same age as our residents, it automatically qualifies you to...
Kelly	No, well. When you put it like that, no; it doesn't appear that I'm overly qualified ...
Julie	Try 'not at all qualified'.
Kelly	Yes ... I mean no, I mean yes, *(pause)*... I mean, but I just thought that it would be so interesting to...
Julie	Miss... *(she looks at the papers she is holding),* Cosgrove. We run a retirement home, not the Big Brother House. This is The Beeches, an exclusive retirement residence for gentlemen formerly of the stage.
Kelly	What Theatre?
Julie	Yes, my dear, Theatre.
Kelly	That's brilliant! I want to be an actress and...
Julie	*(Speaking over her).* ... we are not here to provide you with an interest to further your genuine career aspirations. You must provide support, care, engagement, interest to our residents. But before you can interest them, you have to interest me. Added to which, our residents are... how shall I say... challenging
Kelly	Oh, I don't mind wiping up shi... sorry, mess
Julie	Shit. The word is shit. And I have managed this home long enough to also know when somebody is talking it. We don't dress it up here Miss Cosgrove and yes, at times there are plenty of occasions to engage with shit. Similarly, there are just as many occasions when you feel like it and – to be honest – are treated like it.
Kelly	I don't mind. Really I don't. Having three older brothers and a chocolate Labrador with Crohn's disease, I've had my fair share of sh...
Julie	Yes, I think I am getting the idea...
Kelly	You see with our Labrador being chocolate coloured you sometimes couldn't tell what was Labrador and what was actually sh...
Julie	*(Interrupting with urgency).* Yes. As I said, I get the idea. What you clearly lack in professional experience, you make up for in, well, other ways. If you are

7

	given this position, I'll expect you to find time to speak one-to-one with each of our residents as soon as possible. Get to know them. Understand them. Discover what makes them tick. Right, let me show you around, you can meet some of our residents and we can take it from there.
Kelly	Thanks. *(Pause. Both take a step apart and then turn to face each other).* But I do want to be honest with you. I don't intend to spend the rest of my life here.
Julie	*(She looks at Kelly and then looks front).* Neither did I Miss Cosgrove. Neither did I.

LX: lights come up almost immediately. We are in The Beeches. The morning room to be exact. As the lights come up, Julie is leading Kelly through the lounge.

Julie	This way
Kelly	What's that bloody smell?
Julie	Age. Welcome to the care of the elderly Miss Cosgrove. As you can see, this is our Lounge. We tend to find the majority of our residents spend their day in and around this area, mostly reading. *(She leads her to a well-stocked bookshelf up stage).* As you can see, complimenting their professional backgrounds, the selection of books comprises most of the classics
Kelly	Barbara Cartland?
Julie	I think not. William Shakespeare is the norm and you find that our gentlemen are often quoting him. But in consideration of the behaviour of some of our residents, you might not be that wrong about Barbara Cartland

Tom enters. He is wearing a garish wrap/bath robe, a towel around his head, sunglasses and a bright coloured face pack. On his feet are the most outrageous pair of slippers and on his head, a large pair of headphones and he is carrying a portable stereo in front of him to which the headphones are wirelessly connected. He has a cigarette hanging precariously from his mouth. He is humming tunelessly, along with what is playing. He takes up position facing the audience and is oblivious to Julie and Kelly at the back, initially due to the earphones and moreover, what is playing on them. He occupies his time whilst Julie speaks, rummaging in his bag and 'preparing' and then warming up elaborately!

Julie	That is Tom, as you can see, aptly fulfilling your Barbara Cartland question. But do not be fooled. This is not just a home for any old people. Our residents such as Tom over there have spent their lives surrounded by some of the most famous people that have ever lived. Theirs was a life of opulence, grandeur of a by-gone age; of standards and manners. These are men who know how to behave socially within any sphere, men with keen minds and sharply honed intelligence. Theirs is a language of beauty and charm, of Keats and Milton; of Shakespeare. Of articulation, of eloquence, of...
Tom	*(Still with his back to Julie and Kelly and suddenly shouting off stage).* Will somebody open a bloody window. This place smells like a goat's fanny.
Julie	... as I was saying, of articulation and eloquence.

Tom then takes off his earphones and positions his stereo on a chair and presses the 'play' button. Facing front, he promptly drops his bathrobe to reveal nothing more than a leopard-print thong. He then strikes a pose as the music comes on - Music: 'Take A Little One Step' - which he then proceeds to depict in an elaborate and very camp dance/mime/exercise routine. After no more than 30 seconds of this and at a key point Julie and Kelly stare transfixed, he bends down providing courtesy of his lack of attire, a more than graphic rear view. Kelly screams. Tom turns. He screams at the 'sight' of Kelly. Kelly screams at the 'sight' of Tom. Julie is unfazed. This is normality and she is numb to it. Tom quickly puts his robe on, turns the music off and removes the sunglasses. Julie and Kelly move downstage.

Tom	What the bloody hell do you think you're doing spying on me?
Kelly	What were we doing??
Tom	And what in God's name are you supposed to be?
Kelly	What am I? What are you? You cheeky sod.
Julie	Just a minute!
Tom	Your friend Boadicea *(he pronounces it bow-di-see-a)* called me a cheeky sod.
Kelly	Well, what did you call me?
Julie	It's actually pronounced Boo – dicka.
Kelly	*(To Tom).* Boo-dicka.
Tom	Charming!
Julie	What on earth were you actually doing?
Tom	My morning-light-exercise-improvised-mime-dance-musical-theatre-extravaganza-session … thank you! *(He curtseys).*
Kelly	You call that dance?! I did dance as part of my college drama course.
Tom	Oh an expert eh? I take it this course didn't include beauty and makeup?
Kelly	Y'what?
Tom	And you clearly missed the lesson on elocution.
Alan	*(Entering and then seeing Kelly).* Morning Tom and... Bloody hell!
Don	*(Entering after Alan).* Morning all. Dear God, its Boadicea, *(He pronounces it correctly as Boo-dicka).*
Kelly	Not you as well!
Don	I beg your pardon?
Tom	I was just doing my morning workout with the voyeur twins spying on me, when this one screamed. Screamed! At the sight of me? I ask you? *(He opens his gown at Alan and Don).*
Don	Dear Lord!
Alan	You didn't get the memo did you?
Tom	What memo?
Alan	The one entitled 'growing old gracefully'.
Tom	*(To Kelly, as if nothing has happened).* Rubbish. You're old as you feel, and I feel like a twenty-one-year-old. Trouble is there are none in here. Anyhow, let's get the formalities out of the way. Hello love, I'm Tom. This is Alan and Don. *(He sits in the armchair).*
Alan	Charmed I'm sure. *(He sits on the sofa).*
Don	Enchanted. *(He kisses her hand which leaves her nonplussed and he also sits on the sofa).*
Kelly	*(Crossing to move opposite Julie).* I'm Kelly. I've just had an interview and...
Julie	... and I have just offered her a job as the new Care Assistant.

Don, Alan and Tom all look from one to the next as the exchange of the next dialogue takes place 'a la Wimbledon'.

Kelly	Job?
Julie	Yes
Kelly	When?

Julie	Just now.
Kelly	You didn't.
Julie	Just accept that I did.
Tom	When?
Julie	A second ago!
Alan	*(To Don).* Did you hear her offer Boadicea the job?
Kelly	Kelly!
Don	This is jolly fascinating…
Alan	Nothing surprises me in 'ere any longer.
Don	*(Standing).* … Boadicea was queen of the Iceni tribe …
Tom	Oh bollocks. Here we go … he's off. Take a chair whilst Bamber Gascoigne regales us.

Julie sits. Kelly sits on the arm of the chair next to Tom.

Don	*(He is in his own world).* … she led an uprising against the occupying forces of the Roman Empire. Her husband, Prasutagus, was ruler of the Iceni tribe who had ruled as a nominally independent ally of Rome, left his kingdom jointly to his daughters and the Roman Emperor in his will. However, when he died, his will was ignored. The kingdom was annexed as if conquered, Boadicea was flogged, her daughter's raped and Roman financiers called in their loans.
Kelly	*(Pause).* Just like my Mother said. Bank Managers? Bunch of gobshites.

There is a pause and the three men suddenly laugh – it is lost on Kelly. Don sits.

Tom	I think you are going to fit in just fine my love.
Julie	I am sure she will. Kelly told me earlier that she is interested in a career as an actress. Kelly, these are just some of our residents, but all are professionals, retired entertainers, actors, directors, managers, impresarios; treasures of our stage heritage and what one might call our 'treasured theatrical artefacts'.
Tom	Artefacts?! More like Farty Acts if you ask me.
Alan	Speak for yourself.
Julie	And they are so funny. All of them. Especially dear Tom, aren't you Tom?
Tom	Julie, I might have the bladder control of a two-year-old but you don't have to talk to me like one.
Julie	*(Standing. To Kelly).* Well?
Kelly	*(Standing).* What?
Julie	*(Trying to regain some semblance of normality).* Job?
Kelly	*(Being cocky and moving to sofa).* Thinking.
Julie	Answer?
Kelly	Staying. *(Smugly, she sits down very deliberately and slowly in between Alan and Don).*
A/D/Tm	Ooooo!
Julie	<u>Stop!</u> Just … stop. For once in this place can we just have a normal conversation that does not make me feel I am in a sitcom, a lunatic asylum or both. *(Silence. She stares at Kelly, almost demanding a civilised and appropriate answer).*

Kelly	*(Exaggeratedly demure and standing politely as if she is 'in service' and curtseys).* Yes, madam, I'll take the job thank you. *(Julie beckons Kelly to her and then speaks to her, unheard, whilst the dialogue continues).*
Tom	Ooh, it's just like 'Upstairs Downstairs'.
Alan	No, 'Downton Abbey'.
Tom	Well. What she lacks in haute couture, she makes up for in decisiveness.
Don	And balls.
Tom	Not an expert in these things my lovely, but them certainly ain't balls.
Julie	*(She is frayed by her latest dalliance in the world of her resident).* See me in my office and we can sort the paperwork. I've told Kelly that she needs to speak to each of you in turn to get to know you. And God help her. *(She exits).*
Alan	Thank God she's gone.
Tom	Jesus. VT's on form today.
Kelly	VT?
Alan	Vinegar Tits.
Don	*(Standing to address them again).* Vinegar Tits is the name given to a sour faced old hag, typically from Rochdale or Oldham *(can be changed at director's discretion to other local areas)* who was usually pregnant at the age of 46. It was also the nickname given to Officer Vera Bennett in the Aussie TV show 'Prisoner Cell Block …
Tom	For god's sake Don, not again, you bore for bloody England.
Kelly	That's not very nice.
Don	And neither are some of the residents in here when they put their minds to it. *(He scowls at Tom and Alan and sits).*
Colin	*(He enters, reading a newspaper. As he crosses to 'his' armchair, he stops dead. He looks Kelly up and down and then carries on walking, sits and holds the paper in front of him reading; and then to Kelly).* Are you a vampire?
Kelly	Eh?
Colin	Well dear, nobody in their right minds would go out in daylight dressed like that.
A/C/D/Tm	*(Spoken as if this is a well-worn joke/response, as if this is their standard repertoire).* The old ones are the best.
Colin	Thank you, thank you, I'm here all week.
Kelly	That was a bit rude.
Colin	You ain't seen nothing yet dearie.
Don	I think she is more a Lilly Langtree.
Tom	No, a young Emily Pankhurst.
Alan	Emily Pankhurst didn't have tits like that.
Tom	Oh and you'd have remembered?
Alan	Oh and you'd have noticed?!
Don	I would have noticed her.
Tom	You would have wanted to shag her…
Don	Please ladies, remember a real lady is present.

They all look around to see, oblivious to Kelly.

Kelly	Erm … When you've all finished I am still here? *(Pause).* Is it always like this?

11

They are silent as if pondering a weighty question.

Don	No. It's normally worse than this.
Kelly	You lot can be worse?
Alan	Not us luvvie. *(They murmur in agreement and look as one towards Colin who still has the paper in front of him).*
Colin	*(He slowly puts the paper down).* So then boys. Do tell. What do we have here?
Alan	This is Kelly, another Care Assistant.
Kelly	Another? How many have you had?
Tom	More than you can imagine.
Kelly	And why have they left?

Silence.

Colin	We've had the likes of this before and we'll have them again. *(He takes money from his wallet and places it on the coffee table).* Four weeks – twenty quid.
Tom	I'll take that.
Alan	I say three and make it thirty.
Colin	Done.

They carry on with their business.

Kelly	*(She moves behind the sofa. To Don).* What was that about?
Don	A small wager on your longevity in this establishment. *(Kelly looks confused).* How long you will manage to stay here.
Kelly	And what do I get if I stay longer?
Tom	A medal.
Don	Committed!
Kelly	And what do I get if I leave?
Alan	Freedom. *(He says the word with a flat, almost painful longing. The others pause for a moment as if struck with the possibilities of the word).*
Colin	Nobody lasts dearie. Not here. Not with us. We've seen them come and we've seen them go. If VT doesn't finish them off, then we always do.
Don	You always do. *(To Kelly).* Welcome to the firm, love.
Kelly	Don't you mean family?
Alan	No, we call it the firm. Families are, well …
Colin	*(He stands).* Families! Families don't come here. Families are an anti-climax, a let-down. They're one long drawn out disagreement about disappointment and which side scores the most points. You can depend on the firm, but not on the family. At our age, the only interest family have in us is what we've got and how much of it will be left when we snuff it. You might appreciate then that they don't have a great interest in the birthdays we clock up. For them, a birthday is another debit on their savings account.
Kelly	That's a bit harsh.
Colin	*(Pointedly).* No dear, its life. *(He takes another note out of his wallet and bangs it on the coffee table).* One week fifty quid. *(He exits).*
Kelly	(Returning to sit on the sofa). Christ. I've never worked in a place like this – I don't really know what I'm doing here. It was this or the transport cafe.
Alan	*(Theatrically stands).* 'Us or The Transport Café'. And still, we prevailed *(He exits taking the note with him).*

Don	Then welcome to our world. It's not as bad as some of us paint it. Some of us like it here. It's all a matter of perspective. At this time in one's life there's a very fine line between contentment and resignation *(He exits).*
Tom	It's actually quite lovely … *(He trails off and looks around. He is out of sorts, like he is uncomfortable and then).* At our age the difficulty is coming to terms with, well, the terms. Don't worry love. This place is just another chapter of a book called life. The pages might be a bit creased and faded, but there's still a story there waiting to be read, longing to be told … desperate to be heard. And you're never really alone. *(He looks around again and exits).*

She is alone. She looks around. She has her bag on her lap clutched to her. An innocent abroad. Fade to black. Music: 'Wilkommen' from 'Cabaret'.

Scene 2

Previous music fades out during black out. Music: changes to 'Oh What A Beautiful Morning' from 'Oklahoma'. The following day. The lights come up. The morning room is empty. The curtains are closed and it is in semi-darkness. Julie enters muttering under her breath.

Julie	*(She calls out).* Kelly! *(Muttering).* Bloody music left on again. (She turns off stereo – track stops abruptly). Kelly! *(There is no answer. She goes to the window and opens the curtains. LX: the room lights up).* Kelly! Kell… *(She is interrupted by the entrance of Gordon).*
Gordon	*(He sees Julie).* Oh shit! *(He does an about turn – but too late).*
Julie	Gordon, a word please. Have you seen Kelly? *(Gordon doesn't respond).*
Gordon	*(He looks intently at her and then as if he is concentrating on the greatest question ever asked of him. He stands pondering, facially contorted, mulling over the answer to the meaning of life and then).* Eh?
Julie	Have you got your hearing aid on, oh forget it, Kelly? The new care assistant? I told you about her this morning? *(Gordon slowly shakes his head as if lost on this subject).*
Julie	Outrageous makeup? So high? Late 30's? Spikey hair? *(Gordon doesn't answer).* Large breasts?
Gordon	Oh yes!
Julie	Have you seen her?
Gordon	Eh?
Julie	Kelly?
Gordon	Who? *(Julie gestures Kelly's proportions).* Ah, yes, yes, yes, yes!
Julie	You have seen her then?
Gordon	No.
Julie	But you do remember me telling you about her.
Gordon	Who?
Julie	Gordon, when will you sort out a battery for that bloody hearing aid? *(Kelly enters. She is now wearing 'the uniform' comprising some loose-fitting trousers and the standard nursing/residential home top and sensible shoes. The make-up and hair are the same – as is the cleavage).* Ah Kelly, there you are. Can I introduce you to Gordon? Gordon, this is Kelly.
Gordon	*(He moves to her and stares at her cleavage).* Bloody Hell … hello boys.

Julie	Gordon, this is clearly Kelly who has just started with us. She is the person stood closely behind the breasts you have just met. Gordon is our maintenance man, odd jobs, looks after the grounds etcetera. Very hard of hearing.
Kelly	Alright? *(Gordon doesn't respond).* Alright?
Gordon	*(He stares at her intently, through her, lost. Then looks behind himself).* Who?
Kelly	You can't hear proper, I don't speak proper, what a pair eh?
Gordon	*(He is still transfixed by her cleavage).* Y'tellin' me.
Julie	Kelly, that's meant to be humour. Don't worry about it. He promises never to do it again.
Tony	*(Entering and moving between Gordon and Kelly).* Julie, can I have the chequebook please, I need to pay for some… *(He stops dead).* I say. And who are you?
Kelly	I'm Kelly, the new care assistant.
Tony	And what a pretty little filly...
Kelly	No, Kelly.
Tony	And where, pray, have you come from … Kelly? *(He advances on her, eyes transfixed on her breasts).*
Kelly	Oldham.
Tony	Really.
Julie	Tony, that's a place, not a request.
Tony	What? Oh, I say, very funny, very …
Julie	Tony can you rearrange something for me?
Tony	A meeting?
Julie	No, a phrase: off…sod.
Tony	What?
Julie	Off.
Tony	*(He pauses as it sinks in).* Right-O. *(He goes to leave and then).* About the er…
Julie	Off.
Tony	Gone. *(He exits).*
Julie	My husband. Ancient. Bit simple. Family money. In bred. Pig shit. Thick as.
Kelly	Lovely.
Julie	Not really. *(Loudly).* Gordon!
Gordon	*(He is startled).* Huh?
Julie	Bed! *(He looks horrified. Julie advances on him).*
Gordon	What????!
Julie	The one under the bay window? Needs watering. *(She exits).*
Gordon	*(He is relieved).* Thank god for that.
Kelly	*(Speaking quite pronounced as if on holiday speaking to the locals).* It was lovely to meet you Gordon. I'm sure you and I are going to be good friends. I can tell you're a really nice person and I hope we get the chance to have a proper chat sometime.
Julie	*(Off stage).* Kelly!
Kelly	Got to go. See you later love. *(She touches him on the arm and exits. Gordon lights up and almost grows in stature. He goes to exit walking like John Wayne, repeating: "See you later love" to himself, acting out the persona of a screen god. Colin enters and almost collides with him; he backs up to centre stage followed by Tom and Alan. They encircle him like prey. For Gordon this is hell on earth and he stares front, frozen with fear!).*

Colin	Well boys, if it isn't Lady Chatterley's Lover.
Tom	No, I think Mr Darcy, striding boldly across the lawns … *(leaning into Gordon, speaking provocatively)* … slightly moist.

Kelly walks in on them, for now unnoticed. They begin what is for them, a routine; their daily skirmish with an unprepared world. They throw quotes at each other, theatrical one-upmanship

Colin	Ah, what a piece of work is man!
Tom	How noble in reason!
Alan	How infinite in faculty! In form and moving how express and admirable!
Colin	In action how like an angel!
Tom	In apprehension how like a god!
Alan	The beauty of the world, the paragon of animals!
Tom	Though this be madness, yet there is method in it!
Alan	And it must follow, as the night the day, thou canst not then be false to any man!
Colin	Ah, Brevity is the soul of wit!
Tom	*(Moving slowly into Gordon).* Doubt that the sun doth move, doubt truth to be a liar, but never doubt …I love.

Pause. Then Gordon bumbles backing away from them, almost collides with the table and exits. Alan, Colin and Tom burst out laughing and sit in their respective chairs reading.

Kelly	What was that all about?
Tom	Sport.
Alan	The hunt.
Colin	It was Hamlet dearie – the play, not the cigar.
Don	*(Entering with a newspaper).* Morning all. By the expression on Gordon's face I take it he stupidly came into the house whilst you three were out marauding? And what was it today? Romeo and Juliet?
Alan	Hamlet actually.
Don	Well, just remember, the smallest worm will turn, being trodden on.
A/C/Tm	Oooo!
Colin	Get the stagehand quoting Hamlet.
Don	… Manager thank you.
Colin	Whatever.
Alan	Henry the fourth – part two?
Tom	Three.
Colin	Act two, scene two to be exact.
Kelly	*(She has been watching and then addresses them like a school kindergarten).* So, you're all having a nice time then?

Alan, Colin, Don and Tom slowly stop what they are doing and stare at her: the imbecile has spoken.

Colin	Did it speak?
Don	Let the girl be Colin.
Colin	Be what? An imbecile? A continual drone? A claim upon my irascibility?
Kelly	I don't understand what he just said.
Alan	Be grateful for small mercies mon petit chou.
Kelly	I don't understand what you just said either.

15

Colin	In plain and simple language that even a single celled organism like you could understand: shut up.
Kelly	Oh, right-o. I see what you mean. That's always been my problem, jabbering away like, well, I don't know what. My mother used to call me a silly little chicken and I guess that was me. Cheep cheep cheep. Mind you I don't know what noises they really make 'cos I've never been around them - chickens, not mothers - except when I've been to KFC but I expect that doesn't count…
Colin	*(Shouting).* Be quiet!
Kelly	Am I speaking too loudly?
Colin	No, you are speaking. And at the moment I fear that an even greater issue is that you are breathing.
Tom	Colin …
Colin	So do us all a favour and <u>get out</u>!
Don	Kelly, that will be all my dear. Check the conservatory and make sure it's tidy. Julie can be a little touchy about …
Alan	*(Speaking under his breath).* Julie can be touchy?
Colin	Ah, The Great Pretender speaks.
Tom	Leave it be Colin.
Colin	What? Let the family secrets out? Air the dirty dresses in front of the children?
Alan	I'm going to my room. *(He goes to exit but pauses as Colin speaks).*
Colin	That's right. Go back into the closet you never left. *(Alan cannot, will not turn around to face him. He exits, holding back the upset, broken again).*
Tom	*(He gets up and goes to follow him. Stops and turns to Colin).* You know what Colin? You really are a son of a butch! *(He exits after Alan. Don picks his paper up again and starts to read it, clearly blanking Colin. Kelly observes, lost in the politics of personalities).*
Colin	*(He stands defiantly).* I'll be in the conservatory – where it's quiet! *(He exits).*
Kelly	Bloody hell, what was all that about?
Don	Its … complicated. No, it's very simple really, but we have made it complicated. I wouldn't normally discuss such matters as they are private, personal. Such matters are for the individual concerned to voice, not for gossip and …
Kelly	Do you mean about Alan being gay?
Don	He's told you?
Kelly	He doesn't need to!
Don	Doesn't he? *(Gordon enters).*
Kelly	He might as well wear a chuffin' T-shirt with it written on - I am Gay, I am Gay.
Gordon	Oh not another-one! *(He exits).*
Kelly	No Gordon, not me … oh shit! He thinks I'm one of them now!
Don	One of them? Well, apart from you, me, Julie and her husband, we are in the minority here.
Kelly	<u>All</u> of them? All of the residents are … you know …
Don	Not all Kelly. And you can use the word. I think we stopped gaoling them a number of years ago now.

Kelly	I know. I've got a few mates who are queer, but I've never been around so many of them.
Don	It doesn't make this an isolation hospital.
Kelly	I know. I don't have a problem with them sort. My dad would have.
Don	Them sort. Forward thinking type then is he your father?
Kelly	Was. Well he wouldn't watch Coronation Street.
Don	Ah!
Kelly	I'm not biased. Not me.
Don	Oh, of course, I can see that.
Kelly	It's just …
Don	*(Interrupting).* Kelly, never be frightened of a person just because they are different to you. But be very wary of those who take delight in pointing those differences out
Kelly	I'm sorry, I don't …
Don	Understand? No. Understanding is a long journey that we have to choose to take. Look beneath Kelly. Find the men behind the mask. When you do, you might find it is not just them that are wearing one. *(She is speechless).* Yes, I know. You still don't understand. Welcome to life – welcome to the journey and welcome to finding out for yourself the answer to that great question.
Kelly	What question?
Don	'Where is the life' – the life you want for your own. And welcome to a job that might teach you more than you expected.
Tom	*(Entering).* You know, Colin can be such a tosser when he wants to be.
Kelly	I think it's got nothing to do with wanting to be a tosser.
Tom	Crying his bloody eyes out in his room is Alan.
Kelly	Is that because Alan won't admit he's …
Don	Kelly… *(He shakes his head at her).*
Gordon	*(He enters quickly, speaking urgently as he walks and makes his way to look off stage through the window).* Taxi, taxi! *(The others go rushing to the window, leaving Kelly behind, bemused at what is going on).*
Tom	Who is it?
Gordon	Dunno.
Don	Which company?
Tom	Looks like Simpsons.
Alan	*(Enters running).* Taxi, taxi!
D/G/Tm	We know.
Alan	Who is it?
D/G/Tm	Dunno.
Colin	*(Enters running).* There's a…
A/D/G/Tm	*(Without even turning).* We know.
Colin	But who is it?
A/D/G/Tm	Dunno.
Colin	Who…?
A/D/G/Tm	Simpsons. *(He joins them).*
Julie	Guess what? *(Enters running and joins them).*
A/C/D/G/Tm	We know…Simpsons…no idea.

Tony	*(He enters).* I say…
A/C/D/G/Tm	Sod off!
Tony	Right – O. *(He exits).*
Kelly	Will somebody please tell me what is going on?
Julie	*(She has picked up the phone).* Marjorie, who are they here for. I see. When? Thank you.
Kelly	*(She walks over to the window and joins them all looking out of the window).* That's not a taxi, it's a bloody hearse.
Tom	No love, it's a taxi from where we're standing.
Julie	*(She has put the phone down and joined them).* Mr Grainger in room 7.
A/C/D/G/Tm	Ahh!
Tony	*(He enters).* I say, I know who …
A/C/D/G/Tm	Sod off!
Tony	Right – O. *(He exits again).*

Alan, Colin, Don and Tom break position and simply carry on as if nothing has happened. They move to their respective seats and sit. Gordon exits.

Julie	*(She prepares to exit).* Kelly, I'll be back shortly. Out for lunch with our bank manager. Lovely man. Picking me up in his Jaguar.
Alan	*(Speaking aside).* Didn't know Jaguar made fork-lifts. *(She pauses as if to say something but thinks better of it and exits).*

And for a perverse moment, normality returns.

Colin	Well.
Don	Right.
Tom	Time for tea me thinks.
Alan	Indeed.
Don	Has anybody seen the remote?
Colin	No, got to be the Archers, surely.
Tom	What about Radio 3?
Don	Radio 3 on a Tuesday? German tone poems and scratchy period instruments?
Tom	You're right. He's right. Archers it is *(He goes to the radio and is turning it on/tuning in).*
Kelly	But…I'm sorry… I think I have missed something … has someone not just…are you all not feeling a bit, y'know …?
Alan	What?
Kelly	You know?
Colin	No?
Don	What is she saying?
Tom	God knows.
Alan	What is it girl?
Kelly	With Mr Grainger well, dying. I thought you might all be a bit, well…
Colin	What for god's sake?

They all have paused carrying on with life and stare at her.

Kelly	*(Kelly moves to the window and looks out at the hearse and then back at the scene, a little nonplussed).* Nothing. I thought something had happened. But, nothing.

They resume normality. There is a hum of low chatter. Kelly is again left bewildered, wondering what has just happened. Music: 'Archers' theme begins.

A/C/D/Tm   Ahhh…
Kelly   But surely…
A/C/D/Tm   Shhh

The day is perfect again and the lights fade to black with the music.

Scene 3

Alan is sat in an armchair and is picked out of the darkness by a special. He puts down the paper he was reading, the Archers theme fades as dialogue starts.

Alan   *(Speaking to the audience).* Please Kelly. Must we do this? Why is there a need to have 'confession'…alright, sorry, not confession: 'a one to one getting to know me session'. *(He starts singing, theatrically).* Getting to know you, getting to know all about you. Getting to like you … Sorry. Occupational hazard here. Now and again we all just burst into one of many scripts, songs, roles we have all played. Pathetic, I know. Musicals are a particular favourite - The man that hath no music in himself nor is not moved with concord of sweet sounds is fit for treasons, stratagems and spoils. Anyhow, beats playing 'me', whoever 'me' is. Not Don though. He doesn't do luvvie. Years as a stage manager were like a shot of immunity. He lives in the real world and grounds us all. He's as normal as it gets in here. Our rock. Our conscience. Our memory. Mine's bloody awful. *(He laughs and then speaks the lyrics).* Getting to like you. That's rich. That's what all of us really want. To be liked. The great character flaw of all luvvies. The need to be loved. The need to be yourself never crops up thankfully. Too frightened to be yourself. Shit scared to be me. Bugger. No confessions I said. So, 44 years on the stage and 5 years 3 months and…13 days penal servitude in here. No family. No marriage, no children… no goods, no chattels, no ox, no ass… Lots of yesterdays, who knows how many tomorrows. *(Singing again).* Too many mornings… Stephen Sondheim. Musical Theatre. Seemed appropriate somehow. Right, I'd like to speak to my solicitor now. *(He laughs).* Sorry. Humour. Fills the void created by awkwardness. They're all a good bunch here. Apart from, well. Colin can be…well …hurtful. He picks. Finds flaws. Takes pleasure. Discovers weakness. Exposes secrets. Teatime I think. Must do this again. White. One sugar. There's a love. *(He picks up his paper and begins to read. The interview is most certainly over).*

Music: 'I am what I am' from 'La Cage Aux Folles' begins to cover scene end. Fade to black.

Scene 4

Music fades out. Lights up

Tom   *(He is stood in the dressing gown and slippers from earlier. He is drying a teacup with a tea towel).* What do you mean Kelly do I mind talking about myself? You can clearly see from my conservative attire I am a violet of the shrinking variety. *(He strikes a camp/OTT pose).* Not. Don't worry love, I don't bite. Don? I met Don when he was ASM at the Vic. By god he was attractive in those days. Surprised aren't you? Thick wavy hair and steely eyes. Utterly wasted on an unappreciative, heterosexual world. If he told you to be quiet in the bloody wings you did. Moved here when his wife died. That nearly killed him. He spent the first six months keeping himself to himself. You could tell every day he had been crying though. Still does now and again without any warning. Emotional type. He has a daughter and son-in-law you know.

Right pair of gobshites. It kills him that they ignore his calls and when they do visit, it's clearly a real hardship for them. *(Sarcastically)*. Not. Can't wait to get out the bloody door. But he won't have a word said against them. He worships her. You just want to cry. You can understand family ignoring the likes of me. No? Well I can. Trust me. But not Don. He says I should still be working. Says there's still at least one good drama left in me.

Me. An old fag-been. I only ever wanted just one serious role. Panto, soaps and shitty adverts was my fayre. The low point was being a dancing courgette on the Benny Hill show. But at least it paid for this. This. *(He looks around)*. Colin? We've known each other for years, loved each other, hated each other. Alan? Alan, Alan, Alan. An enigma, wrapped up in a puzzle and dressed in a sequin ball gown of the 'Emperors' New Clothes' variety. He's that far back in the wardrobe he's in bloody Narnia. Alan will never be at peace. *(He's distracted)*. Christ I've nearly rubbed the bloody glaze off this cup. Alan, yes. If you do nothing else Kelly, look out for him. We take him and his baggage for granted but he worries me. There's something else going on inside him. No, I've said enough on the subject. But if you hide something for that long, it's got to take its toll somehow, some time. And it's a toll we will all pay… and if you stay here long enough, so will you. Because at some point we will either be one of two things to you: your living or your life. And one way or another, it will come at a price.

Fade to black. Music: 'Stranger in Paradise'

Scene 5

A couple of days later. Lights come up as music fades. Alan, Colin and Tom are sat in their places watching TV. Kelly is sat in the centre seat of the couch next to Alan.

Alan	Oh, there must be something else on TV than this. What is entertaining about people showing their bits to a doctor and several million people watching?
Tom	I suppose if it helps them. It's made me feel better just knowing I've not got a willy like that.
Colin	No comment.
Tom	What happens on tour stays on tour!
Colin	Precisely.
Kelly	Shall I tell you from the TV guide what's on?
Colin	Deep joy.
Kelly	Seven o'clock is that new reality talent show about bus drivers wanting to be rock stars.

Alan	Why do they call it reality TV when everybody is pretending to be something they're not, in the hope they will end up being something they don't have the talent to be?
Colin	You managed it for 40 years.
A/K/Tm	Ooooo!
Tom	Bitch.
Colin	Queen.
Tom	Slag.
Colin	Whore.
Alan	Enough, for goodness sake.

Don enters, fully dressed except for his trousers. Alan, Colin, Kelly and Tom are concentrating on the TV.

Don	*(He also concentrates on the TV).* Evening all. *(All continue to watch the TV and don't look at him).*
Tom	Don?
Don	Yes?
Tom	Trousers.
Don	*(He doesn't look down).* Bugger. *(He exits).*

The others continue watching TV whilst talking.

Kelly	Is Don alright?
Alan	Don't worry, he's not lost his marbles.
Colin	And even if he had, under no circumstances do we mention it to VT, understand?
Kelly	Yes but?
Colin	Understand?
Kelly	Yes!
Tom	To answer your question Kelly: because this is a retirement home, not a nursing home.
Alan	And first sign of 'barmy'…you're out.
Kelly	It seems like most people here have got their marbles. You know, there are no real barmy ones.
Colin	Well. Thank you for your clinical assessment.
Alan	I don't know though. You remember that quite dapper chap last year?
Tom	Oh yes. Very well to do. Ex RADA teacher. Room 11. A Capricorn on the cusp. We thought he was very intelligent until Don found him struggling with the remote control.
Kelly	Were the buttons too small?
Alan	No, he was trying to get BBC 1 on the fish tank.
Tom	Bless. He thought he was watching 'Wildlife on One'. Thought the little deep-sea diver was David Attenborough on location.
Colin	Oh come on. There must be something to watch. Are there no films on?
Kelly	*(Reading).* The Great Escape?
A/C/Tm	No, bloody hell, how old is that, how old are you! etc
Tom	Oh I don't know. Might give us some ideas!
Kelly	What about that film, 'The Queen'?

21

Tom	I could have been me in that.
Alan	Wouldn't that mean calling it 'The Old Queen'?
Tom	Careful what you wish for.

Gordon enters carrying a box.

Kelly	Here's one. What about 'Free Willy'?

Pause. It's all in their silent expressions.

Colin	*(He realises Gordon is there and pounces)*. What do you think Gordon? Gordon?
Gordon	Eh?
Colin	*(Walking close up to him)*. You look like the type of man who'd like a bit of free willy.

Pause and then stifled giggles. Gordon is embarrassed – again – and bumbles out to safety.

Kelly	*(Calling after him)*. Gordon. *(To Colin)*. Why must you be so cruel to him?
Colin	*(Pointedly and very deliberate to Kelly)*. Because I can. *(He sits)*.

Alan goes as if to speak. Colin cuts him dead with a look. Kelly changes channels on the TV and after a few uncomfortable seconds.

Colin	No. Leave it on this. The Remembrance Parade.
Tom	Oh, look at the Queen. Good for her age. God save the Queen! – no, God save <u>all</u> Queens!
Alan	I can't find me glasses what is she doing?
Tom	She's laying a wreath at the senokot.
Colin	Taph, <u>Taph</u>! For God's sake.
Alan	The Queen's Scottish?
Tom	No, she's never Scottish. Anyhow, 'Taff' would make her Welsh. But she does wear a lot of tartan.
Alan	Och aye. Sometimes she looks like bloody Lorna Doone! And what was that musical?
Kelly	Macbeth?

Alan, Colin and Tom immediately respond, screaming wildly OTT, bizarrely camp, frenetically theatrical at the mention of 'The Scottish Play'. Tom kneels down and blesses himself with the sign of the cross over and over again repeating to himself: "Angels and ministers of grace defend us!". Alan shouts out: "break a leg" over and over. Colin spins around on the spot, spits on the floor and repeats this saying "Thrice around the circle bound, evil sink into the ground". Kelly watches them bewildered.

Tom	*(Breaking the moment and snapping them back to their pseudo-reality)*. Oh, I remember. It wasn't Lorna Doone, it was Brigadoon! *(He starts singing)*. Brigadoon, Brigadoon…
A/C	*(Joining in)*. Brigadoon, Brigadoon…

Kelly is lost by it all. Alan, Colin and Tom resume their seats and start watching the TV again.

Colin	Who is that dreadful woman who's stood next to Princess whats-her-face?
Alan	She's got some money.
Tom	She's got some testosterone as well by the look of that 'tache.
Colin	She's only rich because she's had a few husbands.
Alan	Aye, but none of 'em, were hers!

Kelly	Is she a bit of a slag then?
Tom	Oh no, no. More of a lot of a slag.
Don	*(He enters now wearing his trousers and looks at the TV. He collects a dining room chair and sits next to Tom).* Lovely, I do like a bit of good old British state occasion. Oh look Tom, that woman looks like you in, what was it called when you played the female impersonator?
Tom	La Cage Aux Folles.
A/C/D	*(Singing).* Oh Tranny Boy, the tights, the tights are calling.
Tom	So funny.
Kelly	Glad to see you never dress up like a woman now.
Tom	Not on my own then am I?
A/C/D/K	Ooooo!

They all laugh apart from Colin.

Colin	*(Interrupting the laughter. He has been reading the paper. Sarcastically and loudly).* Why is that funny? Does the truth hurt?

The mood changes.

Kelly	And what does that mean?
Colin	Well, I mean. Look at her. Hardly feminine are we dear. No sense of dress, no sense of occasion, no sense of taste…no sense.
Don	Come on now Colin.
Colin	Come on? Come off it! It's embarrassing.
Kelly	*(She stands and starts to exit).* I'll go and see if afternoon tea is ready.
Colin	Off you go - little orphan Kelly.
Kelly	*(Turning to Colin).* What did you say?
Colin	Saw her personal file on VT's desk. Had to have a look. Shame. No Mummy, no Daddy any longer…hides here with the old folk because she's not capable of owt else.
Kelly	Don't you talk about…
Colin	Off you trot, little orphan Kelly.
Kelly	Don't you…
Colin	You're dismissed! *(He picks up the newspaper and starts to read it again).* And if you hadn't realised the hired helps only speak when they are spoken to and you are being spoken at, not to.

She moves quickly towards him.

Don	Let it go Kelly.

Julie and Tony enter unnoticed.

Colin	*(Deliberately, smugly and almost an aside to himself).* That's right Kelly, let it go, like yourself.
Kelly	You bastard!
Julie	I beg your pardon?

Kelly spins round in horror to look at Julie and Tony.

Colin	*(Sanctimoniously).* Fifty quid coming my way I think.

Tom	*(Pause. Then suddenly, in a flash of inspiration, he stands and claps).* That's it Kelly love, well done! Beautifully delivered line. Just like a pro. We'll make an actress of you yet. What do you think, Alan? Alan?
Kelly	What?
Alan	What? *(Standing, cottoning on and joining him).* Oh yes! Indeed, but it should be delivered with the same passion as in the full line from the play - I am a bastard, too. I love bastards! I am bastard begot, bastard instructed, bastard in mind, bastard in valour, in everything illegitimate.
Don	*(Pause. He stands and explains to Julie).* William Shakespeare. Troilus and Cressida.
Julie	Oh, I see.
Alan	But consider the intent when you say the line. It sometimes helps to add additional words into dialogue to assist you in rehearsal with the emphasis. Why don't you try it?
Kelly	*(She strolls purposely up to Colin in his seat and speaks into his face).* You ignorant, miserable, old, bastard.

Don, Alan and Tom begin to applaud. Julie and Tony unwittingly join in. Colin stands and begins to march out.

Tony	Well done, bravo.
Colin	Sod off. *(He continues to exit).*
Tony	Right-o.
Alan	And of course there is that simple, all-encompassing quote from Troilus and Cressida which I always feel captures the moment and the intent perfectly… *(Colin pauses but does not turn).* 'Farewell, bastard'.

Julie and Tony start clapping again – Colin exits, fuming.

Julie	Well, this is jolly exciting. Just like theatre, but a little bit more camp – if that were at all possible. Well done everybody. Keep up the good work Kelly. *(She exits followed by Tony).*
Don	I best go and…you know. Ladies and gentlemen, this is not good. *(He exits after Colin).*
Alan	'Double, double, toil and trouble' comes to mind.
Tom	*(He joins Alan).* Yes and, 'Misery acquaints a man with strange bedfellows'.
Kelly	*(She moves to stand in between Alan and Tom. Speaking without warning and unexpected passion).* 'Cry havoc and let slip the dogs of war'.

Tom and Alan look at each other, incredulous and then stare at Kelly.

Kelly	What? They said it on Corry last night.

They all look front. Music: 'Everything's Coming Up Roses' from 'Gypsy'. Fade to black.

Scene 6

Lights come up on Tony. Music fades out.

Tony	Well, well. I didn't expect to receive the same pleasurable treatment as the residents, Kelly. Don't think Julie included me in your one to ones, but I'm not complaining. It won't take long. Been here for ten years now. Bought the place for Julie. Was an old sanatorium-come-asylum

when we got it. Not changed much in that respect. Still full of bloody lunatics. Present company excepted. They don't like me very much. The residents. They've inherited that from Julie. Sorry, I won't insult your intelligence. Doesn't take a genius to figure that we are no longer love's young dream. Never were actually. Marriage of convenience was the old-fashioned term that was used. She should have married somebody her own age not an old git like me. She used to refer to me as her soul mate – for a short while. It didn't take me long to realise that there were two ways of spelling 'soul'. And by the time I did, I didn't have a 'sole mate' left. Bad joke. Just like us. One twelve-year-old bad joke. But at least the business needs me. And do make sure you stay on the right side of old VT ... ah, sorry. Yes, I do know what they call her. Bloody funny if you ask me. If you need anything, just stop by. My door is always open as they say. And if you're lucky, it might not stay open. *(He gives a rather slimy laugh, whilst adjusting his tie as if he has finished. He continues).*

I do try hard with them all you know. Try to help them belong. That's all one can ever hope for. To belong. Just being useful isn't enough sometimes. Don is an old gent isn't he? Tom, well, is Tom. But harmless. Alan is, God knows; he certainly doesn't. And Colin is a man with whom you have to achieve the impossible by staying on his right side. And if you can figure which aspect of the nasty old bastard that is, then you're a better man than me Gunga Din. Well, not 'man' ... clearly. Steer clear of him Kelly. You'll only end up being the loser and believe me, one member of that club is enough. I should know. And thank you for one thing, you're the only one in this place not to have told me to sod off. Yet. I believe the world is a stage where every man must play a part, but my part is a sad one. Shakespeare. Playwright. Apparently. Don't really understand a word of it. Just like life really. Don't you think?

Fade to black. Music: 'Mr Cellophane' from 'Chicago'.

Scene 7

Sunday. Lights up. Kelly is alone in the lounge, tidying things, plumping cushions.

Julie   *(She enters).* Ah, Kelly. Good. Just make one final round of the place before family and friends arrive to visit. I hate Sundays. It's not how many families come to visit that's the issue, it's how many that don't. I've asked Gordon to help out today. God help us. I've told him he doesn't have to speak, just serve tea, coffee, juice and circulate with nibbles. It took me twenty minutes to get through to him that 'nibbles' wasn't a person. And remember, he does <u>not</u> engage anybody in conversation or grunts. Anyhow, he has made an effort and looks very, well, presentable in a Gordon-esque sort of way.

Gordon enters. He looks like a character from a Jeeves and Wooster novel. Plus fours, etc., hair combed to look like he has made a bizarre effort.

Kelly   Well. You look very ... 'Gordon', Gordon.

Gordon	Who?
Kelly	*(Persevering).* Is that a special suit?
Gordon	Eh?
Kelly	The suit. Is it special?
Gordon	Brothers.
Kelly	Oh that's nice. Are you close?
Gordon	Who?
Kelly	Your brother.
Gordon	Where? (He turns around).
Kelly	No, you and your brother. Are you close?
Gordon	No.
Kelly	Argument?
Gordon	Dead.
Kelly	Right. So that suit must be a very appropriate and treasured memory of him?
Gordon	Who?
Julie	So Gordon, are you happy with what I asked you to do?
Gordon	Where?
Julie	That's a yes then. Kelly, keep an eye on him. Make sure he doesn't eat anything, anybody.
Gordon	Who?
Julie	It's going to be a long day.

Julie exits as Colin, Alan and Tom enter. Gordon is immediately uncomfortable.

Tom	*(As he enters he looks Gordon up and down first and stops).* Are we filming 'Hound of the Baskervilles'?
Colin	Gordon, you have something stuck to the bottom of your shoe.

Gordon lifts his left foot out to the side to have a look at his shoe whilst at the same time holding his hands up in front of him, striking a rather unfortunate Shirley Temple pose.

A/C/Tm	Ooo, hello sailor! *(The three men laugh and then, led by Colin).* The old ones are the best.
Colin	Thank you, thank you, I'm here all week.

Alan, Colin and Tom go to sit and Colin almost collides with Kelly. There is an uncomfortable moment as they look at each other and then he sits as do the others. Kelly moves away. Gordon bumbles backwards, again embarrassed.

Kelly	*(She goes to Gordon).* Gordon, just ignore them. You know what they're like. No matter what happens or what they say, you just do what Julie told you. There's no need to be nervous. *(Her words of encouragement are not working).* Look, anytime you feel they're getting too much, just wink at me and leave the room so that I know that you're not happy. Why don't you try it? *(Gordon does a most elaborate and pronounced blink with both eyes).* Yes, well, I think I'll get the idea. So, if they start being rude to you, just do your blink-thing and I'll come and help. No need for you to suffer. That's what I'm here for apparently. Remember, it's just a job we do. It's not life.
Gordon	Y'reckon? *(Kelly stares at him).*
Don	*(He enters, excited and goes straight to the window).* No sign yet then I take it?
Colin	Of?

Don	Our guests of course. Jolly exciting. My daughter and son-in-law are coming today. Did I tell you Kelly?
Kelly	A few times.
Don	Awfully good of them. They are just so busy and taking the time to drive all that way to see me. Well, it just makes my day, actually.
Colin	Try month, actually.
Don	*(He is distracted, absorbed)*. Sorry?
Colin	*(Speaking under his breath)*. Aye, they should be.
Don	Think I'll wait out front. *(He exits)*.
Kelly	*(To Tom as she sits on the arm of his chair)*. What was that about?
Tom	They do it to the poor bastard every time – like I told you. Promise they're coming and then don't. They haven't been now for six months, but as it's her birthday, I can't imagine that she'll miss.
Kelly	Why? *(Tom makes a money sign with his fingers)*. The rotten sods.
Tom	Oh no dear. Worse. Much worse than that. You wait and see. Mind you, going off what condescends to come through those doors calling themselves family, they're just one example of many like them. She in particular is a nasty piece of work. You just watch and listen. Clearly some history there but Don has never told us what it is and it isn't my place, or yours, to ask.
Kelly	It might be nothing. You know, with them living hundreds of miles away, surely …
Tom	Oh no love, try miles. Ten at the most.
Kelly	The rotten sods.
Tom	Well done love. You're learning.
Colin	*(Breaking Tom and Kelly's conversation)*. We always have a basket of fresh fruit for visiting, where's the fresh fruit?
Kelly	It's here. *(She moves to the fruit bowl on the table)*.
Tom	Hang on, what are we having? Those bloody nectarines were like golf balls. Last time I had one I looked like a demented hamster.
Colin	Not a problem for us with real teeth.
Tom	None taken I'm sure!
Alan	What is there Kelly?
Kelly	I don't know really. Just loads of different apples…
Colin	*(He moves to Kelly)*. Out of the way. Let someone with a brain have a look. There's Golden Delicious? *(Alan and Tom mutter in disapproval, which is continued after each suggestion)*. Gala? Granny Smith? Braeburn? Pink Lady? Red Delicious … *(Gordon enters, uncomfortably)*. Cox! Who likes Cox?
A/Tm	Yes, Yes! Yes, please! *(Gordon is horrified)*.
Colin	What about you Gordon? *(He moves towards Gordon provocatively)*. You look like a man who likes Cox?

Gordon starts to wink furiously at Kelly and then exits sharpish as Julie enters. Kelly goes after him. Alan, Colin and Tom laugh.

Julie	*(She is carrying a tray of sandwiches and speaking to Kelly as she leaves)*. Has Gordon got a problem?
Kelly	Yes. This bloody lot. *(She exits)*.

Julie	Here we are. Lovely assorted sandwiches for you all. *(She leaves the sandwiches on the table and also exits).*
Alan	Boiled ham. How uncouth. Boiled ham on the same plate as the rest. That'll please Mr Goldberg in room nine. And tongue?! Bloody hate it. I was always made to eat it by my mother. I suppose what knocked me sick was the idea of where it had come from.
Tom	What, the butchers?
Colin	You really are quite scary aren't you?
Tom	Aww, thanks Colin. Ooo, do you think I've got time to nip to that new Jewish deli on the corner and get something for Mr Goldberg? Bit insulting expecting him to pick what he can eat out of a tray of ham and tongue, don't you think?
Alan	What Jewish deli?
Tom	The one on the corner next to the off-licence.
Colin	Can't think which one you mean.
Tom	The Jewish Deli. You can't miss it, it's called 'something-about-Jewish'. What is it? In bloody big letters on the window! I know, it's called 'Everything Hebrew'.
Colin	No, you silly old sod, it's called 'Everything Homebrew'!
Tom	Oh. Explains why they looked at me funny when I asked for half a dozen bagels.
Don	*(He enters, followed by Mary and Kevin who are his daughter and son-in-law. Tom has stood up momentarily to get a sandwich).* This way, this way. Everybody, I am sure you recall but this is Mary my daughter and this is Kevin her…
Mary	Yes, yes father, I think they know who we are. *(She sits in Tom's seat who returns to sit back down in it. Abruptly to Tom).* Yes?
Tom	Nothing. Can I get you a Sandwich?
Mary	What do you think?
Tom	Don't think I'm allowed to say.
Mary	What? I'm sorry?
Tom	Accepted. *(He glides away and nearly collides with Kevin).*

Kelly and Gordon have now entered. She is carrying two cups of tea.

Kevin	*(To Tom).* Watch it!
Alan	*(Holding out his hand to Kevin).* I don't think I've had the pleasure.
Kevin	And you won't. *(Ignoring the handshake, he takes the two cups from Kelly unceremoniously and goes to Mary).*
Tom	So, you must be Don's devoted son-in-law?
Kevin	Eh?
Tom	First letter of the alphabet my love. Don't struggle with anymore. *(He glides away again).*
Kelly	I'm sorry, the teas, they're not for you.
Kevin	Then get two more. *(To Mary).* The kids they get in here still aren't up to much I see?

Kelly exits with Gordon. Tom is with Alan and Colin, all pretending not to listen.

Mary	What do you expect? Peanuts and monkeys comes to mind.

Alan	Monkeys? The cheeky bastard.
Tom	I'll deal with this. *(He walks towards Mary and Kevin with the tray of sandwiches Julie brought in and makes a monkey sound).* Ooo…ooo…ooo…who would like a sandwich? *(Kevin reaches for one and as he does so, Tom sneezes on them).* Oops, sorry. Would you like one without dressing on?
Kevin	Don't think I'm that bothered now.
Tom	Yes, but that happened some time ago didn't it?
Kevin	Eh?
Tom	Aw. Still stuck on the next one are we chicken? Bless. Let me see if I can help. 'B'. It stands for banal, boorish, bastard, belligerent, buffoon…
Kevin	I'm sorry.
Tom	Accepted. *(He glides away again).*
Don	So love, how are you? *(Mary doesn't respond).* What's new?
Mary	Nothing.
Don	There must be something.
Mary	What did I just say?
Don	I see…and how's work?
Mary	Works work.
Don	Are you busy?
Kevin	Is she busy? What do you think?
Don	I don't know, that's why I'm asking.
Kevin	Don't you be clever with me.
Don	I wasn't.
Mary	And here it comes; the first argument.
Don	I'm sorry.

Kelly and Gordon enter with teas for Alan and Tom. Colin picks up the tray of sandwiches to break the moment and walks over to Gordon.

Colin	Now then. Little Lord Fauntleroy here is going to come around and see to you all with some sandwiches. *(Gordon stares blankly).* Off you go, Gordon! Go!
Gordon	*(He hesitantly goes to Mary first).* Eat.
Mary	Tongue please. *(Loudly).* <u>Tongue</u>! *(Gordon slowly sticks his tongue out).*
Kelly	*(Intervening).* For shits sake. Drinks anybody? Gordon, go and find some juice. *(Loudly).* <u>Juice</u>. *(She exits taking Gordon with her).*
Tom	*(He stands, singing, very OTT).* If I were a rich man, do-be-do-be-do-be-do… 'Fiddler on the Roof'. *(Pause as they all stare at him).* Sorry, I thought…one of Mr Goldberg's favourites. Sorry. *(He sits).*
Colin	You deaf old sod. She said <u>juice</u> not <u>Jews</u>.
Tom	Oooo, Pardonne moi!
Don	*(Pause).* I thought you might have brought little Jamie and Georgia to see me…
Kevin	Here? Not likely.
Mary	Father, why would the children possibly want to come here? They get anxious.
Don	Anxious? I'm sure they don't…
Mary	How would you know? You never see them.

Don	*(He is confused, overly conciliatory).* I know love, but that's the point, I never do …
Mary	Don't start father.
Don	I'm not love.
Kevin	Told you this would happen. Every time.
Don	Look, let me nip to my room and get your birthday present.
Mary	You mean you don't have it here? How long will you be? We are in a rush. We haven't got all day.
Kevin	Pubs did open at eleven.
Don	Right love, two minutes. *(He bumps into Mary and knocks her tea which spills onto the floor).*

Kelly enters.

Mary	Brilliant.
Kevin	Told you it would be like this. *(To Kelly).* You. Clean this up. *(Kelly kneels on the floor near Mary and starts cleaning up the mess with cloth from apron pocket).* And don't bring any more of that crap tea. Where's the half-wit with the orange juice?

Gordon enters carrying two glasses of orange very carefully. He is spilling some so licks the side of the glass. Colin intercepts him and we observe him putting something in the drinks, which he then takes off Gordon.

Colin	*(To Kevin and Mary).* There we go. Can't think of a more appropriate drink for you, Mary. Fresh orange: a little tart, not very sweet, can appear bitter and full of pith.
Kevin	Pith?
Colin	As in 'taking the'. *(Kevin is nonplussed).* Don't worry. You needed to be there.
Kevin	Think you're funny?
Colin	To quote the bard Kevin - I would challenge you to a battle of wits, but I see you are unarmed. *(He sits).*
Kelly	*(As she is wiping the carpet).* Lovely man is Don.
Mary	I'm sorry?
Kelly	Lovely man, your Dad.
Kevin	And what's it to you?
Mary	What are you after?
Kelly	Nothing.
Mary	Trying to worm your way in? Wait 'til I tell your boss. Seen people like you on the telly. Taking advantage of old men and their money.
Kelly	No, I'm just saying…
Kevin	Think we're stupid?
Alan	Oh no, none of us <u>think</u> you're stupid.
Kevin	You what?
Mary	Ignore them Kevin. What do you expect from people like them? *(Mouthing the words to him).* All queer.
Kevin	I know what they all need.
Tom	Cheeky.

Kevin and Mary finish their drinks. Gordon walks over to get the glasses and then remains staring at them.

Kevin	What's your problem? Cat got your tongue? *(Gordon slowly pulls his tongue out again).* Eh?
Gordon	Where?
Kevin	Who?
Gordon	Eh?
Alan	Nothing more exhilarating than two great minds meeting.
Kelly	Thank you Gordon. *(and She gets up and walks him away).*
Don	*(Entering).* Here you are love, happy birthday. *(He hands Mary a card and goes to kiss her on the cheek).*
Mary	*(She stands ignoring Don's attempted kiss).* Where have you been? I told you we're in a rush. Leaving us here with all … these.
Tom	None taken, I'm sure.
Don	I think you're being a little…
Kevin	That's right. Told you they mean more to him than you. Your only daughter. Your only family.
Tom	That's rich.
Mary	What did he say Kevin?
Kevin	What did you say?
Alan	Merely corroborative detail, intended to give artistic verisimilitude to an otherwise bald and unconvincing narrative.
Kevin	What are you lot talking about?
Tom	Pooh Bah.
Alan	The Mikado.
Tom	Gilbert and Sullivan.
Alan	Operetta.
Tom	You won't have read it.
Alan	No pictures.
Tom	Just lots of lovely words.
Kevin	Eh?
Tom	That's one of them. Well done son! Not as stupid as you always come across are you?
Mary	Leave it love. Their sort aren't worth it. Let's get going. We're in a rush. *(Kevin suddenly stops. His demeanour changes. He holds his stomach and groans and makes a series of elaborate noises, facial expressions, contortions etc.).* What is it Kevin?
Kevin	I don't feel well. My stomach. I think I need … I think I need …
Tom	A personality?
Alan	A lobotomy?
A/T	*(Singing).* 'If I only had a brain'.
Tom	How exciting! Wicked Witch and Scarecrow have come to see us!
Alan	No. Widow Twankey and Simple Simon surely.
Mary	What are you going on about. This isn't funny… *(She suddenly stops. Her demeanour changes. She holds her stomach and makes noises, the same as Kevin).*
Tom	Well, well. They sound a little bit like monkeys, ironic don't you think?

31

Alan	Irony abounds dear boy.
Mary	*(To Gordon).* You. Idiot. Where's the…
Gordon	Who?
Mary	You know, the er… *(She pulls her hand down as if flushing a toilet).*
Gordon	Eh?
Mary	*(To them all).* We need the, you know…
Alan	Sorry. Hearing aids playing up.
Tom	So has mine. Think it's gone a bit queer.
Alan	I think they've gone a bit queer.
Tom	Must be catching.
Alan	Speak for yourself!
Tom	You both look very pale.
Alan	Is it something you've eaten.
Colin	…or drunk perhaps? Tummies can be a bit like families really. Easily upset. Very delicate. Often neglected.
Gordon	Full of shit.
Don	Can I help love?
Mary	Get out of my way!
Kevin	Shift!
Mary	I need to go before you.
Kevin	No, me first.

Kevin and Mary exit very quickly, holding their stomachs and knees together. Alan, Colin, Don, Gordon, Kelly and Tom look off stage after them.

Tom	Well they did say they were in a rush.
Alan	They're fighting to get in the visitor's loo but can't seem to open the door.
Tom	How unseemly.
Alan	Common as muck.
Colin	It's locked.
Kelly	It wasn't before.
Colin	*(Producing a key).* It is now.
Alan	And they're off! *(They all follow him to the window and look out).* Like the Grand National this.
Tom	But with only two runners.
Alan	A donkey and an old mare.
Colin	A horse! A horse! My kingdom for a horse!
Tom	And off they go across the gravel. Oh bless, they do look a little distressed.
Kelly	Where are they running to?
Colin	Wouldn't call that running. Not with their knees together.
Tom	Looks like they're heading for the outside loo in the garden.
Don	I hope they're OK. Oh dear, Mary has left her birthday present. *(He picks up the card from the chair and sits on the couch).*
Colin	*(He goes to Don, putting his arm around him).* Save it for next year Don. Don't think you'll be seeing them before then.
Alan	I'll bet you a fiver they don't reach the toilet before they …
A/G/K/Tm	Too late.
Tom	Messy.

Kelly	Reminds me of our Labrador.
Tom	Oh dear, what a pity. Not. Gordon, go and see if they need help, there's a love…maybe a hose pipe might help … *(Gordon exits)* … and a stiff brush … and a cork.
Alan	Isn't it around this time that the lawn sprinklers normally… oops, there they go.
Tom	How fortuitous in a cleansing sort of way.
Don	But I don't understand. What caused them to be ill so quickly?
Colin	They'll be fine in a couple of hours.
Kelly	How do you know?
Colin	Because it says so on the sachet. *(He produces a small packet from his pocket).*
Kelly	*(She moves to him, takes the sachet from him and reads it).* Fleet?
Don	Not my bowl preparation?!
Kelly	Oh you didn't?
Tom	Well, they did say they were in a rush.

Gordon enters.

Kelly	How are they?
Gordon	*(Pause, as if thinking of a difficult answer to an even harder question).* Shit.
Colin	In more ways than one.
Don	That he which hath no stomach to this fight, let him depart.
Alan	Dear Henry the 5th.
Colin	Always appropriate.
Tom	Tea?
Alan	Lovely. Kelly?
Kelly	Immediately.
Don	Radio?
Tom	Undoubtedly.
Alan	Archers?
Don	Indubitably.
Colin	Family?
All	Sod 'em!

Alan, Colin, Don and Tom begin to resume their seats and normality.

Kelly	*(To Tom).* I think I'm beginning to get it.
Tom	We're not that bad are we?
Kelly	Not that bad.
Tom	Will you stay?
Kelly	Will you let me?
Tom	We'll see.
Kelly	*(She goes to exit and comes face to face with Colin).* Not a very nice thing to do was it?
Colin	Not very nice people.
Kelly	And you're not a very nice person?
Colin	Exactly.
Kelly	Doubtful.
Colin	Stick around.

Kelly	Intend to.
Colin	You'll lose
Kelly	You think?
Colin	I'm never wrong.
Kelly	And I'm never right.
Colin	What are you trying to say?
Kelly	Nothing. Not allowed.
Colin	*(He moves close up to Kelly).* One week. Fifty quid. Remember?
Kelly	*(She moves still closer to Colin).* One life. Priceless. Forgotten?

Music: 'Archers' theme starts. Kelly exits leaving Colin, bewildered. Chatter and small talk amongst the others as life resumes. Fade to black.

END OF ACT ONE

INTERVAL

ACT TWO

Scene 1

One month has passed. Music: 'Happy Birthday to you'. Lights come up. Alan, Don, Colin, Tom, Julie, Tony and Gordon are gathered. Kelly has a plate of sausage rolls and all of them have a glass of wine. As the music fades they all take over from the track and sing 'Happy Birthday' to Don. They all applaud at the end.

Don	*(He speaks over them trying to interject).* Friends, Friends … Friends, friends.
Alan	Romans, Countrymen…
Tom	Lend me your sanitary pads!
Don	Thank you for that Tommy, Alan. Seriously, you are all so very kind to have thrown this little soiree for me. And I am delighted to be paying for it. I'm just sorry that Mary and Kevin couldn't be here to share the occasion …
Alan	We're not.
Don	… but perhaps they will drop in later.
Tom	Lovely. I'm sure we can all hardly wait Don.
Don	They really are terribly busy you know. Mary is at the dentist …
Alan	*(To Tom).* Having her teeth filed…
Don	…and Kevin is at a cricket match.
Tom	*(To Alan).* Well, he does know a lot about runs…
Don	…but most important of all is to be surrounded by all of you. People I have shared a lifetime with and equally, had the time of my life with. And not forgetting one who has only just arrived for the end of the show. One month Kelly, and you have brightened this place up no end. It's like you've always been here.
Colin	… don't we know it.
Don	Gentlemen, you all mean so much to me and therefore, it only leaves me with one thing to say - We few, we happy few, we band of brothers.

They all applaud.

Tom	Very well said.
Alan	For a stagehand.
Don	Manager!
A/C/D/Tm	The old ones are the best.

They all laugh and break. Kelly has a tray of food and works the room with it.

Colin	*(He approaches Kelly).* So, let's see how it goes: you can fool some of the people some of the time.
Kelly	Meaning?
Colin	Losing the bet isn't losing the battle.
Kelly	Let's get one thing clear shall we? I ain't going anywhere sunshine. And chuckin' clever quotes around and sarcastic comments counts for jack shit with me. I like it here. I'm staying here. And I might not be the brightest star in the sky…
Colin	Well I hadn't noticed…
Kelly	But I'm streetwise enough to have you figured. So get off your high horse, get your attitude from up your arse and grow up.

Colin is just about to explode but Julie wanders over.

Julie	Well. *(Uncomfortable silence).* Isn't this lovely. *(No response from Colin and Kelly).* Both having a good time?
Colin	Lovely.
Kelly	Brilliant.
Colin	Couldn't be better.
Kelly	The company makes it for me.
Julie	*(Pause).* Good.
Colin	So satisfying being surrounded by people with intellect and culture, don't you think Julie?
Kelly	… and people who aren't spiteful and malicious, eh Julie?
Julie	Right.
Colin	And knowing we are serviced by staff who are competent and agreeable, isn't that right Julie?
Kelly	… and residents who are pleasant and caring, who don't have personality disorders and talk out of their ar…
Julie	…absolutely. How…interesting. Stimulating little chat. Good good. Carry on. *(She moves on quickly and then exits to get the birthday cake).*
Colin	Think I'll try the food before things get any staler.
Kelly	Be careful not to choke. Wouldn't like to enjoy myself too much.
Tony	*(He wanders into the exchange between Colin and Kelly, followed by Gordon).* And how are we Colin?
Colin	Sod off. *(He walks away).*
Tony	That good? Right, so. Another memorable heart-to-heart with a resident.
Kelly	Are you having a nice time Gordon?
Gordon	*(He reacts like he has been asked the most taxing question of his life).* Yes.
Kelly	Have you had something to eat?
Gordon	Yes.
Kelly	You look very smart.

Gordon	Yes.
Kelly	Is that all you're going to say?
Gordon	*(Pause).* Yes.
Tony	I wrote Gordon a little guide to keep with him all the time that he can refer to. You know, just to help him in being comfortable with making small talk.
Kelly	That's a brilliant idea. And it seems to be working well Gordon. Is there a knack to it? *(Gordon holds up a small piece of card with the word 'Yes' written on it).* Is there nothing else your guide tells you?

Gordon turns the card around – it has the word 'No' on the back. He ambles off, leaving the card on the table which is used by Tom later.

Tony	Whilst I'm here I might as well take advantage of you and have a little nibble. *(He laughs suggestively).*
Kelly	Right. Try one of these. They're gorgeous. I love hot sausage.
Tony	*(He laughs suggestively).* Is that a euphemism?
Kelly	*(She ponders the question like it is one of magnitude and then with solemnity).* No. I think it's a Wall's.
Tom	*(He has been stood back observing. He walks in between Kelly and Tony and kisses Kelly on the cheek).* Don't you ever think of leaving Kelly. Don't you think of staying Tony.
Tony	Right-o. *(He moves on).*
Kelly	Tommy, Colin's really got one on him with me today – more than usual.
Tom	I know. Face like a Tranny with a blunt razor.
Kelly	No. There's something else.
Tom	Don't let it bother you love. As dear Larry once said to me at The Vic: "Don't let the bastards grind you down".
Kelly	Lawrence Olivier?
Tom	No. Larry the toilet attendant at Victoria Station.
Kelly	Before I forget, I was meaning to ask you. Has Tony been a successful businessman in Australia?
Tom	Julie's other half? I don't think so, why?
Kelly	Nothing. It's just that he asked me earlier if I'd heard about him being big down under.
Tom	Did he now? Where did we leave Don's bowel preparation? I can feel the need for a fresh batch of orange squit. *(He moves away).*

Julie enters carrying a cake with candles on and starts the singing: 'For He's A Jolly Good Fellow'. They all join in.

Julie	Now, here we are.
Alan	Come on now. Take a big puff.
Tom	Form an orderly queue! *(They all laugh).*
Julie	Come along now Don, make a wish. In fact, all make a wish.

They all stop and the atmosphere changes for each of them just for a moment. Colin and Kelly look at each other. Tom touches Alan on the shoulder. Tony smiles at Julie who blanks him. Gordon just looks uncomfortable. Don pauses and blows the candles out. All cheer again.

Don	*(He seems to falter for a second or two).* Sorry. All OK. Think I tried a bit too hard.

Tom	My Donald that was impressive. Think you've been hiding your light under a bushel!
Kelly	Are you OK?
Don	Of course. No need to fuss. Just getting too excitable.
Kelly	What did you wish for?
Don	I think I might make a phone call to see if I can make it happen. *(He picks up a cordless phone on the side table by Tom's chair and dials a number. As the conversation gradually develops, the others stop chatting and listen).* Hello Kevin, it's dad. Dad. Donald. How are you? Oh. Are you feeling…right…can I just have a very quick word with…hello love, it's your Dad. Well, you know thought I'd give you a call today. Why? With it being my birthday of course. No love, I don't want anything. I just thought it would be nice to have a quick chat and…I'm sorry…just thought I'd save you calling and…yes, I know how busy you are…no, I didn't realise you would be eating…sorry…how are the children? Would it be possible to have just a very quick word with…no, alright. Will there be any chance of you calling to…no, sorry, I understand. I'm just having a little party here for my…well, I paid for it…don't get worked up dear, it was only a few pounds…I didn't think I needed to check with you and…it's just sandwiches and…but I only wanted to say…hello. Hello? Hello? *(The call has clearly been terminated. And then, in a much brighter voice when he realises he is being observed).* Oh, that will be lovely. Oh, you didn't need to spend that much. Course you can come around. Anytime. Yes, super. And I love you to. Goodbye love, goodbye. *(He ends the call and turns to find everybody in silence staring at him. He realises that his charade has not convinced anybody. He begins buoyant but gets upset, a little breathless by the end).* Mary and Kevin send their love to you all. Sorry that they can't make it. They've been trying to get through on the phone you see … all day to wish me happy birthday but the line was engaged. So lucky to have family aren't I. *(He turns and looks out of the widow. He is distant).* So lucky to have... people, who care. And that I mean so much to…a great comfort. Knowing you are remembered, loved. Not a burden. Not ignored. Useless. Forgotten. Already buried. *(He turns back to them).* Think I'll just nip to my room for, for.. I think I need my spray. Won't be very…please excuse me. *(He exits quickly, clearly distressed).*
Kelly	I'll just go and …
Colin	No. I'll go.
Kelly	But I know …
Colin	You know nothing. *(He exits).*
Kelly	I just can't believe that happened.
Tom	Welcome to Groundhog Day at Pensioner Central, eh Julie? *(Julie and Tony exit clearly embarrassed. Gordon follows them).* And off they trot. You see, real life events spoil the little fantasy world of their glossy brochure. Times like this I'm glad the only person I need to worry about is me. And as I don't give a shit about me, win-win I'd say. What do you say Alan? Alan? Hello, earth calling Alan.
Kelly	*(Putting her arm around him).* Are you alright my love?

Alan	*(He has been sat in an armchair throughout).* I was just trying to remember something … but now I can't remember what I was trying to remember.
Kelly	Comes to us all.
Alan	*(He is distant).* No. Not like this. Life's memory is a receding tide Kelly. And your life, the footprints you leave on the beach are only there for as long as there are people who saw you leave them. With each tide and each new day after you have gone, time simply washes the memory of you away; makes a new beach for a new generation to make their mark. And within just one lifetime, it's as if you never existed. And now I've realised that, it makes the decision much easier …
Kelly	Decision?
Alan	*(He becomes anxious as if the exchange had not occurred).* I was just trying to find my room key. That was it. Where is it? I had it. I know I had it.
Tom	Is it in your pocket?
Alan	*(He stands, suddenly snapping and incredulous).* In my pocket? Do you think I am an imbecile? Why would I not know where I had put my own key … *(He puts his hand in his pocket, realises it is there, but does not say so. He exits, annoyed, speaking as he does so, leaving his wallet on the chair).* I just wish people would not interfere.
Tom	To think, I shaved my legs for this.
Kelly	For god's sake. What is the matter with everybody today? And what was Alan talking about?
Tom	Not sure love. And that wasn't like Don one bit either. It's never got to him like that before. And I can't remember the last time he needed his spray.
Kelly	I don't understand what was going on with that phone call.
Tom	…oftentimes excusing of a fault doth make the fault the worse by the excuse.
Kelly	Right, I think.
Tom	In other words, I don't know what's worse: what they do to him or how he covers up for it. Concealing how they treat him is killing him Kelly. And what sort of life is that? Living isn't just about passively existing Kelly. It takes effort. And it ain't easy. And sometimes, no matter how difficult it might make things, you can't just allow shit to happen.
Kelly	I think I get it. *(She smiles).*
Tom	What?
Kelly	Understanding is a journey we choose to take.
Tom	My God. Shakespeare?
Kelly	No. Don. Just something he said to me that now makes sense.
Tom	Good on you Kelly.
Kelly	But it still doesn't help me figure out what's going on today – I'm sure I'm missing something.
Tom	We're all just as bad at not seeing what's in front of us. Don, Alan, me; we're all getting older and more peculiar. Even Gordon. He's become very chatty recently with a wicked sense of humour!
Kelly	Really? *(Tom holds up Gordon's card with the word 'No' on it which was left on the table by Gordon).*
Kelly	I don't think you've changed much.

Tom	… no perfection is so absolute, that some impurity doth not pollute.
Kelly	Hmm. And what about Colin?
Tom	Oh, you know. Still a cock.
Kelly	Did Shakespeare say that?
Tom	No love. But I bet he wished he had. *(He exits).*
Kelly	*(She goes to the sofa Alan was sat on and begins to tidy it. There is a wallet on it which she picks up, looks in it and calls out).* Tom, will you give this to Alan … *(Tom has already gone. She puts the wallet back down on the chair. As she touches the cushion on the chair, she recoils back slightly and touches it again. To herself).* It's wet. *(She smells her hand).* Oh, Alan. *(She looks off stage after him. She exits taking the cushion with her).*

Colin enters slowly, smiling, indicating that he had been watching. He picks up the wallet and considers it. He goes to put it back down, but then takes twenty pounds out of it and puts it down again, smiling. Fade to black. Music: 'Ain't We Got Fun'.

Scene 2

The following day. Scene opens to empty stage. Lights come up as music is fading out.

Tom	*(Entering with Tony).* But why does Julie want to see us all?
Tony	Not sure. Just asked me to gather everybody together in here and that she would be through shortly.
Kelly	*(Kelly She enters followed by Gordon).* What's going on?
Tom	We don't know. Have to wait for Julie apparently. Very cloak and dagger. Bit like a TV drama, but clearly, infinitely more talented prominent actors taking the leads daaaaarling!
Kelly	Am I included in that?
Tom	Of course love. Every piece needs cheap extras.
Kelly	A poor player that struts and frets his hour upon the stage and then is heard no more.
Tom	Ooooo! How sharper than a serpent's tooth it is to have a thankless child!
Kelly	Nature teaches beasts to know their friends!
Tom	These words are razors to my wounded heart. *(They laugh. Alan walks in, interrupting, a little flustered).* Alright Alan? *(Alan doesn't answer but he sits, as does Tom).*
Kelly	*(Don enters and she goes to him).* OK love?
Don	Yes thank you. Nothing that a good sleep and a clear head couldn't repair.
Julie	*(She enters followed by Colin).* Morning everybody. Sorry to interrupt your day, but something quite serious has cropped up which I need to speak to you all about. It would appear that some money has gone missing. *(Immediately there is a response from everybody and chatter).* I am sad to say that Alan has had twenty pounds stolen. *(Everybody reacts except Colin).*
Don	Is that correct Alan?
Alan	Is it correct? Of course it's bloody correct. Why would I be sat here if it wasn't.
Don	I'm sorry, I just…

The following three lines are delivered but there is follow up/generated conversation from everybody else.

Tom	But when did you last know you had it?
Tony	Can you be certain you didn't spend it?
Kelly	But how can it have gone? A thief in here?
Julie	*(Interrupting)*. Please, please. The money has gone from Alan's wallet that he left in here yesterday. There was one hundred pounds in it that he had withdrawn from the cash machine in town. He has not had a chance to spend any of it. Somebody has taken a twenty-pound note from it. There is no other explanation.

More conversation and conjecture from everyone except Colin, who is silent throughout.

Alan	*(He is uncomfortable)*. Look. I can't have lost it. I know I haven't.
Julie	The bank notes were all new and sequential, so if it is here, it would be easy enough to identify.
Tom	That's all well and good but that would mean searching us all.
Tony	Julie, I think we need to chat about this before you take this any further.
Julie	I think you need to stay out of this and let me handle it.
Tony	But really. *(Julie cuts him a look that stops him dead)*.
Tom	*(To Don)*. Well. It would appear The Gorgon has spoken.
Gordon	I never did!
Tom	*(Speaking loudly to Gordon)*. Gorgon…oh forget it.
Julie	I don't need to search everybody – do I Kelly? *(They all look at Kelly)*.
Kelly	What?
Julie	Did you take that money?
Kelly	No I did not! Why should it be me who's taken it?
Colin	Shall we start a list?
Kelly	And what does that mean?
Colin	The lady doth protest too much, methinks.
Tom	Now hang on just one minute Colin…
Colin	Did you take it?
Tom	No I bloody well did not!
Colin	Do you think Donald did?
Don	I say!
Tom	Of course not.
Colin	And is Alan just making it up? *(No response)*. Well then. Unless the owners are on the take or perhaps another member of staff…? *(They all look at Gordon)*.
Gordon	Who?
Tom	Don't be stupid. I mean…I'm just saying…Oh I don't know what I'm saying.
Colin	So. Who is there left? I mean. As if I would dream of causing unnecessary problems or issues for anybody.
Kelly	As if.
Julie	There is a simple way of clearing this up. Kelly, have you any money in your apron pocket?
Kelly	Of course not. *(She puts her hand in her apron pocket and then her expression immediately changes as she slowly takes a twenty pound note out)*. That's not mine!
Colin	From her own mouth.

They all look at Kelly.

Julie	*(She takes the note and looks at it).* That is the correct serial number.
Kelly	No! I didn't take it!

Commotion and talking from everyone except Alan. The noise gets louder.

Alan	*(He covers his ears with his hands).* Stop it. Stop it. *(Shouting).* Stop it! *(Pause. He is clearly distressed).* Please! This is all too much! *(Tom goes to comfort him).*
Julie	Kelly, I'm waiting for an explanation?
Kelly	I didn't take it! What else do you want me to say?
Colin	How about 'guilty'?
Tom	Hang on, how did you know the money would be there?
Julie	Let's just say somebody saw it placed there. *(More commotion from everyone).*
Don	Excuse me. Then they are mistaken. I'm sorry everybody. This is all a little embarrassing. I think this is all my fault.
Colin	No it is not!
Julie	How? What do you mean?
Don	How embarrassing. I found that twenty-pound note first thing this morning when I came down. As Kelly must have been the last one in here clearing up, I assumed it was hers, so I went to the kitchen and put it in her apron. I meant to tell her this morning but completely forgot…
Colin	*(Incensed).* You're a liar!
Julie	I beg your pardon?
Colin	Stop covering up for her!
Don	I'm not Colin…
Colin	You can't…he can't have put that money in there.
Tom	Why Colin?
Colin	Because, because …
Tom	And the mists begin to disperse. I think that clears it all up, don't you Julie?
Colin	No!
Tom	Problem solved. Kelly, Julie is very sorry aren't you Julie?
Julie	Well, I…
Tom	Kelly, you appreciate that this was a complete misunderstanding don't you?
Kelly	Well, I…
Tom	Alan, you're as happy as a pig in shit aren't you?
Alan	Well, I…
Tom	Gordon, you haven't got a clue what's going on have you?
Gordon	Who?
Tom	Marvellous. Alan and I are going outside to get a breath of fresh air. Come along Alan. *(He takes Alan's hand and then looks at Colin, pointedly).* After all, the smell of bullshit in here is pretty overwhelming, isn't it Colin? *(He leads Alan, walks over to Julie, takes the money out of her hand and they both exit).*

Pause. Colin is seething.

Julie	Well, no harm done I suppose. Carry on. *(She exits followed by Tony and Gordon).*
Colin	*(He approaches Don).* They shall have wars and pay for their presumption.
Don	Mine honour is my life; both grow in one; take honour from me and my life is done. *(He stares at Colin. This has taken any anger, betrayal out of it. Colin is*

	broken by this. He goes to speak but cannot. Don of all people should find him out and show him for what he is. He bows his head and exits).
Kelly	I didn't take that money – and you didn't put in my apron.
Don	I know.
Kelly	Why? Why did he do it?
Don	Anger, loneliness, habit, power, but above all of them, fear.
Kelly	And I've caused all that?
Don	Oh no. *(Smiling).* Kelly, how have you managed thus far in life so innocent? *(They hug each other. He breathes out, as if a little breathless).* Think I need my spray. *(He goes to exit. Then stops and turns).*
Don	And thank you.
Kelly	For what?
Don	I saw you Kelly, after everybody had gone last night. I saw you cleaning the seat Alan had been sitting in; saw you this morning, first thing, fitting a new cushion cover which I assume you bought on your way home.
Kelly	I…
Don	And I knew then the change in you. Like was said to you all those months ago. If we're not your living, we become your life. We're not just a job any longer are we Kelly? You care. Care enough to conceal that Alan is incontinent… *(he gets a little overcome)*… and care enough to protect the most important thing of all. The one thing that all of us fight to retain above all else. Dignity. *(Kelly is speechless).* And I knew if I claimed to have put that money in your apron, the truth would out.
Kelly	I don't know what to say.
Don	Then doesn't that prove we have both done a good thing. Welcome to the firm my love. *(He kisses her on the forehead, breathes out heavily again).* Think I need to nip to my room. *(He goes to exit, pauses without turning back).* What would I have given for a daughter like you. *(He exits).*

Kelly sits. There is a loud crash. Kelly goes to exit as if to see what has caused it but is intercepted by Gordon, who is clearly distressed.

Kelly	Gordon, what is it? Gordon!
Gordon	Help him, please Kelly, help him.
Kelly	Oh no. Please god, no. *(She exits running and we hear her shouting from offstage).* I need some help here … now. Don, speak to me. Don, Don. Help!

Gordon stands looking off stage, shocked. Fade to black. Music: 'Send in the Clowns' from 'A Little Night Music'. During black out, a church lectern is brought on stage and Colin takes position behind it.

Scene 3

Music fades as light comes up. Sharply focussed with spot. The following week. A church service.

| Colin | Good morning everybody. Following the death of his son, Wordsworth wrote in a letter to a friend - For myself, dear friend, I dare not say in what state of mind I am; I loved him with the utmost love of which my soul is capable, and he is taken from me - yet in the agony of my spirit in surrendering such a treasure I feel a thousand times richer than if I |

	had never possessed it. And it was with that sentiment and with a very heavy heart that we all heard of the passing away of this very dear friend to us all. He was one of those rare breeds in theatre who had no acquaintances, just friends. And in Don's circle of influence, there were no strangers, just friends he was yet to make. Don contributed something to all of us in his own unique way and acknowledging and remembering that one thing, ensures that the memory of such a fine man never fades. *(For a moment, briefly, he is a little overcome).* The last time Don and I spoke, well, it was not how I would have preferred. So I dare not leave him with words of mine, but with words from one we shared a life with and a love of.
Colin *(Cont'd)*	Not a flower, not a flower sweet, On my black coffin let there be strown. Not a friend, not a friend greet My poor corpse, where my bones shall be thrown. A thousand thousand sighs to save, Lay me, O, where. Sad true lover never find my grave, To weep there.

He bows his head and quietly cries. Fade to black. Music: 'Someone to watch over me'. Lectern taken off in black out.

Scene 4

Later the same day. Lights come up and music fades. The Wake. All are on stage including Mary and Kevin. Julie is finishing off speaking.

Julie	… And so in closing, I just wanted to say that Don will be a great loss to us all, and The Beeches will not be the same without him. Thank you. Oh, and the buffet is in the dining room when you are ready. *(Polite applause. No response from Mary and Kevin who remain as unmoved as ever. As Julie passes them, she speaks with them).* I do appreciate the family accepting our invitation to come back to The Beeches for this small reception. I know the residents feel…
Kevin	You did say there was no charge didn't you?
Julie	Oh yes, yes.
Kevin	Then it's alright then.

Gordon approaches with two glasses of orange juice.

Mary	*(Abruptly).* We don't want anything. Especially that.
Gordon	*(Chucking).* Pity.
Julie	Well, if you need anything before you go, just let me know.
Mary	Such as?
Gordon	Toilet?
Julie	That will be all thank you Gordon.
Gordon	*(Walking away).* Gobshites.
Julie	I mean, if there is anything of your fathers you might want to take with you today?

All are now clearly listening as they quietly chat.

Mary	Does he have any money here?
Tom	Disgusting.
Julie	I don't think so, unless he had any in his room. We don't handle cash for the residents. They manage their own financial affairs. Kelly, did Don ever mention anything about money to you?
Kelly	No, I don't think so.
Kevin	And why would you know about his money?
Kelly	I don't.
Kevin	I bet.
Mary	We will want to go through his things to remove anything of value – security you see.
Tom	Oh, we see.
Kevin	Eh?
Tom	Still struggling with those letters? Bless.
Julie	No problem at all. Just let me know and I will take you up there.
Mary	Which room is it?
Kelly	Which room is it? You mean you don't know which room your father was in. He'd lived here for seven and a half years!
Tom	Leave it Kelly.
Kelly	No I won't leave it.
Colin	Yes she will.
Kelly	I don't need your help.
Colin	No. But they do. *(Kelly is taken aback by this).*
Alan	*(In his own world).* Don was a dear friend, a surrogate family to me. You see I never really hear anything from my family because …
Kevin	What are you going on about you stupid old fool?
Kelly	Don't you speak to Alan like that.
Colin	Right. You just listen to me.
Mary	No. We've had enough of you lot and your rubbish. It was because of you and your precious theatre that I never had a father. It was because of you and your precious theatre that Mum and me were always on our own. Off he went, gallivanting around the country. Only came back to give her money, get her pregnant and tell his big stories about the people he met, the famous people he knew and talk about you lot. You lot. Pathetic. A bunch of old has beens who live in your own little world.
Alan	But we love Don.
Mary	Aye. I bet you did. And its 'loved'. He's dead. Freaks. Living in your own little cess pit getting up to god knows what.
Julie	Can I just say…
Kevin	My wife's talking so shut up.
Tony	I say…
Kevin	Shut it!
Mary	We want nothing of his, just whatever money he's got and anything that can be sold.
Tom	But what about his collection? His programmes, memorabilia, a lifetime's worth of memories?

Mary	His memories, not mine. Burn it.

Everybody is mortified and begin to protest.

Kevin	*(Shouting).* Shut it!

Everybody stops talking.

Mary	'The firm'. I know what he called you. You all make me sick. We scrimp and save for a living and he lives here being waited on hand and foot.
Colin	Don paid his way.
Mary	With money that should have been mine! My mother dies and who got it all? Him. What did I get? Nothing.
Kelly	Don would have given you anything.
Mary	Well I didn't want anything off him.
Tom	Well make your bloody mind up.
Kevin	One more word out of you. *(Gordon walks into the middle of it all).* What do you want, freak?
Gordon	Don was my friend too.
Kevin	What? Shut it. Come on Mary. Let's get out of here as soon as we've been through all his things. At least it's the last time we'll be in this dump.
Colin	Ironic that it's the longest time you've spent here. Don't let us delay your grave robbing.
Kevin	*(He turns and starts walking towards Colin. Instinctively, they all step between them to protect Colin).* Pathetic.
Mary	Come on love. They're not worth it.
Gordon	He left something y'know. For his favourite son-in-law. Something he could never give you himself.
Kevin	What?
Gordon	Over there. *(He points in the direction behind them with his thumb. Mary looks in the direction in which Gordon is pointing and walks to the back. All the others, except Kevin, also turn and move to join Mary. To Kevin).* An overdue present from Don, Gobshite. *(He promptly punches Kevin in the stomach causing him to reel back and fall in a chair, dazed).*
Mary	I can't see anything.
Gordon	Neither can bollocks here
Mary	*(She hears Kevin's groans and goes to him).* Kevin! Kevin! What's the matter?
Gordon	*(Theatrically and very OTT).* Overcome with emotion.
Tom	Oh Gordon, you old queen!
Colin	*(Realising what has just happened).* Would I be correct in thinking Gordon, that with all that's gone on, it's all, how shall I say, 'just hit him'?
Gordon	Where?
Kelly	I don't think you're as daft as you make out.
Gordon	Who? *(He winks at Kelly).*
Tony	*(Helping Kevin up and out).* Come along Kevin. Let's get you some fresh air… and maybe a glass of orange.
Kevin	*(Groggily).* No!
Tony	Certainly. Bring you around in a flash … or should that be a flush. *(They exit).*
Mary	You lot won't get away with this. *(Backing away).*

Colin	Get away with what Mary? Love?
Tom	Caring?
Julie	Respect?
Alan	Dignity?
Kelly	Friendship?
Gordon	Kindness?
Colin	Belonging?
Tom	Happiness?
Julie	Family?
Alan	Laughter?
Kelly	Security?
Gordon	Home?
Julie	You know what Mary? There is something he could never say to you, but I feel that we should do now that he has gone.
Mary	What?
All	Piss off! *(Pause. Mary exits in a rush).*
Julie	Is this what it always feels like? You know, how you lot always are?
Colin	A little bit.
Julie	Bloody marvellous! *(She exits).*
Tom	Come on Alan, let's get you some buffet. You too Gordon. *(They exit leaving Colin and Kelly alone, looking at each other).*
Kelly	I'm going to the dining room. God knows what will happen with those three in there. *(She goes to exit).* Would you like something to eat? *(Colin nods and as she is about to exit).*
Colin	Yes – please. *(Kelly turns to him. He is perhaps embarrassed at himself and speaks like the old Colin, abruptly).* Bring it to the conservatory. *(He exits).*
Kelly	*(She smiles. To herself).* You're welcome.

Fade to black. Music: 'Friendship' from 'Anything Goes'.

Scene 5

Some weeks later. Lights come up to reveal Alan. He is clearly anxious, sat holding a telephone directory and the portable phone handset. He is rocking gently. He quickly takes a bottle of tablets out of his pocket looking at it and places it very purposefully on the table next to him. He has a coffee cup next to his seat. He dials a number.

Alan   Hello, is that directory enquiries? Hello. I'm trying to contact my family who live in the Gloucester area. What name is it? I suppose you must get a lot of older people calling who can't. Name please? You see I haven't seen them in such a long time and I just want to…their name please? Yes. That's the problem. You'll think this is most peculiar. I woke up in the middle of the night and that was my problem, I can't remember…their name please? You see, I have the phone book in front of me and I know this sounds bizarre, but I've been looking through it all night thinking it might jog my memory about what they're called. I think I've looked on every, single … are they the same surname as me?

Yes, I think they are, they must be, why didn't I think of that, but that's the problem you see, I'm just struggling a little to remember…which name

	please? *(He becomes upset).* Look, just saying over and over the same question won't help because I can't, I can't … what? Which town please? Which one did I say? Did I say one? I went to school in Lincoln if that helps. Father had a grocer's shop on … Mother had beautiful blonde hair and had a voice like … and my eldest brother was a rear gunner for bomber command and died during the … *(His demeanour changes. He becomes angry and distraught).* … I just need to speak to someone, anyone … anybody, somebody please tell me who I, who I…hello, hello.
Kelly	*(She enters carrying a duster, singing to herself, paying no attention to Alan. She starts dusting the bookcase whilst singing to herself. She is clearly aware that Alan is there but does not look at him).* Hiya chuck
Alan	*(He is distant, removed, not really aware of the questions or the answers).* Kelly?
Kelly	*(Carrying on cleaning).* Yes, my love what is it?
Alan	I need to speak to you?
Kelly	Hang on Alan, just finish this.
Alan	Kelly, I can't carry on like this.
Kelly	That's nice.
Alan	You see, I don't remember.
Kelly	Yes, that is nice.
Alan	I've got nothing left. *(Kelly is still singing to herself).* I keep trying to remember, but the more I try the more of it, of me, goes away.
Kelly	I'll get you a tea in a minute.
Alan	It can't go on like this. I can't. I can't…
Kelly	No sign of any of the others yet then?
Alan	I have to stop it. Yes. Stop. End it. *(He has picked up the tablets and is frantically twisting the lid. We hear the rapid clicks of the child-proof lid and he is very quickly frustrated, emotional, crying, distressed).*
Kelly	*(She turns and for the first time looks at Alan. She instinctively runs across the room and struggles with him and eventually gets the bottle from him during the next dialogue).* Alan! What do you think you are doing?
Alan	Making it go away.
Kelly	Making what go away?
Alan	Helping.
Kelly	Helping!? Stop it you, crazy old man.
Alan	Get off me!
Kelly	Or what, you'll kill yourself? Give them to me. And who is it you're actually helping with this?
Alan	Everybody.
Kelly	Oh, so you think Tom is going to be pleased and Colin will be doing belly laughs?
Alan	Colin doesn't care...
Kelly	Of course he does.
Alan	Nobody cares.
Kelly	But I do!
Alan	You don't know me.
Kelly	And you do?
Alan	I don't know anything any longer. I don't think I ever did.

Kelly	Then I'll tell you something shall I? Something that I know shall I? I'll miss you; I'll be upset, I care.
Alan	*(He becomes lucid again, disbelieving).* Why?
Kelly	Because. Well, I don't know why. Do I need a reason to care? Does caring about somebody need conditions attached?
Alan	Well sometimes, you just need to know, you just need to be told; you just need to be able to remember, remember. *(Shouting).* Who am I? What am I?
Kelly	*(She takes hold of Alan's head in her hands and speaks forcefully to him).* You're Alan, my friend. I care about you. *(Tom enters).* That's all you've got to remember. I care about you, you silly old bugger.
Tom	Well, that NVQ level 1 in 'counselling the elderly' was worth every penny. *(He then begins to take in the melee).* What on earth is going on?
Kelly	Tom, you care don't you?
Tom	About what?
Kelly	Alan.
Tom	Of course I do.
Kelly	How much?
Tom	How much? What's this, afternoon bloody quiz time?
Kelly	I'm being serious. *(She shows Tom the tablets in her hand).*
Tom	*(He takes the tablets off Kelly).* Oh Alan... *(Alan slowly starts sobbing).*
Kelly	What has happened for him to be like this?
Tom	This has building up for a while now. But what are these tablets? I didn't know he was taking tablets? Why didn't we know? *(Reading the bottle).* Oh no, they're Mr Goldberg's from room 9.
Kelly	Get Colin will you Tom. We need to figure this one out. Go. I'll stay with him.
Tom	Will do. *(He exits).*
Alan	*(Kelly kneels next to Alan again and takes his hands. He then speaks, distant but with clarity, oddly lucid and gently).* Whatever comes cannot alter one thing. If I am a princess in rags and tatters, I can be a princess inside. It would be easy to be a princess if I were dressed in cloth of gold, but it is a great deal more of a triumph to be one all the time when no one knows it.
Kelly	'A Little Princess'.
Alan	But how do you ...
Kelly	Know? I might not have a posh voice or be very bright, but like you I can read, and like you ... I can dream. *(Alan begins to sob again).* There's no need to cry. I know Alan. We all know. We know you and who you really are better than you do. We always have. And you know what? We don't care. What matters is the firm get you better. Bit too old not to be who you really are; don't you think?
Alan	Bless you Kelly. Though I know I don't deserve your kindness. Bless you. Kelly, I can't remember anything. It's all gone. With every passing day. Like a thief in the night. Age. It's taking everything away from me. And I'm next.
Kelly	Then I'll help you get everything back. We all will. After all, what's the firm for?
Colin	*(Entering with Tom).* What's going on?

Kelly	Nothing you could ever understand. Tom, stay here with him. *(She exits).*
Tom	Colin, do something.
Colin	What?
Tom	I don't bloody know. He's lost it or, well, I don't know what. Kelly caught him trying to take these. He's rambling.
Colin	He has been for months but none of us wanted to know. We've known for months that something wasn't right. It was just easier to ignore.
Alan	I'm sorry.
Colin	What for? What have you got to be sorry for?
Alan	I don't know.
Colin	Time to stop pretending, Alan. Time to be who you are. Time for us all to be honest. And time to concentrate on getting you better. Jesus, Julie's coming. If she realises how bad he is he'll be out.

Julie enters followed by Tony.

Alan	Mother?
Julie	Oh yes, I'm your mother, very funny. What's going on?
A/C	Nothing.
Tom	Everything's just fine.
Julie	Whose are those tablets?
A/C	Mine.
Julie	Alright, what is going on? *(She takes the tablets. Kelly enters).* Kelly, what did you say was the matter?

Tom and Colin stare at Kelly.

Colin	Judas.
Kelly	I thought... but Alan was... what was I supposed to do?
Julie	Come on Alan, let's get you to your room and get the doctor to you. He's already here seeing somebody thankfully. Tony, go fetch him.
Tony	Julie, do you not think…
Julie	Yes. I think. And you do.
Tony	One day, Julie, you wipe your feet on me for the last time. *(For the first time he stares at Julie with defiance. Julie breaks her gaze. He turns slowly and walks out. Julie starts to slowly walk Alan out).*
Kelly	*(She watches Julie and Alan exit then turns and looks at Colin and Tom).* What? Don't look at me like that.
Tom	Well done Kelly.
Kelly	What have I done?
Colin	Alan will be gone from here by morning. Congratulations.
Kelly	He can't leave. He won't leave. I need to look after him. He's not well.
Tom	Congratulations again.
Colin	'Independent Living' - ever thought what that means?
Tom	When you can't care for yourself you have to leave. That's the rule. The 'contract' that we signed. We told you how it works. We told you, Kelly.
Kelly	But this is his home!
Colin	A gilded cage.
Kelly	But he won't cope.

Colin	Congratulations.
Kelly	Stop saying that!
Colin	Had to go running to Miss didn't you?
Kelly	We have a duty of care to...
Colin	Bollocks! 'Duty of Care'. What does that mean? I'll tell you. It means that my arse is corporately covered. It means that my risk assessment is printed and in a folder ready for inspection: glistening, perfect, shiny, rehearsed… just like my smile and my answers. It means all policies and procedures have been adhered to, boxes have been ticked, quality systems were followed at all times. We have a certificate on the wall to show we care. It has four gold fucking stars on it to show competence, compliance, cleanliness… bollocks. Now and again, just now and again Kelly, we have to step outside the world the likes of you and Julie live in and realise that you have created a vacuum that real people no longer live in.
Kelly	Don't you compare me to her.
Colin	The creatures outside looked from pig to man, and from man to pig, and from pig to man again; but already it was impossible to say which was which.
Kelly	What?
Colin	*(He gets a book off the shelf and throws it at her feet).* Animal Farm. Read it and weep.
Kelly	But… I'm not like Julie.
Colin	And the circle is complete. Life imitating art, imitating life.
Julie	*(She enters).* Can I have your attention a moment.
Colin	And here comes the sugar-coated pill.
Julie	There isn't an easy way to do this so I may as well just come out and say it. Alan has had a stroke. He collapsed the minute he reached his room.
Kelly	I'll go to him.
Colin	No, I'll go.
Julie	No, I think you should both wait here.
C/K	But he needs me.
Julie	It took less than a minute.
Kelly	What took less than a minute? Tell me?
Julie	Alan has passed away. Doctor Fraser got to him almost immediately. Tony is with him and has called for the undertakers. There's nothing that can be done. He's gone.
Kelly	No. But he... he was OK. He was sat here. The chairs still warm. His coffee is… he walked out with you just now…
Julie	He collapsed as we arrived at his room. It was that quick.
Kelly	*(She is rambling).* He can't be. No. The doctor has to be wrong. I've read about people who they thought were dead and they weren't. I remember thinking my hamster was dead one Christmas but...
Colin	*(Taking hold of her).* Kelly. Kelly, he isn't hibernating, he's dead.
Kelly	No, I need to go to him.
Colin	Stop.
Kelly	He needs me.
Colin	Stop! <u>Stop</u>!

Gordon	*(Pause. He comes rushing in).* Taxi, taxi!
C/J/K/Tm	*(Subdued).* We know.
Julie	I'll go and… well, you know. Come on Gordon. I've something to tell you. *(She links Gordon and starts to exit with him).*
Tom	Well. That's that then. *(Life carries on).*
Colin	Julie, you best tell the kitchen. It'd be a sin to waste a whole fresh salmon. *(Julie and Gordon exit).*
Tom	Was somebody saying something about making tea?
Colin	Oh I'm dying for a… well. You know what I mean.
Tom	Pass me the remote Kell', Countdown's on in 5 minutes.
Colin	Oh, that's not been the same since Richard Whitely died.
Kelly	What's the matter with you?
Tom	Beg pardon love?
Colin	Nothing why?
Kelly	Is that it then?
Tom	Is what, what?
Kelly	Have you got no feeling, no…
Colin	What is she going on about?
Tom	What you need is a nice brew and whilst you're making yourself one, you can...
Kelly	This isn't the new man from room seven. This is your best friend, the one you have shared a lifetime with. He died, just five minutes ago. I can still smell his aftershave in the air. And you sit there like nothing has happened; Countdown and a cuppa is that what it boils down to?
Tom	Nothing's boiled until you get your finger out.
Kelly	Has nothing just happened here?
Colin	At our age dear, no. This particular scene has an ending that we've rehearsed many times.
Kelly	Scenes, rehearsing: This isn't your precious theatre. How dare you pretend now. How dare you be normal. How dare you…
Colin	Oh no dear, we do dare. At our age all that is left is to dare. Dreaming is for some piss sodden pensioner sentenced to life in a bed: a duvet that's become a dungeon, a mattress that's become a manacle… a pillow that's their confidante. Oh no dear, I do dare and will continue to dare because life gets to a stage where dreams are pointless.
Tom	To sleep, perchance to dream; ay, there's the rub.
Kelly	What?
Colin	Dreams are to hope, and what would you like us to hope for? A miracle? I think somebody's already got the market cornered with that one and called it Easter. So what does that leave us with? Let's see. A hoped-for call from a doctor saying it was all a big mistake? A cure for something that we have spent a lifetime being told is just around the corner? An injection that will make me happy, or sad when expected of me? No dear. I am what I am…
Tom	*(Softly singing).* I am what I am…
Kelly	Don't sing at me you old queen!

Colin	How dare you. An audience of one is still an audience and at his age, beggars can't be choosers dear. We don't need your applause, we don't need your understanding and don't you ever dare give us your pity. So if all you've got left is anger then piss off. *(Kelly goes to leave).* Get back here!

Gordon enters having heard the commotion.

Kelly	You just told me to piss off.
Colin	*(Slowly gathering pace, getting more pointed, sarcastic, more vitriolic).* So clever, so wise, so mature. You waltz around here expecting floods of tears, wailing old fairies air kissing memories and yearning to be understood. Sliding around like some pain-snail, carrying your little house of angst on your back and trying to off-load it on us. Because you understand, because you've experienced. And now somebody you know has died, we all have to play out a soap episode that allegedly paints a picture of real life. What a farce. The telly parodies life and we re-enact the parody because we have forgotten what it is to live. And now, you stand there expecting the world to be the same as the telly because to you, that's life. Well. No. We are life, this is life. Life is about dying. Death is about living. You live with your own pain and don't infect us with it. *(Kelly begins to cry).*
Tom	Colin…
Colin	*(Angrily).* Shut it! *(He pushes Tom, who falls to the floor and then he turns back to Kelly again).* Oh, have I upset you? Have I spoilt your little illusion of what a crock of shit living can be? Well, this isn't Citizen's Advice or The Samaritans. I'm not here to listen and stroke your hand about how bad you feel; how upset you are. This is a rest home for old fuckers that are waiting for heavenly 'ring and ride' to turn up. And you are the minimum wage girlie employed to brew up, mop up sick and spray air freshener to mask the smell of death. *(Kelly sits, still crying).* Get up! *(Grabbing her arms and making her stand – he is in a rage).*
Gordon	*(Approaching Colin from behind).* Colin, just...
Colin	Get off me! *(He pushes Gordon who falls heavily into the armchair behind him, next to Tom. Julie enters having heard the commotion).* You're not upset for Don, you're upset for yourself. You expect everybody else to play along and carry your baggage on the guilt trip you've set out on. Grief is about loss, but with the likes of you, it's not for the one who's snuffed it. It's the loss of the opportunity to do all the things you meant to do and now can't do because the selfish bastard has gone and died. You're not ridden with grief you're ridden with guilt like all of us are. Your tears aren't for Alan, they're for you. *(Kelly screams and lets rip with a slap across his face. He falls into the armchair onto Gordon).*
Gordon	*(Pause. To Colin, peering around him).* Y' come here often?
Julie	Kelly! Get your coat and your things and get out.
Kelly	I…
Julie	Out.
Kelly	I'm leaving anyway. *(She shouts).* I want to live!
Tom	*(Trying to get up).* Good on you Kell.
Kelly	Drop dead.

Tom	*(Dropping back down).* Aye, most probably.
Colin	*(Standing).* Sometimes Kelly, we need a slap from life before it will hug us. Life ain't easy. Its shit and the only person who can un-shit it is you.
Kelly	So you've done me a favour getting me sacked?
Colin	Yes, I have.
Julie	Kelly, I have asked to you leave. Do you want me to call the...?
Kelly	I'm going. *(To Colin).* I loved Alan.
Colin	I know Kelly. The real tragedy is that you never told him, so he didn't know. But the real triumph is that we did, every day... and he knew it.

Tony enters, but remains unnoticed.

Julie	You have lost me a very capable member of staff and I will have to seriously consider whether I want you in my establishment.
Colin	Piss off.
Julie	I beg your pardon?
Gordon	He said piss off.
Tom	*(Gaining courage. He and Gordon help each other up).* Yes, piss off... VT!
Julie	I beg your pardon? VT?
Colin	Great. The King of Ad-libs strikes again.
Kelly	It's their name for you. The full title being, 'Vinegar Tits the piss witch'.
Julie	I'm speechless.
Gordon	Thank God for that.
Julie	I want both of you out of here tomorrow.
Tom	Reckon do you?
Colin	Four grand a month gone just like that, and do you think you can get two other silly old buggers to pay that? I don't think we're going anywhere somehow, unless of course, you're having it off with the bank manager as well as your business partner.
Tony	What?
Julie	Tony, don't listen to them. I can explain.
Colin	Pull up a chair Tommy. You too Kell – and turn your hearing aid on Gordon. This'll be an Oscar winner. Where's the life? Right here!
Tony	*(Incredulously).* 'Having it off with the bank manager'?
Julie	I, I...
Colin	And the business partner Tony...
Julie	I, I...
Tom	Bet there's more as well.
Gordon	Well don't look at me!
Julie	I, I, I...
Tony	Julie?
Julie	Tony, don't listen to them love.
Tony	Julie, will you do something for me?
Julie	Anything.
Tony	Piss off.
Julie	But...
Tony	Off. Piss.

Julie pauses and then exits.

Tony	*(Quietly to himself)*. "The old ones are the best".
Colin	There's only one answer to that isn't there?
Tony	"Thank you, thank you, I'm here all week".
Colin	*(He walks up to Tony with his hand outstretched)*. No, it's, welcome to the firm Tony.
Tony	You're very kind.
Colin	'bout time… don't you think?
Tony	I think I've served my apprenticeship.
Colin	No, more like a penance. I'm sorry Tony for, well…
Tony	No Colin. What's done and all that. New beginnings Colin, new beginnings. Your job's still available Kelly, if you want it. Ignore what VT said.
Kelly	Thanks Tony, but I think it's time to move on. *(Tony smiles at them all and then exits. Pause as they all stare out front, sat on the couch)*. I still can't believe that Alan has… you know.
Colin	Died. The word is died. It's what people do.
Kelly	Why do you have to make it sound so…
Colin	Real, honest, factual?
Kelly	It's not fair. I know its life. But it's still not fair.
Colin	I'm sorry chicken, you know for, well, everything.
Kelly	Good.
Colin	Look, I'm old and I'm gay. I'm a persecuted minority. One at least should buy me some forgiveness? *(Kelly doesn't respond)*. Makes me very popular at a general election?
Kelly	*(Speaking with great relish and cool sarcasm)*. I'm not Citizens Advice and I'm not The Samaritans.
Tom	Ooo, Trés Touché!
Colin	But I am sorry.
Kelly	I know.
Colin	About Alan, about you and really, about everything.
Kelly	I know.
Colin	What'll you do?
Kelly	Leave – which is more than you can.
Tom	We can leave love, it's just that we have to wear a mahogany overcoat.
Kelly	Don't be morbid.
Colin	Which is another way of saying 'don't be honest'. As T. S. Elliot wrote in 'The Four Quartets' - Human kind cannot bear too much reality.
Kelly	Right. *(She whispers to Tom)*. TS who?
Tom	TS nobody, love. He's more dead than we are, so in your world what he wrote counts for bugger all. You know what the TS stand for?
Gordon	'Talks Shit. I'll be off. *(He goes to leave)*.
Colin	And thank you as well Gordon. For everything. And sorry, for everything. *(He puts his hand out to shake hands which Gordon slowly acknowledges)*.
Gordon	Vinegar Tits eh? *(He starts laughing and walks over to Kelly and gives her a kiss)*. See you later love. *(He gives his over-pronounced wink and he exits 'a la John Wayne')*.

Kelly	What do you two both plan on doing then?
Colin	The most we can possibly hope for; to carry on breathing. And remembering, reminiscing, keeping memories alive and the people that are in them. Oh and making life shite for the next failed job seekers allowance that walks through them grotty doors.
Kelly	Did you ever care about anything.
Colin	Oh, lots of things; sadly, most of them revolved around me. That's why I am what I am.
Tom	*(Singing).* I am what I...
C/K	Shut it!
Tom	Ooh. Pardon me for being happy.
Kelly	But what will you do?
Colin	I haven't got a do in me.
Tom	*(Speaking under his breath).* Aye... until your Sunday laxative.
Colin	You know it's like having some big camp parrot sat on your bloody shoulder.
Tom	*(Sounding genuinely touched).* Aw. Thanks Colin, that's a lovely thing to say.
Colin	*(To Tom).* You wouldn't know the difference between a compliment and a condiment. *(To Kelly).* What I have left is to take the piss as often as possible, reminisce about the past... and now... miss you.
Kelly	Miss me?
Colin	Yeah. Very much probably. When the net curtains in this dump make any ray of sunshine fighting through them turn grey, you filled the place with light Kelly. *(Kelly is filling up).* Eh. Don't start. Never cry in front of him. You'll have to get the fire brigade in to pump out the water.
Tom	Oooh, Firemen. Do you think?
Kelly	Do you ever cry, ever show emotion?
Colin	My mother taught me one thing: cry in private. Tears shouldn't be a spectator event. They show weakness.
Kelly	Then I feel sorry for you.
Colin	Don't. Your personality has left no space for any sadness. Look at me. Honest and sincere! What have you turned me into? Who would have known we could actually teach something to each other? For the last few months... well. You did it by just being you when everything else in here was an act; everyone was an act. I was an act. You've put up with a lot from us, me. And I suppose I'm jealous of what you have.
Kelly	Me? What have I got?
Colin	A chance. A chance to laugh, to cry, to love; to hope. Youth, your health, freedom, an open door, a fresh start…
Tom	A prostate that works…
Kelly	Have you never had that examined?
Tom	Not medically…
Kelly	But you could still pick any of those things and make them happen.
Colin	This is life love, not a football coupon. Get out of here before our air suffocates you. Before our, my envy drags you down.
Kelly	*(She goes to leave, but then comes back and hugs Colin, then kisses him on the cheek. He laughs quietly).* What?

Colin	The last woman that kissed me was a man in drag.
Kelly	*(Speaking in a deep voice).* Shit, you caught me out. *(They all laugh).*
Colin	That. That's what I'll miss. That's the parting memory I needed. Now go out there and show that bloody world who you are and most important of all, be you and find out where the life is that you deserve. What are you smiling at?
Kelly	An old friend of ours once told me that.
Colin	Don? *(Kelly puts her head down, upset and nods).*
Colin	I know love, we miss him too. Every day. We'll let you know when Alan's funeral is. No doubt I'll have another starring role. *(He turns and then pauses).* One thing Kell. Send us a postcard now and again. Doesn't matter where from. But make sure it has the brightest, happiest most colourful picture on the front.
Tom	Ooh lovely. It'll just be like the end of 'The Great Escape' when them soldiers get to Switzerland and send post cards back to the camp and... and I'm waffling again aren't I? *(Colin and Kelly nod).*
Tom	Oh, come here an' give your Gran a hug. Ta ra Kell. *(He kisses her and hugs her and then stares intently at her face for a few seconds, as if in a moment of rare sincerity).* And before you leave love, do one thing for me.
Kelly	Of course.
Tom	Immac that top lip. You've a gob like a Yeti. Ta-ra kid. *(He exits).*
Kelly	I will miss you.
Colin	It's very kind of you to say. Here. *(He takes out his wallet and gives her a bank note).*
Kelly	What's this?
Colin	Payment for a lesson that a very dear friend taught me.
Kelly	Lesson?
Colin	One life. Priceless. *(She goes to hug him and he turns away. She smiles and then walks out. In the silence and stillness and then ever so slowly, he begins to sob uncontrollably with his back to the audience).*

Music: 'Look Over There' from 'Mack and Mabel'. Fade to black.

Scene 6

A week later. A church service. Lights come up to reveal Tom stood in a sharply focussed white light. The church lectern is in front of him which has been placed during the black out.

Tom	Good morning everybody. Here we are again. Same people, different tears. I have been asked to deliver a tribute at today's service concerning our dear friend, Alan. Before doing so, I must pass on the apologies of Colin. He is not very well and has asked me to do this on his behalf. Not like him to be under the weather or to miss this service, but he has been told to stay in bed by the doctor. In addition, Kelly asked to be remembered to you all as she has an interview for a job in London. Well, an audition actually for a part in a play. Lucky cow. Sorry Reverend. As you know, Colin has always written something when one of the firm has passed away. Shit, I'd best double check he's not written one for me already. Sorry, Reverend. It seems strange standing here in front of a wooden box, knowing it contains one of the best friends I ever had. He always said he wanted me to say

something when this day came because he said I made people laugh; more importantly, I made him laugh. I hope to Christ he doesn't laugh now. Sorry Reverend. Alan and I met when we were both playing pantomime dames at Morecambe. So please, if I say anything like: "I can't believe Alan is dead", I don't want anybody shouting out: "Oh no he isn't"; and certainly not: "He's behind you". Sorry again Reverend. Can't help it. Well, at least I haven't said 'fuck'. *(He couldn't help himself. He mouths the words: "Sorry Reverend").* Shakespeare was as much part of our lives as we were to each other. So from us all I simply say - Now cracks a noble heart. Good night, sweet prince and flights of angels sing thee to thy rest.

Fade to black. Music: 'The Impossible Dream'. Lectern removed.

Scene 7

Eighteen months later. The room is in semi-darkness. Tony walks in and turns on a light. He draws the curtains and lets in the daylight. Kelly enters. She is well dressed, smart, successful.

Tony	Hello Kelly. This is a nice surprise. To what do we owe the honour of a visit from our new rising star of the stage?
Kelly	Get away.
Tony	Well, you have achieved so much in what, less than eighteen months?
Kelly	Not made it yet
Tony	Oh no? We all read the papers. Colin in particular. Every column inch, every review. He cuts them all out and keeps them. Ah. Probably wasn't supposed to tell you that. You know Colin.
Kelly	Don't think I do by the sounds of it! I have to admit Tony, I'm surprised to see you still here, you know after, well…
Tony	No, all is well. VT went off with her beloved bank manager. I'm sure they're happy somewhere, making each other deliriously miserable. I, however, refuse to be bogged down in such negative thoughts about the nasty bitch. Joke.
Kelly	Gathered. How is everybody?
Tony	Oh you know. Same old same old. Funny. That takes on an altogether different meaning here. Did you know Tom is in America?
Kelly	America?
Tony	Yes. He was overheard playing himself in the supermarket and by chance, an executive of an American TV network was in getting his groceries. Was blinded by Tom immediately and within a week he had signed a contract for a new sitcom that they have just started filming.
Kelly	Bloody hell. He always said there was one more performance in him.
Tony	Indeed. He's happy, but the place isn't the same without him. He keeps sending bright, garish post cards that are lost on me. Keeps signing them, 'Love from Switzerland'. Anyhow, I'm sure the gentlemen will be down shortly for morning coffee so I'll leave you to play catch up. Do pop in the office and say goodbye won't you. *(He goes to exit).*
Kelly	How's Colin?
Tony	*(Pause before he turns back to her).* Not had the best of health since Alan passed away.

Kelly	But he is OK?
Tony	Don't forget to say goodbye. *(He exits).*

Kelly wanders over to the stereo and turns it on. Music: 'Oh What a Beautiful Morning' from 'Oklahoma'. Whilst she is listening to it Gordon enters. He is pushing Colin in a wheelchair who is clearly very ill. His pallor, breathing, frailty all underline it. He gestures to stop Gordon from instinctively speaking and for a moment, he watches Kelly and smiles. She has her back to them but clearly knows somebody is there. She turns off the stereo.

Colin	Are you a vampire?
Kelly	Well, nobody in the right mind would go out in daylight dressed like this.
C/K	The old ones are the best.

Kelly turns smiling and is immediately taken aback by Colin's appearance.

Gordon	*(He walks over to Kelly and hugs her).* Don't stay too long. He gets tired quick.
Colin	Stop fussing you imbecile.
Gordon	Bugger off you, old faggot. *(Colin coughs. Gordon rushes back over to him and kneels down in front of him to straighten his blanket. He then takes Colin's hand and speaks gently).* I'll get your tea.
Colin	You are very kind.
Gordon	What are friends for? *(He stands and touches Colin on the shoulder as he passes him to exit).*
Kelly	See you later love
Gordon	*(He again grows in stature and speaks as he exits without turning).* If you've got it, flaunt it!

Kelly wheels Colin to an appropriate position centre stage.

Colin	Well, well. What brings you to Crematoria Corner.
Kelly	Was just passing. I was deliriously happy and laughing to myself for no reason, so I thought I'd call in and have a little dose of morbidity. Feeling morosely better already. Might even try and find a guide dog to kick on my way home.
Colin	Point taken.
Kelly	Point won I'd say. *(She moves quickly to Colin and they hug. He appears to hold on to her a little longer than she expected. It takes her by surprise).*
Colin	So what are you up to? Got a job?
Kelly	Yep.
Colin	Good on you.
Kelly	At the local rep' actually.
Colin	What, cleaning? *(Kelly gives him a look to kill).* Sorry, Kell.
Kelly	Thought you might have known what I've been doing?
Colin	Me? No. Not that interested.
Kelly	Really? I've been cast as the lead in a play for an eight-week run. If the box is good, we'll go on tour. You'll have to come and see it.
Colin	When is it on?
Kelly	About six months.
Colin	Shame, can't make that.
Kelly	Social diary packed?
Colin	I'll probably be dead.

Kelly	What do you want, sympathy?
Colin	No, tea with one sugar; there's a love.
Kelly	*(Pause).* You're serious?
Colin	Can't get more serious than snuffing it.
Kelly	What... how?
Colin	The usual way, you know, stop breathing.
Kelly	No please, what is it?
Colin	Why does everybody always want to know what you are dying of?
Kelly	Well, it's interesting to read-up about it on the internet.
Colin	You really need to go out more love.
Kelly	Joking.
Colin	Gathered.
Kelly	How long?
Colin	And there's the second classic question after what have you got, how long?
Kelly	Colin?
Colin	Before you open in your play probably. *(She kneels next to him and goes to hold his hand but he pulls it away).*
Kelly	So how have you managed, you know…
Colin	To still be in here? Change of management meant we had a human being in charge. I shouldn't be here at all but I have paid for a nurse and things, which means I can stay here for now. Tony has been brilliant. Gordon has been a godsend. He comes in early, goes home late so that he can help me and doesn't get paid a penny. He is my rock. Best friend I never knew I had. Surprising the friends you discover when you least expect it.
Kelly	So if you are dying, who am I going to sell a ticket to?
Colin	I'll introduce you to the undertaker if you want. Sorry. Low for even me that wasn't it?
Kelly	You really are serious about less than six months aren't you?
Colin	Can't get more serious than dying.
Kelly	What a shame.
Colin	'What a shame?' You make it sound like you've just laddered your bloody tights... *(She smiles at him).* Cow.
Kelly	Queen.
Colin	Slut.
Kelly	Puff. *(Without warning Colin winces).* OK? *(He nods).* I… I don't know what to say.
Colin	Then say nothing. I spent my life afraid of silence, but these days... I don't know. *(Kelly stands up).* What are you doing?
Kelly	Well if you can't come to see the play, I'll bring it to you. I've got this huge monologue at the end. I'll do that for you. I've already learnt it you know.
Colin	You silly bugger.
Kelly	Yeah. Silly enough to come here and see you. Which reminds me.
Colin	What?
Kelly	Before I start, I've got something to say to you so I may as well do it now. I used to think a lot of somebody who we both knew, and you once said it was a tragedy that I never told him that...

Colin	Please no. *(For the first time, probably in his life, he can't cope and shows it. He begins to get upset).* Don't do this to me. Don't make me do this in public. I can't cope with that now. Just let me be...
Kelly	Just be quiet for once in your life and bloody listen. It really hurt me when you said I never told Alan what I felt about him. What hurt more was that you were right. Alan said you should only ever make a mistake once. Well. You might be a miserable, hard faced, selfish, self-centred, arrogant old shit.
Colin	Careful I'm filling up here.
Kelly	But I just need to say... *(He winces in pain).* Shall I get somebody?
Colin	To do what?
Kelly	I'm not sure. They always say it on the telly.
Colin	Then you go and get somebody. God forbid we betray the trust of the bloody Telly.
Kelly	I'll stay. Really, how long?
Colin	Every time I have one of these funny turns they hurt more. Doctor said I will just nod off most probably and not wake up. That's the drugs they're giving me. Kelly, I'm so tired.
Kelly	Then have a nap.
Colin	What and kick the bucket? Not bloody likely. I've missed having you around here.
Kelly	Just around here?
Colin	No. Around me. *(He takes hold of her hands).* I've spent my life being so independent I was alone even when I was in a crowded room. There was a song in a show about that... that's when I miss Tom most of all. You only hear the loneliness when your ego is not big enough to fill a room on its own. You don't need friends when you think you're the centre of attention, at least, that's what I fooled myself into believing. And by the time I realised many weren't friends at all, it was too late. I think I will have a rest Kelly love. I know it's not like me to say what I feel... but right this minute, I don't feel frightened.
Kelly	You! Frightened!
Colin	I've spent my life in fear.
Kelly	Of what?
Colin	Being caught out.
Kelly	Doing what?
Colin	Doing 'me'. Pretending for a whole lifetime takes its toll. I'm so bloody tired of it all. But I suppose I'm still waiting for that one moment when I can just be me and be liked for who I am – even if it's for a few seconds – and that last sleep won't seem so bad.

They are silent, look at each other and then laugh.

Kelly	Who do you think you are, bloody Lassie? *(They both laugh).* If you ask me, I don't think you need to be frightened any more.
Colin	Why?
Kelly	If I'm not mistaken, I think I have just met the real you.
Colin	Time must be up then.
Kelly	Oh shut it, you morbid git.

Colin	Not happening right now then eh?
Kelly	No it bloody isn't. Now, let's get you enjoying the view from that window. *(She wheels his chair to the window so that he is facing off stage. He is angled so that his face cannot be seen by the audience. She moves to the window looking off stage and at the appropriate moment she moves away from him).* Not having a normal family always made me feel like a freak, like I deserved to be in a home when I was a kid. I had that feeling for years. That was until I came here. Seeing the family, you had all made for yourselves because you had none. And then the ones who were family were more like strangers because they only came to see you when they could be arsed. Visiting for them was a duty, a burden. They didn't care and because of that neither did any of you. The only thing you had in common with family was a name. I came to despise them for what they represented, how they could treat something so precious with such disregard. At first, I wanted to make up for what they weren't doing for all of you because I felt it was my job. But without any warning, the job disappeared and I crossed the line.
	Don said it would. This, all of you, you weren't a job any longer. This home became my home and none of you were residents anymore. You became the nearest to family I could ever have and without warning, without planning, without knowing, you became family; my family. I know, in your own way, you never meant the things you said to me. I could see it in your eyes. But no matter what ever passed between us, I knew that you were trying to toughen me up in a way. Prepare me for making my own way. I only realised that when I had to stand up for myself and realised I could. I'm rambling, but what I meant to say is, it's not just respect, it's not just caring; you're not just a friend. You must have written to me every week since I left. I really do love you Colin. You've given me so much and you don't even know it. Somebody once said that you're the sum of all the people and things that you experience in your life. And because of that, I know you're a part of me and always will be. Just like Alan, Don and Tommy. You can't forget something that's a part of you. And no matter how low or hard things might get, I can always think of four old buggers who were the nearest to a family I could ever hope for; and any one of them that I would be proud to call Dad. *(Colin's hand drops to the side).* You know, when, if, I ever get married, I want Tommy to give me away, apart from the fact that he'd end up having a posher frock than me... what do you think Colin? Colin? *(She stands in front of him. She is quiet for a moment. She turns to the window and draws the curtains. She kneels/sits next to him, takes his hand and places it on his lap).*
Kelly *(cont'd)*	Our revels now are ended. These our actors, As I foretold you, were all spirits, and Are melted into air, into thin air: And like the baseless fabric of this vision, The cloud-capp'd tow'rs, the gorgeous palaces, The solemn temples, the great globe itself, Yea, all which it inherit, shall dissolve, And, like this insubstantial pageant faded,

> Leave not a rack behind. We are such stuff
> As dreams are made on; and our little life
> Is rounded with a sleep.

She holds his hand up to her face and then slowly starts laughing.

Tony	*(He enters).* What's so funny?
Kelly	Colin's dead.
Tony	What?
Kelly	And why am I laughing? Because it's what he would have wanted. It's how we all were. *(Pause).* Do you tell them that you love them?
Tony	I beg your pardon?
Kelly	Your family. Do you tell each of them every day?
Tony	I'm sorry but...
Kelly	Do you?
Tony	Well, not every...
Kelly	Then shame on you. Fix it while you can Tony. Learn from the residents here like I did.
Tony	And what did you learn?
Kelly	One life. Priceless.
Tony	I suppose I best tell his family.
Kelly	No need. They know.
Tony	With Julie leaving, I'm glad I got to know him better.
Kelly	So am I.
Tony	What will you do now?
Kelly	*(She picks up her coat and bag).* Keep on breathing. And discover the answer to that great question.
Tony	Which is?
Kelly	Where is the life?
Tony	Did Shakespeare say that as well?
Kelly	No. Just one of his friends. *(She begins to exit but pauses).* And you know what Tony? There is something that I know both of us learnt from all of them. The old ones really are the best.
Tony	And what shall I tell Gordon?
Kelly	Just tell him… tell him, 'taxi for Colin'. *(She exits).*

Fade to black. Music: 'Where is the life that late I led' from 'Kiss me Kate' which covers the bows.

THE END

'Is There Anybody There?'

Synopsis

Sue has spent her life married to an empty space. Her husband. A man who wasn't ever there; not with her anyhow. And she fooled herself into thinking her manufactured life had been manufactured by her. But a perfect life is not always what it seems, and her husband made her realise that.

When Sue meets Ann, an employee of her late husband, she finds a soul mate in more ways than one. And following a chance conversation, they hatch a plan to laugh, to drink, to joke and to make fun with impunity about the afterlife and those who ask the question, "Is there anybody there?" But life can bring with it unexpected turns and what begins as a joke soon becomes much more.

'Is There Anybody There?' explores a range of emotions, expectations and fears. It questions what motivates us, what we want out of life ... and what we think about what might come after it. It explores friendship and what we expect from it and then within the cracks between relationships, what is really going on and what happens when it goes wrong and why.

Finally, it considers those times when we are alone and assess our lives with that inner monologue we all rehearse; what part of us is actually speaking and what part answers us back? The journey the characters go on begins and ends in two very different places and the question of the piece is not resolved ... that is a matter for the audience to decide. What will you decide? Was anybody there?

Characters (3f)

Sue   35/45*. Attractive, slim. Always well, and expensively, dressed. She is self-assured, hard, bitter, in humour and in anger. Underneath and later, she is vulnerable, and her demons come home to roost.

Ann   35/45*. Business like, 'safe', initially, but there is a feeling that now and again, her character suggests that there is more to her, unexpected, uncharacteristic. In the beginning, she comes across as a person who sees in Sue an opportunity to be somebody very different, have a laugh, take risks. A trusted friend. But in resolution, she is dark, manipulative, chilling.

The Woman 35/45*. A complicated character and very difficult to read, judge, categorise who or what she is. She is controlled, unemotional, expressionless, detached, calm, precise, articulate. At no point is anything said which indicates the nature of what she represents. I think to have the audience never having any definitive answer is the crux of the piece; let them imagine who or what she is. For the premiere she was simply dressed: jeans, white T-shirt and bare feet.

If the characters are younger than suggested by the dialogue, some dialogue comments might need to be adjusted accordingly to accommodate this. No matter what, I would suggest that they all need to be a similar age.

Setting

The play is set in the present day; any location.

Scenes

Act One

Scene 1: Derek's wake, afternoon
Scene 2: A cocktail bar, the following afternoon
Scene 3: Sue's house, one week later
Scene 4: A small theatre, two weeks later

Act Two

Scene 1: Sue's house, two weeks later
Scene 2: Courtroom, some weeks later;
Flashback, small theatre, two weeks later from Scene 1
Scene 3: Courtroom, continued from Scene 2:
    Flashback, Sue's house, one week later from the small theatre, Scene 2
Scene 4: Courtroom, continued from Scene 3

Music Suggestions

These were successfully used in the premiere production.

Track #1	'Never Ever' (sung by All Saints)
Track #2	'Should I Stay Or Should I Go' (sung by The Clash)
Track #3	'96 Tears' (sung by The Stranglers)
Track #4	'Sweet Dreams Are Made Of This (sung by The Eurythmics)
Track #5	'The Sound Of Silence' (sung by Simon and Garfunkel)
Track #6	'Knockin' On Heaven's Door' (sung by Anthony & The Johnsons)
Track #7	'Winter Kills' (sung by Yazoo)
Track #8	'If You Could Read My Mind' (sung by Gordon Lightfoot)
Track #9	'Spirit In The Sky' (sung by Norman Greenbaum)

Running Time

With a 7.30pm start and a 20-minute interval, estimated curtain is 9.45pm.

Direction/Production Notes

For the first performance, a simple black box was the basic structure. High bar table and two stools set downstage right for Scene 2 which were struck at the end of the scene. The opening piece for the first production used a gobo of a cross projected on a black flat downstage left below which, Sue delivered the church service/eulogy. Similar for Act 2 and Ann, where a court crest was projected.

A running black was used part way down stage. It was needed to have the facility to be backlit centre stage to create the effect of the 'audience' being upstage/behind them at times and to enable the action to switch perspective as indicated in the script.

Furniture for Sue's house was set upstage, behind the running blacks: two armchairs; one that swivels, a table, a clothes rail for Act 1, Scene 2. Free standing/abstract panels behind the furniture to represent the walls, sections, of the room and a free-standing door all of which could be seen past/through on either side of them.

Lighting always tightly lit to draw in the attention of the audience. The intent was to focus on the people and their personalities, relationships, tensions and not have it obfuscated by the practicalities of staging. This approach also has the added advantage that it affords the opportunity to play the piece in a range of spaces and not dependant on traditional staging/setting or venues.

The scene transitions were covered by music edits of 70's/80's songs, which are alluded to at an early point in the dialogue.

I have provided certain stage directions, notes, explanations and with them, suggestions of how it might work. But they really are suggestions for a specific staging solution. It works equally well, I hope, in the round if necessary.

The nature of the language is pacey, and it will be seen from the frequent use of ellipses that the intent is for dialogue to have the feeling of being constantly interrupted, predicted, supporting the pace and hopefully, keeping it edgy, spontaneous.

The Woman, it is suggested, is for best effect, either sat in the auditorium at the front from the beginning as a member of the audience or walks in from there. The writing is structured around that premise. It would work with her coming on from the wings, but it would change the nature of the dialogue and is, in my honest opinion, a poor second choice.   *Martin P Roche, 2017*

<u>First Produced</u>

'Is There Anybody There?' was first produced at Guide Bridge Theatre, Manchester between 14th August and 19th August 2017, directed by Martin Paul Roche, with the following cast...

Sue	Tracey Rontree
Ann	Nicky Mead
The Woman	Jennifer Savill

> "Pure brilliance ... Absolutely gripped ... Excellent script ... A very original and entertaining piece of theatre ... A really thought-provoking play. I loved it ... what a mixture of emotions ... Great play, funny and dark at the same time. Highly recommended ... Brilliant in every way. Totally loved it. Well done to all of you. Martin has such excellent writing skills ... I actually couldn't wait to get back in the theatre at the interval to see how things panned out. Totally awesome ... give us more of this writers' plays ... the cast held me all the way through. Brilliant!"
> ***Some of the audience feedback on social media.***

ACT ONE
Scene 1

House to Black. SFX: Track #1 begins which fades as lights come up on Sue. Sue is stood in a special, dressed in black. Running blacks are in.

Sue　　First of all, can I thank you all for coming today. Derek was so close to all of his friends he would be very pleased to see you all here. He spent so much time with all of you. Golf, football, darts, snooker, rugby ... and the do's: stag do's, leaving do's, retirement do's, christening do's, even self-invited himself to hen do's. Fishing weekends, horse racing trips. Office parties, reunions, resignations, dismissals and once, even a decree nisi do. One long inebriated night, weekend, week, fortnight out. I don't think he had a liver. He certainly didn't have one by the end. Now it's his wake and it will be the first do he's ever missed. Ironic really. But he'll undoubtedly be here in spirit – especially as he spent his life supping one variety or another of them. I was about to say: "Ah well, you knew Derek". But you did, didn't you? Better than me. You spent more time with him than me. You had more fun with him than me. He didn't know me. So, thank you for everything you did for him ... and from me? Well. Thanks for nothing. The buffet and the bar are open next door. He paid for that as well so as ever, feel free to help yourselves. After all, you always have.

SFX: applause is heard. Fade to black. Lights back up as Sue moves next to a pre-set table.

Ann　　*(Enters and walks towards Sue with two glasses of wine).* It's Sue isn't it?
Sue　　Apparently.
Ann　　I'm Ann. I'm ... was ... Derek's secretary. Bizarre. I can't believe we have ever ...
Sue　　Met? No. Like I said at church, you were part of his life. I was just married to him.

Silence.

Ann　　*(She gives Sue a glass).* It was a very honest eulogy you delivered. Refreshing. Accurate.
Sue　　*(Weighing Ann up).* Really? Well, well. You're a first.
Ann　　Why?
Sue　　An acquaintance of Derek that isn't a lying, two-faced sod.
Ann　　Thanks. I think. *(Silence. They both take a big swig of their wine and empty the glass simultaneously. Ann studies Sue).* Can I say something?
Sue　　Feel free. I did.
Ann　　Tosser.
Sue　　Thanks. I think.
Ann　　No. Him. Tosser. Sorry.
Sue　　*(She puts her hand out and shakes Anne's who, initially, is hesitant).* Well who'd have thought it? Derek knew a normal person who actually has a spine. Bonus.

Ann	Thanks. I think.
Sue	He had money. And they all knew it. He liked to flash it around. And they all knew it. He liked to splash it around. And my god, did they help him splash. He liked to buy friendship. They enjoyed being bought. Perfect for all concerned. Need I go on? Qualify further? Pursue the obvious for you?
Ann	No. Thanks. But tell me. Did he buy you?
Sue	*(She surveys Ann again, with admiration and laughs).* My. You do buck the trend. I think I'm going to like you. No love. He didn't 'buy me'. He just possessed me. I thought it was love. He thought it was exciting. I saw him as the one. He saw me as the alternative. I thought he saw me as special. He saw me as not his current wife. I was skinny. She wasn't. She was his age. I was younger. We both believed the requisite fantasy and went along with it. And, well, I walked into it, as they say, 'with my eyes wide shut'. And to be honest with you, I wasn't entirely honest with him about me. You see, in his, your business, the car business, what is it you call a car? 'Clocked'? *(Whispering).* I lied about how many miles I had on mine love. And he certainly didn't appreciate how many times this model had been around the block – or how many previous keepers. It worked though. Exit stage left the incumbent lard arse, enter stage right, the new model. Moi. He always liked the car analogy, being in the motor trade and all. He called me his … 'new Vauxhall Diva'. But within a month of getting married, it didn't take him long to go looking for a sleek, newer model with all the extras … i.e., not me. Oh, and did she come with some extras. But he saw the error of his ways and he soon figured that after his first little dalliance with another woman, he was better off with me than without. So here we are now. Good-bye Derek and hello legacy.
Ann	Legacy?
Sue	The proceeds, the wonga, the consequence. The disposal of the assets and with it, the disposal of the arsehole.

Silence.

Ann	*(Ann feels uncomfortable).* Interesting selection of music during the service I thought. Eclectic. Original.
Sue	It was the only thing we had in common. An interest. A passion. Seventies, Eighties and a bit of Nineties music. Quirky, interesting lyrics and a good tune was the rule. Huge collection of vinyl. But neither of us had a favourite band, style, just songs. So to be honest, the playlist today was mine as much as his.
Ann	So a dry run for your funeral then?
Sue	*(She looks at Ann, slowly smiles and then laughs again).* There you go again. Yes. I guess it was. *(Silence. Ann feels uncomfortable again).* It's bloody ironic that his funeral and burial was at St Swithun's you know.
Ann	I'm sorry?
Sue	Well, I always wondered who he was – St Swithun, not Derek. Anyhow, when I booked the funeral, I Googled the name and it was really interesting. Did you know that before they buried him, they divided his body up into

	different bits, relics? His head went to one place, his arm to another. So it got me thinking: we should have done the same with Derek.
Ann	I'm sorry, I'm not …?
Sue	Well as I say, it got me thinking. He caused that much mayhem in life with his penis, we should have had it cut off and just buried it on its own. And his epitaph could have read: "Here lies Derek. He was just a dick in life and he's just a dick in death".
Ann	Well. Interesting. And did he have any endearing qualities?
Sue	You tell me. You along with all that lot, his colleagues, will have spent more time with him than I did.
Ann	*(She turns Sue around and looks at her).* Look love, I spent time with him. I didn't enjoy time with him. And yes, I've come to have a drink and eat food that he will have indirectly paid for. But to fondly reminisce, shed a tear and share a happy story? No. Oh, and I've come for two other reasons as well: make sure that bunch don't take more time off to be here than I've authorised and well, make sure it's true.
Sue	True?
Ann	That he's dead.
Sue	Hmm. It's true.
Ann	He was charming for a dick though.
Sue	Yeah. I'll give you that.
Ann	More wine?
Sue	Is the Pope a Catholic? *(Ann pours two bigger, fuller glasses. Sue looks at them impressed).* Is there anything about you I'm not going to like?
Ann	Speak to that bunch. They'll give you lots of reasons not to.
Sue	Not popular with the colleagues then?
Ann	About as much as Derek was with you by the sounds of it. Put it this way, I've made them all take half a day's leave to come to his funeral.
Sue	*(She stops mid-gulp, looks at Ann and then laughs out loud. She then looks around and speaks loudly, intentionally, to be overheard).* Oh no, the grieving widow is laughing. Hold onto your glasses and buffet everybody. The jolt from the earth stopping spinning might make you spill your free wine. *(To Ann).* Sorry. He's gone and so has the pretence.
Ann	And where have you been all my life?

They both down the wine in one, maintaining eye contact with each other.

Sue	Here's to dicks buried and friends unearthed.
Ann	I don't think so.
Sue	Why?
Ann	No wine.
Sue	Oh my. You just get better.
Ann	More wine then?
Sue	What other type of wine is there? *(Ann fills the glasses).* So. What happens with your job if I've sold his garage business?
Ann	I'll stay on and manage it.
Sue	Have the new owners agreed to that?

Ann	Oh yes.
Sue	Who are the new owners?
Ann	Me! *(Sue looks at her, her mouth is open with shock. Ann closes it for her at the appropriate point in the next dialogue).* I'm not sure if it is true, but I was once told that wine evaporates quickly. So let's not allow it to happen so easily by leaving your mouth open for no reason, eh? All that effort and none of the benefit? Can't be right somehow. You should have learnt that from being married to Derek. And to clarify for you, I had a little nest egg and it just matured very recently. So. Time to dictate my own future and owning a piece of it ensures just that.
Sue	*(She takes a big swig of her wine and looks offstage as if somebody has noticed them both 'enjoying' themselves. She then speaks pointedly to them offstage).* My wine. My do. My business.
Ann	*(She puts her arm around Sue, takes a swig out of the bottle and then shouts offstage in the same direction).* And my new friend. *(They both give the 'V' sign to offstage).*
Sue	What you doing tomorrow lunch?
Ann	Nowt. You?
Sue	Nowt.
Ann	Suggestion?
Sue	Yep.
Ann	Cocktails?
Sue	Yep.
Ann	Owt else?
Sue	Nope.
Ann	Friend me on Facebook and we'll arrange it.
Sue	Will do. Will it be messy?
Ann	Yeah!
Sue	Brilliant. See?
Ann	What?
Sue	The dick ended up having a use after all.
Ann	Laters.
Sue	Laters, hun.

They both start to exit opposite sides. Ann pauses which makes Sue do the same. They both turn and look at each other, consider each other again and then continue to exit. SFX: Track #2 starts as the lights fade to black.

Scene 2

The following lunchtime. SFX: Track #2 fades and bar background noise is heard. Lights up, after several seconds, on Ann and Sue sat on stools at a high bar table. Each have a cocktail and they are both glued to their mobile phones. They don't look at each other. SFX: bar background noise begins to fade as the dialogue picks up.

Sue   I'm not really surprised that you found my profile online. There's not many Prendergast's out there and having my profile picture as the Grim Reaper. Well, not exactly an unfathomable correlation with …

Ann	… with what? A hard-faced cow that's just buried her husband who she didn't much care for and hates everything and everybody? No, not at all.
Sue	Well, when you put it like that. I do love lunchtime drinks. There's just something about not being in work and …
Ann	Not giving a bugger?
Sue	I was going to say, not having a hangover in the morning.
Ann	That as well then.
Sue	I don't know if it's true, but somebody told me once that Prosecco was a Greek God.
Ann	And?
Sue	Well love, if she wasn't she should be.
Ann	She? I would have thought it was a bloke?
Sue	*(She looks at Ann with a scowl).* You are joking?
Ann	You're right. *(Silence. They are both still absorbed looking at their phones).* There really is some garbage on social media though, isn't there? I mean, pictures of babies, cats, puppies, whales, donkeys and men wearing very little … bloody hell. Look at the size of his … *(She turns her phone around to show Sue).*
Sue	That can't be real.
Ann	We can live in hope.
Sue	Life's too short to spend it hoping. We make our own opportunities. *(She resumes browsing on her phone).* And here we go, for some people being online means every post has to be meaningful quotes, inspirational pictures …
Ann	And videos that you are instructed you have to watch immediately because they will 'change your life' …
Sue	… or messages that you have to share to get a year's worth of luck or if you don't, a lifetime's worth of misery.
Ann/Sue	'Type Amen and forward on'.
Ann	Oh, and don't forget, posting pictures of the meal you're about to eat.
Sue	*(Laughing).* And telling the world which café you're in and who's with you.
Ann	Oh no, how much you love your family.
Sue	… especially the one who died twenty years ago.
Ann/Sue	'Hello?'
Sue	And when they just type, 'Fed up', knowing they'll get overwhelmed with questions.
Ann	'What's up Hun?'
Sue	'You OK Babe?'
Ann	And then it starts. Pandora's Box is opened. How much you hate your life.
Sue	Your work.
Ann	Your friends.
Sue	But love your cat.
Ann	And dress it up.
Sue	Yeah, in animal outfits.
Ann	*(Showing Sue a picture on her phone).* A cat in a dog suit wearing a beard.
Sue	*(Showing Ann a picture on her phone).* A dog dressed as Elsa from 'Frozen'!
Ann/Sue	*(Singing).* 'Let it go, let it go'.
Ann	'Laugh out loud'.

Sue	'Smiley face'.
Ann/Sue	'Woop woop'!

They both 'high five'.

Ann	Utter garbage.
Sue	Absolutely.

Silence as they continue to browse through their phones.

Ann	It's brill though isn't it?
Sue	I'd be lost without it.

Silence. They are both still glued to their phones.

Ann	I do not believe it. God give me bloody strength.
Sue	What?
Ann	Candy Crush. Soddin' Candy Crush. If I get one more bleeding request to play it from this silly cow at work, I'm going to buy some real crushed candy and ram it down her throat.
Sue	She might enjoy it.
Ann	She's diabetic.
Sue	'Live by the candy, die by the candy' then, eh?
Ann	You're sick.
Sue	You started it girlfriend. *(They 'chink' glasses whilst still looking at their respective 'phones. Silence, whilst still engrossed).* I'm really glad we've come out today.
Ann	Yep.

Silence.

Sue	Can't remember the last time I had a proper chat with a real person.
Ann	Yep.

Silence.

Sue	I'm just …
Ann	What?
Sue	It's just … nothing. *(Silence).* I'm just bored with it all. With life. With everything. I just want something, but I don't know what. I want to have a laugh on my terms for once. Years of treading relationship water with Derek. I want to stick two fingers up at the world that has kept me back and the petty people in it and just do something, anything.
Ann	Well, what do you want to do?
Sue	I don't know. I'll know when the right thing comes along.
Ann	Let's hope your judgement in ideas is better than your judgement in men.
Sue	Sod off!

They become engrossed in their 'phones again.

Ann	And she can sod off as well.
Sue	Who?
Ann	Eileen. The one Derek appointed to work on 'parts and service' at the garage.

Sue	Not 'Eileen The Moose'? *(They both put their hands on their heads like antlers, pull faces and make a moose noise).* I'm thinking of the right one? The slapper?
Ann	And some. The full title of her job should actually be 'Men's Parts and giving them a Service'.
Sue	Really? Wish I'd known that job was on offer.
Ann	True. The job would have been a piece of cake to you.
Sue	Meaning?
Ann	Well dear, you did write the manual.
Sue	Cow.
Ann	Moo. Anyhow, she keeps sending me invites to go to stuff. Look at this one. *(She shows Ann her phone).*
Sue	A Psychic evening?
Ann	Yeah. She's into it big time. Never shuts up. Always going to them trying to get a message from her mother.
Sue	Is she dead?
Ann	No, she's in Blackpool but hasn't got a phone. You, silly cow! Course she's bloody dead!
Sue	Alright, alright. So, did she ever get one?
Ann	What?
Sue	A message.
Ann	Sue? Hello? Message from her dead mother? It's nonsense! Two blokes do this show every year in the local workingmen's club. Camp as ninepence they are. She soaks it all up. They all do. Please tell me you don't believe it?
Sue	*(Indifferently).* Course not. I've watched it on telly though. Just never been to one so I've never thought about it.
Ann	What is there to think about? Sue. They rake it in. Seriously. And they have a huge laugh. The place is full of people, just ordinary people, clinging to hope and waiting to be told that they are still loved, they're being watched, all is forgiven, the pain has gone, blah blah blah. An audience full of sponges paying a tenner to get soaked. I could write the book. No, I could actually write the script for the show. You and me could do it better. Bit of girly flair, nice outfits, makeover, hair do and mood lighting. Bit of dry ice and music that would crack any stone-cold heart – even yours …
Sue	None taken …
Ann	No, I'm just saying that many of these are a scam.
Sue	Many?
Ann	Alright, all. We could nail it though. I've worked in sales all my life; you've sold yourself all your life.
Sue	Still, none taken …
Ann	We could do it.
Sue	Us? Like, me and you? Really?
Ann	No. I'm not saying I want to. All I'm saying is that two women with a brain, the flair, the looks and the patter, could convince anybody of anything.
Sue	Just need to find one to help me then, eh?
Ann	Cow.
Sue	Moo. But we wouldn't know any of them, anything about them.

Ann	You don't need to. Because we know people. We've been these people.
Sue	*(Interrupting).* Don't bloody compare them to …
Ann	*(Interrupting).* Alright. No. They're not like us. But we know what makes them tick. Spent a life around them. Worked with them. Been bored witless reading the tripe they post on-line. We've been there and worn the tee-shirt. Christ, you've washed the stains out of life's tee-shirt, took it back with the receipt and got a refund.
Sue	I've just consigned one dead person to eternity. I don't want to go looking for anyone else's.
Ann	I'm just saying …
Sue	Do you want me to un-friend you before I really know you? *(Silence).* Still. Interesting though isn't it?
Ann	*(She is engrossed in her phone again).* Yeah.
Sue	But then …
Ann	What?
Sue	When you really think about it.
Ann	What, for god's sake?
Sue	Would be a laugh though.
Ann	No – no - no! Why did I mention it?! I was not suggesting anything.
Sue	I know, but just think about it.
Ann	<u>No.</u>
Sue	Just …
Ann	I am. It would be a laugh but, I'm sorry hun, I'm just kidding you. Talking crap. Look at me. Social media has now got me posting garbage real-time like the nutters do. Forget it. Me on my soapbox again, that's all it was.

Silence. They look at each other, then back at their phones and then as if to speak, but they don't. They look at each other again. They can't hold it back and both laugh with realisation.

Sue	Ann and Sue – with messages for you!
Ann	*(She is now taken with the idea).* Could you imagine it?
Sue	*(Seriously).* Yes. I can actually.
Ann	*(She laughs but Sue doesn't).* Why are you not laughing?
Sue	I'm just thinking, it doesn't have to be funny, but it could just be fun. And how much it soddin' could be. Would be.
Ann	Bugger off!
Sue	*(Pause).* I know. You're right. *(Silence. They do the same routine again, looking at each other, then their phones).* But still – shut it and listen - all those people out there with their high and mighty attitudes and self-importance. Like that, The Moose, off 'parts and service'. The folk who go to it, the ones who make out they have, 'a gift'. The chance to show them and all their bollocks up for what it is, what they are. What a laugh eh? I mean. Nobody would get hurt, would they? A bloody big scam. Us scamming the scammers. The biggest wind-up ever. And I did say I was waiting for the right idea to come along. And after all, I know the real deal when it comes to the dead. I was married to the dead before he had even died.
Ann	But what if they …

Sue	What? Found out? Rumbled us? Who's going to tell them? The spirits? Yeah right. *(Mimicking a conversation)*. "Eh Sue, I've had a message from our Denise that you can't speak to the dead and you're a liar." "But your Denise is dead?" "Yeah, she FaceTimed me from the other side and told me."
Ann	Ghosts can use FaceTime?
Sue	Please tell me you are havin' me on?
Ann	*(She is offended, but clearly covering her embarrassment)*. Course! *(Silence)*. But anyway, why would you want to, you know …?
Sue	The laugh, the sport. For god's sake Ann, I'm fed up. Have you not been listening? I'm bored. It's the idea I've needed. Oh, go on. Think what a laugh we would have. Just once. Being on the edge. I've had years of being married to an empty chair, a broken promise. I just want to throw it all off and just take a risk and, well, oh I don't know. Just have a go at fooling more than me.
Ann	It could be funny. You know. Haven't had a proper laugh in ages.
Sue	And I haven't had a proper life in ages. So?
Ann	So?
Sue	Come around to mine. We need to think it through.
Ann	We need to drink it through.
Sue	Hey, hang on a mo. That could be our niche, our trademark.
Ann/Sue	Wiiiiine!
Ann	Now you are talking.
Sue	Oh yeah girlfriend.
Ann	'The Sozzled Psychics'.
Sue	'After life, after hours'.
Ann	'From Booze to Beyond'.
Ann/Sue	'Spirit with the Spirits'.
Ann	That's the one. This is mental.
Sue	You're mental.
Ann	You started it.
Sue	At least it beats running a candle party, selling knock-off perfumes to your mates or sex toys to your neighbours.
Ann	So, yours next week?
Sue	Dead right.
Ann	*(Laughing)*. 'Dead right'. We'll have to get that one in.
Sue	Well hold that thought and bring your ideas around to mine next week. Oh, and some wardrobe ideas – and a thirst. *(They clink their 'phones together like glasses)*. Here's to having a laugh.
Ann	Here's to finding out if '… there's anybody there'.
Sue	Here's to wine.
Ann	Here's to 'dead right'.
Sue	And here's to us.
Ann/Sue	Cheers!

SFX: Track #3 starts as the lights fade to black.

Scene 3

Sue's house one week later. Items have been set behind the running blacks which open in the black out to reveal the scene. Sue is sat down with a glass of wine, reading a magazine and listening to the radio, which is Track #3 still playing. SFX: a doorbell is heard. Sue turns off the radio. SFX: Track #3 off. Sue answers the door. Ann enters carrying a suitcase of clothes. There are outfits on a clothes rail in between two armchairs, a side table with a bottle of wine and two glasses. Sue is wearing a dressing gown; her outfit for the next scene is hung on the clothes rail.

Ann	I tell you, I have found things in my wardrobe that defy any memories I have of me ever having good taste in clothes.
Sue	That's an absolutely cracker that you've got on.
Ann	This isn't one of them.
Sue	Oops!
Ann	It's a good job I haven't known you long enough to know when you're being a genuine cow.
Sue	Mooo! *(She gets an outfit off the rail. Ann sits in an armchair with the case on the floor and opens it).* I was thinking something like this? *(She holds an outfit on a hangar up to herself).*
Ann	I don't know what's more worrying: the fact that you still own that or that at some time in the past you actually thought it was fashionable.
Sue	What do you mean? This cost number fourteen a fortune.
Ann	Number fourteen?
Sue	Boyfriend number fourteen.
Ann	Are you being serious?
Sue	Not as much as he was. Gutted when I dumped him.
Ann	Number fourteen? What did you get up to?
Sue	Stuff that would make your toes curl.
Ann	No perve, which number?
Sue	We didn't give it numbers.
Ann	You are so wrong in the head. Explains your taste in clothes.
Sue	And friends apparently.
Ann/Sue	Mooo!

Silence as they look at outfits.

Ann	But fourteen? Really?
Sue	Variety, spice, you know how the saying goes.
Ann	So was your husband number fifteen?
Sue	No. I think he was twelve. *(Ann stares at her).* Oh, come off it. I didn't have you down as a prude. He wasn't interested in me after we got married, just his business and there was no way I was going to spend our marriage sat on the sub's bench. I was a possession. I have needs and he came nowhere near doing anything for them. *(Spoken in a southern American accent).* Money might make the world go 'round honey-pie, but it certainly ain't the spice of life. *(Speaking normally).* You add your own spice, Hun. And I think you know exactly what I'm getting at.
Ann	So you played around?
Sue	Don't look so surprised, love.

Ann	But you were married.
Sue	We, were married. He clearly had an opt out clause on the bits that didn't suit him. He had no interest at all in me. He filled his life with everything but me. So, I had to look for someone who could fill the void. And, well, I liked it.
Ann	Did he know?
Sue	What difference does that make?
Ann	Perhaps it was a two-way street.
Sue	Derek wasn't intelligent enough to have an affair. He wasn't interested in having an affair. All he cared about was his beloved business, golf and mates. He was too wrapped up in someone far more important; himself.
Ann	So maybe, what he was doing was all about getting his own back on you?
Sue	Are you saying he knew? He froze me out because he knew?
Ann	No, but it doesn't sound like you were subtle about it.
Sue	*(She laughs).* My, my. You still like to pack those surprises don't you chuck?
Ann	The more I get to know you, the more I get it. Why you want to do this. Why it's not about just 'having a laugh'. And why you clearly get off on the idea of shattering other people's hopes. You never had any hopes so why should anybody else? Bitter and twisted don't you think?
Sue	The more sweetener you add, the more bitter the taste it leaves.
Ann	I call that deep.
Sue	I call that honest. Having cold feet, are we?
Ann	Not at all. Just need to understand why I'm getting into what I'm getting into.
Sue	And what might that be, do you think?
Ann	Dark. Edgy. Risky. A gamble. Dangerous
Sue	Good. But I need to know why as well. I can't have you bottling it and …
Ann	Did you not hear what I said? Darlin' I sell bloody car parts. Call me Miss Dangerous! I work with a group of morons for whom the only stimulation they get is their morning coffee. You're on a mission and, well, I'm joining it for the ride. Thelma, meet Louise. Does that make me as bad as you? I guess it does. Do I understand it? I guess I don't. Do I care? I guess not. Will I regret it? Who cares? Look, if I analyse it too much I'll be out of the door. You've had a life of risk. My idea of risk, until now, was eating something without having looked at the calories on the packet. So, let's bin the therapy session, open another bottle and pick out some outfits we wouldn't be seen dead in - but the dead will hopefully want to be seen around!
Sue	You, my dear are one sick, hard faced sod … and I love it. Forget me. You were born for this.
Ann	And if we don't stop talking and start getting our act together, we won't need to contact the dead because we'll die on that stage without their help. What do you think of this? *(Holding up an outfit).*
Sue	Brilliant. What do you think of this? *(Holding up an outfit).*
Ann	Shite!
Sue	And you've got the gall to criticise my taste in clothes?
Ann	I'm thinking bright, garish, loud, what do you think?
Sue	Not dark, mysterious, intriguing?
Ann	Why not both.

Sue	Like your style. Well, not that much, clearly.
Ann/Sue	Mooo!

They both continue to look through clothes in silence. Ann keeps looking over at Sue, clearly wanting to speak.

Ann	But seriously, fourteen?
Sue	Well, I don't smoke.
Ann	With that much friction, I'm amazed. *(They both laugh).*
Sue	*(She holds up an outfit).* I think I'm going to go with a little black number.
Ann	*(Tongue in cheek).* Will he be number fifteen then?
Sue	Oooo! You see, that's why this is going to work. You're quick.
Ann	*(Pause).* So, have you figured out how it will work, you know, on stage?
Sue	If I'm really honest I've been fascinated by the whole thing for ages. You've just given me the final piece in the jigsaw and a reason to finish it. Watched loads of TV programmes for years and even researched it online during this last week. You just run with what they tell you. These people are desperate for anything, any message, any hint that there is somebody, anybody there. The majority of the time they give you everything you need to know, and they don't even know it. So, after that? Well, it's just telling them what they want to hear. Just start with a name.
Ann	No. We start with an illness, an accident, a tragedy.
Sue	That's sick.
Ann	No, it gives us the best 'in'.
Sue	Why?
Ann	Simple. At least you know they're already dead. Think. These people aren't trying to contact the bloody living, are they? Forget names. All the rubbish psychics go with names. "Is there somebody here with a vowel in their name?" Please. "Does the name Smith mean anything to anybody?" Yeah, probably half the bloody audience. Go straight for the affective.
Sue	So what do you think then, know-all?
Ann	Let's try you for example.
Sue	Me?
Ann	Yeah. Come on. You want to do this, and we need a dry run. You're recently bereaved. You know how that feels – well as much as you can feel. If you can't take it, you can't give it. So?
Sue	Alright smart-alec. Give it your best shot.
Ann	*(She stands and 'prepares' herself).* Right. I have somebody here with me who is telling me there is a woman in the audience they have a message for. Has somebody recently lost a husband very suddenly, without warning? *(Silence).* Well, come on, just answer me?
Sue	This is daft.
Ann	No, this is the act. Get with it. So. Has somebody recently lost a husband very suddenly, without warning?
Sue	*(She is uninterested).* Yes. Me. I have.

Ann	Oh for god's sake. You're not the next patient at the bloody dentists. You are one of a room full of people waiting, desperate to be picked.
Sue	It'll be better than the Lottery draw on telly this.

Ann looks at Sue sternly. Sue mouths the word 'sorry', holds her hands up, takes it seriously and 'prepares' herself.

Ann	Has somebody recently lost a husband very suddenly, without warning?
Sue	Yes. I have.
Ann	Slow down. Talk slowly. That's it my love, I can hear you. I know your anxious but she's here with me and she's listening to you. It is a man that's here with me. He's telling me that the pain has all gone now and he is with people. Other people. People that you will know. But he refuses to talk about what actually happened. He wants to talk about, about, a holiday. He wants to talk about a special holiday, the best time he ever spent with just you and it was in …
Sue	Barbados.
Ann	Barbados. Yes. You said it just as he did so it must be you he is trying to make contact with. And it was not just a special holiday …
Sue	Our honeymoon.
Ann	This is overwhelming. I can feel so much contentment, love, happiness.
Sue	I didn't want it to end.
Ann	And he says that it was the happiest he had ever been in his life. In his whole life. And he's telling me that although you had difficult times, he never stopped loving you. And it was the greatest then. He might not have told you since and he might not have always showed you, but you meant the world to him. He felt frightened towards the end, but …
Sue	We were both in love but couldn't say it. The words, they just …
Ann	He knew. You didn't need to say anything. You don't need to now. He knew. He knows everything. And no matter what happened he never, ever stopped loving you.

Silence.

Sue	*(Breaking the moment).* Good. Well, that's very … good. You certainly have this …
Ann	He just keeps saying he's so sorry for not being there with you and at times, not being the husband you needed him to be, that he should have been …
Sue	Well, I think you've nailed this …
Ann	He didn't mean the things he may have done that hurt you. He did hurt you, didn't he?
Sue	That's enough now …
Ann	… but he says you know that he found it so hard sometimes to say what really mattered, especially at the end, to admit that you deserved better than him …
Sue	I said enough …
Ann	… and in the hospital there just wasn't the time to …
Sue	Stop.

Ann	… to say goodbye, to make amends, to make peace and just let you know that no matter what, love had, love would, love will endure …
Sue	*(Shouting).* Stop!

Sue is breathing heavily by now. She has reached in her bag, takes out an inhaler and uses it to calm and control herself. Ann looks on, clearly horrified at what she has done and caused.

Ann	I'm, I didn't mean to, I was just … sorry. I can't believe …

Uneasy silence.

Sue	I just need to calm myself down. I'll be fine. The legacy of Derek and a lifetime on my own. That, and panic attacks added to asthma that the doctors say could kill me. Well, I don't want to be seeing that bastard when I've just got shut of him, do I? *(Ann looks away in silence. Sue then realises that she has shown too much, her vulnerability, her weakness. She laughs).* That was just, well. It was very, very good. And I found it really easy to … play along and get drawn in. Just imagine what it would have been like if I had been really affected by it all, and had come along to find out if anybody was there? You're right. Illnesses, accidents, let them fill in the details. This will be a piece of spiritual cake if you ask me. Angel Cake. *(She laughs, falsely).*
Ann	Sue, I hope I didn't go too …
Sue	… far? Hell no. Well, hell yes if you believe in it. Perhaps I should practice on you now?
Ann	You don't need any practice. Believe me. You just be yourself. A lifetime as an actress has its benefits. *(Sue is caught off guard and we see a moment when a comment hit home).* Done it again, sorry.
Sue	No. It's fine. Be myself. Yes. And you never know. If I really do play myself, Mr fifteen might be in the audience. And hopefully, living. *(It breaks the moment and they both laugh).*
Ann	You're sick.
Sue	Well, isn't that just life.
Ann	And death, apparently.
Sue	*(Pause).* I've been doing some research this morning and I've found a venue, a small theatre that regularly has psychic evenings …
Ann	Perhaps we can go there a few times and get an idea about …
Sue	We're on in two weeks.
Ann	What?!
Sue	I rang on the off-chance and got the manager and …
Ann	Sue! *(She starts packing her clothes back in the case during the next dialogue).*
Sue	Look, if I'd not done something then …
Ann	I don't believe it!
Sue	If I hadn't arranged it we'd have never done it.
Ann	Two weeks? What were you thinking?
Sue	But we agreed that …
Ann	Two weeks?!
Sue	I'm stupid, it's stupid, we're stupid. I know. I can't explain it, but I just need to do this and now. I'm sorry. I should have asked you. If you're that against it, I'll get back in touch and …

Ann	No.
Sue	OK, I understand.
Ann	Let's do this.
Sue	*(Not hearing Ann).* I'll just ring them and … what, you will?
Ann	By 'no', I mean, 'yes'.
Sue	Then you'll …
Ann	Why not? Sod it. *(Sue jumps up and goes behind the clothes rail to change into her outfit for the next scene).* It has to seem natural and if we plan it too much they'll see right through us, or we'll bottle it. So, sod it. Why not? It's a laugh, isn't it? You said we'd laugh. *(She does a very false, nervous laugh. Pause).* Do you think there's a chance – the smallest chance at all that, well, we might actually find anybody there?
Sue	*(From behind the clothes rail).* Course. They'll sell loads of tickets.
Ann	No, I meant … if it really is …
Sue	*(From behind the clothes rail).* What?
Ann	Nothing. Just, nothing. You're right. Black would be best.
Sue	*(Walking from behind the clothes rail and sitting on the armchair to put her shoes on).* Anyway, what have we got to worry about? The dead can't hurt you. It's the living you've got to worry about.
Ann	Yes. I guess so. *(Sue is still busy getting ready. Ann closes her case, looks at Sue and studies her, deep in thought).*

Blacks in. SFX: Track #4 starts as the lights fade to black.

Scene 4

Two weeks later. SFX: as the lights come up Track #4 fades and audience sound is heard. Sue is at the venue about to go onstage. Upstage is a running black cloth which is closed, giving the impression she is backstage behind the front of house curtains. The dialogue reveals they are part way through their 'act'. Sue is pacing, waiting with her mobile in one hand and a glass of wine in the other. After checking that no one is looking she takes a selfie and then rings Ann. SFX: audience sound fades out.

Sue	*(Speaking on her mobile).* Ann? Where are you? When you pick up this message, just call me or get to the stage or whatever happens first. We're on any minute and I can't do this without you. *(Ann enters quickly, flustered. She is holding a glass of wine).* Where've you been?
Ann	Pee.
Sue	I appreciate your honesty. So. We've got away with it so far, in the first half. And they love the name 'Spirit with Spirits'. And it gives us the chance to have a cheeky drink onstage. Inspired.
Ann	More than one, I hope! Why have they given us a jug of water? Are they trying to poison us?! And you were right about being dressed in black. A certain ambience is added don't you think?
Sue	Oh indeed. *(They toast each other).* This is the best laugh I have had in ages. Oh come on, let's get on with it and get the bloody curtain open. *(She is breathing deeply, clearly trying to calm herself).*

Ann	Wait. I tell you, I nearly wet myself laughing at that woman who started going off on one. She must have spoken solid for five minutes without drawing breath, told us absolutely everything about 'dear Arthur' dying, and what did you say?
Sue	"That's uncanny love, that's exactly what your husband has just told me".
Ann	And bugger me, they all clapped! This has got to be …
Ann/Sue	… the best laugh I have had in ages.
Sue	We'll give them one more session and then it's thank you, good night and a curry.
Ann	Sounds good to me.

SFX: an announcement and audience applause are heard. Sue and Ann immediately turn upstage and face the closed black tab curtain. As the curtains open, the upstage lighting comes up to blind/cover them as they then turn and walk downstage. Stage crew follow them on through the blacks with a table and set it for them to use for their drinks whenever appropriate. As they walk downstage, the lights go off behind and the blacks are closed. Front of house spots come up. Dialogue commences as applause ends.

Ann	Well, you've been a lovely audience ladies and gentlemen. We hope that you've had a chance to relax in the bar at the interval. The theatre has asked me to draw your attention to their forthcoming events listed on the notice board in the bar. Also, that a new Zumba class will be starting here on Monday next week. Which sounds lovely. Wouldn't see me dead at it – and neither, I think would the dead like to see me in a leotard. *(She laughs at her humour. It trails off as, clearly, nobody else has laughed).* Anyhow, we've been very lucky this evening in being able to make connections with the spirit world, haven't we? I hope that they have meant something to, well, some of you. Before we finish for the evening, we will attempt to connect one more time with our spirit guides and, hopefully, bring the world of the spirits into all of our lives and give your loved ones the chance to touch us again. Sue would you like to start? Sue?
Sue	What? Yes. Thank you, Ann. *(She is quiet, 'focussing' and hesitant before she speaks).* I am drawn strongly to the young couple sat on their own at the front of the circle. Please my love, don't cry. I can feel your loss and I know it's so overwhelming. Your mother? Yes, let me see if it is her.

SFX: applause is heard.

Ann	Just give Sue a moment my love and let her establish the connections she needs to make with her spirit guide who will introduce her to your … Yes, yes, I know, I know, the years aren't the healer everybody says are they?
Sue	My love, I do have an elderly lady here and she says that she is your mother, but says you always called her something unique, your own little pet name for her, something only you ever used that was, well, special, private, personal … Mummy? That was your pet name for your mother? Yes, original, well, she says that's right, yes, you knew her as … Mummy. She's agreeing with you. She looks good for her age even now, a beautiful old lady.
Ann	What, say again love? But she was only forty when she died?

Sue	Well yes, my love but what you don't understand is that she is clearly projecting a much older maternal persona to comfort you.
Ann	*(Whispering, aside to Sue).* Nice one.
Sue	Well, exactly, that's what I'll be seeing isn't it? I'm assuming the visual imagery infers age, but we're both right. A forty-year-old lady who looks like, like, well, like a pensioner.
Ann	Oh, she dressed old for her age did she? Well, that just confirms what Sue's saying. Amazing. Amazing really.
Sue	Truly.
Ann	Really.
Ann/Sue	Amazing.

SFX: applause is heard.

Sue	*(Whispering, aside to Ann).* You're telling me. *(To audience).* And I can see that she is gesturing pain in her, I see in her … *(she moves her hand around, hesitating, giving the impression she has no clue and is waiting for a lead to help her)* … legs?
Ann	Oh, she died of a heart attack?
Sue	*(Aside).* Shit, *(To audience).* Correct, she's telling me that it radiated … from her heart … into her legs.
Ann	Uncanny really.
Sue	Really.
Ann	Truly.
Ann/Sue	Amazing.

SFX: applause is heard.

Sue	And so comforted she is, comforted to know you were with her when she died. By her side, holding her hand and she could hear every word you said my love, feel every tear that … what? She died in Benidorm? Really?
Ann	… and you were in Cleethorpes?
Sue	Well, that's spot on … because she could … she's saying she could, feel you with her … across the miles.
Ann	Amazing the connection between mother and daughter. Comes from the womb you know.
Sue	Definitely.
Ann	Absolutely.
Ann/Sue	Amazing.
Ann	'Umbilical association', we call it in the psychic world.
Sue	*(Aside).* Do we?
Ann	*(Aside).* Shut it
Sue	It can't be cheated.
Ann	Infallible.
Sue	What? Oh.
Ann/Sue	You were adopted?

Ann	Then your bond must have been exceptionally close with your Mum. To have been adopted and the miles meant nothing. Her in Benidorm and you holding her hand …
Sue	… in Cleethorpes. Dear, sweet …
Ann	Young.
Sue	Mum.
Ann	Mummy, yes Sue, Mummy.
Sue	She is clearly a dear, sweet, attractive …
Ann	Young.
Sue	Slim …
Ann	Oh, struggled with her weight did she?
Sue	Inside, a slim woman, fighting to get out of …
Ann	… of her wheelchair, you say?
Sue	Which is the reason for me seeing her legs. Unbelievable. Really.
Ann	Truly.
Ann/Sue	Amazing.

SFX: applause is heard.

Ann	Is there anything you would like to say to your mum, Mummy, whilst she is still in our plane? *(Ann and Sue are looking to the back of the auditorium as if listening to the unseen young woman speak).* Take your time love, nobody is rushing you.
Sue	*(Aside).* Much. *(She finishes her wine and moves to the table).*

SFX: a whistle is heard. Sue looks front to see where it has come from and then puts her wine glass on the table. SFX: after a few seconds the whistle is heard again. The Woman appears from a prominent position in the auditorium so that the audience' attention is drawn to her. Ann is still looking to the audience, engaged, listening.

Sue	*(She looks across to where the sound came from, distracted, and then speaks to 'whoever' is whistling in the audience).* Does somebody want to ask a question?
Ann	Y'what?
Sue	The person whistling? It's a little rude to interrupt but now you have …
Ann	*(Aside).* Sue, what are you doing?
Sue	*(To Ann).* Somebody whistled, down there.
Ann	*(She is embarrassed. To the audience).* I think Sue's hearing things, ladies and gentlemen. It has been a heavy evening for us, I'm sure you'll all agree. I do apologise my love, you carry on.

SFX: the whistle is heard again. Woman moves onto the stage into position.

Sue	*(Shouting).* Who is that?
Ann	For god's sake, Sue! Nobody is whistling! I'm very sorry everybody …
Sue	Are you deaf?
Ann	No, but you are. *(Putting her wine glass on the table).* Probably a hearing aid whistling or something. Can we carry on please? I'm sorry everybody. Sorry my love, please continue.

SFX: the whistle is heard again.

Sue	Right, who is that? *(To Ann).* Don't tell me you didn't hear it that time? *(She makes her way to the edge of the stage and looks in the direction of where the sound came from. The woman is next to her, studying her).*
Ann	Sue, what the hell are you doing?

It is clear neither of them can see The Woman, who moves around Sue, looking at her.

Sue	What is your game love? Come on, where are you? You want to be the centre of attention do you? Don't believe, eh? Bit of a childish protest is it? Getting a kick out of spoiling it for everybody else?
Ann	Ladies and gentlemen, I think we're going to have to leave it there. If we can bring the curtains in. Sue is clearly tired by all of this and …
Sue	What? What are you talking about? *(SFX: the whistle is heard again).* Look love, don't ruin this for everybody else. Can somebody find this person and get them to leave please?
Ann	Sue. You're embarrassing us now. *(The Woman exits, touching Sue fleetingly as she does which Sue reacts to).* I'm so sorry everybody. We do hope to see you again and that you support the Zumba class. *(Stage crew remove the table).* Please check the notice board for further details. We do hope you've enjoyed 'Spirit with Spirits' and that you will join us again. Thank you and goodnight and cheers! *(She downs her drink).*

SFX: applause is heard. Ann has taken hold of Sue to 'make' her bow with her. The black tab curtains open, lights up behind them. They both bow to reveal The Woman, now in silhouette stood 'out front' facing them.

The blacks then close in front of The Woman as SFX: a slow applause is heard which fades out. Sue is breathing heavily, looking wildly around the stage.

Ann	*(Parting the curtain to speak to the audience).* Thank you everybody. Apologies again. Thank you. *(To Sue).* Breathe, calm, calm. Right you, off the stage! I don't know what the game is. *(Calling out).* Can the manager come onstage please? *(She gets hold of Sue's arm).* Come on love, let's just get off stage.
Sue	Why? Get off me. I'm not frightened of them.
Ann	Them? Sue, who are you talking to? Can we have the manager please?
Sue	It was a whistle! They just blew on my face.
Ann	What? Sue, there's nobody there! Blew on your face?! Give it a rest. We've finished.
Sue	Oh right, I see, get your own back. You've set me up, haven't you? *(The Woman enters. Sue parts the curtains to speak to the audience).* Sorry everybody, goodnight, all the best. *(To Ann and offstage).* A stage practical joke by everybody is it? Whose idea was this?

Ann is just staring at Sue. The Woman moves slowly and as she does she touches Sue's arm and Sue screams.

Ann	Calm down or you won't be the only one having a seizure!
Sue	She touched me.
Ann	She?
Sue	It's a woman. I felt her. I could smell her perfume just then.

Ann	Smell? What are you on? Manager, I asked for the Manager!

The Woman just observes, expressionless. Ann goes to take Sue's arm and Sue reacts violently.

Sue	Get off me!
Ann	Don't start with me lady. Nice one. Make us look a right pair of idiots why don't you? 'Spirit with Spirits'? More like 'Spirits who've had too much bloody spirits'.
Sue	Me start? Look darling, if you're going to add to the act at least let me know. But hey, you got them going as well as me, apart from the fact you've made me look barmy with your little tricks. How are you doing it then, eh?
Ann	Please tell me this is a wind-up.
Sue	What are you talking about? Who's your partner in crime then?
Ann	What am I talking about? Sue, on my mother's life, nobody was whistling, there was no one onstage, no practical joke, no touching, blowing. I have no idea what you're talking about. There was, always has been, only me and you on this stage.
Sue	But …
Ann	*(She takes hold of Sue by the arms and shouts at her).* Sue. There was nobody here, what part of this do you not understand?
Sue	But I heard. I felt … they touched my ... they came on here. It was real. I heard the whistle as clear as I heard you speak. I don't understand.
Ann	Look love, let's just leave it for now. Leave your car here and I'll drop you off. You're in no fit state to drive.
Sue	What's the matter with me, Ann?
Ann	Nothing. With everything you've been through and what we've got through in that dressing room in booze, it was probably all too much.
Sue	But Ann, I swear to you I'm not lying. *(She is getting worked up again).*
Ann	But if you're not lying.

The Woman gently blows on Sue's hair. Sue reacts.

Sue	I can't breathe. I can't breathe.
Ann	This isn't happening.
Sue	I can't breathe.
Ann	Panic attack. Deep breaths now. Just calm down.

SFX: the whistle is heard again.

Sue	*(Shouting and looking around).* Who is that?
Ann	*(Shouting at Sue).* Who is what? Sue, please you're frightening me now.

SFX: multiple whistles are heard.

Sue	Stop it! *(She is getting more worked up. Spinning around, trying to see who or what it is, finally covering her ears).*

SFX: the whistling heard is now getting gradually louder and then overlapping over the next dialogue.

Sue	Who is that? Who's there? Stop it! Stop it! Stop it! I can't see them, where did you go? Who are you? Where are you? Why are you doing this? I can't breathe.

Ann   Can I have some help please? I'm frightened. Hello, I asked for help? *(She takes hold of Sue who is hyperventilating, getting hysterical and finally collapses into her arms and faints. Ann is crying).* Help, now. Help! Help! For god's sake please, somebody, anybody?!

The lights fade to black with Ann and Sue on the floor and The Woman stood behind, observing. SFX: Track #5 starts and is left to play out.

END OF ACT ONE

INTERVAL

ACT TWO
Scene 1

Running blacks out during interval. Sues house, two weeks later. Track #6: music is playing on the radio as the house light go down and stage lights come up. There are two wine bottles, one empty, one practically empty, a wine glass, a bottle of tablets and Sue's mobile phone, all on a table between the two armchairs. Sue is wearing a dressing gown, sat in one of-the chairs with her knees up to her chest listening to the music and staring blankly ahead. After a short while. SFX: the doorbell is heard. Sue is startled and jumps to her feet. A blanket which was over her falls to the floor. She turns off the radio. Track #6 off. She is still, nervous, looking towards the door. SFX: the doorbell is heard again. She quickly sits back on the chair with her knees up to her chest again. SFX: the mobile phone ringing is heard. It startles Sue but she does not answer it.

Ann   *(From outside the door)*. Sue? Open the door, love. I know you're in there. You can't hide forever from me and I'm not going, so answer the bloody door. It's freezing out here. If I had nuts they'd have dropped off by now. It's been two weeks. Sue? Please? I'm not leaving until I speak to you. I'm worried about you. Please Sue? *(Sue quickly opens the door, then immediately goes back to her chair and sits with her knees up to her chest. Ann slowly walks in. Eyes fixed on Sue and slowly sits in the other chair)*. Thanks. So. How are you? *(Silence)*. Glad you let me in. I think the neighbours were beginning to think I was a member of the God Squad with a quota to fill. *(She laughs to herself but soon stops when Sue doesn't respond)*. I've been around a few times, but clearly not caught you in. Suppose you were out. I'll give you the benefit of the doubt with that, those ones. I've called the house phone loads of times, but your answering machine was off, so I'll give you the benefit of those ones as well. But I've lost count of the number of texts and calls to your mobile and as that's permanently fixed to you I can't let you get away with not knowing I was ...

Sue   I wanted to be left alone. Still do.
Ann   I see.
Sue   *(Quickly)*. Do you?
Ann   Yes.
Sue   *(Sarcastically)*. Really?
Ann   Clearly not.
Sue   Clearly not.

Silence.

Ann   *(She spots tablets on the table which have spilled out)*. What are those?
Sue   Valium.
Ann   Why?
Sue   *(Singing, defiantly)*. 'Just a mouth full of red wine makes the Valium go down, Valium go down, ...' *(Whilst singing she takes some Valium and then washes them down with wine as she stops singing. Once she has swallowed, she sings again)*. 'Valium go down ...'
Ann   I just wanted to ...
Sue   What?
Ann   Well. Just to find out ...

Sue	What?
Ann	To make sure you weren't … alone.
Sue	What? Alone? Stupid. A lifetime alone. What difference will two more weeks of it make.
Ann	I was worried about you.
Sue	Why?
Ann	Why do you think?
Sue	To make you feel better?
Ann	Is that what you think? Honestly?
Sue	Don't start me on honesty.
Ann	It's the truth.
Sue	*(She laughs).* Truth. Now. That's a whole new chapter. No. A book on its own. A lifetime of a conversation. Not enough drink, even in this house, to wash that one down.
Ann	And I was worried.
Sue	And I still want to be left alone.
Ann	Fine. *(She gets up and starts to leave).*
Sue	No. Sit. I'm all over the show. Just … sit. *(Ann sits slowly back down, not taking her eyes off Sue).*
Sue	*(She picks up the wine bottle and pours the contents in the glass. There is literally a drop left. She looks at it and then drinks it anyhow).* Sod it! *(She exits and returns with another bottle, unscrewing the top. She pours herself a drink and knocks it back. She pours another and then sits as before holding the glass to her).*
Ann	*(She weighs Sue up).* Bit early Sue.
Sue	Not when you've been drinking all night, Ann.
Ann	All night?
Sue	All night.
Ann	Why?
Sue	*(Incredulously).* Why? Do you seriously want me to answer that?
Ann	Look Sue …
Sue	No, you look, Ann. Don't insult my intelligence by pretending that what happened two weeks ago didn't happen. That we're going to chat like two old dears at a tea dance, comparing conditions and prescriptions. That's what this is all about, isn't it? The house call? That's why you're here. Drop the bull and the pretence. Don't tell me that what happened meant nothing. That we do niceties. I've had enough of pretending. A lifetime. And please. Don't even try asking me to forget it.
Ann	I wouldn't dream of it.
Sue	Dreaming. Wow. Don't get me on to dreaming.
Ann	*(She becomes annoyed).* Please, give it a break darling. I'm not meaning anything by it, so for god's sake stop looking for reasons to be a cow. *(Silence).* Sue?
Sue	*(Pause. Speaking calmly).* Any concept of reality, of sanity, of, God knows. God, now that is a subject for a whole new bottle. Sorry. It all left me two weeks ago. "Is there anybody there?" you asked me. Remember? You asked me. Sat in that chair. Well. After what happened. What do you think now,

	eh? And you asked me, "… but what if?" Remember that as well? You said that as well. Sat there. Well. There was somebody there. Something there. My god there was. And no friend, no shrink, no case of red will convince me otherwise. Two weeks I've sat here thinking about it. Drinking about it. I might have some baggage but I'm not mad. I know what I saw, what I heard. You won't convince me otherwise. We, I, did something that night. My big joke, my laugh at everybody else's expense. And what happened? Well. I'm the joke and the expense is mine. The question is, how long will I be paying? Who am I paying? What will be the price? And now she's back to collect the balance.
Ann	She's back?
Sue	It wasn't just onstage. It's happened in here. I keep hearing voices. A woman. She says things. Can't tell what sometimes. And the whistle. Same thing every time. Like she's calling a dog or something. And blowing on my face. Touching me. Wakes me up. Her voice is very quiet. Calm. But she's here. I know she is.
Ann	Have you been to the doctors?
Sue	*(She turns very quickly and looks at Ann sharply).* Have I what? Doctors? Are you not listening to me?
Ann	Just because you can't explain it, doesn't mean that the answer has to be so, so, far-fetched.
Sue	Far-fetched?
Ann	You know what I mean Sue.
Sue	No I don't, Ann, and neither do you. You don't know what you're talking about.
Ann	And to be honest, neither do you. *(Silence)*. I didn't see, didn't hear anything. Nobody did. Doesn't that tell you something?

Silence. Then the following dialogue gets more heated and angry.

Sue	I only know …
Ann	You only know, what? Think about it. You saw something. You heard something. You believe something. No one else did. A theatre full of people. No one. And you're telling me that something, some woman, was there? And because it's carried on, it's real?
Sue	And what might that something, some woman have been? What do you think Ann? Come on. Pin your colours to that mast.
Ann	You're not drawing me into this.
Sue	Into what? Speculation? The truth? You can't accept it so 'it' can't be? Is that how it has to be? You can't explain, so I need help?
Ann	So I'm mad, am I?
Sue	So we're bring madness into it are we?
Ann	I'm just saying.
Sue	And if you're clearly not, then I am? I asked you, who brought madness into this?
Ann	I'm not saying that.
Sue	So what exactly are you saying?

Ann	To be honest? I have no idea. I don't know what to believe any longer.
Sue	You mean, you don't know who to believe any longer?
Ann	You said that.
Sue	No, I simply said what you refuse to.
Ann	Word games, mind games. It's your game, not mine. When you've figured the rules of your little game, you let me know. *(She stands and goes to leave but Sue's next dialogue stops her).*
Sue	Well, well. I remember these conversations. Just like having Derek back from the dead. And out the door she trots. Bit of a theme in this house. People always walk out of here when reality begins to fight back.
Ann	*(Incredulously).* Reality? Reality? What are you …
Sue	*(Interrupting)* … if you don't know which way to go, just follow the track on the carpet that he wore out, running away when he couldn't deal with life.
Ann	Life? So, seeing dead people is life is it? *(Sue doesn't answer).* Fortunate you can speak to his friends then. Isn't it?
Sue	Sod off!
Ann	*(She moves to Sue).* So. You can pick and choose reality, but I can't? Is that it? Come off it. Isn't that what this is all about? So, go on then. I'll say it because you won't. You 'feel the presence' of a dead person, a ghost, a spirit, a woman? And worse, you now believe that what we did brought it there and now she's here. *(She turns and moves away. Sue's breathing is becoming anxious and obvious).* You brought her here and she might come back. And I can't see her, so it has to be right. The joke has backfired and instead of being the joker, you're the joke. *(Sue is getting more worked up).* And locking yourself away with a cupboard full of wine, a head full of shadows and a life full of nothing, helps? And ignoring the only friend you've got makes it easier to cope I take it? Because any minute, you're scared that the next person you see might be your dead husband. *(She turns and sees the state Sue has got herself into which immediately diffuses her anger. She kneels next to Sue and takes her hands).* Breathe. Deep, slow. Calm … down. Calm. I'm sorry. *(Sue fumbles in her handbag for her inhaler and uses it. She calms slowly and then suddenly embraces Ann).* Alright. I don't know. I don't understand. And worst of all. Neither do you. Well. Whatever happened was down to us both, so no matter what we've done, we both have to fix it. Don't we? *(Sue sits back and nods).* First step completed. You've let me in the house. Second step, well, think we've done that. But number three - will you allow me to come into your, our problem? *(Sue nods. Ann hugs her again).*
Sue	What time is it?
Ann	Ten. In the morning.
Sue	… in the?
Ann	*(Standing).* Yeah, morning, you piss head. Go and get dressed. We need air. Breakfast. *(Sue picks up the glass of wine and knocks it back).* What are you doing?
Sue	Breakfast.
Ann	Sue?
Sue	One step, one problem at a time. Not all crutches are made of wood.

Ann	*(She picks up the bottle of wine and looks at it. She looks for a glass but can't find one).* Sod it. *(She takes a big swig from the bottle).* See you out front. I seriously need a fag. *(She goes to leave).*
Sue	And Ann? *(Ann stops and turns to look at Sue).* Who, whatever this, she, is. I'm not frightened of it any longer. I guess the reason I'm getting worked up is all about me. But I will find out what's going on. I will.
Ann	Good on you, Doris Stokes. *(She exits).*

As Sue stands and folds the blanket, The Woman appears. SFX: the whistle is heard.

Sue	Did you not hear me, darling? Not frightened. So, do one.
Woman	Really? We'll see!

Sue stops dead in her tracks and drops the blanket. Fade to black. Track #7 plays as running blacks in.

Scene 2

Courtroom. Ann stands facing the audience in a tight spot. This is now her position for the subsequent scenes in the courtroom. She is wearing a different overcoat.

Ann	I swear by Almighty God that the evidence I shall give to this Inquest shall be the truth, the whole truth and nothing but the truth.
	Where was I? So, yes, as I said before we finished for lunch. Two weeks ago, and I hadn't seen my friend Sue for, what, the previous two weeks before that, so we went out for breakfast. We talked. For hours. And breakfast turned into lunch and dinner and, well, the world was well and truly put to rights. We agreed that, well, look … I know you're not interested in what we thought happened that night at the theatre, but what matters now is that we agreed to go back. We agreed to do our act and, well, see what happened.
	She didn't want to go. I guess I convinced her. Wanted to show her it was all in her head. She insisted she did it on her own to prove it was real – as real as seeing and hearing dead people could be. She did explain to me why, her rationale. I didn't get it, understand. And in the end, I gave in and we agreed to see, to see, well, just to see what, who, would be there if we went back and to see if there really was, 'anybody there'. *(She appears to get upset).* Do you mind if we have a break? It's all a bit much, remembering.

Fade to black. Ann exits to remove her coat. Lights up on Sue who is now stood in front of the running blacks waiting to 'go on stage' for her performance as before. She is holding two glasses of wine. SFX: audience sound is heard. Ann enters.

Sue	*(Handing the glass of wine to Ann).* Bloody hell, you're cutting this one fine. We're on any minute.
Ann	You're sure we're doing the right thing?
Sue	No. But I'm doing the only thing I can do and I'm just so bloody grateful that you are here – even though you think it's all a crock.

Ann	This might be a crock, you're not. If we get to the bottom of you then we get to the bottom of this. So, it's worth it. I suppose the problem is, it's just …
Sue	Just what?
Ann	Them. The audience. It started as a joke but we're not laughing any longer. We're taking advantage of them. I just still feel bad about it. Using them.
Sue	Look, it's just one more time. They know why they're here. We know why we're here. Different reasons? Yes. Will they care? No, because they will go home none the wiser. But I will.
Ann	How?
Sue	Because one way or another, I'll know if there is something out there or whether it is all in here. *(Tapping on her head).*
Ann	And one way or another, I don't think you'll be happy with what you find and you'll regret …
Sue	You call it regret. I call it life and I'm used to it. *(She takes a large swig of her wine).*
Ann	Steady Sue.
Sue	Dutch courage.
Ann	I don't think you need any of that.
Sue	Getting into character – 'Spirit with Spirits'. Remember?
Ann	Hmm. More like 'Spirit full of Spirits'. *(They laugh).* Oh, by the way, it's not just the punters in tonight.
Sue	What?
Ann	The audience. Not just the public out there.
Sue	Meaning?
Ann	The Manager rang me on my mobi'. That's why I was late. The local papers are in.
Sue	Papers?
Ann	Yep. Your little encore performance last time. It would appear what happened on tour didn't exactly stay on tour?
Sue	Who? How?
Ann	Not who or how, <u>what</u>. A little matter of a mobile and a little 'ole thing called YouTube. Social Media, my dear girl. YouTube infected Facebook which gave it to Twitter who passed it onto Instagram and the rest is networking history. We took the piss out of those who air their dirty laundry on the net. Remember? Well, it looks like technology has bitten us on the spiritual arse. Just, you went one further, got a lifetimes worth of dirty laundry and chucked it out the window onto the street for everybody to gawp at. In other words, my little Mystic Meg, somebody in the audience got their phone out and you went viral.
Sue	This is bad.
Ann	Not entirely. It's means tonight's sold out.
Sue	Oh bugger.
Ann	Well, this is what you wanted all along. The big laugh, the big scam, that you …
Sue	We! *(She takes a peek through the curtain).*
Ann	Yeah. We.

Sue	Oh double bugger. They've already got their phones out taking pictures. Christ, there's reporters everywhere with big cameras.
Ann	Our adoring public want to see a show.
Sue	Want to see a meltdown more like.
Ann	Whatever you call it, I can guarantee they're gonna get it. And whatever it is will be on YouTube, Facebook and all the rest of them quicker than you can say …
Sue	I want to go home.
Ann	Not quick enough darling. We're on. Stick with the plan. What we did last time. If we don't go wrong, this won't go wrong. *(They turn upstage and face the closed black tab curtain).*

SFX: audience sound fades out, announcement and then applause is heard. Running blacks open, the upstage lighting comes up to blind/cover Sue and Ann as they then turn and walk downstage as in Act One. Dialogue begins as applause ends.

Ann	Good evening ladies and gentlemen. Well, it would appear that for only our second evening of 'Spirit with Spirits' we have a full house. So, thank you for sharing your evening with us. My beautiful assistant has kindly furnished us both with the necessary. *(She holds her glass up).*
Ann/Sue	Cheers!
Ann	And I trust you have all brought in the same from the bar. So. Time to find if there really is, anybody there, assisted of course by 'Spirit with Spirits'.

SFX: applause is heard. Sue moves down stage and stares out into the audience. Silence. She closes her eyes. After a short while, Ann looks a little uneasy as nothing appears to be happening.

Ann	Well ladies and gentlemen, these things take a short while to get warmed up because of the way things work in the spirit world, we can't just turn things on like a tap, can we?

The Woman walks on stage during Ann's dialogue and stands behind Sue. She then moves to the side of her and blows on her face. Sue smiles, but now a little more controlled.

Sue	She's here.
Ann	*(Speaking under her breath).* Oh shit! *(To the audience).* Well ladies and gentlemen, it appears we are ready to commence. We just need a moment for Sue to focus. Just a moment hopefully.
Sue	I can feel her here.
Ann	*(Speaking under her breath again).* Double shit! *(To the audience).* It would appear, ladies and gentlemen, that Sue has made contact with the spirits.

SFX: applause is heard. Ann goes into a freeze just as she is to speak to the audience. LX: lights go down on Ann and highlight Sue and The Woman. The Woman is stood closely behind Sue and they are both facing the audience.

Woman	*(Quietly).* You know I'm here.
Sue	*(She reacts slightly and also speaking quietly).* Yes. I can hear you. I can feel you.
Woman	Who am I?
Sue	I … I don't know. I'm not sure if …
Woman	Are you sure?
Sue	No. Yes.

Woman	You really don't know?
Sue	I …
Woman	Do you believe?
Sue	I'm not sure if …
Woman	*(Interrupting).* Do you believe that I am …
Sue	Don't say it.
Woman	Say what, that I'm …
Sue	Please.
Woman	Then do you believe? Do you? Do you? Do you?
Sue	*(Interrupting first and then shouting her repeated answer).* Yes. <u>Yes!</u> <u>Yes!</u> <u>Yes!</u>

LX: lights come up on Ann and she reacts to Sue calling out.

Ann	*(Almost sounding relieved).* And she's back in the room, ladies and gentlemen. Thought Sue was re-enacting 'When Harry Met Sally' for a moment then. *(She laughs nervously).* So, Sue, what are the spirits saying to us?
Sue	They're asking if I believe in them. Asking if I think they're real.
Ann	Lovely. That's, well, lovely. Isn't it ladies and gentlemen? Don't know about you but I'm not struggling to believe at the moment.

LX: lights fade on Ann as she goes into a freeze and highlight Sue and The Woman.

Woman	Ask the lady who looks tearful on the fifth row the question. You know the question.
Sue	How can I know?
Woman	You know. Think. Consider. You know.
Sue	*(Loudly).* I know.

LX: lights come up on Ann who is confused and laughs nervously.

Ann	Well, aren't we pleased ladies and gentlemen? She knows, something.
Woman	Ask her.
Sue	You, my love. *(Pointing).* Yes, you. Why did you never tell him? *(SFX: applause is heard. Ann slowly turns sideways, mouth open and looks at Sue).* No need to cry, my love. He knew. He always knew. He's just sad you never had the chance to say it.
Ann	*(She is nonplussed and hesitant almost).* Indeed, yes, never saying, sadness, saying what exactly … *(Silence).* Nothing, clearly. Anyway, yes, my love?

LX: lights down on Ann as she turns to the audience and goes into a freeze as if about to acknowledge someone in the audience.

Woman	Look at them all. You know what they are all here for. You can tell, just by looking at any one of them, what they want to know. Why they want to know. It's no longer funny. Think. You feel you now have a purpose in your life. You have a reason. Death has given you life. A life-giving hope. So give them hope. Look at them. Tell them.
Ann	*(LX: lights come up on her. She is speaking as if mid-sentence).* … and I do understand my love, I think the way the spirits work is …

Sue	*(Speaking over Ann)*. You're frightened there was somebody else, aren't you? *(Ann again looks sideways, at Sue, her mouth open)*. I know, I know. Don't be embarrassed to cry.
Ann	*(Nervously, laughing, to the audience)*. Well Sue, I'm glad that you do know.
Sue/Wom	*(Both facing the audience)*. The man in the dress circle. The one in the red top. Why are you laughing? Are you frightened? That I might speak to you next?
Ann	*(Speaking under her breath)*. Shit! *(Shouting in the same direction)*. No love, don't leave, please.
Sue/Wom	Please. Stay. He wants to speak to you. The one you hoped you would never hear from again.
Ann	What my love? How does she know?

SFX: applause is heard.

Sue/Wom	He says he is sorry. And you know who, don't you? And you know why, don't you? Why he is sorry? Why he did it?
Ann	No, don't cry my love, I'm sure that … *(She goes to Sue and whispers to her)*. What the hell are you playing at?
Sue/Wom	He's so sorry. So sorry for everything. No need to be upset. Not anymore.
Ann	*(Hesitantly)*. Well ladies and gentlemen, we are clearly communing with the other side about things that, things, which mean things to you all about, well, things that mean absolutely nothing to me. Yes. Lovely, lovely things.

SFX: applause is heard. Track #8 starts in the applause. The Woman is stood silently smiling at Sue, nodding. Fade to black.

Scene 3

Courtroom. Track #8 fades. Lights up on Ann.

Ann	I'm sorry, thank you for that break. Yes, I understand, still under oath. I just needed to compose myself a little. Where was I? Oh yes. That second performance was another chapter, a new chapter in her increasingly bizarre behaviour. Yes, I know I should have just walked away, but how could I? She was vulnerable, and I was in too deep. I was having a really hard time at work and … *(as if interrupted)* … yes, sorry, I'll stick to answering the question. She was very assured in the theatre that night. She was asking things I wasn't expecting, giving answers that the audience loved, and which freaked me out. It was as if she knew, that – I can't believe I'm saying this – that there might just be somebody there. Anyhow, after the show, we didn't speak for a week. Another episode of unanswered calls and texts. So, I just turned up. Seemed to be the only way I ever got to speak to her.

Fade to black. Ann exits. The blacks open to reveal Sue's home again. Lights up and Sue has a bottle of wine and a glass. She is sat, pouring herself a glass, knocks it back, then pours another and sits expressionless. The Woman enters and stands behind her, staring front. Sue appears to sense her presence.

Sue	What, no whistle, no touch, no blow on the cheek any longer?
Woman	Why? You knew I was here. Was it the perfume this time?
Sue	Hmm.

Woman	Do we need to play games?
Sue	No.
Woman	No. Indeed. Enough games in your life I would say.
Sue	Meaning?
Woman	Meaning exactly that.
Sue	Yes. You're right.
Woman	No, you're right. I'm just helping you see what you already know.
Sue	But how do you know? Are you from heaven?
Woman	Heaven?
Sue	Well, yes. How else? How else could I be speaking to you. You are dead, aren't you?
Woman	Am I?
Sue	Well …
Woman	That's how it has to be is it?
Sue	It's the only rational explanation.
Woman	Rational? To talk to and hear dead people?
Sue	So you are dead?
Woman	More games. Are games better than reality? Does it all fit together when it's a game? All that from a woman who spent her life in a state of pretence and wants to escape one make believe to create a new one? Heaven? Really?
Sue	What other explanation could there be?
Woman	Don't just accept things because it answers your confusion. Think. You know the answers, you always have.
Sue	What? What does that mean? One step at a time. What do I call you?
Woman	What do you think you should …
Sue	*(Standing)*. For the love of god, give me a break, will you? I already think I'm going mad.
Woman	And are you?
Sue	*(Sitting)*. I'm so confused.
Woman	Why? Think.
Sue	Just answer one thing. Are you from heaven?
Woman	Why is that so important to you?
Sue	I just wondered if there really was one.
Woman	Does it really matter to you that much, now, here, after all that has happened?
Sue	Yes, I think. No. I don't know any longer.
Woman	Are you beginning to understand you any better?
Sue	*(Pause)*. No.
Woman	Really? Really?
Sue	Yes.
Woman	Are you happy?
Sue	No.
Woman	Really?
Sue	Actually …
Woman	Well?
Sue	Happier than I've ever been in my whole life?
Woman	Why?

Sue	Because out of all of this, I'm finally beginning to feel I have some control.
Woman	Of?
Sue	Me.
Woman	Then does it matter where I'm from?
Sue	No.
Woman	Do you need to believe in heaven?
Sue	No.
Woman	Does a make-believe place where dead people live actually make <u>now</u> any better, easier to understand?
Sue	No.
Woman	So what do you really need to do?
Sue	What you said last night: "Live in the moment, cherish the moment, believe in the moment. Because <u>now</u> only lasts as long as it takes to say it".
Woman	"Is all what we see or seem, all a dream within a dream".
Sue	That's very profound.
Woman	According to you I'm dead, so what did you expect? Bing Bong. *(SFX: the doorbell is heard. Sue goes to stand but The Woman speaking stops her).* Calm. Sit. Wait.
Sue	Who is it?
Woman	Think. Who will it be? Who is the only person it could be?
Sue/Wom	Ann.
Ann	*(Offstage).* It's Ann, Sue. Let me in love.
Sue	What should I do?
Woman	"Live in the moment, cherish the moment, believe in the moment" – isn't that what you said? Your undertaking? Your resolution? The new You? What do you want?
Sue	*(She stands, walks towards the door and then stops, retraces her steps and sits, knees drawn up to her chest).* No. Not now. Not ready. Need to think.
Woman	Need to think. What else, what else might help. Need to think and …
Sue/Wom	Need to drink.
Sue	Yes, drink, need to drink.
Sue/Wom	Makes everything feel better.
Sue	Makes everything go away.
Woman	Makes Ann go away.
Sue	Yeah, make her go away. *(She moves to stand and call out to Ann).*
Woman	Such a good idea?
Sue	*(She resumes her position).* No. Leave her.
Sue/Wom	Leave her to stew.
Woman	Yes, need to think, need to drink. Need to get to the bottom of problems.
Sue	Need to get to the bottom of the bottle.
Woman	Piss funny.
Sue	No, pissed is funny.
Woman	*(Pause).* But when, why did it all stop being funny?
Sue	Not sure.
Woman	Really?
Sue	I suppose. I guess. Before Derek died. Years before.

Woman	Really? That long?
Sue	I'm … not sure.
Woman	Think.
Sue	Confused.
Woman	Think. What makes us happy, can also make us sad.
Sue	Yes.
Woman	Some people who make us happy also make us sad.
Sue	Meaning?
Woman	Some people who make it right, also make it wrong. *(SFX: mobile vibrating is heard. Sue stares at the phone on the table but ignores it).* And it all went wrong, all seemed to only start going bad when, let me see, when was that, when, when do you think? *(Silence).* Who has made you happy … and now sad.
Sue	It can't be … why would that … I can't believe.
Woman	You can't believe? Happy enough to speak to dead people that you can't see but then disbelieve the living proof in front of you. Which leads us very nicely to …
Sue/Wom	Ann.

The Woman puts her head back and breathes out a very satisfied sigh.

Sue	It was all fine until …
Sue/Wom	Ann.
Woman	Who would have thought it?
Sue	Need to think.
Sue/Wom	Need to drink.

Sue picks up the bottle and starts drinking from it. The Woman smiles. LX: lights fade out and cross fade to Ann, again giving evidence.

Ann	OK. Let me see. Anyhow, I had been to the house again. I knew she was in there, but she just wouldn't answer the door. I thought I could hear voices, but when I put my ear to the letter box, I suddenly realised that it was just Sue. And she seemed to be having a conversation with herself. I got frightened as I then began to put the pieces together. She thought there was somebody on stage, she thought there was somebody in the house with her. It was all in her mind. What other explanation? If only I had appreciated the warning signs then, if only … *(she starts to get upset).* No Sir, I'm fine. I need to get this inquest out of the way, get it all out and move on; tell the truth.

LX: the lights go down on Ann and she exits. The lights come up on Sue who is sleeping. She is dishevelled, looking terrible. There are a couple of empty bottles around her and she is still holding a wine glass in her limp hand. The Woman enters. Sue becomes aware of her presence and opens her eyes. She has clearly had a drink, and this is reflected in her manner and slightly in her speech.

Sue	About time. Where have you been? Have you been away somewhere?
Woman	Away?
Sue	Well, yeah.
Woman	Where could I possibly go, why would I without you?
Sue	So you've been here all along?
Woman	What do you think?

Sue	Why didn't you say something, give me a sign?
Woman	Why?
Sue	Hmm. Guess so. Why should you? *(Pouring herself another drink).* Just knowing you might be around is enough. Knowing I'm not alone, but then again …
Sue/Wom	Always been alone.
Sue	Ain't that the truth. Now there's just me. And before that there was just me and …
Woman	And?
Sue	And? Me and …
Woman	And … who?
Sue	Derek. Me and Derek.
Woman	And?
Sue	What? I'm not sure what you …
Woman	Mean? Hmm. Mean. Very, very mean.
Sue	Where's this going?
Woman	Honesty. The truth. I know you're thinking it. The truth always needs a beginning. But it doesn't always make sense. Bit like Derek. So, what was the beginning? What was the truth of Derek?
Sue	*(Pause).* Well. There was always, you know …
Woman	Something, Some …?
Sue	One.
Woman	Interesting.
Sue	Yeah, someone. It always felt like he was acting …
Woman	Suspiciously?
Sue	Suspiciously. Yeah, that's right. He sometimes behaved like there was a …
Sue/Wom	Secret.
Sue	Secret. That's the word. I was trying to remember it, but yes. A secret. That's exactly it. I knew it was that but never processed it, never thought it, considered it, challenged it. As if he was …
Sue/Wom	Hiding something.
Sue	Hiding something. Of course. How could I have been so … and a suspicious, secret, something. Always, always, hiding …
Woman	Things? *(She moves to stand near Sue).*
Sue	Things, nothing you could, nothing you could pinpoint as, you know, ever point a finger, raise a question. There was nothing ever …
Sue/Wom	Important.
Sue	No, that's right as well. But there was just something about his behaviour, always something …
Woman	Concealed?
Sue	Wary.
Woman	Furtive?
Sue	Preoccupied.
Woman	Cagey?
Sue	Avoiding.
Woman	Busy?

Sue	Late.
Woman	Uninterested?
Sue	Cautious.
Woman	Indiscreet?
Sue	*(Pause. She stands. Her expression is of somebody who has had an unexpected revelation).* Indiscreet. *(She is pacing anxiously and searching for an answer).* Discreet. Discretion. Concealment. Furtive. Hiding. Secret. Concealing, concealing an, an, an …
Sue/Wom	*(Almost whispering).* An affair.
Sue	*(Speaking slowly, deliberately and convincing herself as she says it).* He was having an …
Sue/Wom	Affair.
Woman	*(Breaking position, away from Sue).* Bravo.
Sue	Affair.
Woman	Bingo.
Sue	Affair.
Woman	Outed.
Sue	But …?
Sue/Wom	Who?
Sue	The signs were there. And they were just, so, subtle. *(Pacing).* No. What the hell am I saying. They were blatant, illuminated, almost … speaking to me. Talking, walking, breathing signs. Signs like an attention seeking dog jumping up and down demanding attention. *(Getting louder ending almost in a scream).* An ignored, cheating, dog. And a stupid, stupid, gullible, bitch! *(She is shaking).*
Woman	But who?
Sue	But how could I not have realised? I didn't think him capable, interested. He was never interested in me, so why would he be in anybody else?
Woman	But who?
Sue	It must have been going on all the time. All along. Years. Late nights at …
Woman	Work?
Sue	Work. Of course.
Woman	And?
Sue	And all through it he must have been …
Woman	Laughing.
Sue	He was seeing her, and they were …
Woman	Laughing?
Sue	And I was, I was …
Woman	Blind?
Sue	Stupid.
Woman	Gullible?
Sue	Humiliated.
Woman	Feel?
Sue	I feel …
Woman	Sick?
Sue	I need to …

Woman	Sit?
Sue	Down.
Woman	Please.
Sue	*(She sits).* Head full of questions. Can't think straight. But …
Sue/Wom	Who?
Sue	If it was there all along. If the signs were there all along. If she was there all along. Then it's common sense. It has to be. I must know …
Sue/Wom	Who?
Woman	So what shows us the way?
Sue	Signs.
Woman	Then signs are just numbers. A simple calculation. So just add up the numbers.
Sue	Signs are just numbers.
Woman	See the signs.
Sue	You see the signs and eventually you reach …
Sue/Wom	Answers.
Sue	No. No.
Woman	Ahh. But you know the answer, don't you? You probably worked it out years ago, but you ignored it. A marriage of convenience and with it, a lie of convenience. But behind the lies, there are numbers and numbers have a face value. So, if you add it all up, all the numbers make a, make a?
Sue/Wom	Face.
Woman	And now, at last, you see the numbers, so naturally, you see the …
Sue/Wom	Face.
Sue	*(Pause).* Of course. Work. Eileen. It was Eileen. That's why he gave her the job.
Woman	Really? Has someone done their maths wrong?
Sue	What?
Woman	Is it really that simple? Have you really been that simple? *(Silence).* A lifetime as a wife, blind to the obvious. And now a widow who wants to remain blind. Does it make it all easier?
Sue	No. I'm not sure …
Woman	Sure. Hmm. We're never sure. Truth and deception. You deceived Derek, made him believe what you wanted him to. So why couldn't he have done the same? 'Dear Deceiving Derek'. 'Dear Deceiving, Departed, Derek.' What's the difference? He's died and nothing's changed. Except, well, he's dead but his deceiving lives on.
Sue	You mean. His lie was also a lie? He made me want to think it was Eileen if he was found out, when he was found out.
Woman	And has 'if', now become 'when'? *(Silence).* Ah, but it has, hasn't it? So. Time to revisit our calculation. You did the calculations and you saw a face, but not the face; you worked it out to get the answer he wanted you to, saw the one he wanted you to; then ignored the one he wanted you to … *(She moves close to Sue, both in profile and almost touching).* If you face the truth you see the face. So, see the face. See the truth. *(Chanting, loudly but getting quieter).* Who do you see? Who do you see? Who do you see?!

Sue/Wom	*(Pause. Whispering).* Ann.
Woman	*(She breaks position, away from Sue).* Bravo. Bingo. Outed!
Sue	Ann.
Woman	Ann.
Sue/Wom	Ann.
Woman	Bing Bong. *(SFX: the doorbell is heard. Sue jumps. She is nervous and frightened).* Think; calm, control, breathe, breathe. Think. What stands behind that door? Questions and answers. Door. *(Sue is neutral, blank. She goes to answer the door but The Woman stops her in her tracks when she speaks).* Sue. Payback. *(She exits).*

Sue answers the door and then immediately sits; upright, composed and waiting. Ann walks in slowly, looking around. She does not take her eyes off Sue as she takes off her coat and sits. Silence.

Ann	I've been around a couple of ...
Sue	I know. Twice.
Ann	You didn't answer the ...
Sue	Busy.
Ann	Right. So how have you ...
Sue	Fine.
Ann	Have you been ...
Sue	Nowhere.
Ann	Right.
Sue	Fine. *(Silence. Sue stands and moves downstage).* How long?
Ann	How ...?
Sue	Long.
Ann	I'm sorry, I don't know ...
Sue	*(Speaking deliberately and slowly).* How, long.
Ann	How long was I ...
Sue	Having sex with Derek? *(Ann stands and begins to move to her).* Stay back from me; sit down.
Ann	*(She moves slowly to sit down. She looks tense).* Sue I don't know ...
Sue	Don't lie to me. I know everything. Everything.
Ann	But ...
Sue	Everything. But I want to hear you. Your words. Details. Sordid. Everything.
Ann	Look, I ...
Sue	*(She suddenly loses her control and screams at the top of her voice).* Don't lie to me! Don't lie to me! *(She moves quickly to Ann who goes to get up and Sue pushes her violently back into the chair. She goes behind her and holds her in the chair, aggressively).* Oh, don't worry Ann, we're mates, remember? You hated the bastard more than me, remember? We're having a good laugh, remember?
Ann	You didn't love him.
Sue	You lied to me!
Ann	You were happy that he had died.
Sue	You lied to me. All along you wanted me to think it was Eileen.
Ann	*(She breaks her grip and now there is a change in her demeanour, delivery, personality. She composes herself and is cold, calm, calculated).* Such a small lie compared to a lifetime of deceit. And you betrayed every wife of the

	husbands you slept with. The only difference between you and me, lady, is capacity and anonymity. And you beat me hands down on both counts. So, don't you dare build yourself a pedestal because there ain't one small enough for you to deserve.
Sue	Don't look at me. And get out of my house. Get out! *(She sits huddled on the swivel armchair).*
Ann	Not so quick lady. You want an honesty session, well you're gonna get one. And more, so much more. *(She circles Sue in her chair, like a predator waiting to pick at her prey).* Not nice is it? Being on the receiving end? Oh, I knew about you. Knew all along. Derek told me. Every word. About every victim you made of all those women. Oh, he knew your history love. And now being on the receiving end, you just can't hack the truth. Consequences love. Consequences. In a way, you couldn't hack your own sordid life, so you picked on the vulnerable to hide you from yourself.
Sue	*(Screaming).* Get out! *(She begins to cry, and her breathing becomes laboured).*
Ann	You pushed out your predecessor, I pushed out you. Natural selection, survival of the fittest. Darwin would be so proud. You slept your way, your life through this town you sick, demented bitch and tore him to pieces in the process. But faux victims like you are all the same. Create your own little alternate reality to make yourself feel better about being the biggest shit of them all. You believed the lie you created. And I helped you. And you didn't even realise. Puppet on a string. *(Sue's breathing is now erratic).* Aww. Is little asthma girl getting all worked up? Not looking good this kid.
Sue	I need my inhaler, please, help me.
Ann	*(She picks up Sue's bag, rummages through it and then empties it in Sue's lap).* Find it yourself, bitch. You're a big girl.
Sue	*(She is now clearly in distress and frantically rummages through what is on her lap).* Can't breathe, can't breathe.

Through what follows, Sue is clearly succumbing to the attack and slowly becomes motionless apart from her breathing which is slow, shallow and noisy.

Ann	Oh dear. Can we not breathe? Is that asthma finally going to take its toll do we think? No inhaler either. Dear, dear, dear. This isn't looking good is it? Not really how you planned all of this is it? Not funny any longer is it? Well, for me, it was funny at one point, but that was before I met you. It was when Derek was alive. When he was still with you. And still with me. Oh, but you had figured that hadn't you? And in your sad, sick little mind, you thought it was a ghost, a spirit, even Derek. Let you into a secret love. There're no such things as ghosts. *(She turns Sue around in her chair so she is now facing upstage).* It's not the dead you need to be worried about. It's the living. Talking to yourself all along, weren't you? And that lunchtime with the cocktails, I realised there was a way to find an opportunity to settle-up with you for keeping me from what I wanted. You were the last person I ever wanted to be around. And funnily enough, the other <u>last person</u> who ever wanted to be around you was Derek.

He hated you more than I did. The advantage was, I had never met you until recently. It didn't have to end up like this you know. It could have been so different. So very different. *(She picks up a cushion from the other chair, slowly walks around to face Sue and stares at her).*

Here you go my love, this will help you. *(She takes the pillow as if about to put it behind Sue's head but suddenly holds it over her face and continues talking, nonchalantly, neutral. Sue is struggling slightly but not enough to stop her).* We could have been friends, you and me. Then again, no. Obviously not. Maybe in a different set of circumstances. But you had what I wanted. The man and the money. Well, the money. But what you didn't know, my pet, was I was bleeding him dry over the years I worked for him and slept with him and when he died, all the money I had been given or just taken from him, I used to buy his business. Ironic really. So many ironies. And to top it all, the cherry on the Bakewell, meeting you and getting to know all your issues. And then it all just fell into place. Just had to wait for the opportunity. And to think, you spent your life taking men from their wives with impunity and you then had the gall to want to get your own back on a world that had done nothing to you other than give you a selection of people to sleep with; a world littered with your victims, your spite, your <u>sluttishness</u>. Cheap, dirty, little, slut.

(Sue stops what little struggling she has been attempting and falls silent and still. Ann drops the cushion on the floor. During the next dialogue she straightens Sue's clothes and her hair). And there we go. All done. Now. Wasn't hard was it? Sorry that took so long. Couldn't hold it too tight as we wouldn't want anybody thinking somebody had helped you on your way, now would we? Don't want you spoiling anything would we? Let's just have a little check ... *(Shouting in Sue's face).* Is there anybody there? *(She laughs).* Oops. Think not. That's a cracker. You kept asking me that, remember? "Is there anybody there?" Oh, and you said it sat in that chair as well. And now I'm saying it to you. Piss funny. Who would have thought by the end, your death could have brought me so much happiness? How happy can one death make a person? I just don't deserve it. So much good fortune. Still.

(She puts her hand in her pocket and takes the inhaler out of her pocket and then continues). Oh! Look what I've found. Would you credit it? I had it all along. Must have fell in my pocket when I went in your handbag. To think I could have helped you in your hour of need. Then again, no, probably not. What am I like eh? Mooooo. Remember how we used to do that? How it made us laugh? And to think. I was the real cow all along. The killer cow. Who would've thought it? You've eventually been killed by Mad Cow Disease. *(She takes her mobile out of her pocket and starts to dial).* Here we go now. Pity you're not here to see this because it is inspired. And the award for best actress goes to ... *(Suddenly sobbing and hysterical she speaks into her mobile).* Help, please God help me. Send an ambulance. Forty-two Cherry Tree Gardens. Sue's asthma. I can't help her. She can't breathe. I think she's dying. I think, I think ... And disconnect. *(She starts putting her coat back on).*

You know what? You will never know how I enjoyed that little call. Liberating. I always wanted to be an actress. But hey, I think I've done pretty well so far. And you'll never know how happy I am that you're dead. Have I told you that already?

Fade to black. As the running blacks close, Ann walks into the courtroom area and the lights cross fade.

Scene 4

Ann   … and this inquest will never know how sad I am that Sue is dead. Have I told you that already? But she was clearly troubled. All I will say is that I know my opinion counts for nothing, but I still feel she had an undiagnosed mental condition. Hearing voices, sounds, wanting to speak to dead people. What was that about? So confused. So unhappy. But I had to play along. I thought it would help her. So very, very sad. *(She takes a handkerchief out of her pocket and wipes her eyes).*

No, I'm fine thank you. It was so unfortunate, her dying of an asthma attack. So preventable. I blame myself. If only she would have taken my advice and kept her inhaler with her. I emptied her bag on the floor, tried to find it. If only she would have been to see her doctor, got referred to a psychiatrist as I pleaded with her to do. If only I could have found the inhaler when she was fighting to breathe. It's the guilt you see. That I could have done something to help my best friend. My only friend. But it wasn't to be. That poor woman. Voices in her head, imagining things. Just another tragedy to add to the loss of a husband who she was devoted to. She worshipped him and him likewise. *(She appears to become a little overcome).*

No, I'm happy to have helped, it's been no trouble. I'm just happy my evidence to this inquest has been a help, brought closure for everybody, especially her family. No need to thank me, Sir.

And yes, I'm more than happy to answer any questions that Sue's poor relatives may have. *(She looks in a different direction as if somebody is speaking to her).* Aww, that is so kind of you Aunty Joan. She often spoke of you. So comforting to know Sue's family feel I did all I …

SFX: the whistle is heard. She looks front as slowly, realisation dawns on her face. Track #9 starts. Light fades on her as the backlighting comes up. The blacks part open. The Woman enters from behind the blacks to stand in the gap and she is then joined by Sue. Very slowly during the introduction part of the song, one reaches out to the other and they hold hands. They swing their hands in time to the music. Lights fade to black as the music continues. Cast move to centre stage and lights up for bows. Cast exit and lights fade to black. Track #9 plays out as audience leave.

THE END

'Soul Without End'

Synopsis

It is 1940 and a young French woman and her brother have escaped the ravages of the second world war and destruction of their tiny village. Fleeing the atrocities and the death and loss of all they hold dear, they find themselves in the remains of Chateaux Tatar. It is inhabited by the last remaining member of the family who owned it. But they also find it is the home of a small group of soldiers from apparently different sides who appear to be seeking refuge from... what?

They soon come to realise that with the chateaux, its owner and the soldiers, there are many unanswered questions and secrets.

Old secrets. Dark secrets. Secrets which, as they are disclosed, will shake their relationship, their faith and all they hold dear. More importantly, secrets which will challenge their understanding of good and evil, of life and death, of love... and of Chateaux Tatar.

Finally, they discover that it is not only people who have memories. So do places. And the reasons are darker, much darker than they could possibly ever think.

Characters (6m, 2f)

Paulette : 50 or older, composed, dignified, passionate, elegant

Younger Paulette : 20's, fiery, passionate, questioning, inquisitive, attractive

Captain Howard : 30/50, British Army Officer, English, well-spoken but not overly so; more educated, articulate. *(Also plays 'The Man' at the opening and the end)*.

Claude : 25-35, Good natured/humoured, strong, balanced, attractive

Antoine : 25/30, the voice of reason, uncomplicated and honest

Klaus : 20-60, an ordinary German soldier who changes to become a dark, foreboding, acolyte of the Captain

Geneux : 20-60, an ordinary French soldier who changes to become a dark, foreboding, acolyte of the Captain

Carter : 20-60, an ordinary British soldier who changes to become a dark, foreboding, acolyte of the Captain.

Casting

Accents are a matter for discussion and agreement. Either all use them, or none.

Older Paulette: 50+. Age is a function of the time period decided on and the age of the younger Paulette. French accent. Composed, dignified, passionate, elegant. Must be a good storyteller and able to paint vivid pictures for the audience. Because of the static nature of the playing, it needs detail, mannerisms; if she is a smoker, then all the better.

Younger Paulette: 20's. Fiery, passionate, questioning, inquisitive, attractive. Sister of Antoine (see below). Devoted to each other. Is attracted to Claude. Casting needs to bear in mind that she is the younger version of older Paulette.

Antoine: 25/30. Priest. Brother of young Paulette. Slightly older than his sister (or could be played older and as her Uncle with the appropriate changes to the dialogue). Initially composed, calm, naïve, he has his faith challenged by the rigours of war and the secrets of the chateaux. The voice of reason, devoted to each other. Uncomplicated and honest. His character goes on quite a journey or emotions, of faith, belief.

Claude: 25/35. Remaining member of the family that owned the chateaux. Good natured/humoured. Strong, balanced, attractive, immediately attracted to Paulette, youthful vigour and passion; thoughtful, honest.

Captain Howard: 30/50. British Army Officer. English, well-spoken but not overly; more educated, articulate. Initially, he is approachable, business like. But he is cold, unfeeling, ruthless, takes delight in pain and inflicting it. He is the lynchpin to what takes place and the secrets disclosed and he evidences the evil within him in an almost matter-of-fact way.

Klaus, Geneux, & Carter: 20/60. German, French and English soldiers respectively. Carter could have a strong regional accent to separate him from Howard. All are initially nervous, reasonable, 'ordinary' soldiers with the camaraderie that would demonstrate such. However, they soon become dark, foreboding, acolytes of the Captain and all he represents.

Wardrobe

For the premiere production, uniforms of the correct period were used for the soldiers. Experience, feedback and common sense illustrated that this worked against the plot, and as such it is not imperative that nationality is represented by such. Uniform trousers, shirt/vest, braces, boots would be sufficient for the three soldiers, with the addition of an overcoat for Howard. This assists in supporting the storyline that initially they are all part of World War 2. The weapons mentioned comprise three rifles and one sidearm for the Captain.

One costume per character for the remainder, representative of the period.
Younger Paulette, Antoine, Claude are, as a function of the story, dishevelled and unkempt. Older Paulette is smart, elegant and refined. Howard's outfit as 'The Man' at opening/end is simply achieved by the addition of an overcoat and a hat.

Staging

The play was conceived with one main set which does not change and which represents a ruined chateau with the main action/story taking place during the 1940's (World War Two) in France. However, the story begins in an antique shop in 1970's Paris, some thirty years later.
The main character (Older Paulette) recounts her story and the events which happened to her during the period she took refuge at the chateaux. For this purpose, the premiere production had an area apart from the stage, completely separate to the main action, from within which she tells her story. The action and lighting switching between her antique shop in 1970 and war-torn France in the 1940s. An important prop required is the 'Anima Saeculorum' book, of which there will need to be two identical copies: one is retained by Older Paulette throughout, the other is used in the action on stage.
A 2m deep platform was created at the centre-back of the stage, some 1.8m above floor level which had a working door with opaque glass to allow for a figure to be seen behind/through it. Walls formed the shape of a room and a single armchair which Paulette remained in throughout the play. This was all contained behind a gauze which allowed the lighting to reveal her in her 'present' day. Given the height of the 'antique shop' an upstage entrance to the chateau was possible underneath it.
There is a great reliance on lighting and sound effects to create the required atmosphere and texture. The ruined chateau must provide visuals of shapes, levels, shadows, character. Combined with the lighting and sound effects (see below), it presents a very dark, moody, atmospheric ambience. A gun that fires blanks is required.in Act Two, Scene 3.
The above is merely one staging solution. The writer also conceived another approach in which the older Paulette acted within and around the action, reliving it as part of her storytelling.

Sound Effects

The sound effects suggested here and detailed in the script form a complementary soundscape to the play and were used in the premiere production. All are royalty free except SFX #11 which requires a PRS royalty payment. The twelve effects below can be purchased as mp3 files from Stagescripts Ltd.

SFX #1a: voices / tuning into a radio broadcast
SFX #1b: tuning into a radio broadcast
SFX #2:   a crack of thunder
SFX #3:   a crack of thunder
SFX #4:   sirens, broadcasts, Hitler, battle noise
SFX #5:   distant artillery fire / rumble of thunder
SFX #6:   distant battlefield noises /strange noises
SFX #7:   rainfall
SFX #8:   battlefield and wailing noises
SFX #9:   battlefield sounds
SFX #10:   unearthly sounds
SFX #11:   curtain calls & playout

First Performed

The play premiered at Guide Bridge Theatre, Tameside, Greater Manchester in February 2017. It was directed by Martin Roche with the following cast:-

Older Paulette	Joy Siddall
Younger Paulette	Mary Platts
Captain Howard	Mike Sammon
Claude	Dominic Peberdy
Antoine	Vince Bowers
Klaus	Ken Redfern
Geneux	Ian Ball
Carter	Jack Lyon

"Was gripped from the start ... Eerie, well written, great performances, amazing set. Thoroughly enjoyed 'Soul Without End'; great piece of theatre ... Deep and meaningful ... A Triumph. Applause to the cast and crew for keeping us transfixed ... Eerie tale with a surprise twist ... suitably eerie to create an atmosphere of suspense, drama and intrigue...a play that certainly left the audience something to think about"
Some of the audience feedback on social media.

SOUL WITHOUT END was an ambitious, epic and theatrical piece of work which connects on a number of levels through its exploration of the universal theme of struggle between good and evil in the complexity and contradictions of human life. The theatrical structure is operatic and grand and has an ambitious sweep across the narrative. It is a thought-provoking piece in terms of its exploration of conflict and human barbarism which resonates with so much of today's world news."
Royal Exchange Theatre, Manchester (May 2016) – script feedback.

Optional Prologue

The auditorium and stage are in complete darkness. SFX #1a: a pre-recorded voice is heard which segues into a radio broadcast and into Scene 1. [SXF #1a replaces SFX #1b if this opening is used]

Voice   Do you believe the adage that history repeats itself? Or does the frailty of humankind mean we are destined to repeat our mistakes over again because we are incapable of learning from them? That time is somehow complicit? But what if there is more to it?
What if the lessons learnt were not just captured on the memories of those who experienced them... what if they were also etched into the very fabric of the place and time in which they occurred? That the joy, happiness, anger, fear... even the wickedness wrought by people living out their destiny, was indelibly imprinted on that place, like a chapter in a never-ending novel called history?
We may want to keep memories of places, but the places also want to keep memories of us... and the reason may be darker, much darker, than you could possibly ever think.

ACT ONE

Scene 1

The lights gently come up. As they do so...

With Prologue: the voice fades into the sound of a wireless being tuned, and once tuned, the sound of 'Non, Je Ne Regrette Rien' (sung by Edith Piaf) playing on the radio is heard.

Without Prologue SFX #1b: the sound of a wireless being tuned, and once tuned, the sound of 'Non, Je Ne Regrette Rien' (sung by Edith Piaf) playing on the radio is heard.

Sat in the chair asleep is Paulette Devauchelle. On the table next to her is a wireless and a table lamp. The light through the door gives the impression of a streetlight outside. The figure of a man can now be seen on the other side of it. There is a knock at the door. Paulette awakens, turns the radio down a little, wearily goes to the door, and looks through the window seeing the man. Throughout what follows, his face must not be visible; it is obscured by positioning and lighting so that he is in silhouette. He remains within the doorway.

Paulette	We are closed. Please call in the morning. Call back at...
Man	*(Interrupting).* Madame, I apologise for the lateness of my call.
Paulette	Monsieur, we are closed. Please call in the morning.
Man	Madame, I...
Paulette	What?
Man	I must speak with you about...
Paulette	I can't hear you, please wait, Monsieur. *(She returns to her seat, turns the radio off, [SFX #1a/b out], and then goes back to the door).*
Man	Madame, I am sorry but I need to leave something with you for valuation; a book. I would not normally bother but I have a buyer for it who is most insistent that it is available. Please, Madame, I am away on business after today and need to have it valued before I leave for...
Paulette	*(Interrupting).* Again, come back in the morning *(She tries to close the door).*
Man	*(Insistently).* Madame, please, I implore you.

109

Paulette	Yes, yes, Monsieur, wait there.
Man	*(Handing her an object wrapped in a cloth).* Merci Madame
Paulette	Let me go to my chair, into the light. *(Unwrapping the cloth, a small book, ornately decorated, is revealed. As she opens the cover her expression is one of curiosity and alarm.* SFX #2: *a crack of thunder is heard).* Dear God. Monsieur, where did you get this?
Man	I bought it several months ago in a shop not dissimilar to this whilst on business in Verdun-sur-Meuse. It was a tiny place on the outskirts of the town; a village containing the ruins of an old chateaux you will never heard of called…
Paul/Man	Tatar. *[Pronounced Tah-tah].*
Man	But how did you know?
Paulette	It must be over thirty years since I have heard that name, Monsieur. I prayed to God that I would never hear it again.
Man	Madame, my sincere apologies, I never meant to cause any offence, I merely…
Paulette	*(Interrupting).* Tell me, Monsieur, did it still contain a dedication inside the cover?
Man	Why yes, it reads…
Paul/Man	'A gift, for all time'
Man	How did you…? But this is incredible! The coincidence! What are the chances that…?
Paulette	There is no coincidence, no chance. All things, all places in life have a purpose, a reason, a time, a story to tell. But not all ever give up their secret. Your visit to that… place, to the shop. The choosing of this book and now, bringing it to me: people, events, places. Oh yes, places most certainly have a story and a secret. But the dedication, is it still in the book?
Man	But you still have not told me how you knew about the note? Who would have thought that you could ever…?
Paulette	Is it still there?
Man	Why yes, Madame, just open the cover.

SFX #3: a crack of thunder is heard as she opens the book and reads.

Paulette	"My love. I loved you for days and have lamented you for years. And over thirty years ago. *[Adjust this number to suit the actor].* 1940. It was on a night not dissimilar to this that the story began. Oh my love. Thirty years and it is as if it were only yesterday, a different world, a different person. Such memories. So much love and hope at a time and place that such had no right to exist. And at the same time such pain… such evil". Oh yes, Monsieur, all four can live hand-in-glove if you are unfortunate to be at the wrong place, at the wrong time… or should I say, in the wrong place, in the wrong time. Time may pass, but love? Never. *(As the street lighting fades out in the doorway, the man backs away into the shadows and disappears. The lights fade on Paulette. The door is struck and Paulette takes her seat. SFX #4 commences as soon as the stage is dark; it is a mix of air raid sirens,*

broadcast recordings, Hitler and battleground noises. [NOTE: It is important that throughout, any effects which underscore the dialogue do not interfere with the clarity of that spoken dialogue]. She begins to speak immediately as the effect segues into rain/thunder. Lights up).
And then one morning, youth, innocence and happiness left my home, my country, my heart, for what I thought would be forever. The cancer of humanity had discovered my little corner of paradise... war. My brother and I fled our home leaving everything, everyone we held dear and we ran. As hard and as fast as we could. The Nazis took our lands, our lives, our loves. We ran like animals pursued by their prey. But how were we to know that in leaving one bloody conflict behind, we would stumble into something far worse? A war deadlier and more sinister than anything we had escaped from and that the world had ever, would ever know. I think the time has now at last come to tell the story and reveal... a secret.

Scene 2

The lighting comes up to reveal the scene is of a burnt out, semi-destroyed structure. It was clearly quite opulent in its day, the remnants of Chateaux Tatar.

Paulette	As we reached that place, the smell of smoke and fog invaded all of the senses: acrid, penetrating, almost consuming. It seemed to be part of the darkness and gave the darkness its own unique aroma, its own texture, like a blanket... a shroud with a myriad of tastes: soil, damp, a hint of something metallic... sulphur, bitter, decay, stinging eyes, heaving, laboured breathing, as if this cocktail of darkness might easily overwhelm at any moment. Overwhelming. Yes. Unrelenting waves of overwhelming, but what? Foreboding? Slow, unforgiving waves. And not a shore in sight to take refuge. And with it, no hope of a sunrise. No hope of a salvation. Just... no hope.
	And amongst the incessant bombardment of the land and the senses was a feeling that there was something else about that place. Something indiscernible, unquantifiable; a presence beyond anything I had ever known or would ever encounter again. Every shadow felt like it had the capacity to speak, an identity waiting to be revealed, a past longing to be discovered, a story aching to be retold. But still there was something else. Hidden and yes, uncanny. A secret. *(A young bedraggled couple enter the scene, running, as she speaks. It is the Younger Paulette and her brother Antoine, both exhausted, slowly falling to their knees, unpacking, and then frantically referring to a map. SFX #4 fades out).* Finally, we stumbled through that interminable blanket of darkness into a place without ending or beginning and into... only God could truly know. But we simply came to know it by its name on a map. *(She remains seated and observes all that then ensues, sometimes in darkness, sometimes not).*
Paul/Young P	Chateaux Tatar.
Young Paul	That's what it says on the map. So that's where we are.

Antoine	At least the rain and thunder has stopped. And thank God, the shelling. I have no idea how we found ourselves here
Paulette	Maybe it found us.
Young Paul	But it's of no relevance now. This is where it ends. This is where we stop.
Antoine	Just a few more kilometres and I am sure there will be a…
Young Paul	*(Interrupting)*. What Antoine? What are you sure there will be? A meal? Sleep? Freedom? Peace? What Antoine? What will there be that will make this hell any better or bearable? Will this journey of salvation bring Mama and Papa back to life? Will it make the German invaders who shot them disappear? Will it rebuild your church and resurrect your congregation, Father?
Antoine	Please do not blaspheme, Paulette
Young Paul	Do not blaspheme? Can you not hear yourself and your pretence at the sanity of good manners? If blasphemy is the last of the hardships we are to deal with, then I will endure it with a demented smile. You took Holy Orders, not me. If clinging then to a meaningless hope of divine intervention makes this living nightmare any more bearable then please, be my guest. You carry on and I hope you find God at the end of your quest. I am your sister, not your keeper and not a member of your murdered flock. I cannot go on. I will not.
Antoine	We must. We need to
Young Paul	*(Shouting)* To where? What is the point?
Antoine	We are the point; you are the point. Life, living is the point
Young Paul	Life? What life?
Antoine	Stop! Just stop. We have each other and I say nothing else matters. For no other reason than that. If this war is the end of us, of the world, then so be it. I will give up on all I have and yes, all I believe, but I cannot, I will not, give up on you for a second. My faith in God may be on the brink, but never my faith in you. Each other is all that we have. And as long as I have that, I will never stop, never give up… and never stop hoping, believing in you, Paulette.

She begins to cry. They embrace. Older Paulette turns to the front.

Paulette	And as we held each other, one by one, the players in the unfolding tableau of darkness would begin to appear. Like a chess game in which you did not know your opponent; which piece you were, but above all else, who was moving the pieces, or indeed, that you were even part of the game. Was it the hand of fate who dictated the moves, or something else…?

Enter Klaus, wandering into the scene carrying a rifle, completely oblivious of them being there. Before they see him, he freezes, fumbles with his rifle and they frantically break their embrace as they hear him pull back the bolt on it. What happens then is pandemonium that segues into confusion, panic, fear. They all begin to speak then shout over each other. The following lines should be repeated if needed and may be added to, but they form the principal text. It begins with Klaus:

Klaus	Halt! Achtung! Halt!
Antoine	Please we are unarmed.
Young Paul	Dear God no, please, no, not after all we have been through.
Klaus	Do not move!

Antoine	Do not shoot.
Young Paul	We mean you no harm.
Klaus	Do not move or I will shoot!
Antoine	We surrender.
Young Paul	What have we done to you?
Klaus	Stay where you are!

After a moment Geneux enters, running into the scene, frantic, having heard the commotion, fumbling with his rifle.

Geneux	Mon Dieu!
Klaus	They are French, but I do not understand…
Geneux	*(French accent).* Where did they come from?
Klaus	God knows!
Antoine	Please. We mean you know harm!
Geneux	Who are you? What are you doing here? <u>How</u> did you get here?
Antoine	I am Antoine Devauchelle. This is my sister Paulette. My God. You're French?
Klaus	Keep your hands up!
Geneux	Are they from the village?
Klaus	They cannot be. It is not the right time.
Geneux	Then that makes them…
Young Paul	What in God's name is this? A German and a French soldier stood side by side, pointing guns at us, demanding answers! Who are you? How dare you! Answer me!
Captain	*(Entering).* For the time being, Mademoiselle, we ask the questions and we decide the answers.
Young Paul	An English Officer! What in hell… *(She continues to shout, extempore, as the Captain calmly speaks over her tirade).*
Captain	…and as there appears to be a lack of understanding, perhaps this will assist.*(He draws his side arm from its holster and points it at Young Paulette's face which silences her abruptly).* Be quiet. Do you now understand me?

Pause.

Paulette	The principal architect of what was happening and what would now unfold.
Captain	Good. Très bon. Sehr gute.
Carter	*(Entering, running on with his rifle).* What's all the shouting about… bloody hell!
Captain	Indeed. And what a bloody hell it is. Put your weapon down, Carter. All of you stand down… Geneux, Klaus, you too. I think our visitors understand their situation.
Antoine	Which is what exactly? Visitors? Prisoners?
Captain	I prefer to think of you as our guests. Can I offer you both my sincere apologies for mistaking you for foe? *(To Young Paulette).* You in particular for my appalling behaviour and having the temerity to raise a weapon to you. The front is not far from here. It can change within an hour from a few

Captain/ Paul	kilometres to a few metres away. I am sorry to say it was my only way of making you quiet. We must protect our… Secrecy.
Paulette	And there it was for the first time that word. A word which would underscore what was to come.
Captain	But please understand this. You are guests that are for the time being going nowhere unless they want their status to be reviewed. I now have your safety to consider as well as that of us. So, guests. Welcome to what is left of Chateaux Tatar. *(He puts his side arm away. Claude Durant enters).* Ah, young Monsieur Durant.
Paulette	Dear, sweet, pure, beautiful…
Captain/ Paul	Claude.
Captain	May I introduce, I think I overheard correctly, Paulette and Antoine Devauchelle? They are our 'reluctant' guests for, well, let us leave it open-ended, shall we? Claude's family own what is left of the chateaux before the advancing German line took its toll on it. Young Claude is all that is left and kindly looks after our every need. So. Please take a seat in our desirable billet.

The other soldiers laugh.

Claude	How in God's name did they get in here?
Captain	All in good time my young friend.
Geneux	They're not villagers…
Claude	What?
Captain	QUIET!
Paulette	Within all this ugliness, such beauty, such hidden beauty
Captain	But a few words of advice, again. I implore you do no attempt to leave. This is a theatre of war and you will get killed if you stray out of our, well, call it our protection.
Klaus	So make the most of Monsieur Durant's hospitality and our kind services, and I also apologise for frightening you. We all do. I know what you must think of me as a German soldier. Do not condemn a nation for what we are all enduring.
Antoine	Easier said. You think a well-phrased sentence can wipe away an abomination?
Klaus	I… No.
Young Paul	And are we permitted to know who our hosts are?
Captain	I see no reason not to have formal introductions. I am Captain Julian Howard of His Majesties Expeditionary Force along with Carter here. Klaus is a German soldier and Geneux is clearly a French soldier. That is sufficient for you to know at this time due to, how shall we say, operational exigencies. I am sure you understand. But let me say for the first time and with all sincerity. We are not your enemy.
Carter	*(In a smarmy insinuating manner).* Absolutely.

The Captain immediately turns and looks at Carter who in a second becomes subservient.

Captain	'Good manners' and all that, Mr Carter… 'Good manners'. My men are not used to non-combatant company. Especially one so demure, pretty lady. They will remember their place. Come along, men. We have guests to protect, preparations to make. We will leave them with you Claude. Delighted to meet you both. Please be at ease and if you can, rest and make yourself comfortable.

The soldiers exit, leaving Claude and the young couple alone.

Claude	Claude Durant.
Young Paul	Well. I can safely say that this war is, yet again, full of surprises.
Antoine	So, what is the story behind your friends?

Claude begins to gather together some pieces of wood which are lying close at hand and placing them in a hessian sack he has with him and continues to speak. This device is used to cover the times when older Paulette speaks.

Claude	Not my friends. I have no side, no politics, no interest in them. They are here because they are. They do what they do. War demands questions but does not always provide answers and I have learnt to live with that. The first thing is to survive and I guess you have already learnt that painful lesson. I would also guess that like me, you are all that is left of what was once your life. I don't know how you found us or how you managed to get into here… and how we can get you out of here is a wholly different matter. But the sooner I can figure that, the better for us all.
Young Paul	What do you mean 'get into here'?
Paulette	The first chink in the armour of mystery, of polite untruths and in Claude's case, his desire from our first meeting to try and keep us, me, safe. But I would never allow anything to be left. It was my way. Especially after all we had been through. Lies shone like a beacon. And I would not allow myself to be blinded by them.
Claude	I merely meant how you managed to find us
Antoine	Then what do we do?
Claude	The only thing you can.
Claude/Paul	Wait.
Paulette	The only thing we could do.
Young Paul	Do we have the time?
Claude	Time is the only thing in abundance we have here.
Young Paul	And what do you do here?
Claude	Survive.
Young Paul	And how have you managed that?
Claude	By not asking questions.
Paulette	Confusion, riddles, intrigue, darkness…
Paul/Young P	Secrets.
Young Paul	No answers, just secrets. What is going on here?
Antoine	You mean you don't know?
Young Paul	And you mean you do?

Claude pauses. He is nervous, uneasy.

Antoine	Simple. I would have thought it obvious. How could men of three different nationalities on two opposing sides be here together? What else would tie them? And poor Claude is stuck in the middle of it all with clearly no option but to acquiesce.
Young Paul	And what must they have done?
Antoine	Deserters.
Paulette	How desperate we were to find obvious answers within the wholly inexplicable.
Claude	Why yes. You have seen through it. At least I do not need to conceal anything, break an undertaking. Deserters, yes. Please excuse me. *(He exits).*
Young Paul	Claude…?
Antoine	Yes, deserters. They don't need to have done anything other than walk away from war. And now they have no side but their own, they have but one enemy.
Young Paul	Who?
Antoine	Everybody.
Paulette	The naivety of fear. And we drank it down like a fine wine, to wash away our concerns at the end of a long journey and with it, our sense of reality.
Antoine	We are no threat to them. They are no threat to us. On one hand you could say they are the epitome of cowardice. Others might say that they are the bravest men of the highest principles. So…
Antoine/Paul	Status quo.
Paulette	I remember that clearly. The phrase. It was the first time it was said, but it would not be the last. Status quo. How were we to know that it meant something far more important in that place? But still I had doubts, convenient versions of an alternate truth.
Young Paul	This is all too accepting. Forced normality. This, they, could be something far more dangerous. A special operation perhaps? Yes. Spies of different nationalities, but working for whom? Against who?
Antoine	Hmm. You might be right.
Young Paul	Either way. We leave as soon as possible, Antoine. We leave now.
Antoine	Paulette, no! Did you not just listen to what I said, what he said? I have no idea what is going on here, deserters or spies, but it scares me enough not to even attempt to leave at present. We may be in danger, but we need to know from what before we innocently put our lives in even greater peril. And you do not even think of mentioning that we believe them to be spies, deserters, whatever. That would most certainly change things for all of us. There is clearly a balance here which we must not upset. They have secrets and we cannot, must not, compromise them.
Paulette	If only he knew then, what that really meant.
Paul/Young P	He was [You are] right. Of course he was (you are). He always was (You always are).
Antoine	I have never known such darkness. It must be a combination of the mist, the burning, the artillery. But it chills me to the core, fills me with…
Antoine/Paul	Dread
Antoine	I can't describe what it is, it feels almost…

116

Antoine/Paul	Uncanny.
Antoine	Why yes. The very word. But what that means in this place…
Young Paul	God only knows
Paulette	And we would soon discover that it was only God that could know.
Antoine	We keep saying that, 'God only knows'
Young Paul	Yes. And I hope he at least does.
Antoine	God? Why?
Young Paul	Because I hope he remembers that you still work for him.

They both laugh, briefly, forced.

Antoine	It feels good to laugh.
Young Paul	Make the most of it, dear brother. They're in short supply these days.
Paulette	And there was certainly one other thing that was in short supply at that time. Answers.

Fade to black.

Scene 3

SFX #5: distant artillery fire mixed with a low rumble of thunder is heard. The lights come up on older Paulette.

Paulette I recall now that from the moment we had arrived there, I struggled to remember. Bizarre. Just the simple act of remembering. How odd is that? It was the first thing that I began to notice. Facts, memories and above all else, a sense of time were all unknowingly slipping away. The day never arrived. The night was eternal. And we never questioned it. We can only have been there for a day at that point but it felt a lifetime but equally, a mere breath. And for the first time in such a long time, a glimmer of light. We ate with Claude. *(Lights up to reveal Young Paulette, Antoine and Claude. They have a basket of food and are sat eating, drinking, chatting; normality).* Since escaping our home, it was the nearest to what normal must have felt like. Despite the orchestra of war constantly playing their instruments in the background, with the relentless crash of the percussion section, it might as well have been a band playing, serenading an unpretentious lunch of simple food, simple French folk. We could have been in any park, any café on a tree-lined boulevard in France. Three new friends chatting, learning of each other, enjoying the moment. Relaxed, no expectations, no judgements. But it was far from normal. And with reality shunned for what seemed like an hour, pretence brought sanity and with it, no need to consider hope. And for a brief spell, the noise of war ebbed away. Or had we made it so? *(SFX #5 starts to fade out).* And it was made all the more normal by Claude. I was instantly drawn to him and I could tell from the way he looked at me that it was reciprocated. Dear, sweet, honest, accepting

Paul/Young P	Claude/Claude?
Young Paul	How long has this house been in your family?

The lights fade on older Paulette.

Claude	What is left of it? Centuries at least
Antoine	At least?

Claude	Yes. Many, many centuries. It has seen much, witnessed such happiness in an area which has, well, it is old. My family is old.
Young Paul	You don't look that old.
Claude	I feel it!
Antoine	As do I!
Young Paul	OK. So you're not old. Then what does that make you? How about mature, distinguished?
Claude	My father was mature and distinguished!
Young Paul	Then how about experienced, wise?
Antoine	Now he's an owl?

They all laugh again. It slowly subsides.

Claude	I was about to say that it is some time since these walls echoed with the sound of laughter. But that was when we had walls. *(He says it so seriously. Silence. Then he bursts into laughter and Antoine and Young Paulette begin to join him in laughing).* And when did you leave home on your journey?
Young Paul	Our escape, you mean. It was last… it was about a… strange… When was it, Antoine?
Antoine	Oh Paulette; it was at least two, no three… oh, I don't remember.
Claude	Journeys do that.
Young Paul	We are not on a holiday.
Antoine	No. And your family?
Claude	Dead. Yours?
Antoine	Dead. By the Germans?
Claude	Does it matter?
Young Paul	Does it matter? Of course it matters!
Claude	Why?
Young Paul	Because they are responsible. Murderers. Worse. How could you not think any other way?
Claude	Because when you explore the idea of sides, you miss the bigger picture.
Antoine	Which is?
Claude	Humanity. Bizarre. It is a word also used to express our greatest qualities, yet as a label for what we are, it sums up our worst. I am beyond rationalising right and wrong. We either kill, or allow killing to happen. We commit or we observe. One side calls it an invasion, the other a liberation. Good, evil, what do they really mean?
Antoine	I think Claude that is an overly simplistic…
Young Paul	'Explore the idea', 'bigger picture'? Murdering scum. Bastards. Animals. The French, the British, the Belgians. I did not see them pointing a gun at my mother and father and slaughtering his congregation. Enjoy your academic theorising, your moral high ground Mr Durant. I believe you will be the only person sat there. And I think history will not be interested in how that ground was formed.
Claude	Please, I…

Silence descends as Young Paulette looks away from Claude. The lights rise on older Paulette.

Paulette	We were dancing around the subject. Avoiding the question that would lead onto what we needed to know, what I needed to know: the truth. I, however, could not wait any longer.
Paul/Young P	Claude, what is happening here?
Claude	Lunch. A simple meal, I think, I hope. I am still good company I hope?
Young Paul	Yes, yes… God yes. Oh, Claude I am so sorry. I think… I don't know what I think. What must you think of me? My problem is that I don't think!
Antoine	Hmm. Your problem, dear sister, is that you think too much.
Young Paul	And is that the official response from the church?
Antoine	Hmm.
Young Paul	Oh, shut up, Antoine. I am sorry if I offended you, Claude
Claude	*(Pausing, he then stands, bows and holds his hand out to Young Paulette).* Bonjour, mes amis. Claude Durant. Orphan, Chateaux owner, ruin keeper, collector of over-ripe fruit, assembler of the worst picnic you will ever find this side of the Seine and offender of guests. You are?
Young Paul	'Sorry'. New beginning?
Claude	New beginning

They both smile at each other and he kisses her hand. There is a moment. They continue.

Young Paul	One question
Antoine	Paulette!
Young Paul	Would one question hurt?
Claude	No. Please. Any conversation is good conversation. I had almost forgotten what good conversation and good company was like. And attractive company. Question away. You won't hurt my feelings
Antoine	Hmm.
Young Paul	Oh, Antoine, stop grinding your teeth. *(To Claude).* There is something about this place. I know it is your home. But something else. It is not you. You are… you don't fit.
Claude	None taken!
Young Paul	I am explaining this badly.
Antoine	Hmm.
Young Paul	*(She glares at Antoine).* But all this is a façade. There is something else here, around, within. What nonsense this must sound like. I am just trying to ask …
Claude	Then just ask.
Paul/Young P	What is the truth of this place?
Paulette	I knew there was more to it but it was as elusive as Claude was mesmerising to me. Both were part of something bigger
Claude	*(Pausing, he considers).* Does a place need to have a truth about it? Can it not just be accepted for what it is? I think… I think there is no truth here to be discovered.
Young Paul	Then what is the lie?
Claude	Does the absence of one mean the other must prevail? Truth. Lies. What does any of it mean now?
Antoine	What do they mean here?

Claude	The world is tearing itself apart and you want to have an academic debate about the meaning of life?
Young Paul	No, just mine. Claude, why do you stay here? Why are those soldiers here? Why do you provide for them? What are they to you? What are they up to?

In the darkness of the upstage shadows, the shapes of the three soldiers slowly rise to standing positions in silhouette from the darkness and behind the ruins. Unseen, unknown to the others and if possible, achieved by being back-lit.

Claude	For now I have already said too much.
Antoine	You have said nothing.
Claude	And that is too much. Please excuse me. I must go. Chores.
Young Paul	What chores? For who? What do they involve? Conversation! Is it so much to ask?
Antoine	I think enough questions and not enough lunch. Please, Claude. Don't allow my overly inquisitive, imaginatively fertile sister to drive you away. Please. *(He sits).*

Pause.

Claude	Lovely weather we are having for this time of year. Champagne? *(Pause. Laughter breaks the moment).* I am sorry if …
Antoine	No.
Young Paul	No. I am sorry… again. It is fine. I again find myself apologising for being…
Claude	For being you? Never be sorry for who you are. Inquisitiveness has its own charms. And I am sorry for your family, your friends
Antoine	*(Then, uncharacteristically).* What is done is done. They are dead. All that is left is us now. Bizarre. How so much can be summed up, dismissed in one sentence and we do it now without thinking.
Young Paul	Antoine? Where did that come from? You are sounding like me! Nothing is dismissed. Don't keep beating yourself up. All that matters are us now. You keep telling me that. One would think you were losing your faith.

Pause. The light fades on the three soldiers in silhouette and they exit.

Paulette	Strange. How could I have been so ignorant? All that time we spent together running for our lives and I never saw it. Never saw the change that our experiences were having, as a consequence, on Antoine. And only now, in that place. I had been wrapped up in my own loss. It had been slow, again innocuous, unnoticed. And I, we, had become numb to it, magnified in that place. Numb to how quickly people can change… can be changed. And equally, blind to who, or what, would bring that change about. But for a brief moment, I didn't care. Except for something, someone
Claude	And all that is left of my family, my life is what you see before you. Kindred spirits.
Young Paul	Then why not be kindred pilgrims? Come with us, leave them, this place and its shadows of the past. Be a pilgrim with us.
Claude	I cannot.
Antoine	Or will not?

Claude	I cannot leave this place. They do not compel me. The soldiers. I am not afraid of them. I think I have no fear left in me. War has even cheated me of that. This place is in my blood. It is me and all that is left of me. I will not abandon their memory, their history, the spirit or their life. I have nowhere else to go. And I have no reason to fear the future – if one does exist. And neither have you. In another world in another time.
Paul/Young P	In another time?
Paulette	How easily we do not see, accept, the picture a jigsaw makes when all the pieces are not in their correct place. I heard but did not see, sensed, but did not appreciate. Surprising how the ease of acquiescence, acceptance, beauty, can obscure the mind to the frighteningly obvious.
Claude	In another time? *(Quickly correcting himself)*. At. I meant, at. Do you pick up on everything?! You remind me of my sister, you know.
Antoine	And where is she? *(Pause)*. I'm sorry.
Claude	No need. She was so like you, Paulette. She had your honesty, your vigour, your strength.
Young Paul	Strength!
Claude	Oh yes. And your beauty. *(Beat)*. And now we are both embarrassed. Excuse me. Work beckons. *(He gathers his things, preparing to leave)*.
Young Paul	And what is you work?
Antoine	Paulette!
Claude	At this moment… considering what gastronomic delights are possible with an old courgette, an over-ripe parsnip, and several questionable potatoes! Please just do as the Captain asks. For the simple reason that he is correct in telling you that this area is treacherous. You must stay here for now until we can figure how to get you away.
Young Paul	Any other reason?
Claude	For me?
Young Paul	Then that is enough. *(They smile at each other and Claude stands, making to exit. Antoine stares at her, disbelieving. Claude leaves something on the floor wrapped in a cloth. As he stands she picks it up and looks at it)*. A beautiful book.
Paulette	Beauty… and inside, riddles.
Claude	*(Taken back at first)*. It is very old. Belonged to my father and to his. Priceless and timeless. Reminds me of who I am, what I was and what might be again
Antoine	Exquisite. So ornate. So unusual…

Young Paulette hands it back to Claude.

Paul/Young P	So beautiful.

There is a moment between them.

Antoine	Unusual inscriptions on it. Latin, of sorts? But I do not recognise what it says, though.
Claude	'Anima Saeculorum'. I don't really know what it means. We like to think, well it has always been handed down that it translates to…
Paul/Clau/Ant	Soul Without End

Young Paul	An unusual name
Antoine	An unusual book
Claude	An unusual time.
Young Paul	And does a soul have an end?
Claude	No, like love. But both are accountable. Please, do as I ask. *(He exits).*
Young Paul	We will.
Antoine	That I should live to see this day. My sister doing as she is told.
Young Paul	I think you will find I was asked!

They laugh.

Antoine	So. My sister has an admirer?
Young Paul	So. My brother needs to mind his own business?
Antoine	That's a yes then.
Young Paul	And why not? As it looks like we will be here a while, what's the harm in getting to know somebody that makes me, for a short period, feel I am a woman again?
Antoine	Indeed. A genuine person is a rarity in these days, in this war. And it is good to see my sister smile. And as we appear to be staying a while now…
Young Paul	So it looks like we will be celebrating my birthday here.
Antoine	Your birthday?
Young Paul	Of course! On the, on the… Antoine, how embarrassing. I can't remember. I know it is soon but…
Antoine	And neither do I. It might be worse. I might have forgotten… I can't remember my own birthday?
Young Paul	Antoine. And neither do I. When are they?
Antoine	It is on… they are… I can't remember. *(They laugh, nervously).* We must be more tired than we thought
Young Paul	That will be it. Yes. Tired.
Paulette	Slow, innocuous, innocent. And so it began.

Fade to black. Lights back up on older Paulette.

Scene 4

Paulette	I left Antoine on the premise of finding somewhere to wash. I think in my mind it was a reason. But not the reason. The true reason? I was compelled to find Claude. Compelled to ask more questions of him. Compelled to know him. But more than anything else, compelled to be near him. A man I did not know but who I desired to, desired to… desire. Again, it was not me. To be like that was not the Paulette that I was, that I knew. But who of us was what we thought any longer? War changed us. That place changed us. Changes we did not see, could not notice. Did not remember.

The lights come up to now reveal Young Paulette entering.

Paulette	I called out to him
Paul/Young P	Claude!
Paulette	But instead, I found…

Captain	*(Entering)*. Mademoiselle, I would advise against calling out. The front is somewhere near here and I cannot tell you which side is out there.
Young Paul	Does it matter to you? Englishmen, a German, a Frenchman. Who is your enemy?
Captain	Not you.
Young Paul	Really? And where are your men. Our great defenders.
Captain	They are close by.
Young Paul	Doing what?
Captain	What I tell them.
Young Paul	Which is?
Captain	Not your concern. *(Young Paulette turns to leave)*. Please. *(Young Paulette pauses but does not turn)*. We started off on the wrong foot and it appears that it continues. *(She again makes to leave)*. Just hear me out. I apologise again for my conduct when we met. You must appreciate that at a time of war, who the enemy is can be confused.
Young Paul	Are you confused?
Captain	No.
Young Paul	Yet you do not answer any questions?
Captain	The only questions I have are the ones I ask of myself. And their sole purpose is to ensure the safety of you and my men. Wouldn't you do the same?
Young Paul	Questions answered with questions.
Captain	My men have been through more than you could ever comprehend.
Young Paul	My heart goes out to you all.
Captain	Do not judge me or my men. There are no winners in war, just varying degrees of being a victim, a casualty.
Young Paul	I prefer being a survivor.
Captain	We no longer have 'a side' because of, well, let us say, the mission we have embarked upon. For us, although there will one day be a peace, we will never be at peace. We exist with the knowledge of what we have done, what we must now do… what we have become.
Young Paul	And what are you, what have you done?
Captain	What was needed.
Young Paul	And what must you now do?
Captain	What is needed.
Young Paul	Isn't it convenient when secrecy is for your own good?
Captain	Some secrets must be kept; there is a greater good.
Young Paul	Brava Senor Machiavelli.
Captain	Who I believe also wrote a book called 'The Art of War'.
Paul/Young P	Riddles wrapped in secrets
Paulette	There was something about him which was more than he portrayed himself as. A simple soldier. Soldier, yes. Simple? He was a politician; a storyteller, a spinner of fact into a cloak of fiction. And not only did he wear it well, we unwittingly admired it, accepted it. And somehow, we were beginning to wear it.

Pause. The light fades on older Paulette.

Captain   Mademoiselle. You have clearly been through a lot, as have we. Suffered, as have we. But we exist with the burden of knowing that as soldiers there is a suffering that we will undoubtedly cause others as part of what we are and what we must do. I do not, cannot, expect you to understand. But if you are so adamant about discovering answers to questions, then I will now betray a secret, a trust which I hope will in some way provide, if not answers, then at least the reasons why they are not forthcoming. To do so I feel I must share with you the inner most secrets of my men. Show you how their experiences have shaped, transformed, disfigured them. In doing so I betray their confidence but if that is what is needed for you to just accept that sometimes there can be no answers, then so be it. If that is needed to give you an insight into them, of what they have also been through. Some suffering does not end, it evolves. And it is the worst kind.
Young Paul   So do we now compare wounds to see who bleeds the most?
Captain   How biblical. No. But if you would...
Young Paul   *(Interrupting).* Just say your piece.
Captain   They write a letter to their family every so often. I am obliged to keep them. Pass them on if... well, I am sure you appreciate when. They know it may never be sent or find a family who will ever read it. Equally, they know it is what they will be remembered by. Their parting thoughts, their footprint on life. And it is their way of rationalising the irrational. Of what war has done to them and what they have done in its name. Please. Read. No answers. Maybe, even more questions. But look beyond what you see before you. *(He hands a bundle of letters to Young Paulette. Light back up on older Paulette).* If you must be judge and jury on what we are, then so be it. You have every right. But at least allow yourself to be the arbiter of the evidence before you pass sentence.
Paulette   I took the letters from their stained, crumpled envelopes and read each in turn. With each, I saw the men's faces. I felt the emotion from their pens, seep into my mind... and they were with me.

Young Paulette sits on the floor and begins to read the letters. In doing so, the Captain steps back out of the light but remains in the shadows. The lights fade on older Paulette. In turn, the lights come up on a different part of the stage as in turn, each soldier speaks the contents of the letter that Paulette is reading. As each ends another light comes up, another soldier, another letter.

Klaus   Dearest Father. I sat on a rock at a crossroads today, gathering my thoughts, my strength, and my prayers for our advance tomorrow. As I did, I sat and watched the retiring battalion, returning from the front. But it was quiet, oh, so quiet. Several hundred men, equipment, walking in silence, their eyes never wavered from the man in front and I was overwhelmed by the sight of them. The mud and dust from the battlefield covered them all and they looked just like lead toys, waiting to be painted, yearning to be given a uniform, a purpose, and a life. But these boys no longer had theirs; theirs had been painted out, colour-washed with the brush of battle by that soulless artist called War, who paints in the detail of misery and suffering with the broad and unforgiving stroke of his hand. His palette has only one colour...

	grey; grey for the men, the fields, the flowers, the sky, the sun… and the soul. I've decided when I go over the top tomorrow, I'll think of mother's rose garden, it's myriad of colours and scents. Fear's a marvellous thing, Father, it can make you pretend you are anything, anyone… anywhere.
Carter	My dearest Edna. We advanced towards the German lines under cover of darkness last night and bedded down beneath a ridge until dawn. I was first man up and the Captain told me to recce the line. As I climbed the ridge and peered into the distance across the valley beneath, the stillness of the morning and the warmth of the sun felt like being on the hills where we have so often walked. But as the sun burned away the morning mist that had gathered, I had to keep rubbing my eyes as I could not take in the sight. All I could see covering the battlefield, was horses… no men, no equipment, just dozens and dozens of dead horses. Why, Ed? What had those beautiful creatures ever done to anybody? They didn't deserve this. The guns had just mown them down on purpose so the cavalry lads would be useless. Such beauty and nobility had been turned into an ugly, twisted mass. I didn't think it was possible to make a creature so innocent look so abhorrent. But they had, we had, for bringing them to this place. I want to keep horses when I come home, Ed, I have to, I must… or that scene will stay with me to the grave; it'll be my way of saying sorry.
Geneux	My Dearest. I keep reading your letter you gave me before we left. No, don't be sad, sad is not a word a soldier ever uses, ever knows. We can't afford to be. Tired, hungry, frightened, angry… yes. But if I'm honest, I suppose the only time you get close to it is when you meet the refugees. The ones who are not part of this war; tired, lost, weary. Shuffling, hopeless, despairing. Column after column wandering like animals, yearning for… I don't know. Peace? No, not peace from battle, just peace for their souls. I think if they just had the opportunity to lie down on fresh green grass in the sun and be allowed to sleep and never awaken, they would do it now and not miss a second of the life they would give up. *(Almost matter of fact)*. An old woman refugee asked me to shoot her and her husband today. I tried to ignore her but she grabbed me and spat in my face as I tried to walk past. She cursed me and then, in the same breath, blessed me for what we were trying to do for them and collapsed on the floor asking for my forgiveness. My forgiveness? Who am I to forgive anyone? God forgive all of us for what we have done… if there is a God in this place.

Silence. The lights rise on older Paulette and fade on the soldiers. The Captain walks towards Young Paulette. She slowly hands the letters to him without making eye contact, staring at the floor. She then gets up, making to leave.

Captain	Winners and losers. They are the convenience, the device of historians. It is the people in between the two which are the untold story. A premise which explains why some questions do not have answers.
Young Paul	What a simple, acceptable and conveniently packaged world you must live in, Captain.
Captain	No. It is just the letter home that I have never had the courage to write.

Paulette	That one sentence took my breath away. It gave him humanity. It gave us affinity. I was overwhelmed with a sense of loss, of despair accepted, of a lot bigger than mine which made me and all my questions, my doubts, mean nothing.
Captain	And to quote Machiavelli: "The ends justify the means".
Paulette	And in that final sentence, my roller-coaster of perceptions, of the truth, of the status quo was swept away again. And I realised that with Chateaux Tatar, I did not, would not ever know the ends or the means. Moreover, the idea of discovering them filled me with dread. *(The Captain walks upstage, turns, looks at the letters, tears them up, puts them in his pocket and exits).* And slowly. Ever so slowly. Without us ever even realising. The darkness began to notice us. *(She exits).*

Fade to black.

Scene 5

Lights up on the three soldiers. They are sitting together cleaning their weapons, chatting.

Carter	Germany? What would Germany know about football?
Klaus	More than you could ever know! And what has England ever achieved? You are about as good at football as the French!

Silence.

Geneux	*(Suddenly realising what has just been said).* Hey, hey!

Klaus and Carter laugh.

Carter	Bloody got you again, Geneux. Like a bloody fish on a hook. We reel you in every time! And here it comes…
Cart/Klau/Gen	Sacre bleu!
Klaus	And you say that every time!

Carter and Klaus start laughing and Geneux reluctantly joins in. Antoine and Paulette enter, wandering into the scene to break it. The three soldiers immediately stand. As they do the lights rise on older Paulette.

Paulette	Having read the letters didn't really answer anything. What annoyed me more was that the Captain said they wouldn't and that he was right. I decided that Claude, Antoine, everyone really, everyone but me was right. We had to make the best of whatever this was and be thankful when providence allowed us sleep… and more importantly the chance to awaken from it.

The light fades on Paulette.

Antoine	Please, do not let us disturb you.
Young Paul	Whilst you are all here, I just wanted to say, well, I am sorry for well, how I was.
Carter	No need, Miss. I think we need to apologise to you.
Young Paul	We were looking for Claude.
Geneux	He will be around somewhere.
Carter	Aye. Back soon. Went looking for your dinner, I think.

Klaus	Ah yes. Monsieur Durant's specialities. A hundred and one ways to cook a parsnip!
Geneux	I don't think we have had them mashed in a while.
Carter	Bloody hell, don't let him hear you, he might do it!
Geneux	If I never see a parsnip again I would not be disappointed. Roast…
Klaus	Boiled…
Carter	Chipped…
Geneux	Grated…
Klaus	Fried…
Carter	Raw…
Geneux	Stewed…
Klaus	Steamed…
Carter	Mashed…
Three Soldiers	Ugh!
Geneux	There is one way we have not had them and I would gladly provide the service.
Carter	What?
Geneux	Shot!

They all laugh. It subsides and the soldiers get on with attending to their guns.

Young Paul	You all appear in good spirits.
Geneux	What else is there to be?
Young Paul	Doesn't it frighten you?
Geneux	What? Parsnips?

They laugh.

Young Paul	No.
Carter	What then?
Klaus	War?
Young Paul	No. Death. *(The soldiers fall silent and look at each other, clearly nervous).* I'm sorry…
Carter	We…
Geneux	We don't discuss it
Carter	;Operational exting, exit, ex… that thing the Captain always says.
Antoine	Exigencies.
Carter	That's the one.
Young Paul	And what does that mean?
Klaus	It means we don't talk about it.

Pause.

Antoine	So what were you talking about when we arrived? You were all laughing. Can we share that?
Carter	Football. We always tease each other about it. Do you play? *(Paulette and Antoine shake their heads).* There's a shock. The French can't play football.

Pause, before Geneux catches on.

Geneux	Hey, hey!

127

Klaus	*(To Geneux)*. Don't worry. Neither do the British.
Gen/Klau	Hey, hey!

They all laugh then Carter realises who the comment was aimed at.

Carter	Hey, hey! Now hang on a minute…
Geneux	Different when… how you say… the boot is always on the other feet?
Klaus	Its foot.
Carter	Yeah. But you Jerries still don't know how to use them!
Geneux	Just the left one, remember?

They all laugh.

Klaus	Oh really? We showed you at Christmas.
Carter	Nah. That didn't count.
Geneux	Oh, I see. Doesn't count when you get beat!
Young Paul	What happened?
Klaus	We had an unofficial ceasefire. Played football. Even exchanged gifts. But most important of all… we beat the British two-nil!
Geneux	And we beat the Germans three-nil in a re-match!
Carter	Rubbish, we beat both of you! *(There is good hearted banter between them; laughter, raised voices, and then).* Your memory is as bad as your football!
Geneux	How can I forget? The only thing you lot did was sing that bloody 'Pack Up Your Troubles' song.
Klaus	And they didn't do that very well! And what about 'A Long Way To Bloody Tipperary'!
Carter	I remember perfectly what happened with those football games on the front. It was just before we ended up here and… *(He stops in his tracks. The other two look at him).* Nothing. Getting confused. Nothing.
Young Paul	Christmas? You mean you've been stuck here since Christmas?
Antoine	What? Last Christmas?
Carter	Yeah…
Klaus	That's right.
Geneux	Yes, since last Christmas.
Antoine	I remember my parents talking of that happening before, in Christmas 1914 and the football games in no-man's land. Who would have thought that history would repeat itself?
Carter	Not hit the papers yet probably.
Geneux	Yes. Probably won't for months.
Klaus	Yah. The tradition carried on. Not that our superior officers liked it.
Captain	*(Entering)* What didn't we like?

The soldiers stand very quickly, nervously. An uneasy silence descends.

Young Paul	Parsnips. Claude's one hundred and one ways of cooking them. We were just hoping he hadn't remembered how to mash them.

Another uneasy silence. Then the Captain unexpectedly laughs. They all join in.

Captain	Hasn't taken you long to get the measure of this place and how we pass the days.

Antoine   Indeed. How you have managed being here since Christmas is beyond me.
The atmosphere changes.
Captain   Christmas?
Antoine   Your men were just telling us…
Captain   Were they…
Antoine   How they played football at Christmas on the front. It appears even war has its traditions.
Captain   Doesn't it just…
Antoine   And as Mr Carter said…
Captain   What did Mr Carter say…
Antoine   Merely about the football, the songs they sing, sang, the…

Carter is suddenly, abjectly overcome with fear, hysterical. Without warning he practically throws himself at the Captain's feet.

Carter   I said nothing, Sir. Please believe me, I said nothing. I would never tell them anything about it. Please don't send me there, don't…

Carter continues to babble and the Captain just keeps saying quietly, measuredly, slowly "Be quiet" over and over again. The Captain draws his side arm and places the muzzle against Carter's forehead. Paulette screams. Antoine takes hold of her. Carter is shaking uncontrollably and quietly crying. The other two soldiers look on in fear. Claude suddenly enters the scene, unaware, buoyant, good humoured.

Claude   Alright, cut out the dramatics. I have potatoes, you will be pleased to hear. No mashed parsnips tonight… *(He stops dead in his tracks and drops the basket he is carrying).*

The scene is frozen, silent, apart from Carter sobbing. The lights rise on older Paulette.

Paulette   And this was when it revealed itself. I remember it as vividly as if it were happening now. Fear. Abject fear on the soldier's faces was inexplicable. Why did he do that over what appeared inconsequential? Why were they so frightened of him? And against that, Claude. Entering the game in a way that I could never have expected. A manner, an intervention which was incomprehensible. My mind began to race, competing with my heart.

Claude then walks slowly over to the Captain and speaks in a low, calm voice.

Claude   Captain. Put the gun away. Please. You know the consequences. You know what will happen. *(The Captain suddenly cocks the revolver. All quickly flinch. Paulette cries out, Carter whimpers loudly).* Captain. Remember where you are. Remember who you are. Remember what you are. Remember when you are. Please. For the sake of everything. There is too much at stake.
Claude/Paulette   Status quo
Paulette   Where, who, what, when… stakes. A riddle of words which at that time, was too hard to decipher

The Captain re-holsters his side arm. The tension breaks. Carter collapses prostrate on the ground. Young Paulette faints into Antoine's arms. The Captain continues as if nothing has happened. Claude runs to Young Paulette.

Captain	You two take him back and stand guard. Niceties are over. Cosy little chats are over. Treating this place like a bloody holiday B&B is over. You will remember where you are and what you are. And you two are under my command and control. You will do as you are told and you will remain within this immediate area. Do you understand? *(Beat).* I said…
Antoine	Yes.
Captain	Carry on. *(He exits).*

Klaus and Geneux help Carter to his feet.

Carter	*(To Antoine).* Why did you tell him? Why?
Young Paul	We didn't do anything!
Klaus	That's what they said.
Young Paul	What? Who?
Carter	*(To Klaus).* Quiet, you bloody idiot!
Geneux	*(To Paulette).* This is all your fault. Be very careful, Mademoiselle. You don't want to make enemies of us. We know the game you're playing with your questions. Playing us off one against another. Drawing us in with your nice chats, apologies, being friends, wanting to know everything. The last time, I think. Your secret is out, Mademoiselle. And ours are nothing to do with you. Pray to your God it remains that way.
Young Paul	My secret?
Antoine	Please, we have done nothing wrong.
Klaus	*(To Claude).* And as for you…
Claude	*(To the soldiers).* And as for you three, you do not want to make an enemy of me either. Remember? Enough has been said here. On your way. Go!

The soldiers exit.

Young Paul	What in hell…?
Antoine	What just happened here? Claude?
Young Paul	Answer him! For once, give us one straight answer!
Antoine	What are we to do?
Claude	Sleep.
Paulette	Sleep. Claude's answer to everything.
Young Paul	What?!
Claude	I need to think. I need to speak to the Captain. I need to sort this out. *(He makes to exit).*
Antoine	What have we done?
Claude	You have no idea
Paul/Young P	More secrets?
Claude	*(Angrily, for the first time).* Can you not just stop?! For God's sake, woman, there are greater things here than answers to your stupid questions. I am trying to help you and you do not help yourself. *(He exits).*
Young Paul	I don't care what might happen. What side is out there or in here. We leave in the morning.
Antoine	Yes. *(Pause).* When did you last see a morning?
Young Paul	It was… it was, I can't…
Antoine	When did we get here?

Young Paul	I don't…
Antoine	How long have we been here?
Young Paul	It was… I can't…
Antoine/ Paul	Remember.
Antoine	What village did we live in, Paulette? What is happening to us?
Young Paul	Sleep, I need to sleep, I just need to sleep. You need to sleep. It will all be clearer then.
Paulette	And still, darker yet…

Fade to black.

Scene 6

The lights rise on older Paulette.

Paulette	Despite what we had just experienced, we slept, a deep and bizarrely restful sleep for such a restless place. Time still appeared not to exist. Light was still banished to be replaced with shades of grey and black within which the minutes, hours, days were unable to penetrate. We had been asleep for, who knows how long…

Cross fade to Young Paulette and Antoine who lay asleep, huddled, centre stage. The background lighting then comes up and in the gloom are revealed Klaus, Geneux and Carter crouched on boxes, on rocks etc, at different levels around the scene, just looking at them like vultures. Antoine slowly awakes and is suddenly aware of them. He sits up with a start which makes Paulette suddenly wake.

Antoine	What is going on?
Klaus	Nothing, my friend
Carter	Just doing what we were told.
Young Paul	Which was?
Klaus	To watch you, of course.
Geneux	To protect you, of course.

The three soldiers, almost quietly laugh, alien personalities, as if they have become something very different.

Young Paul	Laugh as much as you want. We are not afraid of the likes of you.
Antoine	Paulette, don't…
Klaus	And what are 'our likes'.
Carter	You know nothing of fear.
Geneux	What we are capable of.
Young Paul	But we do know something. You might write heartfelt letters home but they don't fool me.

The three soldiers suddenly stand up.

Klaus	You have read them?
Carter	Our letters?
Geneux	You had no right!
Young Paul	We know what you are!

The Captain enters. The moment he speaks, even without seeing him, the soldiers react, almost skulking back to their places/positions and squatting down again. Like dogs responding to what

131

their master might just do to the disobedient. His entrance is followed by Claude, entering from opposite carrying a bound bundle of firewood. He stops in his tracks and observes.

Captain	And what are we?
Young Paul	And you are the biggest deceiver of them all.
Antoine	Paulette!
Young Paul	And we are not afraid of you either. You are the ones who should be afraid.
Captain	Of…?
Antoine	Paulette. Please…
Claude	Paulette?
Captain	No, Monsieur. Please. Feel free to be candid. If the protected cannot speak openly of their concerns with their protectors… Allow us to know your fear.
Antoine	We are just tired, Captain. My sister, like I, is merely anxious that…
Young Paul	I know a secret.

The three soldiers suddenly, quickly stand up in their positions again.

Captain	Is that so?
Young Paulette	Your secret. Secret missions, we thought. Secret missions! What nonsense. Spies, I thought! I was blind. We figured it out from first meeting you.
Captain	Intriguing.
Young Paul	No.
Captain	Then what?
Young Paul	Disgusting.
Antoine	Paulette.
Young Paul	Dirty little secret.
Captain	Fascinating.
Antoine	We are tired, frightened, we need to leave this place and take our chances with…
Young Paul	What will they do when they find you? Can't imagine a hero's welcome awaits.
Captain	Are we to eventually learn where this is going or…
Young Paul	Deserters!

Everything stops. Silence. Tension. Carter then suddenly breaks ranks and lunges at Claude and strikes him to the ground and pins him down.

Carter	You! It was you speaking to them! Can't keep his bloody gob shut. We don't need him any longer. I told you what we needed to do with him. Bloody French.
Geneux	Hey, hey!

Geneux now attempts to become embroiled, pulling Carter off Claude. Klaus joins in. Paulette goes to Claude and tends to him on the floor. The Captain has an Officer's stick/crop. He turns to Carter and without warning pushes Geneux to one side and begins to beat Carter mercilessly to the ground with the crop whilst Carter screams like a dog in pain. The pleasure of what he is doing is apparent on the Captain's face. The other two soldiers observe, subserviently indifferent, clearly aware of the price of dissent.

Captain	I warned you, Carter. I warned you!

Antoine　　*(Intervening).* Captain, stop, stop. Please, STOP!

The following note explains how this moment should be dealt with: Antoine takes hold of the Captain's arm and turns him around. The smile on the Captain's face is now clearer to see as he raises the crop to strike Antoine, beaming with enjoyment, an epiphany of pain. And then as quickly as it commenced, he withdraws back to being the controlled Captain, slowly lowering his arm. Carter scurries away like an animal behind the other two soldiers. Antoine backs away leaving the Captain and sits next to Paulette and Claude. The Captain turns around and stares at them, studies them all in turn. Antoine and Paulette are in shock. The soldiers look down at the floor and will not make eye contact. The Captain walks slowly over to Paulette who is sitting on the floor with the others. He places the crop under her chin to lift her face to look at him. Antoine moves as if to intervene, but Claude stops him.

Captain　　Deserters? It's all a matter of perspective, Mademoiselle, of language. Are the conscientious cowards because they see where the real battle lies? Is the soldier that discovers the secret of his true vocation to be vilified because he chooses his side and refuses to have it imposed on him? Does it make his letters home, his hopes have less value? There is more than one battle, one side, one war. Choices Mademoiselle. I fear at some point during your stay with us, you too will have them to make, and with them, decisions, sides, futures to consider. And with the choice come the spoils. Spoils that can last for… There are rewards at stake here which are greater than those found on…

Claude　　*(Standing quickly and interrupting).* Captain, please

Captain　　*(Moving away).* Yes. Enough for now I think. All in good time. 'Good time'. What a very interesting, intriguing term, don't you think? Is this time good for you, do you think? Perhaps time will tell, if it can, if it wants to. You will get your answers very shortly, pretty lady. But I hazard that you won't like what you discover. *(Beat).* To your posts men. *(The soldiers respond immediately and skulk away).* Delightful, as ever, speaking with you. I do hope we have the chance, and the time, to pursue this.

Young Paul　And what is your war, your secret? When will be your time?

Captain　　Oh, but you have happened upon it, surely? Too clever by far for we simple soldiers. We are outed, aren't we? You said it yourself. We are deserters. The pretty lady has figured it. What else could it possibly be? I do hope you are uninjured Claude. I would hate anything to happen to you. Your assistance to us is so important. Do feed our guests. Keep them… well. There's a good chap. 'Good chap'. Hmmm. Another interesting phrase. But that's what you are. Good? Our host, our caretaker, our conscience? You and your lamented family. Your dear departed sister. Our 'soul without end'.

Young Paul　And what does all that make you?

Captain　　Time will tell.

Antoine　　God will judge you, remember that.

Captain　　I think not. Remember that, if you can. But do you still hear him, Padre? Does he hear you any longer? Do you care? You can pour out your soul here, you know. No need to keep secrets. They are petty and meaningless when set against where you are. When you are. *(He exits).*

Young Paul　Thank you

133

Claude	For what?
Young Paul	For speaking up. For protecting us from him.
Claude	You are mistaken, Paulette. I wasn't protecting you from him.
Antoine	Then what?
Claude	I was protecting you from yourselves. You had to say something. You couldn't just let things be, could you? Why, Paulette? Why? *(He exits).*
Young Paul	Claude?

Young Paulette turns to Antoine and they embrace. The lights crossfade to older Paulette.

Paulette	It wasn't the fear of death that frightened me. It was the void created by uncertainty. And every event created more questions. But I knew. I knew from that point what it was. It was so obvious. It had been alluded to so many times, stared me in the face, unrecognised. We thought we knew it from the beginning, but we were mistaken. It was a secret. The secret. But not any secret. An old secret. A dark secret. A secret that was about to unravel and with it, any sense I had of what my life had been up to that point. A secret which would find love and lose it. A secret that would deny faith and regain it. A secret which would give life and take it. A secret as old as time. A secret which would be given up in time. But the greatest secret of all had now obviously and without any fight, surrendered itself to us. We had run out of time.

Fade to black.

END OF ACT ONE

INTERVAL

Act Two
Scene 1

The lights rise on older Paulette. SFX #6: distant battlefield noises followed by strange noises are heard. Younger Paulette and Antoine are asleep, lit dimly with their possessions, bags, around them.

Paulette   What amazed me was that, even filled with the greatest fear we had known since we escaped our home and ran for our lives, we slept that night in the rain. And again, we did not know for how long. A sleep of dreams that could not be remembered, and never would. Dreams that anaesthetised, purged, obscured.
The guns and explosions again started at some point but it was impossible to gauge when, where it was coming from. It was distant, but all around. It was above, below, everywhere. Was it inside me? Was that the ground trembling or was it me? And then amidst the gunfire and thunder, it began. Quietly at first in the background and then becoming prominent, blended surreptitiously with everything else so that you didn't really know if it had a beginning. We would come to pray, however, that it would have an end.
For it began to change, replace the sound of war. Unnerving, uncanny, not of this earth. It was familiar, but clinging to sanity would not allow me to believe it. It was breathing; heavy, laboured breathing first of all and with it, whispering sometimes. Then moaning. The sound of pain, fear, despair. Was it the wind dragging itself across the remains of the chateaux? It was one sound, one voice at first but then it became more; a myriad of misery. Their calls, indiscernible. Human yet, almost, inhuman. It was everywhere and nowhere. Their fear, unquestionable. Who were they? Where were they? It would then become louder, louder, then more voices, and now and again screams added, louder, more voices. *(The sound effect still underscores and gets gradually louder).* Competing, unbearable. We then realised: it was the last desperate cries of soldiers dying in whatever bloody battle was waging around us. The battle that Claude had warned us of. At least, we hoped it was, explained it away as that and then... *(SFX #6: fades suddenly).* Silence. Nothing. As quickly as it began. No warning, no event, sudden, unexpected, without theatrical fading, segue, nothing. And that was most disturbing. The silence more overwhelming than the deluge of despair. A cacophony, a conspiracy of silence. The din of the darkness consumed us. *(The lights come up full on the young couple who begin to prepare to set out on their journey, their escape, loaded down with their possessions which were around them).*
And it was then that events began to take a turn in a way that even we could not have speculated upon. The decision was inevitable: we would escape that place. Despite the advice of Claude which I had ignored and clearly angered him, we set out to, we didn't know where. To what? We didn't care. We just needed resolution I guess. Another chapter in the story of our journey in which we didn't hope, didn't care where it took us, as long as it gave us something, anything close to, alright not an answer, just an ending.

Something tangible. Something that we at least could say we had control of. And if we died, it would be at our behest. Heading into the unknown, we expected death. Leaving that place, death was a likelihood. Staying in that place, it was a certainty.

The following describes how this moment was achieved in the premiere: the lights now rise on Antoine and Paulette, struggling to move downstage. SFX #7: rainfall is heard. Paulette is walking and breathing in a laboured manner and Antoine to a lesser extent. They are almost in mime depicting walking, the sensations, the effort they describe as in doing so, their progress grinds to a halt down stage as they begin to speak.

Young Paul	How far have we walked?
Antoine	I have no idea. How long has it been?
Young Paul	I don't know. Have we got away from there yet?
Antoine	I cannot tell. This darkness. This rain.
Young Paul	Listen. Can you hear it?
Antoine	All I can hear is my heart beating and rain falling
Young Paul	The voices, the screams, the shelling, those sounds …
Ant/Young P	Silence
Paulette	Silence
Young Paul	My god yes. It's stopped. We must have finally left that place. Escaped the battle. I had not noticed.
Antoine	Why have they stopped so suddenly? Have we escaped or do you think they have…?
Young Paul	Don't say it
Antoine	Their pain … death can only have been a blessed relief
Young Paul	I need to stop. I, I …
Ant/Young P	Can't breathe.
Paulette	Can't breathe.
Antoine	Neither can I. I can feel it now, can you? Oh no. Oh dear lord no. It can't be? Not now. Not that! It must have killed those poor souls so suddenly.
Young Paul	What?
Antoine	Mustard Gas.
Young Paul	Gas? Now? After all we have been through. To die like this. Not like this. Please not like this.
Antoine	My arms, my legs.
Ant/Young P	Heavy.
Paulette	Heavy.
Antoine	I feel like I am walking, bogged down in thick, mud but there is none there, moving ever so…
Ant/Young P	Slowly.
Paulette	Slowly.
Young Paul	I feel I am surrounded by mud but can't see any. Antoine I cannot move. I cannot…
Paulette/Ant	Breathe
Young Paul	Breathe. I can go no further. Almost like we are being pulled back and
Antoine	And my chest, my eyes

Paul/Young P	Burning
Antoine	Burning.
Young Paul	I feel like I am-
Paul/Young P	Sinking.
Antoine	Sinking. Like a wall. An impenetrable wall that allowed us in, but will not allow us to…
Paulette/Ant	Escape.
Young Paul	Escape. But how can this be?
Antoine	Maybe if we tried to retrace our steps… but I cannot.

SFX #7 fades out and is replaced by SFX #8: battlefield and wailing noises.

Antoine	Gunfire!
Young Paul	Antoine? I cannot lift my legs. Cannot turn. Antoine! I cannot move. I am…
Ant/Young P	Paralysed.
Paulette	Paralysed.

In the shadows at the back the lights come up and the three figures of the soldiers slowly rise into standing positions.

Young Paul	Antoine! Do you hear them? That sound again. Dear Lord. Not again. Poor, bastards. They are still dying out there in the fields. *(Calling out)*. Can you hear me? Hello? I cannot see you.
Antoine	Paulette, nobody is there
Young Paul	I cannot help you. Forgive me. Lost and abandoned as are we. Claude! Claude?! Help us! Help us! God… help us. To go home, any home, anywhere, anywhere, anywhere… *(She begins to fall unconscious)*.
Antoine	God help us? Pointless. Helpless. Your servant? Your fool. Your faithless disbelieving fool. Do your worst, if you exist. I am beyond caring or believing. Nothing can help us now. Nothing. Nothing. Noth…

Antoine cannot continue. He is now gasping for air and eventually succumbs and passes out. As he does so SFX #8 fades out. The lights on Antoine, Young Pauline and the soldiers fade to black, leaving only Older Paulette lit.

Paulette	As I slipped into unconsciousness I remember that defining moment, ringing in my ears with the cries of the damned, hearing Antoine finally giving up on all he had spent his life in believing. All he, we, had been through and still he had clung to any liberation, salvation, being influenced by the divine. But it was over, his journey, both physical and spiritual. And now in my fear, desperation, I had turned to a god I had shunned; blamed for what had happened to us in the hope that forgiveness was indeed at the heart of my faith and not just the ideal, the final hope of the hopeless. But faith can mean so many things. The tables had turned. But they would continue turning, spinning out of control.

Fade to black.

Scene 2

The lights rise on Young Paulette. She is laying, unconscious, in the arms of Claude who is brushing her hair from her face. Antoine is laying to the side of them a short distance away, also unconscious, his back to them and the audience. Young Paulette begins to awaken and with a start, realises, remembers what their situation had been. Claude places his hand over her mouth to prevent the expected scream.

Claude   Quiet, calm, be calm, you are fine. I am here.
Young Paul   Antoine?!
Claude   He sleeps. What you should still be doing
Young Paul   But you walked away. I angered you. I thought you no longer wanted to know us?
Claude   Why would I? How could I?
Young Paul   But I thought…
Claude   You thought what I needed you to believe. *(Young Paulette looks at him, suddenly breaks down, and then without warning, kisses him passionately).* You're welcome
Young Paul   How embarrassing. I don't know what came over me, I'm…
Claude   *(Kissing Young Paulette).* Nor I.
Young Paul   What has happened to the world, to us, Claude?
Claude   War.
Young Paul   No, that is the consequence. What had we become to allow this? I think back not so long ago to a life which does not seem like mine now. A life which I feel I must have read about in a book and never really, truly experienced. A life without hopes and dreams. *(She looks at him intently, like there has been a revelation).* Until now.
Claude   Now? Why?
Young Paul   Until this moment. Nothing made sense. Nothing had beauty any longer. But I see it, suddenly and without warning. It is you.
Claude   Me? What do you…?
Young Paul   *(Interrupting).* No. Let me finish. I need to say this now whilst I am not afraid to be embarrassed. Not afraid to give my soul a voice and simply, no longer be afraid. In your face, in your eyes. In so many ways. You are the missing piece of my puzzle. You are the longed-for warmth on a cold night. The faint glow of light at the end of a dark journey. You are the stranger I have always known. The soul I have always been apart from, but a part of; the reason to finish the book, the anticipated cadence in a much-awaited song; the drug which I have never had but now, can no longer live without. *(They kiss).* Did any of that make sense?
Claude   No. But does anything, must anything? And yet I knew, understood, every single word. Every sentiment, because since our first meeting, you gave this, me, a purpose. We may have no history, but…
Young Paul   But do we really need a history to know what is right, that a person, a time, a place can be right? Can be a beginning? A new beginning? How many people spend a lifetime together only to find at the end of it that it was a wasted life? So why can't two people just know in an instant what takes so many a lifetime to discover?
Claude   What have you been doing all my life?
Young Paul   Simple. Waiting.

Young Paul	Oh, Claude, might this nightmare finally be coming to an end? I was so frightened. Tonight when we decided we needed to run for our lives; I thought that you didn't want to come with us, but the fact you have and found us and… wait… *(Then suddenly remembering)*. How did you find us?
Claude	Find you? I wasn't looking for you. I found you asleep, here.
Young Paul	Then you didn't get trapped in the mud?
Claude	Mud? What mud?
Young Paul	Why, this, it covered us, our clothes… *(Silence, as she looks around and can see no trace of that which had trapped them)*. What? Where is it? Then where are we now?
Claude	You are nowhere. I mean you have been nowhere. I found you lying here.
Young Paul	But we had been walking for hours, miles.
Claude	You walked metres. Several at the most.
Young Paul	*(Looking quickly around and then slumping to the ground)*. We are back? How can this be? Dear God! Is there no escape from this?
Antoine	For now you are safe. I am here.
Young Paul	But how? Why were you not overcome by the gas?
Claude	Gas? What gas?
Young Paul	The gas which engulfed us, almost killed us. Claude?
Claude	What gas? There was no gas, was no mud.
Young Paul	If not gas then what? Claude? What is it?

Claude stands, troubled, not looking at Young Paulette. The lights rise on Older Paulette.

Paulette	Where the courage to kiss him and then pour out my soul had come from I will never know. But even in that moment, the mysteries which continued to appear were not lost on me. I knew there was now something even more unbelievable about the situation. I knew what had happened to me, what we had felt, heard, seen and it was impossible that Claude could have not been affected, understand, unless…
Claude	Of course. Do you not realise? With all that has gone on, all you have been through, it must have all just been a…
Young Paul	Don't you dare! Don't you dare blame it on a nightmare. Not now. Not after all we have been through, not after baring my naked soul to you.
Paulette	I could not accept one moment longer his mantra of duty, of family, of explanation. But I sensed even he realised we had passed the point of no return. A point on this journey which demanded the true destination be disclosed.
Claude	I don't know where to begin. I must and yet I cannot. But believe me, I am protecting you Paulette. By your not knowing, means there is still a chance. But know this. If I tell you there is no going back.
Paul/Young P	Still more secrets
Paulette	I knew he was trying to protect me from something worse than the truth. But there was no way that I was going to allow the fear of fear to cheat me out of not finally knowing it.
Claude	Yes Paulette, secrets. There are many and they are all one in the same; and I am part of it all.

Paulette	And I then remember saying it. My clarity even took me by surprise. I needed to simply understand.
Paul/Young P	Claude, talk. Just talk. I don't care how I will die or when. I just need to know why

The light fades on Older Paulette.

Claude	In doing so this may not mean just the death of all of us but something much worse.
Young Paul	Worse than death?
Claude	Oh yes. There are things worse than death. A death that never ends. A pain that is eternal. A battle between the light and the dark, of good and evil. *(He takes out his book).*
Young Paul	Good and evil? What do you mean… it has something to do with the book? And the Captain referred to you as being good. Why did he say that? Is there more to it, to you?
Claude	Alright. What is the last thing you remember?
Young Paul	It was, well it was when, I don't know. It's so hard to remember…
Antoine	*(Who still appeared asleep with his back to them, speaks without moving).* Nothing. We remember nothing. *(Paulette moves to him and he sits up).* I am fine. Please, continue. And thank you, Claude; however, whenever, whatever it is you did, whatever happened to us, thank you. Whether it was saving our lives or saving our sanity.
Claude	Your lives?! There is something far more at stake here than your lives. Again. What is the last thing you remember?
Antoine	As I said. Nothing. I am now struggling to even remember our names.
Young Paul	As am I.
Claude	There is a reason why you can't remember. And what I am about to tell you, neither of you will believe.
Antoine	Belief, disbelief, both mean nothing any longer. If you were to tell me the Devil lived here I would not argue the fact. *(Silence).* Claude?

The background lights rise to reveal the Captain and the soldiers in silhouette.

Young Paul	You are frightening me.
Claude	Then allow yourself to be, for fear is only just the beginning. Fear is what may yet save us all. The only rational thing we have. The reason you cannot remember anything is the beginning of the secret. The secret of Tatar. This place does not allow memories.
Antoine	What? A place? Absurd!
Claude	Let me finish. This is not just a ruin. It has never been just a chateau. It, this place, exists to absorb them, memories; more specifically, bad memories, the memories of evil deeds, the sordid recollections of the possessor.
Antoine	Ridiculous!
Claude	Please. Like a leach it drains the memories of evil and then adds them to its collective recollection of darkness. Anything that is not dark is erased because it has no place here, which is why your happy, everyday memories have gone so rapidly. Good deeds, good people cannot survive here. I have never known such goodness of heart, such purity in two people. What makes

you who you are has kept you alive but it will soon be gone. If you remain here you will just slip away one day, lie down and not wake up. That desire to sleep is essential. Tatar will not allow it any other way. You must have realised it? That is why you are the only ones that ever sleep. Can you remember what you have dreamt about since you were here? *(Antoine and Young Paulette look at him and then at each other with a realisation).* Exactly. No. Because to dream is to reflect, recollect, remember. Dreaming here is a one-way process. The more you sleep the more you forget. The more you forget, the more you want to sleep. The more Tatar possess you, the quicker you are gone.

Antoine   I simply cannot…
Young Paul   Yes. I believe you.
Antoine   Paulette?
Young Paul   No Antoine. We have sensed it since we got here. The never-ending darkness. The fear. And now, a lifetime of no memories.
Claude   And the reason why I need to get you away from here.
Young Paul   And you also, Claude. Not just us. We. Come with us. Now. Hold on to that feeling we both have waited a lifetime for and now give it a life, a meaning. Have faith.
Antoine   Faith?!
Young Paul   Antoine, just listen to him. Far-fetched? Yes. Fanciful? Yes. But just…
Antoine   No Paulette, let me finish. I am trying to say that I do believe him, but not anything else. Not anymore. I have not believed for some time. Good? Evil? Everything I have based my life on was a lie. Faith? What is it? Meaningless. Death, destruction is now the basis of the world. We are beyond being saved by anyone, anything. And you Claude are beyond saving us. I believe you because rationality has gone. And with it has gone any faith I had. Surviving is what matters. And if killing means survival for my sister, then so be it. Salvation comes from within, from us and nowhere, no one else. So lead on Claude. Point out who I need to kill to get Paulette away from here, how I can add to it. How can I be any more damned than I am here?
Claude   Stop it Antoine! Don't let this place do this to you. Can you not see? You are becoming a part of this. Fight it.
Young Paul   My God, Antoine. What has happened to you? What has this place done to you? Remember who you are, what you are!
Antoine   Come on! Come shadows! Come whatever you are! Do your worst. Where are you? Where are you?!

The light on the silhouetted soldiers fades to black.

Claude   Quiet Antoine! We need to get both of you out. We need to act quickly. But I need to figure out how. The time is getting close. I need to read, understand.
Young Paul   Your book?
Claude   The contents were written centuries, possibly millennia ago, when this place was formed, as a guide, instructions, rules. All about this place is in it. My father once told me that there was also a way to break the cycle of this place, but I need to read. Need to figure out how and more importantly, when.

Captain   *(Offstage).* When 'what', Monsieur Durant? *(He enters from the shadows).*

Paulette, Antoine and Claude instinctively turn to go in the opposite direction, but the three soldiers enter, spreading out to prevent each of them. The lights rise on Older Paulette.

Paulette   I remember him strolling nonchalantly and yet menacingly into the tableau and with it, I sensed he carried with him a truth that could no longer be concealed from us. I stared at him, studied him, tried to decipher that shroud of secrecy. I was not afraid by him or the others. And then, the shroud he had worn so effectively slipped from his shoulders and with it, his mask. *(The light fades on her).*

Captain   No need to dance around the subject any longer, my dear, good Claude. And no need to lie to me of all people. You forget how much we are aware of all that happens here. We are what happens here. We know everything. Alpha and Omega. I know what you have discovered and what secrets have been told. But I feel the time has now come for the greatest secret of all to be told and please, allow me the honour. Verdun, but more specifically, the place where Chateaux Tatar once stood has had such a colourful past which seems to have passed the world by. The Gallic Wars of the first century BC saw thousands die in this place; the rout of the Roman Governor by the Gauls saw an even greater number of innocents butchered; the beheading of thousands of innocent Saxons by the emperor Charlemagne; the massacre of the Huguenots in the 16th century, oh and the latest gay instalment: The Great War and 1916… a small matter of the wholesale loss of eight hundred thousand souls not far from here and all for the sake of an insignificant piece of nowhere.

Klaus   They even had the obscene idea to call the supply road 'La Voie Sacrée'… 'The Sacred Way'. How were we to know that because of what we had all done to each other for two thousand years it would make this place sacred for a wholly different reason?

Geneux   Didn't you think it strange the name of this place? Chateaux Tatar.

Carter   When the Mongol Hordes swept into Europe, the monks spelling of their name gave rise to the naming of the chateaux. This place, or so the legend goes, tells us they had an encampment on this very spot. But legends have a habit of being a version of the truth. Tatar was indeed the spelling given by the monks… to The Tartars.

Captain   And it was no coincidence. King Louis said: "Well may they be called Tartars, for their deeds are those of fiends from …?".

Antoine   Tartarus.

Captain   Indeed, Tartarus. Bravo, Padre! The true name of this place for millennia. And no coincidence that the Mongol Hordes and their slaughtering was drawn to here is it, my dear Father Devauchelle?

Young Paul   Antoine?

Captain   I think your brother is beginning to realise.

Antoine   Tartarus was said to be the final dwelling place for those who had been wicked in their mortal lives. But I can't see the significance of all this to…

Klaus   Tartarus was said to be as far beneath Hades as Heaven was above it.

Geneux	"... where men received their punishments for such misdeeds as deserved everlasting torture".
Young Paul	I think we have heard enough of your ghoulish bedtime tales. I don't know what this all means and I really don't care. Whatever you have done, whatever you're involved in, I don't know and I'm not interested. In the morning we will be on our way and that will be that.
Captain	SIT... down. Mankind has poisoned this very spot and the soil under our feet for thousands of years with hatred until it was that sodden with the blood of the dead. It eventually seeped its way into the furthest reaches of a realm that no mortal soul could ever comprehend
Carter	And we're now the latest custodians of the keys to it whilst this place gathers the souls, the deeds, the memories of the wicked. And we're trapped here until the next atrocity occurs and we then descend into...
Antoine	*(Interrupting).* Enough. I am afraid you have been caught out in your own childish tale. You said 1916 was the latest event...
Claude	Captain. You risk everything...
Captain	Too late dear Claude. Your indiscretion decided that. And to answer your question, how wrong Padre. Such a basic oversight by me. You are quite correct of course. We were the latest piece in this pitiful and perverse jigsaw.
Antoine	In 1916? But how could that involve you?
Geneux	You see we were soldiers. But not the type you would recognise any longer.

The soldiers laugh.

Klaus	We all became split up from our units, but for a different reason. We're all deserters, like you said. We were beyond the edge of sanity by the slaughtering we witnessed. We escaped the trenches and found, stumbled, into each other. We walked by night for weeks, sleeping by day until we reached the nearby village. The locals took us in but one of them overheard us talking one night as we planned our escape. With what they had seen happen around them, they didn't have a stomach for war. But they had less of a one for deserters.
Geneux	The old men and women left in the village set about to betray us to the advancing allied lines... forty or so of them came up here demanding that we surrender.
Carter	We just wanted to run away and hide... me and the lads didn't want to hurt anybody.
Captain	Cowards then and cowards still. Somebody had to be strong; somebody had to save their miserable hides from the firing squad. We are all casualties of war and a few more were not going to make any difference! But these impotent excuses for fighting men pleaded to run away. Look at them! The pathetic, vacant, childlike expressions are still as fresh as the day I did it.
Young Paul	It?
Klaus	He drew his gun because we wouldn't do what he said. He shouted to the locals that for every yard they advanced he would shoot one of them.
Geneux	Before they got within ten yards of the house, they were all dead. We just joined in. Couldn't help ourselves

Klaus	Did you not think what the noises in the darkness were? The screams, the constant cries? Not the war. It is them
Carter	A unit of French soldiers heard the gun fire. When they arrived they found us drenched in blood from head to foot from piling up the bodies
Captain	Did it never cross your mind? Our uniforms? Our ages? Our stories? Our songs? Oh no pretty lady, this isn't our war. The Great War was our glorious achievement; and how great it was. You see, civilisation has perpetuated the myth that ghouls and ghosts are ancient shadows of events centuries past. But in this most unique and most special of places, anything is possible. Anyone is possible.
Carter	We were shot by the French; each one of us.
Antoine	This is nonsense, a sick twisted tale to keep us here.
Geneux	We all died in July 1916.
Klaus	And we have been trapped, entombed here since then by this place; a place with one purpose… harvesting the memories and the souls of the damned.
Captain	*(Proudly).* "Now I am become Death, destroyer of worlds". You see, Padre? It isn't just Christianity which helps us to understand the truth, is it? Now… tempus fugit, Monsieur Durant, tempus fugit…
Antoine	Claude? What does he mean?
Captain	Time to refer to your little book, my dear Claude. The countdown to it happening all over again. Any time soon, it will begin. Read the book. Say the words. Do your job. Remember what your dear father taught you? Nearly time for us to relive. Oh, but now you can both become part of it as we repeat history and do it all again.
Carter	Innocent people.
Captain	Innocent! Did any of you fight me? Did any one of you try?
Klaus	He murdered them. And we let him.
Captain	Yes. And within seconds you all joined in! The blood may have washed from your hands but not from my memory. Cleanse me from my iniquities? Absolve me of my sins? Isn't that how it goes, Padre? Well, not here, not now, and not from the memory of Tatar. *(The sister screams/cries out and covers her ears).* History may help us to recall the people, but the places, and this place in particular, has a memory as well; we are the diabolical shadows of Chateaux Tatar.
Antoine	Shut up! You're all mad… obscene; a ploy to keep us here against our will for some sick and twisted purpose.
Klaus	And by stumbling into it, you have become part of it.
Young Paul	*(Shouting).* But we have done nothing wrong…
Captain	Nothing wrong? Right and wrong seem such petty details when you are in such august company, my dear. But what can one expect; as a gentleman called T S Eliot† is, I believe, about to write: "Humankind cannot bear too much reality".
Young Paul	Please. Just let us go. We won't speak a word, and…
Carter	You can't leave, you stupid cow! None of us can!
Young Paul	You're all insane. *(She grabs a rifle lying on the ground nearby put down by one of the soldiers).* Keep back.

The Captain walks towards her until the gun touches his stomach. Young Paulette fires. Nothing happens. Antoine grabs another and fires again with the same result. Two of the soldiers retrieve them. Young Paulette cries out and she embraces Antoine.

Captain	Congratulations. And now you're both tarred with the same brush, pretty lady, that's how it is. That's how it works. Evil begets evil, and in this place, intentions are just as good as actions. You have just succumbed to its pleasures. I applaud you both on becoming qualified as members of our select little club. Welcome… to Tartarus, and the portal to hell. *(Young Paulette screams and tries to run away, but he blocks her way).* Music to my ears. Tie them up. *(Nobody moves. He takes out his side arm).* Now! Remember boys… they can't hurt you, but I can with this. Any more dissent and mark my words, you will know the consequences by reaching hell, or worse, sooner than you would wish to.
Geneux	Please Mademoiselle. Do as he says. Please believe me, I… *(Young Paulette spits in his face).*
Antoine	*(Moving towards the Captain, holding up his hand).* Satan I command thee to…

The Captain strikes Antoine with the back of his hand, sending him reeling to the ground. Claude, who has been watching helplessly, moves forward. The Captain steps forward to Claude.

Captain	And you forget your place my young friend. Remember who and what you are. Remember what needs to be done. Duty. Responsibility. Heritage. Get the book. Read the book. Say the words. Do your job.
Young Paul	Claude?
Antoine	Are you going to allow the same thing to happen again? Defy him, ignore him!
Claude	I cannot. I… they, must do this. The balance must be maintained.
Antoine	Then one of you. Any of you.
Carter	Us ignore him? You chose to ignore him and his kind all of your life. Evil dressed as the man in the street, stared you in the face every day, and you did nothing. So don't preach to us. We're beyond it.
Captain	If it's any comfort, God does exist, Padre. But he has not lived in this house for some time.
Young Paul	This has to be a nightmare.
Captain	Yes. And yours has only just begun. You have two options, pretty lady: be part of what happens, or simply go to sleep, forget and… who knows what else? I'd hate to spoil that particular surprise.

The soldiers take hold of each of Claude's arms and exit with him as he struggles and resists them.

Claude	Get off me! Paulette! Paulette!
Captain	Know this, woman. Interfere, intercede, do anything to even remotely affect what happens here, and I will rain down on your soul the hordes of hell. *(He exits).*
Young Paul	Claude? Claude! Do something! Bastards!

Fade to black. The light rises on Older Paulette.

Paulette	But he would not… and now, could not? Had he abandoned us to whatever fate they had in store for us? All the pieces were coming into place and we were helpless to do anything. That terrible thing they did was about to happen again, but now, we were to be a part of it, sealing our fate also. The only piece of this secret was now the true involvement of Claude. And only one person had the power to intercede on our behalf. My dear Claude. But to whom would, could, that intercession be made? We sat in the darkness. Afraid to speak. Now even more afraid to sleep. We had become part of the story of Chateaux Tatar; its history but also its future. History was about to again be repeated, and at the same time, rewritten. But what part would we be cast in for this retelling of an old obscenity?

Fade to black.

Scene 3

The lights rise on Young Paulette and Antoine leaning on each other, still bound. The Captain enters and walks towards them.

Captain	Well, well. I take it then that we did not sleep? Shame Mr Durant let you into that particular little secret so soon. It would have made things so much simpler, less painful, less … eternal. So. Welcome to our battle. Our living, well, our hell on, what is left of the earth we were once on. It will all be over soon. Again. I won't spoil the surprise. And then we will all be one angry, at odds, bitter, twisted, hating family. Just like being alive really. No words of encouragement then padre? Any last pleas to please God again? No? Well, well. If this place can make even a priest forget God, then there is hope for us all. Well, perhaps not hope exactly. *(There is silence. Then, loudly, almost preaching).* "What if God were not exactly truth, and if this could be proved? And if he were instead the vanity, the desire for power, the ambitions, the fear, and the enraptured and terrified folly of mankind?"

Pause.

Antoine	Nietzsche
Captain	*(Clapping, slowly).* Bravo, Padre. You are in there. Most impressive. You are full of surprises. Eternity with you might be entertaining yet. *(Silence again).* I find it fascinating that with the multitude of religions and gods that espouse goodness, kindness, respect, tolerance, that the collective religions are the single most significant element in humanity that divides it. Name me one committed Atheist who has committed genocide. Every war that you can ever, will ever call to mind has religion as its core; it has been the cause or the comfort for the victor and the vanquished. For example, I have always been taken with the irony of the crusades, that it was done in God's name! So much suffering and death in the name of one god, to crush the followers of another. Defending one set of spiritual morals by doing the opposite of what they demand and destroying somebody else's. Isn't it ironic that evil is the one thing that binds us? We are all capable of it and every race and religion have gladly pursued it with equal vigour, in the naive belief that theirs was in some way superior. If you think about it, evil provides more commonality

	that any collection of gods. Who would have thought it? Humanity has made evil ecumenical. *(Paulette is staring at him)*. Oh, don't use up all that hatred too soon, pretty lady. We'll have an eternity to hate each other's company. I can hardly wait. *(He makes to leave)*. See you on the other side. How exciting. Chin chin. *(He exits)*.
Antoine	If only I had listened to you.
Young Paul	No. What matters is that whatever happens now, happens to us both
Antoine	God bless you, Paulette. If your purity means anything, God will see it, see you.
Young Paul	God? Have you found your faith again, Father?
Antoine	I think He has found me. I realise that now. He was always there. I think I just chose not to see, to listen because it was easier to hate, than have faith. You only appreciate the test of faith when you know yourself and then recognise your image in Him, appreciate His plan for you.
Young Paul	And what is that plan?
Antoine	Of that I am not sure. But when he is ready, he will show me.

Claude enters the scene urgently, quickly. He stops behind them and kneels.

Young Paul	You. Is it you? Really you?
Claude	Paulette, Antoine, I could not …
Antoine	Not what? Be honest, truthful?
Claude	That's unfair.
Antoine	Unfair?
Young Paul	Let him speak.
Antoine	And what now? You lead us to our fate slaughter man?
Young Paul	Antoine. Do you think he has a choice?
Antoine	We all have choices. The issue is the one we make and worst, the ones we choose to ignore.
Claude	If only life were that simple.
Antoine	And will death be?
Claude	The choice is not mine; it is still yours. But first of all, I am here to help you get free. We can debate what you think of me some other time.
Antoine	Freedom at your hands and death at theirs?
Young Paul	He means it. Please Antoine.
Claude	There is a way.
Young Paul	Claude! I knew you had not abandoned us!
Antoine	Is this true, or another lie of this place? Please do not give me hope and then…
Claude	No lies. I am sorry for not being able to explain. I had to play my part. Convince them. And now you must be convinced. You must trust me now. I am the only truth here. Please believe me, Antoine. No matter what happens, I need at least to know I had your trust, your friendship, if you can give it. And a chance to give us all the life, the love we deserve.
Young Paul	I can, I do.
Claude	If only we were in a different place, in a different time. What would the world hold in store for us?

Young Paul   As long as we were together, would it matter?

He finishes untying them. They stand and then after a pause, embrace as one.

Antoine   Faith has so many obstacles. But a true soul cannot be ignored, erased, obscured. Thank god for you Claude. Which way do we go?
Young Paul   How much time do we have?
Antoine   Will they not know you are with us?
Young Paul   Claude?
Claude   I am not with you. I cannot come. I must stay. I am here to help you, but to do so I must remain here.
Young Paul   You found us, you saved us before. You must know a way out of here?! Did your little speech just now mean nothing?
Antoine   You owe them nothing. You have tried. We know you have tried, god knows that. Forget history and family responsibility. Come with us.
Claude   I cannot.
Young Paul   Claude? Please? Give the future, us, the chance we deserve.
Claude   I cannot just walk away from here, Paulette; and neither can you.
Young Paul   What do you mean? You can. We can. It starts with the first step and before that is the will.
Antoine   More damn riddles.
Claude   It is not that simple.
Antoine   Damn you and your secrets!
Claude   Indeed. I am damned. I hope that some point, sometime in the future, God will forgive me. But more than anything else, I will damn myself for not being able to do anything to help you now. But if an eternity of being damned means I might have helped the one person, the people, that have mattered to me more than anything else in my recent world, then so be it. You are both my hope. You are both my salvation. Don't cheat me of that.

They again embrace again as one.

Antoine   Then what do we do?
Claude   What happened in 1916 will begin again shortly. So has been the case at preordained times on thousands of occasions for the past, nearly twenty-five years as you and I know it, but also for millennia before. To them 1916 was only yesterday. And so it will be again very soon. And before them was another war, another atrocity stretching back into antiquity. Another collection of souls trapped here, playing out their history. And another one of my ancestors. And before you ask, they must kill and themselves be killed again. Tatar is about balance; the status quo. If they do not repeat the atrocity, the balance is upset and they will descend to something far worse than this. Whilst they live a hell on earth, they avoid another hell below it. And if souls are not gathered on this side, then whatever is on the other side could…
Antoine   My god. Hell on earth.
Claude   Yes. And if they do descend, then whoever is remaining here will have to take their place, relive a new nightmare until a new atrocity and a new set of souls replaces them. So is the status quo. So is the secret of Tatar. Now you

	know everything… and now, my dear friends, you also now know that you are a part of it, unless…
Young Paul	Unless?
Claude	Unless we can maintain the status quo, Paulette.
Young Paul	That damned phrase!
Claude	The key is why my family have been in this place since, for ever. We are unaffected by it, by them. We provide the continuity that allows the balance to be maintained. We are the gate keepers of it. The book sets out how it was and will always be and we, I, must be the custodian. A passage from it must be read by me at the exact moment when the atrocity is again played out. I must read as was the case with my ancestors. That's why the Captain keeps saying that damned phrase: "Read the Book, say the words". I and my family are damned as well. We ensure the status quo because we are it. And by our actions we ensure that all good souls have no end by keeping the bad ones away. Good souls like you, Paulette. You made a big play of choices, perhaps you now understand mine.
Young Paul	I did not know then what I know now. That you carry this burden, this responsibility alone. Forgive me. Again.
Claude	And there is one chance.
Antoine	Then what are we waiting for…
Claude	…but at a price. A heavy, eternal price. *(Reading).* "To take, thou must give. To live there must be death. The ultimate sacrifice borne out of love, out of faith, is thine only escape". One of you can go. But one must stay. One can live, but one must die.
Young Paul	Then we both stay. Antoine can leave and …

SFX #9: battlefield sounds are heard.

Claude	It begins. It may be too late. The battle signifies the beginning of the atrocity. The advancing French troops. Any moment the French arrive again. And then …

Paulette and Claude embrace. Antoine stands facing front; blank, unemotional, to himself.

Antoine	It is never too late. If you have faith and love, nothing is ever too late, no one is too late. And no soul can be allowed to end.

In the darkness up stage, the four soldiers and the Captain now appear in silhouette, facing up stage and the advancing unseen French villagers.

Captain	Stand your ground lads! Here they come! The French villagers!
Carter	Not again! *(The lighting that provides the silhouette changes to a deep, vivid red. Paulette and Claude are now knelt, facing each other, staring into each other's eyes, Antoine still facing front, apart from them).* Please! No! No! We didn't mean to do it! He made us! *(He falls to the ground as the Captain shoots him).*
Captain	Get up and fight, Carter. The villagers shouldn't have guns. What is happening?
Klaus	Please, I surrender; we didn't mean to kill them!

Captain	Quiet, you damn cowards! Where are you? Claude! Read the book, say the words! It isn't supposed to happen like this
Geneux	I am a French soldier. Mon dieu! Mon dieu!
Captain	French soldiers? No! This is wrong! They should not be here now. Claude! What have you done?

Geneux falls down. Antoine speaks to himself, aloud

Antoine	We must all make sacrifices. Some are more important than I ever knew at the time. But I know now. I understand. Matthew 10:39. "He who finds his life will lose it, and he who loses his life for my sake will find it". I have found my destiny and with it, their salvation. I now see his plan and my place in it. *(He turns to Young Paulette and Claude).* Until we meet again.

Young Paulette realises Claude is leaving.

Claude	Antoine?

Klaus falls to the ground, shot. Without warning Antoine turns and slowly walks back upstage and stretches out his arms and occupies the position, now also in silhouette alongside the soldiers.

Young Paulette	Antoine? What are you doing? Antoine no, come back! *(She wants to run to Antoine, but Claude holds her back).* Let me go! Let me go… Antoine, please!
Antoine	In his name and for your sake… *(He falls to the ground, shot).*
Captain	What have you done, priest? Claude, it has to be now! Read the book! Say the words or all is lost. Now!
Claude	We can't wait any longer. I need to get you away from here now!
Young Paul	No! Antoine! It is too late
Claude	He did this for you. Don't let all of this be in vain. Take this and with it the secret. *(He gives her the book).* Perhaps the status quo has now at last come to an end. Run, Paulette… Run!

They embrace. Young Paulette kisses Claude, then starts to exit, running off stage. As she does so, she fumbles as she moves and drops the book. She attempts to find it on the floor in the semi-darkness (but doesn't). During all of this, Claude moves up stage and takes the place, in silhouette, with the soldiers. The lights rise on Older Paulette who is standing.

Paulette	As I ran and dropped that damned book. I sensed he was not by my side. But my need to follow his instructions and keep the book safe was all consuming, until…
Young Paul	Claude! I have dropped the book; I can't find it… help me, quickly! Claude? Claude? *(She stops, realising he is not with her).*
Claude	All of this must end and only I can do it.
Paulette	That simple sentence and I realised. I realised that my only hope of happiness had slipped from my grasp, and all for my sake.
Young Paul	Claude?
Claude	For the greater good. For my family. For you.
Claude/Paul	A gift for all time
Young Paul	What are you doing? Claude! Claude! Stop!

Claude falls to the ground shot.

Captain	Claude! What have you done? What have you done?
Young Paul	Claude! Claude!
Captain	Get back, get back! *(He falls to the ground, shot).*

The lights fade on where the soldiers had been. The lights now also slowly fade on Younger Paulette as they are both calling out. SFX #9 fades out.

Paul/Young P Claude! Claude! Claude!

Scene 4

As the lights fade on all but Older Paulette only her voice is heard, speaking softly.

Paulette Dear sweet, beautiful Claude. "A gift for all time", he said. The note he left in the book. He planned it that way all along. I have dreamt of him, that note, and what we might have had all these years since. If those words could have been played out. *(Silence.as she dries her eyes with a handkerchief. The lights now fade up on the open doorway with the silhouette of the man from the opening scene within it).* So that's the story of the book. I ran. As hard and as fast as I could. I didn't stop until 1945. In my haste I left the book where it had fallen, lost, I thought, forever. Until now. Shortly after the war had ended, the German philosopher Karl Jaspers wrote: "That which has happened is a warning. To forget it is guilt. It was possible for this to happen, and it remains possible for it to happen again at any minute". And so he might have also written of Tatar. There is one thing that we must all do: watch. Never stop watching. Evil is the cancer of mankind and one day, any day, it will return. *(She pauses).* I know what you must be thinking. I thought it for years. But it is true. Every word. Every secret. And now, one more person knows of it. *(She looks at the book).* Dear, sweet, beautiful, Claude. All this you did for me. And Antoine; for the love of me and for a lost belief, never really lost. Both paid the ultimate price so that the world would never know, never have to endure again, Chateaux Tatar and the abomination it concealed. And this book is all that remains. Anima Saeculorum. 'Soul Without End'. A book which proves that a soul never dies, but it must be accountable. Status quo. How I still hate that phrase. And this book is the only remainder, reminder of a secret that would ever have stayed such had you not found this and brought it to me. Thank you, monsieur. You will never know what this means to me. I know you have a buyer. But name your price, what would be adequate recompense?

Man *(No longer in a French accent).* Just the restoration of the status quo… pretty lady. *(The lights behind him that provides the silhouette now turns the same vivid red as earlier. She immediately sinks to her seat, apparently struggling to catch her breath and is slowly frozen in position, apart from her facial expressions).* Feel familiar? Fighting to breathe, to move? Are you on the battlefield again? Does the darkness begin to surround you? Can you smell the aroma of death once more? Can you sense Tatar beginning to embrace you? Did you really think we would ever forget you? Moreover, did you ever think that Tatar would forget you? The Chateaux has a long memory, Madame. *(SFX#10: unearthly sounds are heard).* We all miss you. My men miss you. Tatar misses you more. Did you really think you could just walk away so easily? Dear Claude thought his sacrifice was your salvation, but in reality, it was your damnation. No Claude, no status quo. No happy ending. Such a long time since all the players have been available to take up their roles. To you it must seem years. To us, only a few minutes ago that you went away. And how we have all missed you. Time means nothing there. So… Time to come home, pretty lady. And time to take the place you cheated Tatar of: our new Claude. You will be pleased to know that the old place has hardly changed. Except… well, with all that has gone on in the intervening years in the world with death, war, destruction, unholy slaughter, there are so many, many, new faces who are, how can I say, just dying to meet you. Do you hear it calling to you? Oh, and I will be needing the book you borrowed from us. Well, you'll be needing it. We can't have a gate without a keeper, can we? Remember your favourite phrase? Status quo? The book's return is long overdue. And I fear you will have a fine to pay. A debt as old as time, or should I say: "a soul without end".

The light on the Man fades out and he exits. As he does so the light from the table lamp gets dimmer as she becomes more frantic. Older Paulette screams. SFX #10 ends suddenly with a snap blackout. SFX #11: music plays to cover the calls (the main theme from the film 'The Fury'). It continues as the audience exits.

THE END

'The King's Orphan'
Synopsis.
During the Great War, one hundred and sixteen young men who had attended Blackburn Orphanage in Lancashire, went to war to fight for their King and their Country. Ten of them never returned. One of them was only recorded by his name, William North... the forgotten orphan.

'The King's Orphan' tells the story of the life of an unknown, or rather, creates for him a life, an opportunity to be remembered. It is not a factual account but gives a glimpse of lives through the cracks in history; an orphan who died for King and Country and through theatre, is given a chance to take his place in history.

This is one of many stories of how a generation of ordinary men did an extraordinary thing. But this story illustrates how some men went to war to fight for something bigger; to fight for a family they did not know and for the families of men they could never know. And in this case, with a set of values, self-respect, dignity and desire for a better life and a better world which all came from one couple; a man and wife that popular history fights to forget: the orphanage founder James Dixon and his wife, Jane.

Their Boys may have been orphans. Their Boys may have given their lives for their King. But they did so having been given a special gift from special people. Hope

Characters (3m, 2f) – *2m, 2f if characters double as suggested*

William North   18-30, an orphan and later, a soldier, Lancashire accent.
James Dixon   40-50, founder and first Superintendent of Blackburn Orphanage, Scottish accent.
Jane Dixon   40-50, James Dixon's wife, Lancashire accent.
Maude Thomas   18-30, orphan and later, William North's fiancé, Lancashire accent.
Parsons   50, Soldier, Lancashire accent. Written as to double with James.

Context
Only James and Jane Dixon are 'known' historical figures; the remainder are dramatic recreations. Some of the Dixon's language is recovered from historical records, accounts, journals and particularly those belonging to James. Much is created in the style of the people and their era. But the intention is that the blend of real people with a created storyline contextualises the era and the characters. Hopefully, this affords the opportunity to give a grounding and realism to their dialogue and their story.

Although the story of William North is not historically factual and the relationships with the Dixons and the other characters wholly fictional, the intention is that it will be 'true' to them and moreover, the time. The overriding feature is that as far as possible, James Dixon is factually 'untouched'. And if for dramatic purposes it is occasionally necessary to colour the character, it is done in a style and spirit which is sensitive to the man, his mission, values and aspirations... especially those for his 'boys and girls'.

Writer's Note

If the performance of this piece is not animated, is not alive, it will be a dry history lecture. Make it live. Make them live. Give the audience a reason to remember them.

My grateful thanks go to Melanie Warren, the author of 'James Dixon's Children; the story of Blackburn Orphanage'.

Martin Paul Roche

First Performed

The play premiered at Guide Bridge Theatre, Tameside, Greater Manchester in February 2019. It was directed by Tracey Rontree with the following cast:

William North	Nathan Simpson
James Dixon	Michael Lawlor
Jane Dixon	Joy Siddall
Maude Thomas	Kira Richardson

"I have admired the work of Martin Paul Roche for some time now and was really looking forward to his latest play 'The King's Orphan'; I was not disappointed. The script was brilliantly devised calling upon a mixture of well researched fact and truly felt fiction to create a gripping play."

"A very moving story. Portrayed with great empathy."

"To be honest, if you were asked to join up, seeing this play, you wouldn't think twice about doing so."

"A very moving and stirring account brought to the page and stage by the talented Mr Roche!"

"Moments of comedy sandwiched between lovely scenes of tenderness and high drama which were balanced and judged and brought to life by a strong cast, which shared a great chemistry on stage."

"I know from the reaction of the audience tonight, this production, will be … remembered."

"We laughed out loud during act 1 and cried like babies during act 2 … loved it! You should be very proud! Martin Paul Roche"

"Huge well done to Martin Paul Roche for creating such a wonderful play. Not a dry eye in the house … simply stunning … so moving - so brilliant."

"Last night I was in the audience for this premiere. A very moving story, brilliantly written, directed and performed by all. Huge congratulations to Martin Paul Roche and everybody involved. Extremely well done!"

"Just returned home after watching The King's Orphan … TBH if you were asked to join up, seeing this play, you wouldn't think twice about doing so."

"Brilliant play, very moving, superb acting and direction."

"We were there also this evening. Brilliant play, very moving, superb acting and direction."

"What a gem! 'The King's Orphan' at Guide Bridge Theatre. A script that moves an audience from tears to laughter and back again - not just once but again and again. A powerful piece of theatre Martin Paul Roche."

Some of the audience feedback on social media following the premiere.

ACT ONE
Scene 1

The Trenches. SFX #01: the sound of bombardment is heard, heavy guns in the background. Distant flashes are seen.

Parsons   It's started, lad,
William   I'll make you a promise. I'll compose this letter. I'll write this minute to Maude, tell her how I feel; and ask her to marry me when I get home. But only if you'll compose something for me
Parsons   A letter?
William   A prayer.
Parsons   What? For who?
William   The world.
Parsons   Not much, then?
William   From little acorns, Mr Parsons. Little acorns.
Parsons   I'm afraid that with all I've seen, I have little faith in acorns, in prayer, or in God.
William   Maybe. But he's never lost faith in you.
Parsons   Thank you, son. I just wish that, with all you have been through, and now being here, you had someone back home to call you 'son'.
William   I have, Mr Parsons. He's called James Dixon.

SFX #02: the bombardment stops, silence ensues, then a distant whistle sounds.

Parsons   Time for letters is over. And stay by my side... son. *(He climbs over the top of the trench).*
William   Promise me, Mr Parsons... *(He grabs hold of Parsons).* Promise me you'll pray... promise me, promise me?

Snap blackout. SFX 03: the sounds of war begin to fade and are replaced by the sound of children playing, laughing, singing nursey rhymes. William enters still wearing his army uniform but carrying an army kit bag which has his school uniform in it. He looks around and takes in his surroundings. During the early part of what follows he gets changed into his school clothes. He is passionate, animated; equally, when needed, he uses stillness to good effect.

William   By God. It's good to be home. 'Home'. It doesn't matter who you are, what you are. To be back in the first place you ever truly felt you belonged. Well. What more could one ever wish for? Don't you think?

            I am 'Nobody'. You will have met me. You will have been me at some time. I was also 'Somebody'. Once. Very quickly, I became 'Nobody' again. And finally, I was 'Forgotten'. I became 'Forgotten'. Have you ever even considered what it is to be 'Forgotten'? Do you <u>know</u>? Do you <u>care</u>? Oh, you should. Because you will be. Mark my words. But don't get all worked up about it. Because by the time you're one of the 'Forgotten', you won't be here to care. For most people, 'Forgotten' is an eternity. Natural. Expected. That is, unless you just happen to cross paths with a chap called 'Chance' who knows another fellow called 'Coincidence' and then the 'Luck' twins, 'Good' and 'Bad' they're called. You need to watch out for them. Pair of buggers, they are. Excuse my profanity. And if, just if, all those fellows come together in your life in the right order, it becomes irrelevant whether you were 'Somebody' or 'Nobody' because you just might attain a status which is beyond comprehension. You are 'Remembered'. And all that my friends happens if you have been on good terms with the last fellow of all: 'Destiny'. But becoming 'Remembered'. By gum! It is bigger than life or death, riches or wealth, influence or power. Whether you are a King... or an Orphan. And it can connect the two. So, you see, even a 'Nobody' can play a small part in *making* history. Whether history remembers that 'Nobody', well, that's a matter for you. Isn't it? And the fact that you are here and listening to me, now, has already set that in motion. Welcome to making your own personal history, my friends. Welcome to my friend 'Destiny'. And welcome to my story; a story that could so easily have been yours... and still could. *(James Dixon enters and sits at his desk. William's demeanour changes, now warmer, engaged by the man before him).* Now then. Meet James Dixon. Superintendent of the newly opened Blackburn Orphanage in Wilpshire. A Scot. Born in Annan in 1855. And at precisely 4.30pm on the 18th July 1878 he arrived here in Lancashire aged just twenty-three years. He would remain here for the rest of his life. And what a life. Now here was 'Somebody'. He kept a journal, as his father did before him. Even in the early pages of it, the nature of the man is laid down.

James — *(Writing in his journal).* "Note: the average duration of life in towns is thirty-eight years; in the country, fifty-five years. One hundred and fifty children out of a thousand die during the first year of their birth; fifty more during the second year; fifty-eight more during the next three years; and nineteen more during the next two years. Thus two hundred and seventy-seven die in seven years from their birth. Note: more things than what we feel, see and touch: goodness, kindness, modesty, courage, unselfishness... must teach what will stand the wear and tear of life; goodness, God... suffering, all sorts of trouble for nothing else, but to make us good. Note: the delicate threads of life may snap at any moment. See? I think I can speak for myself, laddie.

William — That he can. That he will. And all because of this man, so can I. Formal introductions. I am William North. I was born in 1893 here in Lancashire. I had a father obviously, but not one to touch, to hold, to know. I'm not sure what is worse: having a bad memory of a person, or none at all. Anyhow, good, bad or indifferent, it always felt like I was incomplete, that part of me was missing, until nine years later. Nine years old and I arrived here at the new Blackburn Orphanage having been given up by my pauper family. Oh yes, given up. Love for your child doesn't put food on the table. And one more mouth to feed can mean not enough for all the others. Pushed out by a sibling and the reality of poverty and survival. A tough first lesson in life for a nine-year-old 'Nobody'. *(Jane and Maude enter).* Jane Dixon. James' wife and co-architect of the goodness and charity which was their lives and the orphanage at Wilpshire. A life which nurtured me, created me, saved me. And Maude Thomas. More about her later. *(Jane starts ringing a hand bell*

	that she has carried on with her and which now breaks the silence). 1893. Happy Birthday me!
Maude	1893. The Independent Labour Party is founded just over the border in Bradford.
Jane	Working men wanted a voice and the MP Kier Hardy was elected its first chairman.
James	For the first time they had hopes, expectations, aspirations.
William	And also, in Yorkshire, the founding of the Brontë Society.
Maude	The School Attendance Act raises the school leaving age in England and Wales, to eleven.
Jane	The first students enter St Hilda's College, Oxford, a college founded for women.
James	*(In a well-spoken English accent).* Women? In a College? Whatever next?
Jane	*(As James).* The vote, perhaps?
All	Heaven forbid.
Maude	And in Britain, we invent a process for producing hollow cast, lead toy soldiers.
William	Who would have thought it.
Maude	Hollow cast soldiers.
William	Helping little boys to play at war.
Maude	Do they need any help? To hate? To kill?
William	*(To the audience).* I don't know. Do we?
Maude	We'll see, won't we?

Jane rings bell. Maude sits on the bench.

James	*(Reading from a ledger).* "Blackburn Orphanage Admittance Record, 22nd November 1902. Case number B0109. William North is admitted this day. Age last birthday: nine.
William	*(Waving at the audience).* Hello! *(Jane slaps him across the back of the head).*
James	"The boy's Father worked in a Foundry and died from pneumonia in 1899. Mother is a charwoman and gets two shillings a week from the town. William has four sisters, one of whom is already resident in the orphanage and one younger brother. Grandfather is a pauper aged 80 years. Family belong St Thomas' Church, Blackburn". *(He closes the book and invites William to him by beckoning).* Well, William, welcome to Wilpshire. Lot of w's there wouldn't you say?
William	Well…
James	*(He laughs).* Another 'w'. Sense of humour. Good.
William	Have I?
James	Modesty too. You'll do fine here
William	Thank God.
James	And an understanding of the Lord and his gifts. Excellent. Now on your way to class. *(He exits).*
William	*(He sighs, relieved, then looks out front).* I think I've just said the right thing, but I don't know what I said. Bloody hell!

Jane   *(Clouting him across the back of the head).* Profanity, William. *(She exits ringing her bell).*

Maude stands and moves, leaving her teddy bear on the floor. She and William stare at each, contemplating each other for a moment as only children (or cats) can.

William	What you lookin' at?
Maude	Not sure
William	What do you mean?
Maude	Thick as well.
William	You new here as well?
Maude	What do you think?
William	You forgot your toy.
Maude	She's not a toy. *(She picks it up).*
William	What is she then?
Maude	She's somebody.
William	I'm going to be somebody.
Maude	You're nobody. Like me.
William	Who says?
Maude	People.
William	Well, what do you know?
Maude	More than you, y'daft 'apeth. *(She pokes her tongue out at him).*
William	Well, you're a cheeky… *(Maude exits, running off. Jane enters, making to exit opposite. As she does, he calls after Maude).* Cheeky bugger!
Jane	*(Clouting him in passing as before, and, without stopping she exits, saying).* Profanity, William; profanity.

William goes to call out again.

William   You're still a cheeky… *(He ducks, just in case, looks around and then exits, skipping off).*

At the same time James and Jane enter to different parts of the stage which are initially in darkness and then speak to the audience.

Jane	Beginnings.
James	Stories often have more than one.
Jane	Introductions.
James	Who we meet.
Jane	Impressions.
James	Choices.
Jane	Who we remember.
James	Why we remember.
Jane	If we remember.
James	Shortly after moving to Blackburn, I was walking the streets of the town and witnessed half a dozen boys sleeping out, crouched in a doorway. I resolved there and then that something needed to be done and I established a Ragged School in Leyland Street, Blackburn.
Jane	On the 15th December 1891, James placed his life savings of fifty pounds in the bank to start the building fund for an orphanage

James	It was the first step in a caring career and it would become my life, well, not all of it.
Jane	*(Changing her accent).* "On Saturday 17th March 1891 Mr James Dixon, secretary and one of the founders of the Blackburn Ragged School was married at St George's Presbyterian Church this morning to Miss Jane McLellan who has been a teacher at the Ragged School since its commencement. A number of ladies and gentlemen interested in the school witnessed the ceremony".

SFX #04: church bells are heard. James and Jane come together, holding hands. Maude and William enter, running on, and throw some confetti in the air over the happy couple.

Will & Maude	Hurrah!

William, Maude and Jane exit.

James	Ladies and gentlemen. I thank you for attending today. We receive children into the Orphanage of almost all creeds and denominations and some who have no creeds. Want is the first consideration and needy cases of orphans and destitute children left homeless are admitted at once without formalities. No fatherless and motherless child, mentally and physically fit, is ever refused admission. And the greatest evil of all, the one that runs like a seam of despair in every case and indeed, throughout our society, is drink.

Fade to black. SFX #05: the sound of a school bell ringing and children singing nursery rhymes is heard.

Scene 2

James is sitting at a small writing desk with a pile of papers. Jane enters with cup of tea and a broom. She gives the tea to James.

Jane	How are the bills looking?
James	Still like bills.
Jane	Staring at them won't help us find the money to pay them.
James	I know.
Jane	I love seeing you at this desk. It was a fine wedding gift from the Board.
James	It was our only wedding gift. But then again, some gifts have no price.
Jane	*(Kissing James on the forehead and begins sweeping the confetti up, pausing as appropriate).* Indeed they don't. So. How much have we got?
James	Not enough.
Jane	We have the orphanage. Never lose sight of that. Five thousand pounds, James. That's how much you have raised, and you started with just fifty pounds of your own. You've achieved a great thing.
James	We Jane. We. And God. And we will always have each other.
Jane	Indeed.
James	The list is never-ending. I hadn't appreciated all the things that an orphanage would need. Last night's committee meeting brought it home to me. Fire grates, wash-house fittings, plaster cornices, fifty pine boxes for lockers, boot racks, plate racks, peaked caps for the bigger boys, sailor caps for the

	younger ones. And then there's the tenders to draw up, the contracts to consider and…
Jane	…and the small matter of how much we have achieved, the children we have helped, the good we have done, <u>will</u> do.
James	I know. But how can we be sure that what we are doing is right? That we are getting it right?
Jane	James, I don't know. Who could know? But I know this. I walk around this town and see the poverty and despair, all fuelled by the curse of drink. And then I return to here. And all I have to do is open my eyes and see just one life being placed on a different track. A track which offers no promises about the destination but is paved with hope. Which is lit by the lamps of faith. And has been built by a man who has cared enough to care. I look into the faces of the children whom we care for and remember the story that their eyes told us when they walked through those doors. If just one child is given hope, a life, an opportunity, then what price do we put on that? What measure could show anything else other than we have done right by them? *(James stands and embraces her).* And to prove my point… *(She produces an envelope from her apron pocket, takes out the letter from it, and hands it to James).*
James	What's this?
Jane	A prayer answered. The reason why we have faith, and proof that we are getting it right.
James	*(Reading it quickly).* Is this real? Please tell me this is real?
Jane	It is. A cheque from Mrs Yerburgh. One thousand pounds, James. One thousand!
James	A thousand pounds! The giver of all good again influences the hearts of those to whom He has given the silver and the gold, to give it freely to the Lord's work. The good book indeed speaks to us. He truly is a father to the fatherless.
Jane	So maybe, just maybe, you are getting it right after all?
James	No. But <u>we</u> are. *(He hugs Jane).*

The lights crossfade to Maude who is sitting on a bench holding her teddy bear. William enters and walks past her. He pauses when he sees her. Uncomfortable. On edge. He is wearing a sailor's cap. As he walks past she sings the first few lines of a song from 'HMS Pinafore'.

Maude	"We sail the ocean blue and our saucy ships a beauty…". *(William stops in his tracks, spins around as she stops singing, and glares at her. She smiles back).* Hello. Jolly Jack Tar. Where are you sailing to today then? Setting out on the noon tide perchance… in your hat?
William	Are you making fun of me?
Maude	Me? Goodness, no. Why would I do such a thing? You're managing just fine on your own, I think. *(Beat).* Lovely hat.
William	Sorry?
Maude	Lovely hat. Very nautical. Jaunty. Gay.
William	I don't think I like you.
Maude	I know I don't like you. *(William goes to walk away. She talks to her bear which stops him).* Well then, Bear, we'd best be off.

William	Bear?
Maude	Sorry?
William	Bear?
Maude	Meaning?
William	Bear?
Maude	Have you got a stutter?
William	Like you've got no imagination?
Maude	Meaning?
William	You've got a bear… and he's called Bear?
Maude	She. And what would you call her?
William	Don't know. Never thought about it 'cos I've not got a bear. Called Bear. But I think I could do better than 'Bear'.
Maude	*(Moving towards William, very close, making him uncomfortable)*. Do you know who she is, what she is? *(Beat)*. Well? *(No answer)*. She is my best friend. She is my only friend. She listens. She never criticises. She's an orphan like me. Abandoned. But she will always be there. No matter what. Is that good enough for you, sailor boy?
William	I'm sorry.
Maude	Yes, well, you'd best be off. *(William makes to exit)*. After all, you've got a boat to catch! *(She exits, running off in the opposite direction)*.

William turns to call after Maude. As he does so, James enters behind him.

William	You're still a cheeky bugger!
James	*(Hitting William across the back of the head as he crosses the stage)*. Profanity, William. *(He carries on walking and exits, opposite)*.

As James does so Jane enters to cross back, unseen by William who turns to the front, and, in a rage, takes off his hat, throws it on the floor, and stamps on it. As she crosses, Jane hits him across the back of the head and continues to exit.

Jane	Temper, William.
William	*(Sitting grumpily on the floor he puts his sailor hat back on and sulks with his chin in his hands. He looks off after Maude and then smiles which turns into a laugh)*. I will be somebody, Maude. You just wait and see. I'll make you proud of me. I'll make Mr and Mrs Dixon proud of me. And Bear! *(He exits, running off)*.
Jane	*(Entering, she sits at the desk and looks in James' journal)*. Every hope, fear, aspiration; every good idea, every quote, James wrote in his journal. Every fragment of common sense written by him and others, all were captured by him. Re-reading them all seemed to help him to focus on, well, on everything. To make sense of his own values, his own beliefs, and those inherited, passed down from his father. It shaped him and in turn, he passed it all on to the children of the orphanage, his children, our children. He helped to shape what he hoped they might become.

James enters. Jane hands him his journal and he addresses the audience from it. With each phrase, he changes his physical perspective and delivery, as if they are sentiments repeated on different occasions to different children.

James "You may apprehend but cannot comprehend".
"Those persons or actions we can say no good of, we had best say nothing of".
"Saul lost his kingdom for want of two or three hours patience".
"You may as soon find a living man without breath as a living Christian without prayer".
"Hard arguments do best with soft words".
"Hard words indeed break no bones but many a heart has been broken by them".
"To render good for good is human, evil for evil is brutish, good for evil is Christian, but evil for good is devilish".
War is a tragedy which destroys the stage upon which it is acted".
(Now back to addressing the audience). And no matter what I read, considered and impressed on the children, Jane was more than capable of doing the same. *(He exits).*

Jane "The children of this orphanage are taught the importance of the basic elements of kindness, sharing and friendship. Their thoughts and actions are influenced by lessons from the bible and how the smallest of good deeds can shape the opinions of those around us. We need to treat each other how we would like to be treated and every small act counts towards creating a good first impression". *(William and Maude enter from opposite sides of the stage. As they meet each other CS, he smiles and cautiously presents her with an apple. She takes it, takes a bite out of it, abruptly gives it him back, and exits without speaking. He exits).* "The children of this orphanage are also taught the importance of caring. How each good gesture makes us a better person and brings out the best in other people. How giving something we value to another and without expectation, can demonstrate so much about us".
(William and Maude enter from opposite sides of the stage. As they meet each other CS, he presents her with a flower. She takes it, snaps it in two, gives it back, and exits without speaking. Jane approaches William). And so William, what has today's sermon taught us? If at first we don't succeed, what must we do?

William Give up.

Blackout.

Scene 3

Jane is sitting at the desk, reading from a newspaper.

Jane *(Reading).* "One poor, miserable little girl was found at eleven o'clock at night in a common lodging-house of anything but good repute. Mr. Dixon made enquiries, and, finding that the child was friendless, offered to take her home with him to the Orphanage. The gift of an orange seemed to the little one a proof of the rescuer's bona-fide intent, so she trustfully and gladly agreed to go with him. On passing out into the street however, she suddenly drew back, and looking into her new-found friend's face pleaded: "I wish you'd take my brother too; if you will, I'll give you this orange". *(She puts the paper aside)*. Until then, Mr Dixon had been unaware of the existence of any brother, but such an appeal was not to be resisted. So, guided by the sister, the boy was sought out, and both were taken into the Home. The boy was found to be seriously ill, the result chiefly of neglect, and the doctor, on being called in, solemnly shook his head. "The boy won't live long", said he; "there is tuberculosis in the bone, and even if an operation were performed, it couldn't prolong the poorly little chap's life much". But the Superintendent of the Home and his wife had great faith in Wilpshire air and Wilpshire nursing, and, at their request the operation was performed. For weeks, nay, months, it was uncertain whether the poor little patient would ever recover, but little by little, health and strength returned to him, and eventually, by God's blessing, he was able to make his way about the place on crutches, and, marvellous though it seemed to all concerned, he was able to take his share in the children's much-loved games of football. That lad is today a married man with two bonny children of his own, occupying a responsible and well-paid position in Blackburn. Mr Dixon, some little time since, found opportunity to visit him, but on this occasion the 'Old Boy' insisted on being host, and no host could have fulfilled the title better. He said to Mr Dixon: "You saved my life, sir. No more, no less. And now, look into my children's eyes as you did mine all those years ago; for now they are as much yours as they are mine".

Scene 4

A few years have passed. Maude is discovered, sitting on a bench. William enters aimlessly, he looks at her and she does not look up. She has a bundle of loose paper and is writing on it with a pencil. She has a small teddy bear on her lap. He meanders over to her, clearly trying to pluck up the courage to speak. He is rehearsing it behind her. After a short while she realises he is there and turns around and discovers him 'practising' but he pretends to be doing something else. Eventually...

William	Hello. *(No answer)*. I said hello. I said…
Maude	I heard you
William	I've not seen you around much. I said…
Maude	I heard you.
William	I was just sayin', I've not seen you around. Well. I have seen you, obviously.
Maude	We've both been here six years. Not that difficult.
William	*(Pausing)*. But, well, we've never spoken. Not proper…
Maude	*(Beat)*. …lee
William	Who is?
Maude	Lee.
William	Sorry?
Maude	Proper-<u>lee</u>.
William	Right. Anyhow. We haven't spoken proper-<u>lee</u>. Well, apart from a few times: you pulled your tongue out; I laughed at Bear. You laughed at my clothes. I called you a silly *(whispering)*, bugger. You slapped me across the face, trampled on the flowers I gave you. If all that counts; a sort of speaking. *(No answer)*. But we've not ever spoken, civil like.
Maude	Then you won't be disappointed now then, will you?

163

William	Happen not. *(No answer)*. We came in here on the same day y'know.
Maude	Fascinating.
William	Eh?
Maude	What horses eat.
William	Sorry?
Maude	Accepted.
William	I've wanted to talk to you, but I'm, well, you know. Shy like
Maude	All evidence to the contrary.
William	*(Pausing)*. You'll be fifteen by now, then. I'm fifteen now.
Maude	Congratulations.
William	It's not my birthday.
Maude	Pity.
William	Why?
Maude	You might have been at a party.
William	Party?
Maude	Not here?
William	Oh. Aye. *(Silence)*. What are you doing? Are you writing?
Maude	What does it look like?
William	You're writing.
Maude	Then I'm writing.
William	What are you writing?
Maude	Stuff.
William	Stuff?
Maude	Yep.

William stands, looking over her shoulder. Maude turns the papers over, staring forward. He moves away. She resumes writing.

William	Still writing then?
Maude	I am now.
William	What y' writing?
Maude	Words.
William	And what do they say?
Maude	Stuff.
William	What type of stuff?
Maude	Stuff made from words.
William	But what…
Maude	A poem. It's a poem. Satisfied? Now go away.
William	Poem? That's like, well, what would you call it?
Maude	A poem.
William	Yes, but a poem is like,
Maude	Poetry.
William	I know but poetry is well, it's like,
Maude	Words.
William	Aye, but together it's, it's…

Maude is by now staring at him, and then:

Together	…a poem.

Maude resumes her writing. She has her teddy on her lap throughout.

William	That'll be the teddy bear you had when we first met. Is she still called Bear?
Maude	No. She got married.
William	Really? *(Maude stares at him).* No, right. Bear it is then.
Maude	Good memory.
William	Thanks.
Maude	It was a statement of fact, not a compliment.
William	Eh? I mean, pardon.
Maude	How do you know it's the same bear?
William	It looks like it, so it must be.
Maude	My. You're getting sharper by the minute.
William	Eh?
Maude	Still what horses eat.
William	Bugger.
Maude	Profanity. *(William ducks).* Why are you ducking?
William	Habit. *(Pause).* But why are you writing?
Maude	Why are you breathing?
William	Why? Because I need to. I wouldn't be able to live.
Maude	Then there's your answer.
William	Writing isn't the same as breathing.
Maude	Y'reckon.
William	So you're saying, as I'm not writing, I'm going to stop breathing?
Maude	Well, they do say hope springs eternal.
William	Eh? I mean, what? Pardon? Bugger! *(He ducks again. Maude stifles a smile. Pause).* What's your name?
Maude	You know it. We've both been here six years.
William	Aye, but it's not a proper introduction listening to folk shouting their name out for a register is it? Mr Dixon says that manners maketh the man. So go on. Let's introduce ourselves.
Maude	Why?
William	Just being sociable
Maude	Must you?
William	Must you not be?
Maude	That is a poor use of English
William	Sorry. But I just thought, y'know, chit-chat…
Maude	I don't do chit-chat.
William	Well, call it talking.
Maude	I don't do talking.
William	Well, call it singing.
Maude	You're not singing.
William	'La'. *(Maude stifles a smile by looking away).* But why not? Please? We could talk about the weather; what you've had for tea; how you're feeling; what your plans are now; why a poem; why you don't want to talk to me; why you wish I wasn't breathing; why Miss Bear never got married…
Maude	Maude. My name's Maude. Now go away.

William	Maude what?
Maude	Just Maude.
William	You must have another name?
Maude	Nope.
William	Just Maude?
Maude	Just Maude.
William	Well then 'Just Maude', I'm 'Only William'. *(He puts his hand out, but Maude ignores him. He then steps closer and thrusts his hand in front of her face so that she can no longer see to write).*
Maude	*(Not moving).* If I shake your hand, will this irritating contretemps, indeed, come to an end?
William	Hmm?
Maude	Will you go away?
William	Oh. Yep. *(Silence. Maude folds her papers, puts her pencil away, and stares out front, prepared).* Contre?
Maude	Temps.
William	I don't know what you…
Maude	It's French.
William	Who?
Maude	Not who, what. Contretemps. French.
William	I don't speak French right good.
Maude	Or English, apparently.
William	What?
Maude	Pardon.
William	Sorry?
Maude	Accepted. *(William puts his hand out again in front of her face. She shakes his finger but he doesn't move).* You're still here.
William	You're quick.
Maude	You lied.
William	You don't miss owt.
Maude	I'd like to miss you.
William	Are you being forward?
Maude	No, sarcastic.
William	What does that mean?
Maude	Stick around. You'll figure it.
William	By gum, you're hard work.
Maude	Yep.
William	Say a lot, don't you?
Maude	Nope.
William	This is how it's going to be, isn't it?
Together	Yep.
William	*(Starting a conversation with himself about Maude).* I know, I know. What do you mean? Do you think so? I don't know. Well, look at her. I mean. What would you expect? Someone like her and all. Do you think she would?
Maude	*(Irritated).* Who are you talking to?

William	*(Mimicking her).* Do you mind? I'm having a conversation. Sorry you were so rudely interrupted; please continue and ignore this… contretemps. That's French y'know. *(He looks at Maude, smugly, and then continues).* Really? What was that again?
Maude	But there's nobody…
William	Shhh! You were saying. Hmm. You might be right. That might be her problem.
Maude	I have not got a problem!
William	Has nobody ever told you it's bad manners to eavesdrop?
Maude	There's only you talking!
William	Aye. Different when shoes on t'other foot! *(Maude smiles and then laughs, which he then joins in with).* Can we please start again?
Maude	I think you mean 'may'?
William	I thought you said y'name were Maude. (Maude *looks at him, unmoved by his attempt at humour, but then, can't help herself).* <u>May</u> I start again?
Maude	You may.
William	*(To himself).* What do you think? Aye, alright then. *(To Maude).* William. *(He puts his hand out).*
Maude	I'm…
William	*(Interrupting).* I know: 'Just Maude'.
Maude	No, my name is…
William	No. You'll always be 'Just Maude' to me
Maude	Always is a long time for people who have just met.
William	Always has to start somewhere when it's the beginning of something.
Maude	*(Taken aback).* Is it now?
William	Surprised you that a 'Nobody' knew words like what a 'Somebody' would use?
Maude	Touché.
William	No, it's William. *(Maude laughs at him).* Touché, eh? French?
Maude	French.
William	I know French.
Maude	Go on then.
William	*(He thinks about it, clears his throat, prepares himself, goes to speak a few times, bows formally to her and then speaks).* No I don't. I can't lie
Maude	A boy that doesn't lie. In my experience, that's very rare.
William	A girl who speaks her mind and tells you what she thinks of you. In my experience, that's very common. *(He puts his hand out again).* William. I am very pleased to make your acquaintance
Maude	Maude. I'm very pleased to meet you, William. *(She takes William's hand. They hold hands for that bit longer, considering each other).* Alright then. You've got what you wanted… 'Barmy Billy'.
William	Barmy? My name's… I'm not barmy.
Maude	If I'm going to be 'Just Maude', you'll always be 'Barmy Billy' to me
William	Always, is it?
Maude	Aye. Different when shoes on t'other foot.
William	Alright. But I ain't barmy. I'm going to be something, I am.

Maude	What?
William	Shove up *(He sits)*. Well, I haven't right figured that bit out yet, but you mark my words. Someday, somehow: <u>somebody</u>. And you'll be glad we met, that we became good friends. That this was the beginning of something.
Maude	Good friends, now then, is it? And who said this was the beginning of something?
William	It's taken me six years to pluck up the courage to talk to you. If you think it's going to stop there, you've got another thing coming.
Maude	Six?
William	Years.
Maude	You've wanted to talk to me for six years? I don't know what to say.
William	My, this is a day for firsts.
Maude	Six years? You've waited all that time. Despite how I have treated you, the things I've said?
William	Impressed aren't you. It proves that I'm determined.
Maude	It proves that you're slow. *(William winks at her)*. You're very sure of yourself.
William	Aye.
Maude	And what if I don't want it to be part of your 'something'?
William	Maude. We're orphans. There's got to be something better for you, me, us. We make our own opportunities. Mr Dixon said so. And life is too short to watch it just pass us by.
Maude	You quote Mr Dixon a lot.
William	Mr and Mrs Dixon are the only proper family I've got. That we've got. He's given me, you, a life, something to hope for; he has made me into what I will be.
Maude	That's beautiful.

They are both embarrassed.

William	And anyhow, you need something to write about, my love.
Maude	And I am not 'your love'
William	Not yet. *(He winks at Maude, stands up, and begins to walk away)*.
Maude	Where are you going now? I thought you wanted to talk?
William	I did. We have. I'm done
Maude	So where are you going?
William	Just somewhere, 'Just Maude'. Just coming?
Maude	Just thinking.
William	Just leaving.
Maude	Just a minute… *(She walks past William without answering and then stops and turns, smiles and without warning, kisses him on the cheek and exits, running off and calling out)*. Just gone!
William	Just brilliant. Bloody brilliant! *(Out of habit, he ducks, then shouts)*. <u>Bloody profanity</u>!
Jane & James	*(Offstage)*. William!

William smiles and runs off after Maude.

Scene 5

James and Jane enter. They both have a newspaper from which they appear to read.

Jane	"1904: An 'Entente Cordiale' is signed between Britain and France".
James	"1905: Germany tests the agreement by triggering a crisis in Morocco".
Jane	Germany expected it to crumble.
James	It didn't.
Jane	"1906: HMS Dreadnought is launched at Portsmouth, the most powerful battleship afloat and with it, a new term is also launched".
James	'Arms Race'.
Jane	"1908: Other races were taking place. The Olympic Games open at White City in London. They feature 22 nations, 110 events and more than 2,000 athletes. The world appears at ease with itself. At peace".
James	"1909: Edward VII dies and is succeeded by George V. His funeral brings together the royalty of Europe for the last time before 1914".
Jane	And in a small corner of Lancashire, against a backdrop of an uncertain world, the orphanage continues in its own small way.
James	Shaping lives, making futures. *(He exits).*

Jane sits at the desk.

Scene 6

Maude enters and stands quietly, obediently.

Jane	I have asked you to come and speak to me because …
Maude	*(Interrupting).* Please Miss, whatever Susan Birtwistle has said about me and the way I spoke to her is a lie. I never said the things she said, I don't know such language and would never dream of saying…
Jane	*(Interrupting).* Maude. Please. You have done nothing wrong. I just want to talk to you, about, you
Maude	Me?
Jane	Yes. The reports I am receiving are that you are doing exceptionally well. Your reading age is beyond any other child in the orphanage and I am told that you like languages and have even asked for books to learn more about them.
Maude	Well. It's true. I love reading, Miss. Anything. Everything, actually. About people and places. Their lives, their languages. Well, anything.
Jane	I see. And what do you want to do with all that you have read?
Maude	I don't…
Jane	*(Interrupting).* I mean, what do you want to be, to do, when you leave here?
Maude	Well. I thought I might stay… not for nothing Miss, I want to work and… be like you. *(She sees the expression on Jane's face).* I'm sorry Miss, I didn't mean anything by that. I'm not a lady like you and wouldn't dream of…
Jane	*(Interrupting).* Maude, you've said nothing wrong. I am very flattered; touched by such a sentiment. That you would, could, consider me a role model is, well, it is a lovely thing to say. An honour. A blessing. But I want

	to talk about you. It's 1911 and you are seventeen and not too young to think about the future. So, what are your hopes for your future?
Maude	I suppose either go into the mill or into service.
Jane	But what do you want?
Maude	Does it matter?
Jane	Of course it matters!
Maude	Well. Really? Honestly? And you won't laugh?
Jane	Maude, honesty and sincerity are virtues not just to be spoken of, but practiced, and certainly not ridiculed.
Maude	Well, I want to be a teacher. *(Again, she sees Jane's expression)*. But I know, I can't, could never be. Its vanity I suppose. I've done it again. I'm sorry. I'd best go.
Jane	Child, why are you always sorry? Sit, stay, talk to me. Teaching is a vocation. It is for life; and to nurture other lives. It is the greatest thing one could dedicate oneself to. So. How do we go about it?
Maude	What… I mean pardon?
Jane	Teaching. You. A long road lies ahead of you and so much work. Hard work. Then there's the studying, the examinations.
Maude	I don't mind. Really I don't. But do you think I could do it? I love sitting with the little ones and telling them stories, reading to them at night-time in the dormitory. Their eyes wide, hanging on every word, asking questions; taking them to places and lives that they can only dream about. Wanting to know more, asking for it not to stop, asking me to make up something else.
Jane	You make them up?
Maude	Sometimes Miss. I love to write stories about the places I've read about. What they might be like. Give the children a chance to dream, to escape. For the briefest of moments, to be something else, to be, well, something, someone.
Jane	Really? My word. The ability to be a storyteller never mind a story writer is a gift, a talent.
Maude	But how does writing, telling stories, put bread on the table?
Jane	Maude, somebody wrote the books that you love to read. They did it for love, but they also did it as a job. Mr Dixon writes, you know.
Maude	Really?
Jane	Oh yes. Only in his diary, his journal. Ideas, stories, hopes, fears… jokes.
Maude	Mr Dixon tells jokes?
Jane	Hmm. He <u>thinks</u> so, Maude. But either they are not very good, or he isn't good at telling them! But don't tell him that I told you! Watch and learn. You will figure it from the way I laugh at them.
Maude	Why do you laugh at him if he isn't funny?
Jane	Bless. The naivety of a young, single woman. Laughing at a husband's jokes is a valuable skill for a wife to acquire. But that is a secret between us women! Anyhow, he plans his sermons, his speeches, his addresses in his journal as well.
Maude	All that work. I didn't realise you gave him homework too.
Jane	*(Laughing)*. Now <u>that</u> is deliciously funny.

Maude	'Deliciously funny'. You see? Him, you, you're both so eloquent, so confident, so clever.
Jane	The use of words does not mean 'clever'. Words are just that, words. Words on their own mean little. But from words come deeds. Now, deeds, undertaken for the right reason and the right sentiment, they are something. You know, when Mr Dixon first came to Blackburn, he wrote down a list in his journal of all the things he wanted to achieve. We wouldn't be here in this orphanage if it did not all start with a simple list of words. But enough people turning those words into actions, doing the right thing, can change the world, Maude. From little ripples great waves are born. We are all a gift to this world, you no less so. You are somebody, Maude. You can be somebody. Why are you smiling?
Maude	You sound like Barmy Billy… sorry, William.
Jane	William? Ah, yes, William North.
Maude	He wants to be somebody, not just a nobody as he sees it.
Jane	Yes. I see you both speaking to each other frequently. He is a good young man. Headstrong but passionate to make his own path. Do you like him?
Maude	Miss?
Jane	Maude. You are young, I am older, but we both understand I think.
Maude	He is… a friend.
Jane	Then it is a good beginning.
Maude	He said that as well.
Jane	Then my good opinion of him is well placed. But tell me more of this writing of yours.
Maude	It's nothing, Miss. When I have time I like to write ideas down on scraps of paper but above all… you won't laugh?
Jane	Never. Mr Dixon and I will never laugh at you, Maude.
Maude	Then, it's poetry Miss. I like to write poetry.
Jane	My word.
Maude	You're not laughing.
Jane	You haven't given me a reason to.
Maude	Well. I love working out how things fit together. Words. Rhymes. Thoughts. Turning an idea, a story into something else. Like a puzzle.
Jane	Can I read some of these poems?
Maude	Oh no Miss. I never keep them. I've got nowhere to. And anyhow, it's just for me, and anyway, they're not very good.
Jane	How do you know?
Maude	Well, how could they be?
Jane	Maude, Mr Dixon and I are people of faith and that means we also have faith in others. We have faith in you. We have taken an opportunity to do good, for young people like you. To give you a chance. To give you hope. To allow you to be who you might be…
Maude	*(Interrupting, smiling).* A somebody.
Jane	Exactly. Then is William so wrong?
Maude	Maybe not. But I'm not telling him!

Jane	Not that naive where men are concerned then, are we?! We can't all be something, Maude. But we can simply try to be the best we can be and do good unto others. And with that in mind, I have a mind to give something to you that you might quite like.
Maude	A gift? For me?
Jane	*(Giving Maude a journal).* Here. I want you to have this.
Maude	For me? What is it? A book?
Jane	It's a journal. Like the one Mr Dixon keeps. Like the one his father gave to him. You don't have a mother to do the same for you, so let me do it for her, in her name, with her heart. Whatever you think, your own hopes, ideas, stories, poems, write them down in here. Maybe you could hand it down to your children. Allow yourself to dream, Maude. Allow those dreams to become aspirations. Your writing might not change the world, but it might just change yours. Now. On your way. Lessons begin soon.
Maude	Thank you, Miss. And thank you for this. I'll treasure it. Truly. I will use it. I promise. Every day. I never expect to be a somebody, Miss. But I will try to be the best something, someone, that I can be.
Jane	Never say never, child. Have faith. Have hope. Trust in God. And give those hopes wings.
Maude	'Give those hopes wings'. Yes, Miss.

Fade to black. Maude and Jane exit.

Scene 7

James enters, reading from a newspaper.

James	"1911. The world is changing and at the same time, planning. Newspapers report the funding for five new battleships and: '…a plan for a British Expeditionary army in case of war with Germany'. A war with Germany? Ridiculous. I've got more important things to be concerned with. The roof is leaking in the infirmary and we need seven new bed pans!
Jane	*(Entering).* 1914: Archduke Franz Ferdinand is assassinated in Serbia.
James	An event unknown to a small orphanage in Wilpshire.
Jane	Britain invites Germany to join in solving the growing conflict in Europe.
James	Germany refuses.
Jane	Austria and Hungary declare war on Serbia, and Russia, its ally, mobilises its army.
James	Germany declares war on Russia.
Jane	And then invades France through neutral Belgium.
James	Britain demands that Germany withdraw.
Jane	The ultimatum expires on the 4th August.
James	And on that day, that fateful, that dreadful, wretched day, Britain declares war on Germany.
Jane	But in the orphanage, wholly different declarations are being made.

James moves to and sits at his desk with Jane by him. William enters.

William	Sorry, Mr Dixon, I didn't realise, I'll just go and…

James	No need, William, what can I do for you?
William	I just wanted a chat, Father, about…
James	About?
William	Things.
James	Such as?
William	You know.
James	Not at the moment I don't, William. Not until you tell me.

Jane sits down and they both stare at William.

Jane	Well, William?
William	*(Imitating James)*. "Well, more 'W's William!". *(He forces a laugh)*. Mr Dixon said that to me. On the day I arrived. Funny. A joke. But not just right now then, eh?
Jane	I see.
James	Really.
William	Well, lovely speaking to you. Thanks for your advice. *(He makes to leave)*.
James	I wasn't aware I had given any, so you best come back and tell me what it is that you don't want to tell me.
William	Oh. Right. Well, I thought we could chat in private, like.
Jane	Off you go, then.
William	Just us.
James	Us?
William	As in you.
James	Yes.
William	And me.
James	Yes.
William	And me
James	Yes.

Silence.

Jane	I think, my dear, that there is a conversation which is required between the men.
James	Really?
Jane	Between you men.
James	Oh.
Jane	I think so. *(She makes to leave, and then, on exiting)*. Be gentle with him, William. He is a little slow at times. Not aided by the fact that he is a man. *(She exits)*.
James	I will never understand women, William; what do you think?
William	To be honest, Father, that's why I'm here.
James	Then sit down and tell me what is on your mind.
William	I don't know what to say, where to start.
James	Then shall I commence for you? You love Maude and you don't know what to do about it.
William	That obvious?
James	Well, to the rest of the living breathing community of Wilpshire, but clearly not you!

William	Aye, well, yes, that's about it in a nutshell.
James	Well, that's saved us at least an hour of word games and semantics.
William	But I don't know what I should do, say, to her.
James	William. You know Maude as well as Mrs Dixon and me. Just tell her how you feel.
William	Me? Tell Maude? How I feel? Maude?
James	She is direct and to the point.
William	You've noticed?
James	And she loves you, William. The world can see that. When you're not at the mill and she is not in the school, you spend your waking and non-working time wrapped up in each other. You both know how you feel. Just say it.
William	Just say it.

Maude enters.

James	And there's no time like the present.
Maude	Morning, Mr Dixon. Morning, William.
James	Maude, William has something he wishes to say to you. William?
William	I haven't actually.
James	William.
William	Nope. Can't think what that could be.
James	William.
William	What?! Now?
James	Carpe diem, William, Carpe diem. *(He exits).*
Maude	Well? What day are you seizing?
William	Pardon?
Maude	'Carpe diem'?
William	*(About to burst but can't speak, and then garbles out).* I love you, Maude, and I want you to be my lass!
Maude	I know that. *(She makes to exit, then shouts back to him).* About bloody time
James & Jane	*(Offstage).* Profanity, Maude!

Blackout.

Scene 8

James is discovered at a lectern.

James	Mr Chairman, members of the Board. I am pleased to present to you this, my annual report for 1914. Notwithstanding the trying time we have had financially in the last quarter, caused by the terrible European war now raging, we are thankful that our friends have nobly stood by us and have so enabled us to close the year with a balance on the right side. Reference to what we are now calling the Great War gives an opportunity to report that Blackburn Orphanage is worthily represented in His Majesties Forces, several old scholars who were in situations having joined the Army or Navy. When the 'Old Boys' list is completed we shall have over thirty who are serving their King and their Country in this crisis. We pray that God's

protecting care may surround those who are at the front as well as those who are ready to go there.

The lights crossfade to William and Maude who are sitting, holding hands.

Maude	I've got a present for you.
William	For me?
Maude	Yes. *(It's a small brown paper package)*. Well open it, then!
William	A bear.
Maude	Not any bear! Do you not recognise him?
William	So this one's a 'him' then?
Maude	Naturally. William, meet Mr Bear, fiancé of Mrs Bear.
William	So, they're getting married, are they? Nothing about it in the papers.
Maude	It was a quiet affair, just family know.
William	How many of them are there? In the family?
Maude	Just two. All you need is two. Soul mates. For life. Orphans, like us.
William	You've thought this one through, haven't you?
Maude	Well, y'know. I thought if two bears can get engaged, then there's hope for us all.
William	*(Embarrassed and uncomfortable)*. Aye, well, y'know…
Maude	Well, if you don't want him…
William	I love him. I love you. *(He kisses Maude)*.
Maude	Wherever you go, wherever you are, you will have Bear and you will think of me; and maybe, us.
William	Well, Maude, it will certainly be the topic of conversation when he's sat on my loom in the mill.
Maude	I'm serious. Bear introduced us. And Bear will stay with us. A reminder of who we are. What we are. Wherever life takes us… and, please God, it will always be together.
William	Aye.
Maude	I can tell we're not having that conversation today, are we? Right, well I've got some apples, a sandwich each and a blanket. Pity to waste such a grand Sunday. I thought a picnic by the bandstand in the park would be nice, don't you think? Will? Me, you, Mr and Mrs Bear? Hello?
William	Aye.

Silence.

Maude	Penny for your thoughts? I've not upset you talking about us, well, getting…
William	Sorry. I've been thinking about how many of the old boys have enlisted.
Maude	Yes, very noble. Indeed. But they will be home soon, and this nonsense will be over.
William	Nonsense. Aye. *(Silence)*. Alfred Burns has already fallen.
Maude	Yes. I heard. Very sad indeed. Is an apple each enough, do you think?
William	Charlie Gray was wounded in both arms in France.
Maude	Egg and cress. Nothing else like it on a sunny day.
William	Aye. Nothing like it.

The lights crossfade back to James.

James	Moving on, Gentlemen, we are pleased to hear from time to time from those who are away and particularly those engaged in the war. One, who is a signal boy on HMS India writes…

The lights crossfade to Jane who enters and reads from a letter.

Jane	"You will please excuse me for not writing before, but we have been at sea for some time and I could not write sooner. I thank you very much for the parcel of good things you have sent me. I think it is very good of you, looking up your old boys like that. I must say you have a good few at the front. I have never heard anything of Harry Parker yet. Perhaps he is in another depot. I am quite well myself and hope everyone at Wilpshire Orphanage is the same".

The lights crossfade to William and Maude.

Maude	Egg and cress. Nothing else like it on a sunny day. *(William stands, beside himself).* Will?
William	It's just… I was just thinking that… Us. Behaving so, normal, like. Presents, picnics, talking about the future.
Maude	<u>Our</u> future.
William	Aye. But then there's the old boys. I feel like I should, you know. That I should…
Maude	Stop worrying, William. There's no need. This will all be over soon. This isn't our war.

The lights cross fade back to James.

James	Another on active service with the British Expeditionary Force says.
Jane	*(Reading another letter).* "Please accept my sincere thanks for your kindness in sending me a parcel. I am extremely proud to be able to count you amongst my friends. Allow me to say that your gift arrived in time for Christmas Day. We made it look as much like Christmas as possible. The weather out here is rough. First it's rain, then its frost, then snow, then it will thaw and freeze again. You will have an idea now what it's like. Of course, I forgot to mention the mud. That is one of the biggest items, I think. Apart from the unpleasantness which arises from the above-mentioned discomforts, I must say we fare pretty well. We have almost everything necessary under the circumstances, so we must not grumble, because there is many a poor fellow worse off than what we are".

The lights crossfade to William and Maude.

William	I feel helpless, Maude. I feel so bloody helpless.
Maude	*(Jokingly, imitating James).* Profanity, William!
William	This isn't funny, Maude. War isn't funny.
Maude	And it is a war which will soon be over, my love. We've talked about this. Mr Dixon agrees. You're doing your part by being here, at home in the mill. Working hard for your King and Country.
William	Working hard for King and Country. Aye.

The lights crossfade to James and Jane.

James Jane	One of our Old Boys with the Cavalry Division in France writes: "When duty calls we must be ready to respond and sacrifice all. I am here to do my best and by God's help, I will do it. We want no half-hearted men over here; we want whole-hearted men… men who will face the foe willingly. God grant that we may all return home safe, rejoicing with victory. We all got a present from Princess Mary, and a card wishing us a Happy Christmas and a Victorious New Year".

The lights crossfade to William and Maude.

William	But how can working in a Mill be enough, Maude?
Maude	Well, we just need to save as much as we can and…
William	No I don't mean that.
Maude	Then what?
William	I've had a letter.
Maude	Who from?
William	Arthur. My friend Arthur.
Maude	You never told me he had written to you?
William	Well, not to me like. But to Mr Dixon and all of us. I asked if I could have it.
Maude	Why?
William	Well, I just wanted to… I thought… Shall I read it to you? He says: "The Indian soldiers are a fine set of men. Most of them can speak English very well…". *(The lights crossfade to James as he now takes over).* It opens one's eyes to see the many different …
James	"It opens one's eyes to see the many different sights as we travel along the country. I have not been very near to the firing line yet, but I can hear the roar of the big guns day and night continually. I often think that I would like to see the little cot that I used to have when I was in the Orphan House at Wilpshire. I was working in Barrow shipyard when the war broke out and I straightaway went to enlist and was accepted".

The lights crossfade to William and Maude.

William	He enlisted, Maude. So many of the Old Boys have
Maude	And a very noble act. And working in a mill supporting them, us, is just as noble, isn't it? We are building a new world for when they get back.
William	Aye.
Maude	Now, egg and cress will not keep in this weather. Get the bag, William. There's a love.
William	Aye.
Maude	Well come on then! *(She exits).*

James and Jane approach William, standing behind him.

Jane	I hear the roar of the big guns.
James	Day and night.
Jane	Continually.
James	Egg and cress.
Jane	I would like to see the cot I used to have.
James	Get the bag, William.

Jane	There's a love
James	When duty calls we must be ready to respond.
Jane	And sacrifice all.
James	There's a love.
Jane	We want no half-hearted men over here.
James	We want whole-hearted men.
Jane	Men who will face the foe willingly.
James	Egg and cress.
Jane	There's a love.
James & Jane	There's a love. There's a love. There's a love.

William exits, running off. Fade to black. James and Jane exit.

Scene 9

The following day. Maude is by the bench, pacing, impatient. William enters.

Maude	Where have you been, Will? I've been waiting for you for ages. You said one and it's nearly half past two. 'One o'clock by the mill gate', your note said. I was here and you weren't.
William	I had stuff to do. Let's get going now.
Maude	No, wait. Stuff? What stuff?
William	You know.
Maude	No... *(Silence).* Unless this is a Musical Hall act and we're going to read each other's minds then... Well?
William	I had, you know.
Both	Stuff.
Maude	Yes, you said that, so what does that...
William	*(Interrupting).* Some people to see.
Maude	Is that it?
William	I guess so.
Maude	Not a bit of this story missing, then?
William	I don't think so.
Maude	'I keep six honest serving-men, they taught me all I knew; their names are What and Why and When and How and Where and Who'.
William	*(Pausing).* We need to go.
Maude	Will, what's the matter. Has something happened? Will?
William	I've joined up. *(Pause).* Well, say something?

Maude stares at him, then without warning, she slaps him hard across the face. William does not move or speak. Maude slaps him again. He grabs hold of her.

Maude	Get off me. Get off me! *(She breaks away and steps back from him, staring, shaking with rage, before shouting).* <u>Are you completely insane</u>?
William	Shush! People are staring at us, Maude.
Maude	Why?
William	Look, I know we talked about...
Maude	Why?
William	I must.

Maude	Why?
William	Because.
Maude	That's not an answer. Why?
William	It's the right thing to do.
Maude	Why? For who?
William	Look Maude…
Maude	*(Interrupting)*. No you look, see what you have done, realise what you have done. Do you know? Do you care? All we talked about, all we dreamt of? Was it all a lie? Did it, us, mean nothing to you?
William	Maude, everybody is joining up.
Maude	No! No! No! You're not everybody. We are not everybody. You're the nobody that's going to be somebody. Remember? The man with nothing to prove, with no history, but with a future, my future, our future. You told me. You promised me.
William	I had…
Maude	*(Interrupting).* You promised me.
William	But…
Maude	*(Interrupting, louder).* You promised me.
William	It was…
Maude	*(Interrupting, shouting).* You promised me.
William	*(Shouting back).* Some things are bigger than promises. Men are dying!
Maude	And I don't want you to be one of them! *(William goes to hug her).* Get off me.
William	I love you. *(Maude goes to slap him again but he catches her arm, preventing her).* Some things are bigger than promises.
Maude	Like what? Lies?
William	Not lies. It was never lies. I would never lie to…
Maude	*(Interrupting).* No. Don't you dare. Don't you dare say that after what you have done. The first thing you ever said to me was that you don't lie. Years ago. All the things we said. You promised me. So tell me. Enlighten me. What is more important than promises?
William	The right thing. Doing the right thing.
Maude	According to who? For who? For you? Certainly not me.
William	There's more than you and me.
Maude	Name names. Who are these people more important than us, the unknown you seem so passionate about?
William	Well, I don't know. Look. The world is going to war, Maude.
Maude	But we aren't! So strangers matter more?
William	Strangers are the rest of the world. We're a grain of sand in a desert, a drop of water in an ocean of, of…
Maude	*(Interrupting).* Of lies? Dress it up how you want, soldier boy. The King has an orphan fighting his lot for him now. One orphan against the world and for the world. Brilliant. One orphan who will make a difference above anybody, above everyone else. 'The King's Orphan' who had a chance for a future. A chance to be something, somebody, with someone. With me.
William	And I still can.

Maude	And what about me? Well? Did you ever in your wildest little dreams ever, for one second, think of me? Of us?
William	This isn't about you and me.
Maude	No! It is all about you!
William	Is that a bad thing?
Maude	Well. Thank you. At least I now know and understand.
William	You don't understand.
Maude	And you clearly do?
William	Maude, others of the lads have gone. If they can go, then why am I so different? The Old Boys from the orphanage must do their bit in this war, for the only family we have ever known. A family of our own making. The best family an orphan could ever hope for. War can't tell the difference between a King or an orphan. But this orphan has a job to do for his King. And I will do it. I am resolved. *(Silence).* Will you write to me?
Maude	Yes. Because writing is all I have ever had; all I've ever been good for, isn't it? And it would appear that it is to carry on.
William	Please, Maude. We're going over it again. We're more important than just words.
Maude	Apparently not.
William	So all your scribbling in the book Mrs Dixon gave you, all those big words were always just that. Words. All nice ideas and no actions. Well, I've taken action.
Maude	Don't you dare turn this on me.
William	I'm not, Maude.
Maude	So action has made you the man you need to be. Congratulations. Words are all I have, William. Books have given me a soul. I'm sorry that is all I have. But they have given me things I never dreamt I could ever have: an understanding of me, of what I want to be, and, please God, how I might one day be it. You're that busy trying to be something else, somebody else, you can't see anybody else. How stupid I've been. It's clear there's no space in your life for us, for me.
William	Maude…
Maude	You don't understand me, William, and you won't understand anyone until you can understand yourself. Perhaps it will take someone else's war to help you to see.
William	This is <u>our</u> war.
Maude	William, you have been at war all your life. One more won't make any difference. *(She makes to exit).*
William	Maude, don't leave me like this.
Maude	It isn't me that's leaving.
William	Maude, please, we can't say goodbye this way.
Maude	We already have.
William	When?
Maude	The day we met.
William	But I want you to be my, my…
Maude	What?

William	Be my, my... *(He can't say the words and puts his head down, silent).*
Maude	How so much can be said with a silence. *(William exits. She is alone, quiet, still. She sits on the bench, and then suddenly stands and calls after him).* William! Will! Will! *(She exits, chasing after him).*

Fade to black. SFX #06: the sound of a brass/marching band is heard interspersed with cheers and applause which then fade and lights the come back up on Maude, alone.

Maude	Twelve abreast they marched the streets, the day they left the town.
	The band competed with our cheers that echoed all around.
	The biting wind upon my face, excused the flowing tears.
	All spoke loud of King and right, too proud to voice our fears.
	Twelve abreast they wove through town, festooned with flags and pride
	Squabbles and petty arguments were gladly set aside
	For we were there for unity as they marched to catch the tide
	No one spoke of war or death, though both gnawed deep inside.
	Twelve abreast they past the school, the factory, then the mill.
	Each had come from one of them; I longed that they were still.
	A part of one or all of them, to keep them in our stead.
	No one spoke of why they went, none dared think of them dead.
	Twelve abreast they left as boys, in weeks they would be men.
	Not knowing what would happen; if we would meet again.
	All knew their reason was to fight, defend for all our sakes.
	No one spoke of their return, reunited at their wakes.
	Twelve abreast were brothers, workers, husbands, sons and friends.
	With one hope, one prayer one wish: to come home at the end.
	I beat through crowds to make sure that I kept sight of his face
	Dear God when twelve abreast return, don't let his be the space.

Fade to black.

END OF ACT ONE

INTERVAL

Act Two
Scene 1

The Western Front. Parsons and William are discovered sitting behind some sandbags. Both have a rifle and wear a tin hat.

William   Are you afraid, Mr Parsons?
Parsons   I believe I am, William.
William   Why?
Parsons   Why? Why wouldn't I be? Thousands of men somewhere not too far away and whom I have never met are pointing guns, shells and bombs at me. And you. I have never done anything to them. I'm sure you haven't. They, as far as I am aware, have never done owt to me. The issue is that the big men we have never met on both sides want things that the other disagrees with. So. The first question should be, why am I here?
William   Well?
Parsons   I guess because I <u>am</u> afraid. Fear brought me here. Fear keeps me here. Fear will make me kill a man I have never met; and the reasons? Where do we start? I was told to be here, it's my duty to be here, I do it for me and I do it for my family. And the last one my young friend is most important. Because if I don't stop them on the other side of that hill, they might try and do to the ones that I love at home, what they are trying to do to me. And whilst there is breath in my body, I will not allow that to happen.
William   Blimey. Never thought of it in them terms. But that's me. Act first, think later. But I don't have a family. I don't have kids, a wife. I had parents, but they didn't want me so the only reason I'm here is because my friends are and I guess ...
Parsons   Well?
William   Well, I suppose I'm here for my King and my Country. My duty.
Parsons   Then thank you from the bottom of my heart.
William   Why?
Parsons   Because it means you are here for my family.
William   But I don't know your family. I don't know you that well.
Parsons   Do you need to? You said you came for your King and Country. I am not your King. But so many people you have never met are your duty. A duty, a country depending on you and me. So no matter who and what we were at home, you and me are equal.
William   You wouldn't think so the way you boss me around. *(They laugh).* Bit odd. An orphan fighting for someone else's family, don't you think?
Parsons   Not from where I'm sat. Is there no one?
William   No.
Parsons   Really?
William   Well.
Parsons   Go on, lad.
William   There is someone back home.
Parsons   A girl?

William	Aye. But we're just mates, really. Now. Not, y'know. We've known each other all our lives. Well the bit of my life that mattered. In the orphanage. And I should've, you see, I meant to ask her if, if…
Parsons	I know. War makes us do that, lad. Makes us remember all the things we should've done, meant to say.
William	So I guess because of that, we're just good friends.
Parsons	I met my wife when I was nine and we've been together ever since. We started off friends and have always been ever since; good and bad! But that's love for you.
William	Yeah, but you're old.
Parsons	Be very careful what you say, young man. *(They laugh again, then, silence).* Do you like her?
William	Oh, I don't, y'know, she's just like, well, we've been like, well, and I don't think she cares much for me now that I…
Both	Yes.
Parsons	So. Not just fighting for King then, are you, orphan boy?
William	I guess not.
Parsons	The King's Orphan has a <u>potential</u> family.
William	I wouldn't say…
Parsons	A family worth fighting for. Seems it needed a war to make him realise it.
William	'The King's Orphan.' That's what she called me before we, y'know…
Parsons	Fell out?
William	Aye. Before we left for France. I promised I wouldn't sign up. I signed up. We argued. She gave me a bear. I left.
Parsons	So you're engaged, then?
William	What? No!
Parsons	Sounds it to me.
William	I haven't asked her yet. Well, not proper like.
Parsons	She gave you a bear.
William	That doesn't count.
Parsons	It's a token of her love.
William	How would you know?

Parsons produces a small bear from his pocket. William sheepishly then produces 'Bear'.

Parsons	My wife gave me this the day we left. And I'm not the only man in this war with one. What do you think to that, young orphan?
William	It doesn't mean we're engaged.
Parsons	Not yet.
William	I haven't even given her a ring.
Parsons	Not yet.
William	*(Smiling).* Aye. Not yet.
Parsons	So get your pen, paper and bloody finger out, lad. 'Not yet' doesn't linger around these parts very long. Make sure you turn it into a 'when'. And then it might just turn into the family you've never had.
William	Give over…

Parsons	…and this good old war might end up being far more than you think it is now, young orphan.
William	A family. I never, ever, dreamed I might, y'know…
Parsons	Not yet. Dreams are to hope. And hope is what your friend Mr Dixon always told you to have. Give it time, son. But not too much, eh? Even an orphan deserves dreams. And it all starts with that letter, remember?
William	I just hope to God this place will give me the time to do it.
Parsons	Aye. Ain't that the truth. It's just words, son.
William	'Words are all I have'.
Parsons	Pardon?
William	Something she said to me.
Parsons	Then give her more than words. Don't just give her somebody. Give her you.

SFX #07: bombs and explosions start. William cowers, but Parsons slowly stands, holds his stance with his hand out to William.

William	What are you doing?
Parsons	Tek mi hand!
William	Get down! You're gonna get killed!
Parsons	Tek mi hand!
William	Get down, yer daft bugger!
Parsons	While I've got this one chance, one moment, one pause in this madness, I want to shake your hand.

They shake hands as the sounds of war underscore them. A loud explosion is heard. They both dive for cover.

William	What was all that about, y'silly sod?
Parsons	Son, I told you. I am one of millions that you do not, did not, know, but you have enough sense of pride, loyalty, enough heroism to do this for me and now, for you. For <u>our</u> future. You, a young boy with no family, no roots, no reason. But a family I pray to god you will one day make for your own. Stick by my side, son. We will see this through, mark my words.
William	But I'm no hero. I'm afraid to be.
Parsons	Then you are one of the greatest heroes of all.
William	Rubbish.
Parsons	Is it now? So, despite not having had a family, despite being afraid of dying…
William	Don't say that.
Parsons	What?
William	That word.
Parsons	Dying?
William	Stop!
Parsons	Is that what you're afraid of?
William	Please! I'm just a nobody.
Parsons	*(Grabbing hold of William).* Wash your mouth out. Everyone in this war matters. Everyone is somebody. You are somebody. Don't just think of yourself as a nobody, young orphan. You are one of the greatest somebody's this good old war has never heard of. Now just keep your head down and

	start planning the memories you are going to make with, with, what's her name? *(SFX #08: an explosion is heard as the sounds of war get louder. He shouts over it)*. Her name. Tell me her name?! I must know it.
William	Maude!
Parsons	What?
William	It's Maude!
Parsons	Then keep saying it, orphan. Remember why you're here. Remember her.
William	Maude… Maude… Maude!

The sounds of battle fade and the lights crossfade.

Scene 2

James and Jane enter.

Jane	*(Writing a letter)*. "Dear Sir. Whilst the terrible European War has greatly increased our responsibilities, the kind and generous help made by many of our dear supporters, such as you, has made it possible to extend and increase our good work. We have therefore been able to grant unrestricted access to motherless and homeless children of soldiers and sailors. Over thirty of such children have been received into the Orphanage, and the fathers of some of them have been killed in the dreadful conflict".
James	1916: Conscription is introduced for men aged 18-41. Around the country, Pals battalions are formed with work colleagues, men from the same town, even from the same football team, enlisting together.
Jane	And in Wilpshire, a wholly different set of pals were answering the call to arms in Europe, even though it sometimes felt like the war was closer than Europe.
James	*(Writing)*. "About ten-thirty tonight, the Orphanage children, one hundred and thirty, being all asleep, loud noises were heard, as of bomb shells exploding some distance away in the west. The Orphanage windows rattled after each explosion as if the glass would break. Thinking it might be German Zepp's dropping bomb shells, I got all the children and officials downstairs into the basements of both buildings, where they sang many hymns and songs for three hours. The noise from exploding shells continued till after two am. We then had Evening and Morning Prayers together with a short address, and all the children, without undressing were put to bed, where all slept soundly 'til seven-thirty am. This evening I was informed by a Police sergeant that the noises we had heard were caused by Lancaster Munitions Works accidentally taking fire and the large store of Munition Bomb Shells etc exploding as the fire travelled through the extensive Works. If that is a fraction of war sounds like… God help them".

Scene 3

Jane sits at the desk looking at paperwork. Maude enters.

Maude	Post has arrived Mrs Dixon.
Jane	Thank you, Maude. *(Maude puts some letters on the desk and is makes to leave)*. Have you heard from William?

185

Maude	No.
Jane	Have you written to him yet? *(Maude does not reply)*. Oh Maude, why have you not written to him?
Maude	Because he doesn't deserve to get a letter after what he did.
Jane	But if he was here, he would have been called up by now. So what difference does it make?
Maude	It's the principle.
Jane	Principle? You talk of principles when a war is waging in Europe? *(Maude makes to leave again)*. Maude?
Maude	I just… he hurt me Mrs Dixon. He lied to me
Jane	Yes he did. So?
Maude	He went against all we had decided.
Jane	We?
Maude	Yes. We decided that he should stay here, in the mill.
Jane	You both discussed it and agreed exactly that?
Maude	Well, not exactly that but…
Jane	Oh, Maude!
Maude	…but he knew how I felt about it. What I wanted.
Jane	Marriage is not about always getting what we want.
Maude	He didn't even have the guts to ask me. Well, we won't have to find out my answer, will we?
Jane	Meaning? *(Silence)*. You mean to tell me that with that young man in Europe, fighting, not just for us, but for his life in, God knows what circumstances…
Maude	*(Interrupting)*. I think you need to …
Jane	*(Interrupting)*. I am speaking and you will stay silent. You are telling me that your relationship is over?
Maude	*(Taking out an envelope)*. I've written him a letter saying just that, and I intend to… *(Jane gets up quickly and marches over to Maude, snatching the letter from her hand)*. Mrs Dixon, what are you doing?
Jane	The right thing.
Maude	That letter is for William.
Jane	That letter is for the bin. *(She tears it up and puts it in her apron pocket)*.
Maude	Mrs Dixon!
Jane	How dare you. How dare you write such a wicked, wretched, unforgiveable letter. What gives you the right to…
Maude	*(Interrupting)*. He lied to me and…
Jane	*(Interrupting)*. And I am still speaking!
Maude	But…
Jane	Silence! You selfish, ungrateful, wretched girl. Abandoned by his parents when but nine years old. That boy is at war with nothing to his name other than you. Nothing other than the hope of what is here for him when he returns. And you dare, dare to take that hope away from him? You, with your high principles and your noble plans? You who led that boy a merry dance all those years and now, because you couldn't have your own way, you throw him to one side? Dear God, girl, use the brain God gave you and the soul I thought you had! He loves you, you love him, and for the sake of pride you

	will cast all that to one side, just to be right? Have you no decency, no compassion, no sense of where we are in history? We are at war! Instead of your pride, have you considered his bravery? Have you for one moment thought how frightened he might be? For all you know he could be…
Maude	What?
Jane	I've said enough
Maude	But…
Jane	He could be dead!
Maude	I thought…
Jane	Enough, I say! You thought. Think of the life you had and what brought you here. Think of the opportunity which is within your grasp, and which you not only plan to cast to the floor but stamp on with a heel of spite. If I ever, ever find out that you have even considered composing such a letter again… get out.

Maude turns to exit and then stops. She turns to Jane, with an expression of horror, a dawning of what it all means.

Maude	What have I done? William, what must he think of me? What must everyone think of me? What was I thinking? Of course I love him. *(She begins to cry).*
Jane	*(Rushing to Maude and holding her).* I'm sorry, Maude. I don't know what came over me.
Maude	But you're right. What was I, have I, been thinking? God forgive me. I must write to William now, apologise, seek his forgiveness and…
Jane	Just take a breath, take a moment, and do one simple thing which will set this right.
Maude	What? What must I do?
Jane	Just remember him and your time together. Remember that feeling, that excitement, that love you have for him. And prepare for the life you will have when he comes home and put all this nonsense out of your mind.
Maude	I'm so sorry. What was I thinking?
Jane	Too much, that's all. Absence doesn't always make the heart grow fonder; especially when there is a mind racing away with itself, confusing what really matters. You and William. Your future. That is all that matters. And simply remembering what your love for him feels like will wash away any anger, any pettiness. Now, dry your eyes.
Maude	Thank you. *(She makes to leave).*
Jane	And Maude? You have such a soul, an inner beauty and capacity to love. Allow it to shine; for William's sake, and your own?
Maude	Yes, Mrs Dixon. I'd best hurry then.
Jane	Hurry?
Maude	I've got a very special letter to write. For someone who I forgot for a time how much I loved, so very much. And Miss, I understand now. What he, all of them have done for us. He'll be a hero when he gets home.
Jane	No he won't.
Maude	Why?
Jane	Because, Maude, he was a hero the day he left.

Maude exits. Fast fade to black.

Scene 4

The Western Front.

Parsons	What are you doing, lad?
William	Writing. To Mr Dixon.
Parsons	The man from the orphanage?
William	Aye.
Parsons	What for?
William	I do. We do. All the old boys. We keep in touch with them about how we are. Publishes them in the paper that the orphanage prints so that everyone knows you're OK. See? *(He shows him a copy).* And then, he writes back with letters about how the orphanage is doing, all the people there. My orphanage family, y'know.
Parsons	No sports page, then? *(They both laugh).* But what about your mother, brothers and sisters?
William	Some of them are in the orphanage as well. I write to them too, well, will. When I get around to it.
Parsons	Of course. You being busy with dinner parties and all. *(They laugh again).* And Maude?
William	What about her?
Parsons	Have you written to her yet? *(Pause).* Well?
William	No. Not for now. Let things settle down with her I think.
Parsons	Settle down? You've been here six months! How bad was that argument? *(SFX #09: an explosion is heard. He and William drop down. He looks over the top and then sees that William has just carried on writing. Shouting out front).* I say? Do you mind awfully, that nearly made my friend smudge his ink. Just give the war a breather for a mo' will you? Thanks ever so. *(He looks at William, who carries on, obliviously).* Excuse me old chap, if it's not too much trouble and all, might you possibly do something for me?
William	What?
Parsons	Give us a lift with a little war I've got on. Y'know? Small matter of a few thousand Hun a couple of hundred yards over there pointing guns at us? *(They both laugh).* I know. Perhaps you could write them a letter too. *(He pretends to write).* "Dear Mr Hun. Just thought I would write to ask how you are and how this jolly old war is going for you and yours". *(They laugh again).* "Do send us word of Mrs Hun and the little Huns. Oh, and some fags".
William	Chocolate, if you don't mind!
Parsons	*(Crossing out on his pretend letter).* "Oh, and some chocolate for Master William who is feeling a little home-sick and rather peckish". *(They laugh again).* "And PS. Don't kill us today". *(He laughs. William does not).* What?
William	I wish you wouldn't do that.
Parsons	Do what?
William	Say that.

Parsons	What? Don't kill us?
William	*(Interrupting, speaking loudly over 'kill')*. Don't say it!
Parsons	When are you going to grow up, lad?
William	I have. I am. Just don't like talking about it.
Parsons	Well, William, what do you think we are going to do? Jump over the top when the Captain blows his whistle to advance, hit each other with feather pillows and then have a tickle fight? *(He keeps a straight face as William laughs)*. I'm not laughing, son. It's time to stop laughing about it. Pretending all the time to make you feel better, to make this war seem like a day trip for wakes weeks. Why do you think the King gave you a bayonet? For peeling apples?
William	No, I know what…
Parsons	That's the point, lad. You do know, but you won't listen to yourself. To the shells, the blasts, to the screams of men dying. *(William doesn't reply)*. Do you know one of the ways we make sure we get home? *(William shakes his head)*. By remembering on the days the sun shines and the guns fall silent, why we are here and why them lot over there are here and what both sides are trying to do to each other. I've told you this. We're here to win and so are they. But it will be the small matter of who is left behind that'll decide it, not a penalty shoot-out in no-man's-land. *(William laughs again and Parsons grabs him violently, shouting at him in his face)*. Stop laughing, you fool! Stop finding war funny. Stop finding excuses to ignore what will happen to one or both of us! Stop ignoring that we're probably going to die! *(He lets go of William and turns away)*.

Silence.

William	I'm sorry.
Parsons	And stop being sorry and start being angry. Sorry won't keep you alive. Sorry will find you dead with a bayonet in your gut and your face in the mud. Bugger. Now I'm sorry. *(They again sit in silence)*. Have you finished the letter yet?
William	I just need to wish Mr Dixon the best and…
Parsons	*(Interrupting)*. Not that letter. The letter. The one the Captain told you to write last week to Maude. *(William does not reply)*. William! Why?
William	I don't want to. It's just tempting fate
Parsons	Rubbish. We all must write a letter for home in case the worst does happen. So they have something from you to read, to remember.
William	I know, I know.
Parsons	*(Turning quickly to William, angry again)*. That was an order from the Captain, not a request.
William	But I thought…
Parsons	You and I are not here to think. We're here to do what we are told. Now write it.
William	But I…
Parsons	Write

William	But what? What do I say? "By the time you read this you will have been told that I'm, that I'm …
Parsons	Dead? *(William does not reply).* The letter isn't about you, lad. It's about them. It's for them. It's a connection, it's not a memento. It might be the only thing of you they have. It's a piece of a real person, of somebody; of all the things that were and might have been, happy times. When they read it, they will see you, hear you, remember you. And keep remembering. Because it will be in a purse, a handbag that will never leave their side. They'll hear your voice when they read and in a very short time will know that letter by heart. Recite it quietly from memory as they drift off to sleep. Quote it to loved one's years later without taking a breath. A window on the past, on a person. A person who was more than a soldier, or an orphan. A simple letter. That gives them strength, gives them hope; gives them you.
William	But who do I write it to?
Parsons	Who do you think? Have you forgotten her so easily? Maude. I told you.
William	But how do I start it?
Parsons	What would your Mr Dixon say to you?
William	He'd say that the Lord placed me on earth for a reason, for a purpose. That I take a path that he guides me on, but is with me on it, always. That he will watch over me and no matter the circumstance, he is at my side, in my mind, in my heart, and that she is in my heart all day, every second of it; and that I love her so very much.
Parsons	And I think you've just started your letter, young orphan.
William	Aye. I think I have.
Parsons	I wish I'd met your Mr Dixon.
William	You will. When we get home
Parsons	Aye. Reckon so. He means a lot to you, doesn't he?
William	He made me who I am. He gave me all I have.
Parsons	Money?
William	No. More, so much more. Hope. A reason. A chance. I'd have died in a workhouse or in a gutter if it wasn't for him and Mrs Dixon. They showed me what being part of a family was like. They taught me the value of life, hard work, knowing yourself and learning to know God, to talk to him.
Parsons	I stopped talking to him a long time ago.
William	That may as well be. But he never stopped listening.
Parsons	For such a young 'un, you have an old head on them shoulders.
William	And for such an old 'un, you can be such a big daft kid!

SFX #10: the sound of bombardment, heavy guns in the background, is heard. The flashes of them in the distance are seen.

Parsons	It's started, lad.
William	I'll make you a promise. I'll compose this letter. I'll write this minute to Maude, tell her how I feel; and ask her to marry me when I get home. But only if you'll compose something for me.
Parsons	A letter?
William	A prayer.

Parsons	What? For who?
William	The world.
Parsons	Not much, then?
William	From little acorns, Mr Parsons. Little acorns.
Parsons	I'm afraid that with all I've seen, I have little faith in acorns, in prayer, or in God.
William	Maybe. But he's never lost faith in you
Parsons	Thank you, son. I just wish that, with all you have been through, and now being here, you had someone back home to call you son.
William	I have, Mr Parsons. He's called James Dixon.

SFX #11: the bombardment stops. Silence. A distant whistle sounds, then the sounds of war return.

Parsons	Time for letters is over. And stay by my side... son. *(He begins climbing over the top).*
William	Promise me, Mr Parsons... *(he grabs hold of Parsons)...* promise me you'll pray... promise me, promise me?

Cross fade. Maude is knelt down, praying. She has Bear with her.

Maude	And I pray you will bring my William home so very soon to me. And, dear God, if you can, make sure William gets the letter I have sent him. I know you are watching over so much anger and hatred in the world at this time. But I love him, so very much. Please make him sense that, know that, and help him to forgive me. Amen. And PS: When twelve abreast return, don't let his be the space. Promise me? Promise me?

Scene 5

Cross fade. At the appropriate moment the light comes up on Jane who is sat at the writing desk and who picks up the line as the sound of war fades.

Jane	*(Speaking to James as if he is offstage).* Promise me, promise me, James that we will at least find a brief time to, well, I don't know, travel to the coast. *(Pause).* Blackpool! Yes, the very thing. *(Pause).* Just one day that's all, one day; just you and I. May we? *(Pause).* Just some fresh air away. *(Pause).* Oh I don't know, a brief respite from bills and bed pans!
James	*(Entering, carrying some letters).* And the small matter of a war, my dear?
Jane	I know, James. How could I forget? But would one day make so much of a difference?
James	You're right. But only one day!
Jane	Has the post arrived?
James	Yes. Let me see. Bills. Bills. Oh look, that makes a change!
Jane	What does?
James	Another bill! And... bless me, I recognise that crooked hand. How this letter has reached us with such a scrawled address, heaven knows.
Jane	Why? Who is it from?
James	*(Opening it).* Young Master William North, I think.
Jane	William? Thank God. Is it addressed to Maude?

James	No. I think he's still frightened of what he did, how he upset her and the way they left things.
Jane	Dear Lord. Those two and their pride.
James	It's not pride, Jane. It's something bigger. They're scared. And who isn't in this world at the moment. And it looks like Master William North has sent us a gift.
Jane	A gift?
James	I do believe he has sent us a lovely example of French mud, on and in, the letter!

Mud dust falls out of the envelope. They laugh. Jane gets close to James and reads with him. The lighting changes and comes up also now on William, sat in the trenches. As he reads, both James and William speak it out loud for the first sentence; the lights fade on James and as his voice trails off it is just William.

Will/James	"Dear Father. Just a brief note today. My friend, my only real friend over here, died this morning at first light".
William	"Mr Parsons volunteered to go out over the top and rescue one of the lads who was caught on the wire. He was carrying him back when enemy machine guns killed them both. He's taught me so much: about him, about war, about death and about me. He was not a man of God. I thought. Well, they were 'estranged acquaintances' one might say. But last night, we talked for a long time. We then sat in silence for what felt like an age and then, without warning, he knelt down in the mud and began reciting 'The Lord's Prayer'. They asked what he was praying for and he said: "The World." Others sat nearby, just knelt down, joined him in the mud and said it over and over again. And then once the silence had descended again, he started singing 'Abide With Me' and we all joined in. Not everyone knew the words to all the verses so they just hummed the tune. We've never done that before. The lads all wandered off leaving Mr Parsons and me. And slowly, ever so slowly, he began to quietly cry. The tears leaving stains on his muddied cheeks. Then he stood up and took my hand and shook it for what seemed like an eternity. That was the last time I saw him. His parting request was that I thank you. Thank a man whom he had never met, but whose faith had, through me, "brought him home", he said. So, from a man you never met and will now never know, thank you father. PS: I've finally figured something out and that you were right. There were two wars I came here to fight. One with the Germans and one with me. I think I've got me sorted. The easy bit is the Hun. Sincerely, William".

The lights fade on William. A doorbell sounds.

James	Thank God. At least he's safe. *(Jane exits).* Who would have thought that slip of a lad, in fact, all of those small boys would have grown up so soon and be doing all that they are for us, for their country?
Jane	*(Entering, carrying what is clearly more post).* More post has arrived. Two letters. And a telegram.
James	I'll read the letters. The telegram can wait. No doubt my family wishing to visit!
Jane	But James…

James	What is it?
Jane	More post from William.
James	Why would he have written again?
Jane	What's the postmark? Can you read it?
James	I can't decipher the one I have just read, hold on. Let me look. This, the first one… dear Lord.
Jane	What, James?
James	That first letter was six months old. Now this other one is from July and the third one is postmarked August.
Jane	The oldest one first then I think.
James	Aye. It's been opened already. *(He opens the first letter and starts to read it aloud. Cross fade on the lights as William takes over).* "2nd July 1917. Dear Mr Dixon. Well, I don't know when you will get this letter or when I will ever have the chance to write again.
William	"Things are desperate, Father, but I cannot speak of it. It is the 2nd July as I write. A letter is the wrong time, especially with this war continuing like it is. We have been told that loose lips sink ships. What that means here in the middle of France in a field of mud, I don't know. Worse, I guess. I am at a place you will have never heard of but we are camped near to a river called, the Somme. Yesterday we engaged the enemy in a major counterattack along the river. We've been shelling the German lines for what seems like an eternity before the order was given and we advanced. We laughed that it would be like a walk in the park, a very wet and muddy park with all this rain we thought. But it wasn't. The Germans had sat out the aerial bombardment in underground bunkers and it would appear they were largely unaffected. As we advanced, the incessant rain was replaced by a deluge of machine gun fire; a hail of hot metal which, like the rain, was impossible to escape. By the end of that first day, me and the lads reckon twenty thousand were killed or lay injured on the battlefield. But, I don't know. More, I think. You so often talked of the eternity of hell which awaited the unrepentant sinner. Well it seems that the innocent faced it all in one day in a field. Over seven hundred of the boys from our regiment 'went over the top' at about 7.20am that first day. Forty minutes later, only two hundred of us were left standing. I lost my new friend in that number. George he was called. From Clitheroe. Younger than me. He has been my rock, my sanity. Looking at the age of the lads now landing here, it is time for me to quickly grow up and look after them now, as Mr Parsons did for me; as you did for me. I daren't write to Maude. I don't want to worry her. And I can't lie to her. I promised that I would not ever do that again. A lie brought me here and a lie nearly took her from me. So, if I don't write I can't lie, can I, no matter how well intentioned it might be. Tell her you managed to get a letter from me. Tell her I am writing soon to her and most important of all, tell her that Bear is still with me, albeit a little muddy now. But above all, tell her that I would be honoured if, on the very day I return home, if she would consider being…"
James	"…consider being". The other page is missing.

Jane	Then just read the other letter.
James	But we don't know what else he was…
Jane	For the love of God James, even you must know what he was asking her to do! Read the other letter. Now! How you ever managed to ask me to marry you isn't a mystery, but more a miracle!

They laugh. He opens the second letter. He and William read as before.

James William	"31st July 1917. Dear Mr Dixon. I apologise for not being in touch sooner. I know it is a month since I wrote to you. And it may be months before you get this letter. But I am alive. That is all I can pray for and my prayers have been answered. Everyone says this dreadful war will be over soon and I will be back with you and importantly, my beloved Maude. Give her my love as ever. Tell her I'm sorry for still not writing. But I have written and hope it will arrive with this one to you. I am hoping that this next push will be the last and I will then be on a troop ship home. We move out soon. I cannot tell you all the details, but the area sounds so beautiful. Some names have that sense of beauty don't they? Every time the Captain mentioned it I saw in my mind rolling hills and serenity, a peace that we have not had since we landed in France. I saw in that name, Lancashire and its green fields, farms and family; I saw all of you. More importantly, I saw Maude and the life we will have. So. Here's to being home soon and here's to having that dream realised and that this next camp and next offensive will be our last. Here's to the end of the war. Here's to being amongst loved ones again. Here's to finding out if Maude answered the question I asked in my letter to you. And here's to our next stop. I don't know how you spell it, so excuse if my spelling now offends the eye, but here's to my final sojourn before home, the beautiful and idyllic sounding… *(The light fast fades on him)*
Jane	What James, what… what, tell me where is he? You are such a tease! Then give it me! *(James drops the letter. She runs to pick it up and frantically scans it to get to the end)*. Clumsy man! Now let me see: "…the beautiful and idyllic sounding… Passchendaele". *(She and James are still, silent.)* Open the telegram.
James	I can't.
Jane	James.
James	Please don't make me.
Jane	James! *(She runs at him, grabs the telegram, opens it and reads it)*. "I deeply regret to inform you that Private William North was… 31st July 1917 at Passchendaele. The Army Council express their sympathy. Yours Faithfully. Secretary, War Office".
Maude	*(Entering, she bursts in, full of energy, talking at full belt)*. I tell you, Father, how you have kept your patience with all of us over so many years is beyond me. But how you dealt with our parents, well, you are both saints. Mrs Hodgkiss sent Daisy to school today and you know how they dressed her, just guess; how do you think? She looked like a clown in a circus! A long red skirt, striped blouse and green shoes that would have fit you, never mind… *(She stops, looking at them for a response)*. What's the matter?
Jane	Nothing.

James	Nothing? Nothing?
Maude	What is it?
Jane	I need to go.
James	Stay where you are
Jane	James, please don't make me.
James	*(Shouting).* Stay where you are, woman!
Jane	Please!
James	You will do as I say!
Maude	Father, what is it? Why are you both shouting? What could have possibly…? *(They all stand in silence, numb, scared, apprehensive. James holds out to her the bundle of letters).* What is it? What's that you're holding?
Jane	Letters from William.
Maude	*(Suddenly, she lights up, excited).* Well, let me see them. Has he sent one for me? Did he get mine? About time! *(She walks over, takes the letters and the telegram and reads them but is clearly not taking anything in, randomly scanning them. She drops each letter in turn).* Well at least he's apologising! Aww bless him, he's too beside himself and wanted you to tell me! And what's this? "Tell her if I would be honoured if she would consider being…", being what? Honoured if what? The other page is missing. He wants to marry me when he gets back doesn't he? Oh, thank you God, thank you, thank you. I thought he didn't love me anymore. That I'd ruined everything. But he loves me, Mrs Dixon. He loves me and does want to marry me! *(She turns the letter over and goes down on her knees, frantically picking up the letters and, shaking, tries to find the missing page).*
Maude	Where's the rest? Is there another letter? The last line is missing, he might have put something else in the other letter.
Jane	*(Almost matter of fact).* Yes. The first envelope had been opened so the last page must have been taken out or lost. I wouldn't be surprised if the army had…
Maude	*(Interrupting, reading the letter).* "My beloved Maude". "Give her my love as ever". Well, it's took him long enough; still not an apology, exactly, but it'll do. Who'd have thought it, eh? He proposes in a letter and the most important bit gets lost! But he loves me. I hoped, but I knew all along he couldn't have given up on me. He going to ask me to marry him. I don't deserve to feel like this, to be so happy.
James	Give it to her.
Jane	James, I…
James	*(Shouting).* For the love of God!
Maude	What! Why do you keep shouting at Mrs Dixon? What is it?
Jane	There's another… it's, a, …
James	It's a telegram.
Maude	Telegram? From Will? He's coming home! *(Silence. Stillness. She runs over to Jane, takes the telegram and opens it).* Is he home and letting me know that…?

As Maude he reads the telegram James approaches, and stands behind her. She goes to faint but he catches her.

James	You will not hear what I am going to say, but you need listen to it, now, before one more word or tear invades this moment. Child, when we lose somebody that we love, we also, for a time, lose ourselves. We choose to forget because remembering is hurting. We remember all the wrong things at the wrong times in the wrong places. We remember the things which hurt. We remember the things, the people that we feel we need to blame. And when you choose to spend all your time on your own, the only person left to blame is yourself. If we're not careful, all we have are the memories that caused the hurt. So we just hurt. But with effort, with time, we are capable of a simply wondrous thing. We remember laughter; we remember love. We turn away from loss and we remember life. And then, child, a miracle happens. We remember how to live again. And with it, we bring the one we mourn back to life by allowing them to live within us, through us again. And we are alive. Be alive, child. Remember a life. Remember how to live. Remember the one who has died. But the hardest thing of all. Remember it wasn't you.

Maude exits, running off. James and Jane embrace. Lighting change.

Scene 6

Jane	On the 11th November 1918, peace was declared. An occasion that a small, insignificant and little-known orphanage, along with the rest of the world, thought would never arrive. And James recorded the event in his diary.
James	"1918, November 11th. Peace Day. End of the Great War. Went to the dentist".

SFX #12: church bells are heard.

Jane	The church bells around the town rang out resoundingly with sounds of thanks and acclamation. We decorated the orphanage with streamers and we ran the Union Jack and the Stars and Stripes up the flagpole on the front. And there was a band. A beautiful, shining brass band. It glistened and gleamed in the bright light of the day, as if the reflected rays carried the music into our very souls. The children ran home from school singing patriotic songs to find a party waiting with sweets and fireworks, followed by a service in the school room. The sun shone in shafts through the windows picking out expectant faces and behind them, lives to be lived, dreams to be realised, hopes to be satisfied and new families just waiting to make a new world. A better world. A remembering world.

SFX #13: children singing 'Abide With Me' is heard.

James	My dear children. I would like you all to think on the words of a hymn, not the new one you have just sung, but the one from this morning which had the words: "God bless our soldiers, Guard them each day, Make them victorious, O'er all the way: In the great conflict, may they endure; God bless our soldiers, Make victory sure". Well. That they have. So, after our celebrations have ended, remember that the aftermath of the war is yet to be addressed. Thousands of bereaved and saddened hearts and homes. And sometimes I ponder and think: Are we as a nation any nearer God and better and nobler

living than we were? There is still the selfishness, greed and lust; and the hateful Drink still holds sway, apparently unheeded and unchallenged by many professing Christians. God grant that after this sacrifice of blood, tears and agony, there may yet rise a nobler race.

The lighting changes.

Jane   One hundred and sixteen Old Boys had enlisted in the Army and the Navy.
James   One hundred and sixteen members of families.
Jane   One hundred and sixteen members of <u>our</u> family.
James   Ten of whom never came home.

Enter Maude.

Jane   In November 1919, at the eleventh hour of the eleventh day, the flag at the orphanage was, at the King's request, lowered. We all gathered to observe two minute's silence. And there began a new tradition, a tradition repeated throughout the land. A tradition repeated in a tiny orphanage, by tiny children. The reading of the names of the fallen.
James   Ensuring none are Nobodys
Jane   Ensuring all are Somebodys.
James   Ensuring that we remember.
Maude   Jacob Aspin.
Jane   Alfred Burns.
James   William Cowell.
Maude   John Thomas Crook.
Jane   Thomas Hutton.
James   John Hutton.
Maude   Joseph Marsden.
Jane   William Siddorn.
James   William Wilcock.
Maude   William North.
James   I hear their names. Read their names. Remember their names. And yet, all I still see, are the faces of children.

Fade to black. SFX #14: in the darkness children singing 'The Lord's My Shepherd' is heard, during which Jane speaks. Exit James.

Jane   And so children, now in 1920, on this second anniversary of the end of the Great War, the war to end all wars we are told, we give thanks, we pray, we remember. And now I ask our own Maude, no longer resident with us and one our newest local teachers, but always a part of our family, to come forward and address us, as she now wishes to deliver her own Act of Remembrance and in her own poetic way. *(She exits).*

A light appears on Maude as she moves forward. She has her bear with her and also her journal. She speaks, addressing the audience as if they are a group of children. Nothing which now follows is tragic. It has an air of calm, of warmth, of happiness, of hope.

Maude   It's funny children. All I came in with when I came to the orphanage at Wilpshire, was a teddy bear. I can't remember how or why, or who gave her to me now. And I was going to say that all I am left with is my teddy, my bear, my friend. But within her, surrounding her, because of her, is so much more. She represents love, a chance, hope, opportunity and yes, happiness. And I found all that here, with Mr and Mrs Dixon, and all of you. And for a brief time when all of those things seemed to slip through my fingers, I did a simple thing. I closed my eyes… and I remembered what Mr and Mrs Dixon gave me and have given you. Hope. And today, I keep my eyes wide open, and with it, keep an open mind, an open heart and all for a memory that I will not allow to slip away. I remember. And nothing will ever stop that. For I have so much love, so much to be thankful for. As do all of you. You cannot ever stop folk from pitying you when you tell them you were, are, an orphan. Well, you just remember this day. This time. These people. You are an orphan because of the past. But the future will make you so much more. I, we, are truly blessed. *(She places her bear on the floor in front of her).* I would like to introduce you children, to Mrs Bear. She had a friend… but he went away and that made me, us, very sad. *(She opens her journal).* So I wrote a poem, children. A poem that Mrs Bear helped me to write. A poem to help me understand. A poem to help me remember. A poem that helped me to recall happiness… and to recall Mr Bear; and never to forget him…

Maude   It now seems true what people say:
An empty space can fill your day.
And then with silence will consume
The sanctuary sought in every room.
For loss has ways, or so they say.
To pause the time that makes the day.
And make each longing, longer still.
Against our hopes, against our will.
And empty words, well-meaning said.
To comfort the living about the dead,
With promises "… pain will go away"
That "… grief subsides with every day."
Not knowing, really, how I feel.
How I cope, how I deal,
The effort needed to conceal.
To fix a smile and not reveal;

William enters upstage as she continues to read. He watches her, smiling.

Maude   That other death so well I hide
The one that's hidden deep inside.
The one that happened on that day.
The day that took my soul away.
And yet within this darkness tide
That overwhelms the place I hide
A spark of light grows brighter yet.
A spark that that won't let me forget;
It holds reflections, voices bright.
That tell the story of the light.

The light of memories, times before
Hidden just behind a door,
That readily opens with no fuss.
Revealing not just me, but us.
Immersed in joy and laughter yet.
Which no matter what, I can't forget;
Proving even though you're gone
Your spirit lives forever on.
Inside my soul, my mind my heart;
So that I know we're not apart.
The one I love who went away;
The one I think of everyday day.
Who's with me now, but deep inside
And proves there is no need to hide.
For once an orphan without a thing.
No silver spoon, no wedding ring.
Will make this soul for ever sing.
And now and always, be my King.

During the above James and Jane enter and join Maude again. They are happy. Truly. They take hold of her arms and walk Maude up stage to exit. SFX #15: 'The Last Post' is heard. William who has been observing all this moves to centre stage places his bear next to Maud's, makes to leave but stops and turns to the audience.

William   Remembered. *(He exits).*

Slow fade to black.

THE END

'Changing #1'
(One act play)

Synopsis
One appointment.
One funeral home.
Three funerals to arrange ... or so the women think.
When it comes to arranging your husband's funeral, it's a job many women would face with trepidation.
Some would fear it.
Some might want it to be over.
Some can't wait.
Some see an opportunity and a chance to live and to laugh.
'Changing #1' explores how a simple but daunting task might have an obvious objective but then meeting others in the same circumstance can change all of that.
And changing in more ways than one would think.
NB: Any similarities between persons or businesses living or dead is purely accidental!

Characters
3f
Kate, Joyce and Alison
Playing ages are flexible

Running time approx 45 minutes

Music: David Bowie 'Changes'
Starts with an empty couch on stage.
There is a freestanding sign which simply reads 'CHAPEL OF REST' and an arrow pointing off.
Kate is pre-set at one end of the couch. Second woman (Joyce) enters and sits at the other end of the sofa. They are both dressed in black.
She picks up a travel brochure from the seat next to her and begins to read.
Both eventually look at each other, acknowledging with a simple, expressionless nod and Kate stares forward.
Silence.
Joyce is still reading.

Joyce	They always look so good in the pictures, don't they?
Kate	Who?
Joyce	Not who, what. Hotels. Holiday destinations. Bit like cookery books or clothes catalogues. They always make everything look good, amazing. The photographs; perfect, dreamlike. Better than anything of your own. Better than your own pictures. Your own life
Kate	Yes, I guess
Joyce	Not that they are. Better. Never what you expected. Invariably. Hotels. Never look like it when you get there, do they? Not when you get off the transfer coach at your package, all-inclusive, respite from reality at two in the morning. And it's

	raining and humid and you're tired and all you want is a proper cup of tea and a pee. And after being herded like mindless farm animals into the reception area by what looks like a 15-year-old holiday rep', you have time to stand there. And wait. And notice the detail. The stains on the reception carpet. The dead insects in the light shades. The badly hand-written notice on the wipe board for the dreaded 'welcome meeting.' They always miss a picture of all those in their glossy brochure somehow. And someone wearing a badly fitting polyester uniform and smelling of sweat is thrusting a champagne flute into your hand containing an unrecognisable, ambient fizzy liquid
Kate	I would think it's supposed to be …
Joyce	Bucks fizz, I know. But odd though, don't you think?
Kate	The drink?
Joyce	Having a holiday brochure in a funeral home. You'd think they'd have catalogues of coffins and headstones lying around to tempt you. Handles and linings to entice you. Mahogany or walnut. Choices of floral arrangements in every conceivable design to whet your appetite. Orders of Service templates to choose from with meaningful poems about meaningless people; which read so well, but bear no resemblance to the reality of the person who has, the person who has …
Kate	Died?
Joyce	Yes, that'll be the word

Silence

Kate	'Funeral Home'

Joyce looks at her, waiting for something more

Kate	Odd name isn't it? Don't you think? 'Funeral Home'. Are you supposed to feel like you're at your own home or in someone else's I wonder?
Joyce	Too tidy to be my home
Kate	Or that you just want to go home
Joyce	And hide
Kate	From family
Joyce	From everybody

Silence

Kate	Or 'Funeral Parlour'… never understood that one either. I'd expect it to look like my gran's front room or something. Y'know. 'Parlour'. Just an odd word to use, don't you think?
Joyce	Especially when you have ice cream parlours
Kate	Beauty parlours
Joyce	Dog grooming parlours
Kate	Massage parlours

Silence

Joyce   'Rest Home', that's another one isn't it? Who's having the rest? You or the person who has, the person who has …
Kate   Died?
Joyce   Yes, that'll be the word
Kate   Not a word you'll be able to avoid hearing in here though is it?
Joyce   But outside here, hardly ever
Kate   Thankfully
Joyce   Thankfully

Silence

Joyce   'Chapel of Rest'
Kate   Oh, I've always preferred that one
Joyce   Me too
Kate   But not 'Undertakers'
Joyce   What does that mean? 'Under-takers'? Are they promising to do something for you or, I don't know
Kate   Perhaps, it's all about putting them under and taking your money
Joyce   Never thought of it like that
Kate   And 'Funeral Directors', like you're on a film set
Joyce   "Stand by pallbearers, stand by incense, roll the tears and … action!"

They both force a laugh and it trails off

Joyce   Flowers. I've always wondered about them too. Such a faff and an expense, all for what? And the tributes that people have made up and placed in the side window of the hearse. You know which ones I mean? Words, names, phrases. Can they spell any word or a name with any flowers, do you think? I wouldn't know where to start, how to do it
Kate   Just like clever flowering arranging really, I guess
Joyce   I guess
Kate   As long as you're prepared to pay, they'll put together whatever you want. Y'know. Pay by the letter like a telegram or engraving. Keep it short to keep it cheap: 'Mum', 'Dad', 'Nana'.
Joyce   Expensive then if 'Great Granddad' has snuffed it
Kate   Quite. If you want to make a statement and you're prepared to pay, you could have what you want, a declaration, an affirmation of what the person meant to you, like, well, what might someone want?
Joyce   'Useless piece of shit'
Kate   Well. I was thinking of 'With love'. But if that's what you wanted, I suppose …
Joyce   Or 'Why couldn't you have died sooner and made us all happy'
Kate   … and tag 'RIP' at the end so they know you're just a bit sad?

Joyce looks at her and then bursts out laughing, which trails off

Kate	I wonder what they do with them afterwards
Joyce	The bodies?
Kate	The flowers
Joyce	Not sure really. You see them all laid outside the Crem' don't you. A window on someone else's loss and how they felt they needed to express it; the message in flowers they wanted to give the world. But no, you're right. You never see where they go at the end of the day
Kate	Perhaps they use them again
Joyce	Never thought of that either
Kate	I mean, you wouldn't collect them all up afterwards like buffet at the end of a birthday party and take them home with you in a box, would you?
Joyce	Only so many lilies you can have in your lounge before you're overcome by the smell
Kate	But I'd struggle what to do with those floral tribute words though. Do you give them as a gift to the Nana or Granddad that's left? Like a floral consolation prize for having outlived the other one? A thank you for having stayed alive. Bunches of flowers I get, but the words?
Joyce	I'm not sure that …
Kate	You know. Where you'd put them afterwards if you did take them home. What use are they? 'Nana', Granddad', where would you put them afterwards? Why would you want to? Couldn't exactly put them in your front window
Joyce	If you've got a long mantlepiece, then my idea would be fine
Kate	Idea?
Joyce	'Why couldn't you have died sooner and made us all happy.' That would fill the length of my mantlepiece perfectly
Kate	Wouldn't even get 'RIP' on mine. Wood burner you see
Joyce	I see. You could always cut the floral letters up and make up a new word or phrase from them. You know. Like criminals do with newspapers for ransom demands
Kate	"Pay your bill or the corpse gets it?"
Joyce	But I'd always still see the original words in it. Like those word-puzzle books. Or them 'Magic Eye' pictures they had years ago. Hidden in plain sight. Speaking to you. Reminding you
Kate	Yes. Because if it originally said, 'Once a shit, always a shit', you'd struggle not to still see the shit
Joyce	Even though he's buried
Kate	No escaping the shit then
Joyce	Not now that he's, that he's
Kate	Died?
Joyce	Yes, that'll be the word.

Silence. Holds her hand out

Kate	Kate
Joyce	Joyce

Kate	Come here to organise a funeral?
Joyce	Is that what this place is? I just saw the word parlour and assumed they did massages
Kate	No, this is a funeral … right
Joyce	Sorry. Nice to laugh sometimes don't you think? Even when you're not supposed to, when people don't think you should. Reminds you that the world is still spinning. Even when someone has, someone has …
Both	Died
Joyce	Yes. I do know the word. Just can't get used to saying it
Kate	Or thinking it
Joyce	What it means
Kate	What it means has to be done
Joyce	And here we are
Kate	And here we are

Silence

Kate	I sat in the car outside for a while you know. Got here a bit early
Joyce	What time?
Kate	Half past five
Joyce	This morning?
Kate	Well, last night would have been a bit odd
Joyce	And half past five this morning isn't? It didn't open until nine-thirty
Kate	Well. I had nothing else to do. If I'm going to sit at home on my own and stare at four walls, I thought I might as well stare out of four windows. At least you get a change of scenery through them
Joyce	But half past five? That's life I suppose
Kate	That's death actually

Silence

Kate	Is it a parent you've lost?
Joyce	Sadly not. They keep finding their way home
Kate	Right. Funny. I guess
Joyce	Husband. Yes. Sorry

Silence

Kate	When did he pass?
Joyce	Pass what?
Kate	You know?
Joyce	Not at the moment
Kate	Pass, you know
Joyce	A driving test, a kidney stone?
Kate	Pass on
Joyce	Don't think he played rugby

Kate	You're not making this very easy
Joyce	Not the only one. Sorry. I'm just …
Kate	It's fine. Not the place for having to explain the need to behave oddly
Joyce	Or arriving four hours early

They both laugh politely. Silence. Kate instinctively reaches over and takes Joyce' hand, but she takes her hand away. Then,

Kate	Cancer?
Joyce	Cancer. Yours?
Kate	Cancer
Joyce	What sort
Kate	The sort that kills you
Joyce	Did he last long?
Kate	No. He sort of gasped a bit and that was it
Joyce	I mean, did he live with it for long
Kate	Yes. <u>We</u> did
Joyce	Where was it?
Kate	Where was what?
Joyce	His cancer
Kate	In his body. Where do you think? We didn't keep it in a box and take it out when visitors came around
Joyce	Look. I can understand that …
Kate	No. I'm sorry. You can't … just like I can't. I've come here to arrange a funeral, not analyse why it all happened to him. Us. How I feel now. Had enough tea, sympathy, hugs and understanding for a bloody lifetime
Joyce	Sorry
Kate	No I'm sorry. You've no need to be. Ignore me. I'm fine. Honestly. No excuse for bad manners
Joyce	Ah well. You're bound to be cranky. You know. You have been up five hours

They both laugh. Alison enters and interrupts the moment. She stops as she enters, looks around and then remains standing, uncomfortably. Silence, then

Alison	Good morning
Kate	Hi
Joyce	Hello
Alison	Have you both come to arrange a funeral?
Both	No, we've come for a massage … (they trail off and then both smirk)
Joyce	Sorry. Yes, we have. Ignore us. I'm Joyce and this is Kate. We've just been putting the world to right and you came in mid-flow
Alison	Oh, I see. Right. Am I interrupting?
Joyce	Not at all. Sit down

She does so, in between them. Silence, then

Alison	Has anybody been out to see you yet?
Kate	A lady came out and said they would be a little while and to tell anybody who arrived to take a seat
Alison	Have you been here long?
Joyce	One of us has

Kate and Joyce both lean forward and look at each other and smile

Kate	I got here at 5.30 this morning
Alison	Why, have they got a sale on?
Joyce	No. She was that excited, she couldn't sleep
Alison	Really?
Kate	Ignore her
Alison	I was just passing. Several times actually. I did the same yesterday. Just kept walking past looking in the window and in the end I thought, well, I've got to do it sometime, so here I am. Are you both here about your…
Joyce	Husbands?
Kate	Yes.
Alison	Yes. This is for my late husband. I've never been in one of these places before. I knew where it was because we always get pizzas from the place next door. Always found that a bit odd as well, when they built this block. Why they'd put a funeral, a funeral, you know …
Kate	Home?
Joyce	Parlour?
Alison	… Directors, why it would be next to a pizza delivery shop
Kate	Oh I don't know. At least it means I don't need to think about lunch when I leave
Joyce	Pizza for lunch. What a good idea
Kate	Eh. Pizza Parlour – Funeral Parlour. Do you think that's why they put them next door to each other? A bit of a theme going on?
Alison	Well, 'parlour' certainly fits with what's coming
Kate	Coming?
Alison	What they're going to be opening next door-but-one
Joyce	You don't mean
All	A massage parlour
Kate	Food, funerals and fornication all in one block
Alison	How biblical
Joyce	Isn't there a hymn about that?
Kate	There should be
Joyce	*(singing)* "All things bright and beautiful,
Kate	*(singing)* "All vices great and small"
Alison	*(singing)* "Deep Pan, Thin Crust, extra cheese"
All	*(singing)* "And garlic bread for all"

They all laugh which trails off. Silence

Joyce	Anyhow, you'll have to be quick if you want to make the most of that pizza place next door
Kate	Why?
Joyce	It's for sale. They were putting the sign up as I arrived. Closes this afternoon
Alison	You're joking!
Joyce	So this place is doing well because their business is the dead, and the pizza place is closing because business is, well …
Kate	Dead?
Alison	Aye. That's the word
Joyce	So what's moving into there instead?
Alison	A DIY shop so I'm told
Kate	Food, funerals, fornication and now, Formica
Joyce	DIY. Pity they don't have do-it-yourself funerals. Be better than having to do all of this
All	Abso-bloody-lutely

Silence

Alison	Anyhow. As I was saying, I've never been in one of these places before. Have either of you?
Kate	No
Joyce	No
Alison	So what do you do?
Kate	I'm assuming they'll give us some options of what we can have, look through some brochures; we choose, we pay, we're done
Alison	You make it sound like a business, a production line
Joyce	Because that's what it is. You can dress it up as much as you want but at the end of the day, it's just another supermarket
Kate	Without the loyalty card
Alison	Or a nice café

Silence

Alison	I was just thinking. If you can have frequent flyer points and shopping Clubcard points, then I'm surprised that you can't have a reward card for frequent funerals
Joyce	What a good idea
Kate	'Save for the grave'
Joyce	'Pall Bearer Bonds'
Alison	Well, it's not as if someone's going to come along with a completely different way of doing this and do away with the need for a funeral, are they? We all, you know
Kate	Die?
Alison	Yes, that's the word
Joyce	Not as if they'll ever go out of business then, is it?
Kate	Never heard of a funeral director getting made redundant
Alison	Certainly not a dying business, the dying business

Kate   But not, it would appear, like the pizza business
All   No

Silence

Alison   But it would be handy wouldn't it? You know. If you could arrange a few at a time
Kate   Pizzas?
Alison   Funerals
Joyce   Aye. If you're a serial killer
Kate   I suppose it would save time
Alison   I was thinking more about saving money
Kate   So if you can have bulk buy, then why not bulk bury?
Joyce   Bog off
Alison   No need to be personal
Joyce   No, BOGOFF
Kate   Bury one, get one free
Alison   Oh yes, sorry
Kate   Can you imagine, if you went to the Co-op funeral people and they still did stamps like years ago?
Joyce   … and with all the money we're going to spend
Kate   That little stamp machine they used to have on the tills would burn out
Joyce   Think how many stamps we'd get!
Alison   It was my job every Saturday when we got back from shopping. To sit at the kitchen table and lick them all and stick them in the books
Kate   Oh, I had to do that
Joyce   And me
Alison   It was all about savings stamps in those days. What about those ones your mum would collect for a Christmas savings club? You know, for Christmas hampers
Joyce   Exclusive hampers in our house if you don't mind
Alison   Executive in our house thank you
Kate   Perhaps now, they could combine the two: funerals and festive delicacies. You know. All your groceries arrive on Christmas Eve, paid for with your savings club stamps, but to add a twist, they're packed in a coffin
Joyce   To have in, in case there's an unexpected emergency
Alison   Certainly a conversation piece for when the relatives call around
Joyce   Christmas Hampers. Them were the days. Tins of ham
Kate   Bags of brazil nuts
Alison   Big jars of mincemeat
Joyce   Tins of expensive biscuits
Kate   That you'd never dream of buying in the weekly shop
Alison   And your mum would give some away to an Aunty who you only ever saw once a year
Kate   Not because she liked her
Alison   But just to piss her off

208

Joyce	And a big ham joint your mam would show the neighbours to make her look something special
Kate	And a box of deluxe crackers with dead posh gifts inside that your dad wouldn't allow you to pull
Joyce	And Belgian chocolates covered in gold leaf
Alison	But they'd never let you eat any of them
Joyce	But now, handily, all packed in a nice mahogany casket that you can save for a rainy day
Alison	Inspired
Kate	Yes, them were the days. All changed now
Alison	When all mums and dads were the same
Kate	When we still had mums and dads
Joyce	Not now they're all gone
Alison	Not now they've all, they've all, you know…
Kate	Died?
Joyce	Yes
All	That's the word
Allison	It doesn't feel like things have changed, that I've changed. It's only when you talk about years ago, the people, their lives: my life. You realise how changed we all are
Kate	And not for the better
Joyce	Do you think this has changed us?
Alison	I don't feel any different by being here
Kate	I do. Just not sure how
Joyce	If only we could change what and who surrounds our lives; control them, shapes them. Take control of this, now
Alison	But we don't have that much control, do we? Look at us, now, here. Why we're here and what we need to do. We can't influence that, change that, can we?
All	Pity

Silence

Kate	Did any of your family offer to come today and help you?
Alison	Mine don't live near by
Joyce	Mine do
Kate	Where?
Joyce	Next door. Back-to-back actually. Typical. You dream of fairies or a pot of gold at the bottom of the garden. I got my bloody daughter
Alison	Do you see a lot of her?
Joyce	Only when she wants something. So, yes. All the time.
Kate	I've only got my sister. I don't see her since I told that her that I'd done my will and left everything to the local dog's home
Joyce	Bloody hell. Good on you!
Alison	Didn't go down well then?
Kate	You could say that. She was only ever interested in me because I had a bit of money put away. The advantage of leaving it to the dog's home is, well, at least

209

	there won't be a homeless poodle sat on my death bed saying, "Has she not gone yet?"
Joyce	Shouldn't be allowed
Kate	Leaving money to a dog's home?
Joyce	Allowing a dog on your bed
Alison	And it wouldn't sound like that either, would it?
Kate	What wouldn't?
Alison	A talking dog. More like *(does a gruff voice as her best talking dog impression)* "Has she gone yet?"
Joyce	Do you think they all sound the same when they talk?

They both look at her

Joyce	Sorry. Sounded a bit barmy then didn't I?
Alison	Barking

They all look at each other and laugh

Joyce	Do you think they go to the same trouble?
Alison	Who?
Joyce	Dog funeral directors
Kate	'Dog funeral directors'?
Alison	Where did that come from?
Kate	You are joking?
Joyce	No. There was an advert in a Sunday magazine I was reading. You can have your pet cremated. They put the remains in an urn and you can have it interred and they do plaques and commemorative stuff; all sorts
Alison	That's nice
Kate	Do all their friends come to the funeral do you think?
Joyce	Whose friends?
Kate	The dogs. Do they organise a mini-wake?
Joyce	Mini-wake-walkies
Kate	With dog treats for the buffet. All standing around in the park, reminiscing
Alison	Yes. All standing around sniffing, straining to be somewhere, anywhere else
Joyce	So, not that different from us then really
Alison	Suppose not
Kate	That's the one thing I am dreading. Having to stand around at the end. Having to endure being hugged and patted on the back
Joyce	And the garbage that they all say to you
Kaye	I might play 'commiserations bingo' to stop myself going mad
Alison	What do you mean?
Kate	We did it at my Gran's funeral. You know. Count how many different ways people can say 'I'm so sorry' (she then repeats it several different ways)
Alison	And 'I feel your loss'
Joyce	'It was a blessing'
Kate	'They've gone to a better place'

Alison   'No more suffering'
Joyce   'No more walkies'

They both look at her

Joyce   Oh, sorry. Thought we were still on dog funerals
Kate   And then the worst bit: sat in a funeral car with everyone staring at you. Like a bloody goldfish in a bowl. How the funeral directors put up with dealing with it day in day out, week in, week out. Beyond me
All   Hmm

Silence

Kate   Where do you think funeral directors go to arrange their own funerals?
Alison   Is this the start of a joke?
Kate   No. Just wondered
Joyce   Never thought about it
Alison   Perhaps they get their colleagues to do it
Kate   God. Could you imagine? People that you know doing - that - to you
Joyce   Well, it's not as if you're going to be embarrassed, is it?
Alison   Suppose not
Kate   Perhaps they get a staff discount
Joyce   What's the point of being eligible for a discount if you're, y'know
Alison   Dead?
Kate   You're right. She's right
Joyce   Be nice to know that it's there though. Just in case. A staff burial scheme I mean. A comfort
Alison   For a rainy day
Kate   Like having your Christmas Hamper Coffin

They snigger. Silence

Alison   So what else do they arrange for you? The staff here? The coffin, flowers, cars, the church, printing. What else is there?
Kate   Will you have a wake?
Joyce   Oh I never thought about that
Alison   Do you have to have one?
Kate   You don't have to do anything. It's all up to you. If you're paying, it's your choice
Alison   What are you having yours' in?
Joyce   Bugger. Never thought of that either. What do you put them in?
Alison   The ground?
Joyce   No you silly sod. What clothes do you put them in?
Kate   Mine loved going to these big fancy dress do's, so I thought I might put him in one of his outfits

211

They both turn and look at her

Alison   You are joking?
Joyce   Seriously?
Kate   Why not? It's not as if he's going to be laid out in state, is it? We've got a wardrobe full of them. Well, not really fancy dress. That's not a very good description of them. More like 'historically accurate costumes'. No use to me now. Cost him a fortune. He did those re-enactments you see
Alison   Re-enactments?
Kate   He used to go to these big events where they played out famous battles and wars. He picked a side and wore the outfit which went with it. He was shot, run through or beheaded at least three times a month. So, I'm thinking. I could put him in one of his costumes. But which one? He had three particular favourite battles. I think I'm stuck between him dressed in the theme of Custer's Last Stand, the Battle of Agincourt or the Roman Invasion of Gaul
Alison   You're going to bury him in fancy dress?
Kate   'Historical re-enactment, authentic period costume' if you don't mind. If Julius Caesar could be buried in Roman military uniform, I can't see why my husband can't
Alison   But your husband wasn't exactly famous for conquering the ancient civilised world though was he?
Kate   No. But he was very popular with the crowds last summer in Cleethorpes
Joyce   And will you, y'know, dress up for the funeral too?
Kate   Don't be daft. I was never into that rubbish. I do like dressing up though. I'm more into film-themed parties and costumes for concerts and shows. Hey, now there's an idea!
Alison   So what will that mean? Dressing as a character from a film for the funeral?
Kate   I'm thinking more of a musical theatre theme for the mourners
Joyce   Musical theatre?
Kate   Rocky Horror Show. I'll wear a Basque. Black, naturally. After all, I am in mourning
Joyce   Naturally
Alison   Got to be respectful
Kate   Picture it: as the curtains shut at the Crem', I'll have them play 'The Time Warp'. And the mourners could get up and do the dance
Joyce   The dance?
Kate   The dance
Alison   You know. Even I know it

Kate and Alison stand up and sing/do the moves

Ka/Al   "Let's do the time warp again"
Joyce   Lovely. I think. And if they're not comfortable with doing that, what would you have them do?
Alison   Ooo, how about 'Agadoo'?
Kate   Or 'The Locomotion'

Alison   'YMCA'
Ka/Al   Love that one
Kate   I could film it on my mobile and put it on you tube
Alison At least the family who couldn't get there would be able to watch it then
Joyce   And I thought I was pushing it with having 'All things bright and beautiful'
Kate   Could you imagine that hymn at my husband's funeral? With his hobby? (*singing*) "All things bright and beautiful"
Joyce   "All costumes great and small"
Alison "Firing bows at Agincourt"
Kate   "Or killing folk in Gaul"

They all laugh and again, it trails off

Joyce   You've got me thinking you know. I might put mine in his favourite suit?
Kate   Dinner suit?
Joyce   Diving suit. He loved his scuba
Alison Would they let you dress him in a rubber suit if you're going to cremate him?
Kate   She's got a point. It could start a fire
Joyce   Never thought of that. Could you imagine? Setting the smoke alarm off in a crematorium

Silence. Alison is by now looking at her 'phone

Joyce   But that is the main point, isn't it? The big decision we have to make? Funeral or cremation?
Kate   I'm still not certain what's involved in it all. I understand burying, because you dig a hole and just put them in, don't you?
Joyce   I think that's the general principle
Kate   So, not much to that. But cremations must be a bit more involved
Joyce   I would expect so. I guess it would be rather technical as well
Kate   Do you think the people who actually do the cremation have a sort of manual to tell them what to do? I know that it's just a big oven, but there's ovens and ovens aren't there? And you always get a set of instructions when you buy a new oven at home. You know. Telling how to do stuff and for how long
Alison They always have a chart with those don't they? My new oven did. Telling you exactly that. You know. Which food took how long
Joyce   Oh yes. Never thought of that. After all, how would the cremation people know, you know, how long to well, do them for?
Alison Could you imagine the instruction book: "For a 5'10" husband weighing 16 stone, place on the middle shelf for 5 hours"
Joyce   "Turn regularly"
Kate   "Until golden brown". Sorry, I shouldn't have said that
Joyce   I should think not. We want to burn them not bake them
Alison I was beginning to wonder where you were taking that one
Joyce   So did I. I was expecting you were going to baste him with egg
Kate   No. Don't be daft. You'd do that before you put them in

213

Alison I could do that job. Working in a Crem'
Joyce   Really?
Alison Well, during my married life, all my oven ever did was cremate things
Kate   You don't need a book or instructions for how to use an oven. 220 for 20 minutes. Perfect for everything that goes in my oven
Alison *(who has been looking at her mobile, then reads aloud)* Here we are. Found it. "On average, it takes about one to three hours to cremate a human body, thereby reducing it to 3-7 pounds of 'cremains'. The cremation remains are usually pasty white in colour. These cremains are transferred into a cremation urn and given to the relative or representative of the deceased."

They are looking at her

Alison What? It tells you all about it on this website
Joyce   One to three hours. Quicker than doing a turkey at Christmas
Alison Taste a damn sight better than my turkey at Christmas
Kate   'Cremains'? Is that what they call what's left?
Alison That's what it says on this website
Joyce   They have a word for everything now. I'm surprised they don't give you instructions on how to do it yourself
Kate   Hey. I tell you who could write a cookbook about making the perfect DIY cremation
Alison Who?
Kate   Mary Bury!

They all burst out laughing which, as ever, trails off

Kate   Oh, come on. How long does it take? What are they doing?
Alison Who's first to be seen?
Joyce   Kate I would say … as she's been camped out in the car park all night
Kate   You 'd think they'd have one of those little ticket machines to avoid confusion
Alison Ticket machines? Are we back on Co-op stamps again?
Joyce   For parking do you mean?
Kate   No. For knowing who's next to be seen. Like they used to have in the Post Office. Our butcher had one too
Joyce   Oh, I know what you mean. You'd tear the next number off a roll at the counter and they'd call the next person out. I remember
Alison Listen to us. Waiting for your number to be called, for your time to be up. I guess that's what brought us all here
Kate   So the modern version would be one of those automated voices that they use
Joyce   That who uses?
Kate   The Post Office
Alison I'm sorry?
Kate   "Cashier number four please"
Joyce   So ours would be "Mourner number two please"
Alison "Please collect your Cremains from desk A"

214

Kate	Just think then. If you could do all of this at the Post Office
Joyce	That would save so much time, wouldn't it?
Alison	Be so much easier. Take your catalogue stuff back at the same time
Kate	"A packet of envelopes, a book of second-class stamps and a mahogany coffin please"
Joyce	Or just go to the Post Office and let them do it all for you. Because they are always so helpful, aren't they? The staff. Be so much easier if you dropped him off and they, well, sent him off
Alison	Dropped who off?
Kate	Sent who off?
Joyce	Your dead husband
Alison	Seriously?
Joyce	His final journey, the big send-off. Only it would be second class
Alison	"Let Parcel Force take away your pain by taking away your husband"
Kate	If I'd known they offered that service, I'd have packed him off years ago
Alison	No faffing with funerals
Joyce	Wakes
Kate	Dinky pies
Alison	Sausage rolls
Joyce	Fake smiles
Alison	Just a debit card
Kate	And a bar code from Parcel Force
Joyce	Casket Force, surely
All	Oh yes
Alison	Interesting though, isn't it?
Kate	What?
Alison	Options. Ideas
Joyce	For?
Alison	Oh nothing. Don't mind me. Mind just working overtime

Silence. Alison takes out her mobile 'phone and starts browsing the internet again

Kate	How many stamps do you think?
Joyce	Stamps?
Kate	Yes. How many stamps would you have to put on a box to send a dead husband through the post?
Joyce	And how much string would you need to use?
Alison	Hang on, I'll have a look

She is still on her mobile browsing the internet

Kate	What are you doing?
Alison	Looking on their website
Joyce	I was only joking
Kate	Who's website?
Alison	Parcel Force.

Joyce	What?!
Alison	Here we are. Right then Kate. How heavy?
Kate	Who?
Alison	Your husband
Joyce	Seriously?
Kate	16 stone
Alison	In new money
Kate	101 kilos I think
Alison	Is the item worth more than £200?
Joyce	What?
Kate	Not any longer. Never was come to think of it
Alison	Now then. Which service. Did he like to be punctual?
Kate	Yes
Alison	So it'll have to be guaranteed next day delivery
Joyce	Look, I was only joking earlier
Kate	No harm in shopping around
Alison	Right, where to. Do you know anyone in London?
Kate	No
Alison	London it is then
Joyce	Come on now girls
Alison	So. Based on your order, that'll cost £145 plus VAT
Joyce	What will?
Alison	To give Kate's husband the send-off he deserves
Kate	Send off?
Alison	By guaranteed next day post to London
Kate	But who would I post him to?
Alison	Who cares? If you bury him or cremate him, you'll never see him again. So not much difference if he gets lost in the post
Joyce	But you can't just post him off. There must be a law against doing that?
Alison	There probably is. But without a return address, who'd know?
Kate	They wouldn't take a parcel without an address
Alison	Then we make one up
Joyce	But we couldn't. We can't
Alison	Look love. Have you read the leaflets here about how much a funeral costs?
Kate	On the internet it said the average one is £3500
Joyce	You can't. We can't
Kate	But Joyce, it's a saving of three and a half grand
Joyce	No
Alison	Each
Joyce	Ridiculous
Kate	No hassle
Joyce	Absolutely not
Kate	That's over ten grand between us
Joyce	*(pause, then)* Show me your 'phone. That's fantastic
Alison	That's a small fortune
Joyce	Ten grand!

Alison	That's a large holiday
Kate	And a bloody good one too
Joyce	And if we sent all three in one box …
Alison	You've changed your tune
Joyce	Can't turn down a bargain. Husband would kill me
Kate	In one box, that's an extra saving of £250
Joyce	Don't forget the VAT
Kate	Even better, £340
Joyce	Oh that's very good value for money. Well done Alison
Kate	It just shows how much you can save by shopping around
Alison	I only made the same comment to Frank this morning
Kate	Is that your son?
Joyce	A neighbour?
Alison	My husband

Silence

Joyce	Your …
Kate	Husband?
Alison	Yes
Joyce	But he's dead
Alison	No he isn't
Kate	But you said you'd come in for your late husband
Alison	I have. He should have been here at 10. Lazy bastard. He'll be late for his own bloody funeral
Joyce	So is he dying?
Alison	I hope not
Kate	But he is ill?
Alison	Not that I know of. But I wouldn't be surprised
Kate	Why, has been complaining?
Alison	Never stops
Kate	No, has he been complaining about being ill?
Alison	Fit as a fiddle. What a bugger eh? Anyhow. He's got to pay for it yet
Joyce	Hang on, hang on one chuffin minute. Rewind lady. So, I still don't get why you're here. What did you mean when you said he's got to pay for it?
Alison	It's my birthday present from him. Well, I never know what to ask for. He said to get something for myself that I'd really like
Joy/Ka	His own funeral?
Kate	No use getting an unwanted present I suppose
Alison	That's what I said
Joyce	Your birthday present is your husband paying for his own funeral?
Alison	Original, I know. I did think of asking for a nice set of luggage. But this is better
Kate	How?
Alison	He can pay by instalments
Joyce	And he was coming to meet you here, knowing all of this?

Alison	Oh no. We've agreed he's going to pay for it but not exactly when. I thought I'd surprise him
Joyce	I can't believe what I'm hearing
Alison	He thought he was meeting me for a coffee. We'll go later. Don't want him to think he's missed out on a little treat. I'll get him a pizza for his tea from next door too. That'll cheer him up. You know. Spoil him a bit. A thank you like. And I thought, anyhow, this way, he can get to choose his own coffin
Kate	That'll be nice for him
Alison	And we have to be careful with the lining
Kate	Why?
Alison	Some fabrics bring him out in a rash. And I did ring another place last week to ask if they did a fitting service
Kate	Fitting service? What did they say?
Alison	Put the 'phone down
Kate	How rude
Alison	I said to the woman "What sizes do they come in?" I mean, he's got an unusually long inside leg measurement for a little bloke. I can't have him being in a coffin that doesn't fit right. I mean, it'd be uncomfortable. I never let him pick his trousers for that reason. Always underestimates his proportions. And he's bad with colours. If I left him to choose a coffin, god knows what he'd pick. He'd look terrible in mahogany. Make him look pale
Kate	Coffins and cappuccinos. It's better than Desperate Housewives. Or should that be Desperate Widows?

Joyce stands

Joyce	I'm sorry Alison. But I just need to say something. I think this is appalling. You sit here next two grieving…
Kate	ish
Joyce	…widows. You listen to us talk about plans and options, when we're both making decisions which are important
Kate	ish
Joyce	You listen to us go through some very private things about people who have been our world
Kate	I wouldn't exactly say that
Joyce	And you even join in and make suggestions - and your own husband isn't even dead?
Kate	Bloody selfish of him if you ask me
Joyce	I had everything straight, rationalised. I was ready, prepared in my own mind about taking that big decision
Alison	I'm sorry Joyce
Kate	Burial or cremation?
Joyce	No. Lanzarote or bloody Benidorm! You've got me looking forward to a nice holiday! How can I now afford that holiday if your husband isn't even dead? He's ruined it
Kate	Like I said Alison, selfish. Typical bloke

Joyce	Absolutely
Alison	You're right. I'm sorry. This is just like him. Only ever thinks of himself

Silence

Kate	And I'd really got into that Idea of posting them all off too
Joyce	And saving all that money
Kate	And having a holiday
Joyce	Without them. Ever
Kate	And now we have to change our plans
Alison	No we don't
Kate	What?
Alison	Sod it.
Joyce	What?
Alison	You're right. There's more to life than paying for death. We were happy five minutes ago and look what he's done? Made me miserable and upset my new friends by having the gall to still be alive
Joyce	Spoiling our fun
Kate	I don't know why I ever married mine
Joyce	Or mine
Alison	This is just like him. Self, self, self. He's late, he's upset my new friends, he's ruined my birthday and to top it all, he can't even be considerate enough to be dead when he should be
Kate	Who would have thought it? That meeting up like this could change the ideas of two women so much
Alison	Three
Joyce	But yours isn't dead
Alison	Yet
Kate	But he's not even ill
Alison	Yet
Joyce	What are you saying?
Alison	Three women on holiday it was and three women it will still be
Kate	Where's this going?
Alison	Look. We all die. It's just a matter of timing. Usually it's bloody inconvenient
Joyce	So?
Alison	So, all I'm saying is, what's so wrong by making it convenient for all concerned?
Kate	You mean...
Joyce	You don't mean you're going to
Ka/Jo	(*Whispering*) Kill him
Alison	No
Kate	(*Laughing*) For a minute then, I thought
Joyce	So did I
Alison	No. Just bring his death forward a bit
Kate	To when?
Alison	Well. How does today suit you both?

Joyce   I'm sorry to sound a bit of a purist, but it's a naturally accepted convention in most cultures that you have to die first before you're buried?
Alison I know that. I just was thinking about sometime this afternoon
Kate   So you are going to kill him?
Alison I wouldn't say kill him. More like hurry along the inevitable
Joyce   Well. We've all got to die some time I suppose
Alison But our time isn't now. Just his
Kate   Meaning?
Alison We've got a holiday to plan girls. Can't begin a new friendship founded on disappointment and disagreement, can we? He's gotta go

Silence. Then, they huddle together

Kate   So. Say, just for instance
Joyce   Hypothetically
Kate   What sort of things might we be talking about, you know, in a very vague, roundabout not-going-to-prison sort of way?
Joyce   You know, innocent conjecture like
Alison Just for instance?
Jo/Ka   Just for instance
Alison Hypothetically?
Jo/Ka   Very

They huddle together even more

Alison I was thinking of buying …
Kate   A gun?
Joyce   A knife?
Kate   A hitman?
Joyce   All three?
Alison A pizza

They look at her

Ka/Jo   A pizza?
Alison You've given me the perfect solution girls. Lunch. Or to be exact, pizza. When it was mentioned earlier. It got me thinking. I need to get him his lunch. That'll fix everything
Joyce   Lunch? For the husband you want to get rid of? You're thinking about meals, now?
Kate   I'm lost
Alison I was thinking more like 'means' than 'meals'
Kate   Still lost
Alison Killing two birds with one stone. Or more correctly, kill one husband with one Marinara pizza

They look at her

Alison	He's allergic to fish
Joyce	So?
Alison	Marinara
Kate	Meaning?
Alison	Meaning, bringing forward lunch with the right topping, might quite nicely bring forward …
Ka/Jo	His topping
Alison	Yep. He only needs to smell a tiny bit of fish or seafood anywhere near him and he starts wheezing. Imagine what a whole prawn buried under extra cheese will do to him?
Kate	Wonder what time the last post is?
Alison	Get those passports and bikinis on standby girls. Our husbands are sending us on our jollies!

They all cheer

Joyce	Shush! One of the staff is coming
Alison	Shit. What do we do?
Kate	Look sad

They all strike a pose for a beat until the unseen member of staff has gone by

Joyce	Look. We can't stay here. They'll think we want something
Kate	Like a funeral?
Alison	We did. But they've done so much more for us than help with a funeral. They've given us …
Joyce	Ideas
Kate	Options
All	Us
Alison	Nothing like a bit of professional advice to help you change
Kate	Your mind?
Joyce	No. Just change
Alison	For the better
Joyce	For the future
Kate	For a better future
All	Together
Kate	You know, when you think about it, they've been really good for us here haven't they?
Alison	Great choices and ideas
Joyce	We could all leave them a nice review on Trip Advisor
Kate	What a nice thought
Alison	You are a very thoughtful lady, do you know that?
Joyce	Thanks Alison
Kate	Perhaps they have their own version

Joyce   Of what?
Kate   You know. Trip Advisor. Like Funeral Advisor or something
Alison Leave feedback like they do on eBay
Joyce   "Very speedy service"
Kate   "Highly recommended"
Alison "A+++ cremators"

Silence

Joyce   Thin crust or deep pan do you think?
Kate   Deep pan
Alison His favourite
Joyce   Stuffed crust?
Alison Stuffed husband more like
Kate   With extra toppings?
Alison Oh Yes
Joyce   Prawns?
Alison A must
Kate   Mussels?
Alison Undoubtedly
Joyce   How long will it take?
Alison About two minutes
Kate   To bake his pizza?
Alison To cook his goose
Joyce   Will he not realise, you know, see the seafood on the pizza?
Alison Bloody glutton. By the time he's bitten into the first slice, it'll be too late
Kate   Does he puff up with the reaction?
Alison Ironically, a bit like a fish
Kate   Pity
Joyce   Why?
Kate   It's just so hard on Alison
Joyce   Meaning?
Kate   Well. Us doing it this way. She'll have missed getting a present from him
Alison Trust me. This is the best present he could ever give me
Joyce   Oh hang on a minute (goes in her handbag). I've just remembered something. Here
Alison What's this?
Joyce   A voucher
Kate   What for?
Joyce   Next door. A free pizza
Alison That's really kind of you. And he does like a bargain. He'll be so grateful to you for saving us £5.99. Thrifty type you see. Hey. I've got an idea. Have you got time to meet him?
Joyce   Who?
Alison My husband
Kate   Oh that'd be nice

222

Joyce	Lovely
Kate	Nothing worse after all
Joyce	Than what?
Kate	Going to the funeral of someone you never met
Alison	Well come on. Busy busy. All our plans have changed
Joyce	All of us have changed
Alison	We've got so much to do
Kate	Holiday outfits
Joyce	And no funeral outfits
Alison	Trips abroad
Kate	Trips to the Post Office

They stand up to leave, then

Joyce	Hang on a minute. Just hang on.
Alison	What?
Joyce	Post Office. How does he get from anaphylactic shock to next day delivery?
Kate	What do you mean?
Joyce	How are we going to get him, from her house, in a box and then to the Post Office Alison?
Kate	And what's more, how are we going to get our two out of here and get them there as well?
All	Oh shit

They all sit down again

Joyce	How stupid could we be? We've forgotten the obvious aspect. How we get them all to the Post Office in the first place and in one box?
Alison	We could just tell this shower we're having them at home for a wake so that family could see them. That would get them out of here
Kate	And then just forget to tell them to come and collect them again? What do we say? That we're just hanging on to them for a bit?
Joyce	Why not?
Alison	But what about the even bigger matter of coordinating getting them all to the Post Office?
Kate	Can't just stick 'em in a taxi
All	Double shit
Alison	We've let business sense get in the way of common sense

Silence

Joyce	So. Let's think. We can't post them. We can't bury them ourselves. And it's not as if we could cremate them ourselves
Kate	But there's no way this lot are having ten and a half grand off us
Joyce	Goodbye holiday girls
Kate	We're stuffed

Alison   Not entirely

They look at her. She is on her 'phone again

Alison   Well, I'm just thinking. You've got me thinking
Kate   What?
Alison   Hang on a minute. Just let me get back online. When did you say that DIY shop is taking over from the pizza place?
Joyce   I didn't. It just said in the paper they were buying it
Alison   Then let's stop thinking of putting them in a box. Let's think out of the box. Here we are. I thought so. Right Kate, how tall is you husband?
Kate   Only short, 5'5"
Alison   Yours?
Joyce   The same I think
Alison   And funnily enough, so is mine
Kate   Meaning?
Alison   We might need the pizza shop to stay open a bit longer… but under new management
Joyce   Why?
Alison   Well, perhaps not so much stay open, but do a little bit of out of hours work for us
Kate   You've lost me
Alison   I'm just on the estate agent's website. The pizza shop closes today for good and according to the description of the business and the equipment in there, the pizza ovens are 5'8" deep and 17" high. The perfect size for …
All   A husband
Joyce   Or three
Kate   You mean…
Alison   You said a DIY shop was going in there and we talked about DIY funerals, so why not DIY cremations?
Joyce   And you know what else that means?
All   No post and packaging
Joyce   That's at least £10,500 we'll then have in the kitty
All   Get in
Alison   I do love it when a funeral plan comes together
Joyce   So let's think. We need to get the bodies out of here. So, if we …
Kate   Broke into here
Alison   And took the bodies out tonight
Kate   Then force next door open
Alison   And if anyone disturbs us say we're getting the place ready for the new business
Joyce   No one would be the wiser
Alison   And I can still go and get the pizza before next door shuts, feed him sat in the car behind here
Kate   And save £5.99!
Joyce   Bob's your Uncle
Kate   Fanny's your Aunt

Alison	And holiday here we come
All	Get in!
Kate	Alison, you are a genius
Joyce	Should start your own business
Alison	So that's it then?
Kate	Can it all really be that simple?
Joyce	Can't see why not
Alison	So you know what this means girls (*singing*) "Oh this year we're off to sunny Spain"
All	"Y viva, no funerals!"

They burst out laughing again, then,

Joyce	Shit, she's coming back! Look sad again

They strike poses again

Joyce	Shush! I don't think we're supposed to be singing and laughing in here. Let's get out of this place

They get up to leave

Kate	You know what? When I was sat on that car park for four hours this morning, looking out of the window, I never thought the day would end like this
Alison	I didn't think my husband would either
Joyce	Does that make us weird?
Kate	No
Alison	Not at all
Joyce	I say, ingenious
Kate	I say, thrifty
All	Changed
Alison	And for the better
Kate	Here's to the future
Joyce	To our future
Kate	And thank God for pizza
All	Here here!
Joyce	But hang on a minute. This all depends on one crucial thing: what if he doesn't want to eat a pizza for his tea?
Alison	Oh, he will. Trust me
Kate	How do you know?
Alison	I promise you. Over his dead body

They start to leave and then, quietly

Alison	It's just a bit disappointing that we've missed out on the funerals. You know. The chance to meet up with family and friends. Have a drink. Reminisce about the good times. Because there were good times. For all of us, wasn't there?

Kate	I guess
Joyce	I suppose so
Alison	They'll ask questions. The families
Joyce	So what do we tell them all?
Kate	I know. We each put an advert in the paper. "A quiet family service was conducted, and his ashes were scattered privately, abroad.'
Joyce	Mine always wanted to go abroad
Kate	Then you've just fulfilled his lifetime ambition
Alison	Now he's dead
Joyce	What if people want to make a donation to a good cause in their names? Folk like to do that
Kate	Benidorm Dogs Home
Alison	Have they got one?
Joyce	They have now
Kate	We could deliver the money personally
Joyce	Mine always wanted a pet
Alison	Then that's another ambition fulfilled in death
Joyce	The bastard will have achieved more in death than he did in life
Kate	Do you think anyone will question it? You know. No funeral, us not being here?
Joyce	I think not. After all, we'll all be abroad, getting over our loss, won't we?
Alison	Helping good causes. Those poor abandoned pooches
Kate	Seeking solace in the company of friends
Joyce	New friends
All	Best friends
Joyce	But, dignity must prevail girls. We should still have at least one hymn
Alison	That's right. After all, we have been practising one
Kate	Oh yes!
Joyce	Shame not to in the circumstances, don't you think?
Kate	I love it when you find a song that is appropriate for the moment, don't you?
Joyce	Allow me
Alison	Sing it like you mean it sister
Joyce	Sister Joyce will now lead the congregation in our final hymn. Hymn number 10,500
All	'All things bright and beautiful'
All	(*singing*) "All things bright and beautiful"
Alison	"All pizzas great and small"
Kate	"As long as there are prawns on top"
All	"It's Benidorm for all"

They burst out laughing and the 'Changing' track comes in again as they exit. BO

THE END

'Changing #2'
(One act play)

Synopsis
Three men.
One shopping trip.
One changing room.
One couch.
One hour to wait. Or so they think.
When it comes to clothes shopping and accompanying women on it, many men have the attention span of a wood lice. Some are resilient, some have coping strategies, some enjoy it and many abandon hope.
'Changing #2': A salutary lesson concerning the take some men have on the ritual of women shopping for clothes and what can happen when two unacquainted husbands, left unattended and unsupervised whilst their wives 'try it on', will do the same.
And changing in more ways than one would think.

Characters
3m
Eric, Ron and Wayne
Playing ages are flexible

Running time approx 45 minutes

Music: David Bowie 'Changes'

Starts with an empty couch on stage. There is a freestanding sign which simply reads 'CHANGING ROOMS – LADIES' and an arrow pointing off.
First man (Eric) enters and sits at one end of the couch. He is loaded down with shopping bags. Sits, exhausted, laden down.
Picks up a newspaper from the seat next to him and begins to read. He looks confused as he does so, flicks the pages and then discards it on the seat next to him.
Second man (Ron) enters in a similar burdened state, sits on the other end of the couch. Both eventually look at each other, acknowledging with a simple, expressionless nod and then stare forwards, silent.
Ron then picks up the paper and starts to read.

Eric	A week ago
Ron	Sorry?
Eric	A week ago
Ron	What was?
Eric	The Home Secretary
Ron	I'm sorry, I don't…

Ron points at the paper's headline

Eric　　A week ago. He was stung by that paper. They caught him dressed as a schoolgirl in a massage parlour. A week ago? The Home Secretary? Remember?
Ron　　Sorry, I don't…
Eric　　*(points at the date)* A week ago? You're reading last week's paper son
Ron　　Oh, I see.
Eric　　I only realised when I saw that pop star on page two who died from a drug overdose and remembered reading it before. I can understand the Home Secretary being thick enough to get caught twice within a week with his pants down, but not a pop star dying twice
Ron　　Skirt
Eric　　Sorry?
Ron　　Skirt down, not pants…see?

Shows him the picture

Eric　　Oh aye. You're right

Both now study the paper

Ron　　Where would a bloke find a schoolgirls outfit that would fit him?
Eric　　Never thought about it
Ron　　Probably off a big schoolgirl perhaps?
Eric　　They were bruisers at my school.
Ron　　Who?
Eric　　The girls
Ron　　Really?
Eric　　Bigger than the lads. I always said that if they'd have played rugger instead of us, we might have won a bit more

He puts the paper down and again, they stare forward in silence

Ron　　Maybe a charity shop
Eric　　What?
Ron　　For the schoolgirls outfit

Eric looks nonplussed

Ron　　Home Secretary *(He strikes a 'girly pose')*
Eric　　Yes of course
Ron　　You can get anything in a charity shop. And you get all sorts in them. Folk I mean.
Eric　　Yes, of course
Ron　　I mean, he couldn't have gone in a school uniform shop and asked for a schoolgirls uniform could he? "Hello. I'm the Home Secretary. Can I get a 46-inch chest in this white blouse please? And whilst I'm here, have you got those red sandals in a 12 and a half?" Yes. "And I'm a 32 inch inside leg"
Eric　　On a pleated skirt?

Ron   No. Perhaps not then.

Silence, then

Ron   Internet
Eric What is?
Ron   Where he got the uniform from. Website. Plain brown package. 'We guarantee complete discretion'. You know
Eric No. But you clearly do
Ron   NO! I'm just...
Eric I'm pulling your leg

Silence, then

Ron   But how would you get there?
Eric Where?
Ron   Massage Parlour. Home Secretary. Incognito. Paparazzi. Y'know.
Eric 'bus? Taxi?
Ron   Dressed as a schoolgirl?
Eric Maybe he drove
Ron   But you'd still have to get in and out of the car. In public. In daylight.
Eric And then you would be seen. You're right. Maybe an overcoat?

Ron picks up the paper and shows it to Eric

Ron   No. See? Blond plaits, drawn on freckles. And that straw boater would give him away at 100 yards, even at nighttime
Eric "She may very well pass for 43 in the dusk with the light behind her"
Ron   Who?
Eric Katisha
Ron   I thought the Home Secretary was called Douglas?
Eric He is. Katisha was in the 'The Mikado'. Gilbert and Sullivan. G&S. It was a line from it. You know. Streetlights? Shadows? "She may very well pass for 43 in the dusk with the light behind her" Wouldn't tell it was a bloke? Humour?
Ron   Oh right. Yes. Sorry. With you now.

Silence, then

Eric 'Ruddigore'
Ron   Pardon?
Eric 'Ruddigore'. That was my favourite G&S. 'The Sorcerer' was another favourite. And 'Cox and Box'. Was never a fan of the popular faves like 'Mikado', 'Pirates', 'HMS Pinafore'.
Ron   Yes. I see. Gilbert and Sullivan
Eric Yes (singing) "When the night wind howls in the chimney cowls. And the bat in the moonlight flies." Great stuff. Ruddigore. Far more tangible and intelligent than

	(singing) "We sail the ocean blue and our saucy ships a beauty." All a bit too camp for me.
Ron	The navy?
Eric	No. HMS Pinafore
Ron	Of course. G&S.
Eric	You into G&S?
Ron	I'm more a 'Les Mis' type of person

Eric turns and looks at him aghast

Eric	Les Mis? Not into music then?
Ron	Course. Les Mis, Phantom, Cats
Eric	I hate Cats
Ron	Is it the story?
Eric	No. They shit in my herbaceous borders
Ron	Cats? The show? You mean Elaine Paige shit in your garden?
Eric	Bonnie Langford actually
Ron	The dirty…

Eric looks at him

Ron	Right. Humour.

Silence, then

Eric	But why would you want to wear a schoolgirl's uniform?
Ron	I wouldn't
Eric	Well I wouldn't. But what does a grown man get out of dressing up like that and …
Ron	*(reading from the newspaper)* "… and being spanked on the bottom by sultry Denise, a buxom and leggy 21-year-old vixen from Croydon, who was also dressed up but as a police officer and had secured him in pink furry handcuffs. Neighbours alerted the real police when they recognised the Minister's voice from a TV interview which had been shown moments earlier. They allegedly heard him through the bedroom wall scream out "I've been naughtier than that officer" and then began barking like a dog"
Eric	Can't remember him barking like a dog on News at Six
Ron	No. But I remember him whining like one on News at Ten
Eric	Hmm

Silence, then

Eric	Barking like a fox surely
Ron	What?
Eric	If she was a vixen, it would have been a better play on words to have said he was barking like a fox instead of a dog

Ron   I don't think the tabloids were aiming for intelligent satire
Eric Probably not

Silence, then

Eric Eric by the way
Ron   Ron
Eric Waiting for the wife?
Ron   Yep. You?
Eric Yep.
Ron   How long have you been …?
Eric Half an hour
Ron   Half an…?!
Eric Hour. Yep. If she isn't out in an hour, I will sign a piece of paper giving my consent for you to select the heaviest stiletto shoe you can find from that display over there and beat me to death with it
Ron   Mine told me she'd be out in 10 minutes

Eric roars with laughter

Ron   What?
Eric How long have you been married?
Ron   Four weeks

Eric roars again with laughter

Eric I am at the stage in my life where female shopping habits are concerned, that I would be rated in any other profession, as a consultant
Ron   How long have you been married then?
Eric Put it this way. If I'd have done her in, I'd have been out by now
Ron   So. How long do you reckon then?
Eric Twenty years with good behaviour

Ron laughs at him and then realises Eric is staring at him and not laughing

Ron   Why are you not laughing?
Eric Is a statement of fact supposed to be humorous?
Ron   Suppose not. Anyhow, it's not too bad. Shopping. You see I have this little tactic that I use that she's never figured out
Eric Really?
Ron   Oh yes. You see when we go up the escalator to the second floor, she goes left to look at home products, bathroom accessories and miscellaneous fancy goods and I go to the right to the electrical section
Eric Inspired
Ron   Yes. I then get the chance to browse uninterrupted, in my own little male world of gadgets and every imaginable thing you could buy which uses a remote control.

	Free from her gaze to roam amongst hi-fi, electrical goods, home entertainments systems and discount action DVDs. In that way I get my own little piece of, well, peace for at least, almost, probably …
Eric	An hour?
Ron	Five minutes usually
Eric	And you say she's not figured this genius ruse of yours out then?
Ron	Not up to now
Eric	Well, make the most of that five minutes because she'll be more than that now.
Ron	Why? How long?
Eric	You need to apply the formula
Ron	Formula?
Eric	Indeed. I worked it out years ago. Changing and changing rooms in particular have a formula. Never let me down yet. Should patent it really. Would have saved so many marriages. *(He takes out a pen, picks up the paper and makes notes on it as Ron speaks)* So. Let's give it a whirl. How many baskets? Your wife?
Ron	Two
Eric	How many garments in each basket?
Ron	About ten I think
Eric	Any of the same items but in a different size?
Ron	I don't think so
Eric	*(he tuts)* Any in the same colour?
Ron	No
Eric	*(he tuts again)* Any items she is planning to make outfits from?
Ron	Yes
Eric	*(he tuts again)* Nature of items selected for trying on?
Ron	One basket had just tops in and the other had three dresses, five skirts, two pairs of slacks and … er …
Eric	Slacks?! Slacks?!
Ron	What?
Eric	Please tell me you did not refer to them by that name to your wife?
Ron	Well, I can't …
Eric	NEVER say that word to a woman. Slacks. A fate worse than death. Makes them feel old
Ron	Well how old is your wife?
Eric	Old. But in her mind, in her vocabulary and in her mirror, she is 21. Slacks do not go with 21
Ron	Right. Point taken
Eric	Anyhow, I digress. Reasons for the purchases?
Ron	We're at a wedding next week. Oh, and she has an interview. And we're going away for a midweek break
Eric	Midweek break? When the Test Match is on? I see. Moving on. Did she pick up any hats, shoes, handbags?
No	We didn't look at them

Ron stares at him in disbelief and tuts again

Eric	Dear God man. You naïve, unwitting, unfortunate fool
Ron	What, what?!
Eric	"Abandon hope all ye who have entered here"
Ron	Tell me, is it bad news?
Eric	Free advice son: get them to do it all in one hit. NEVER in stages and NEVER in different trips. And ALWAYS be at work the following day
Ron	Why?
Eric	Because, my young inexperienced innocent of the world, that my son is the day they take it all back because it doesn't fit
Ron	But she'll have tried it all on. Why would she need to take it back?

Eric laughs again

Eric	'Need'? Dear oh dear oh dear. She really fooled you. It's part of the experience. Women apply a holistic mind set to shopping which can last a whole week. She has the idea of shopping, the discovery of an event to link it to. Then an opportunity to trap you into taking her. Oh, and not forgetting the preparation – usually involving lists. Lots. Then getting everything out of the wardrobe that she already knows she has and laying it out on the bed to make 'mini-me's'
Ron	Mini-me's?
Eric	Yes. Yours must do it. When they make a version of themselves out of clothes laid out on the bed to soak up the ambience of the outfit. It's at that point you are banished from the room whilst they try them on, decide they don't fit, convince you that they've never really liked them, that it was your fault that they bought them, and then the fateful shopping trip is initiated
Ron	Is that why she told me I had to go out last Sunday?
Eric	Exactly. Following which would have been discussions with her girlfriends, online research, posts on Facebook. Then getting mentally prepared on the day. Did she shout at you this morning and tell you off for getting on her nerves before you set off?
Ron	How did you …?
Eric	Know? Experience son. Priceless. It's how they cleanse their soul of any guilt related to cost. It will all be your fault, so one way or another, you are going to pay. Then you arrive. She tries to con you into staying with her. You whine.
Ron	That's right!
Eric	She dumps you in the café. You agree to meet up at the hallowed changing emporium. Voila. Then this joyful exercise within which you are happily immersed takes place
Ron	So what's this about the following day?
Eric	Oh no. We're not up to that point yet. Much more before that stage
Ron	Shit
Eric	Then when you get home, the best bit of all. The bedroom fashion parade.
Ron	But I've seen her buy it?
Eric	Ahh. But you haven't seen her wear it. And that is the most dangerous moment of all
Ron	Why?

Eric	Because at that moment my dear Dr Watson, your life and happiness are in the gravest of danger. She will ask for your opinion
Ron	So? I just tell her they all look fine
Eric	Fine? Fine? Look. This is a whole different course of instruction. We'll cover this in detail on another occasion. But take it for granted from me. No matter what she says or how much she shouts at you concerning these precious purchases, these creatures she perceives as her new-born children, items of beauty personified, you must never use the words 'fine', 'lovely' or worse of all, 'OK' to describe them. And NEVER, EVER say that you will be happy 'as long as she likes them'. Death will ensue. And then, as Autumn follows Summer, at least half of them will be brought back the following day
Ron	That's madness
Eric	No. It's called clothes shopping. It's called marriage. It was the vow the Vicar never read out but was in small print at the bottom of the licence. And it's all about changing. Changing into the clothes, changing out of them and subsequently, changing them for something else and in the process, changing you into her father.
Ron	What?!
Eric	Oh yes. It's all connected. You will never measure up to her father, so by stealth she moulds you into him and then she turns into her mother and evolution continues unabated
Ron	That's perverse!
Eric	It's life. Preordained by God. Like clothes. You are another possession. If you don't conform to the order of the universe, she'll fall out of love with you quicker than she will those clothes which you are going to end up paying for. And you will end up in life's charity shop sooner than what she buys today
Ron	But I'm not … oh shit. I can't win
Eric	Indeed. Know your place in the food chain Ron. Like I said, it's all about evolution. Remember, the first domestic in the Garden of Eden happened because Eve asked Adam "Does my arse looked big in this fig leaf?"
Ron	What am I going to do?
Eric	Be calm. One thing at a time. Let's finalise the formula
Ron	So how long do you think she will be now?
Eric	I have to apply the formula first. Union rules
Ron	Be honest. Don't be gentle. I'd rather just have the bad news
Eric	Well. Your difficulty my son is the fact that she hasn't included different sizes and colours. If she had, it would be simple. But dear, dear. No accoutrements or accessories selected either. It looks bad
Ron	Just give it to me straight Doc'
Eric	Well. Two minutes to take each item off and put the next one on. Then two minutes looking at it. That's forty minutes already by my reckoning
Ron	Shit
Eric	Indeed. Welcome to clothes shopping. Then she has to try them all on with every combination of the things she is planning on wearing them with. We're at an hour now
Ron	Double shit. But I'm at the match at three
Eric	'Were' son, 'were'

Ron   I'm done for. The lads will kill me. I'll just have to tell her I've got to leave

Eric stares at him in disbelief

Eric Leave? Leave? 'The lads will kill you.' Are you completely insane?
Ron   Well she's got the joint account credit card with her, she doesn't need me
Eric 'Joint Account Credit Card'?
Ron   Do you have one?
Eric Do I bollocks! You're telling me that not only does your wife have a card on which she can spend your money, but you are seriously telling me you are going to leave her to shop with it, alone, unsupervised with no effective command and control in place?
Ron   Well, I ...
Eric I feel sick
Ron   Have you caught something?
Eric No but your bloody wife has.
Ron   What?
Eric You!
Ron   What have I done? What am I going to do?
Eric Let me think. If you must leave her, ring the bank and tell her the card has been pinched.
Ron   What?!
Eric They'll cancel it and she won't be able to use it
Ron   She'd kill me
Eric Aye. But that costs nowt
Ron   I best stay
Eric You're a quick learner son
Ron   So how long then, y'know, the formula?
Eric Well. We need to factor in the other colours and sizes
Ron   What do you mean, other colours and sizes?
Eric Well, when she figures out that at least half of them don't fit her – sorry – "... don't sit properly on her frame" or the other gem, " ... it's not a label for normal shaped women like me", then that's where you come in
Ron   Me?
Eric Indeed. She'll need you to go back out there into the jungle and get everything in the sizes either side of the one she's picked up plus, in all the other colours it comes in
Ron   But I don't know what size she is
Eric Easy. When you first go back into the battlefield, come back with a couple of things in a size 8.
Ron   I'm sure she's not a size 8
Eric Course she's not. But when she bollocks you for being stupid, you say that because she has such a good figure, you've always assumed she was a size 8
Ron   That's genius
Eric No, that's bullshit. But you will, for a brief moment, be a god

235

Ron	But anyhow, I can't remember whereabouts in the shop she got them all from. I was bored witless. I pretended to be answering text messages I hadn't even received, to stop her asking me questions. Yeah. And then she started asking my opinion on colours. Colours! But I'd never even heard of some of the colours she was talking about. And when she picked up this frock …
Eric	Frock! Frock! That's like calling a luxury liner a dingy
Ron	Well they're all just boats aren't they?
Eric	How are you still married? Terminology Ron. Do your homework. Know what things are called in the ancient clothes language women speak in. And importantly, which shops sell all the labels she likes. When you know that, you know where to avoid
Ron	Am I allowed?
Eric	Allowed? She expects it! Next time you're here, say you need a coffee, a pee, anything to distract her. Notice a child and say it looks cute.
Ron	Why?
Eric	Floors them every time. Makes you sound like the husband she wishes she'd married. Language, distractions. The best weapons in your arsenal to engineer 'The Great Escape'
Ron	The Great Escape?
Eric	Home Ron. Like Steve McQueen on that motorbike racing along the barbed wire to get across the border to freedom and sanctuary
Ron	But he got caught
Eric	Exactly. You're stuffed
Ron	Anyhow, we're getting off the point. I said that this fro…sorry, dress looked red and she hit the roof. "It is NOT red" she said, "on the colour scale it is somewhere between Falu and Amaranth."
Eric	And what did you say?
Ron	I tried to be funny. I said, "Falu? Isn't that near Fuengirola?" She took a swing at me with her handbag! And then these women stood nearby all started having a pop at me as well for joking about colours. One of them called me a stupid husband. I went to say something back to her and her husband stood behind her back and made a sign to tell me to keep quiet. He looked petrified! Like he might get blamed as well for being a stupid husband even though he'd done nothing wrong
Eric	Word of advice son. 'Done nothing wrong' is an artificial construct of reality, created by men who are in denial of their marital status and fate. You have always done something wrong. Your life hence forth is comprised of mistakes, events, moments in time which are banked, available for your wife to redeem at will. You are simply a glorified Loyalty Card loaded up with misdemeanours which she can cash in at any moment
Ron	Perhaps I shouldn't have got married.
Eric	Don't be daft. We'd be lost without them. It's all like that film
Ron	'Brief Encounter'?
Eric	'Fatal Attraction'

Silence

Ron   So, come on, what's the damage? How long have I got here?
Eric Three hours I'd say. At the very least.
Ron   Bollocks
Eric Then she'll look for shoes
Ron   No!
Eric And bags
Ron   Bags?
Eric And then there's the earrings…
Ron   I don't get paid for another week
Eric "And on the eighth day, God created Visa."
Ron   I'm done for
Eric I think that happened four weeks ago son
Ron   What have I done? What am I going to do? Help me Eric! It couldn't get any worse could it? For God's sake!

Third man (Wayne) walks into the scene and flops down in the middle seat.

Way   Hi guys! How's it goin'? I LOVE department stores. Don't you just love shopping with the little women?

Eric puts the newspaper on his head and sits back in his seat. Ron puts an empty shopping basket on his head. The sound of faint sobbing. Blackout.
Lights up. Wayne is mid-flow. Still. Ron has his head in his hands and Eric is staring forward, blank. Mouth open. Zombified by the banality of it all. Wayne speaks quickly. Always. Without drawing breath. Ever.

Way   …and she says to me "Look Waynibabes" that's what she calls me. You know. Did I tell you that? She says that 'Wayne' is so formal. Did I tell you that already? Can't remember. Anyhows. So. Waynibabes. It's like a pet name, but let's be clear, I'm no pet. *(Wayne barks like a dog and then snorts laughing at his own joke)* Do you hear what I'm saying? Equal shares. Stable relationship. Mutual respect guys. That's what it's all about. Like shopping. This is her space, her zone but what I say is *(shouts)* 'Big Respect'! *(Ron and Eric are startled by it but then settle back into their catatonic state)* You know what I mean? Respect to her and her space. Her needs. Because she is *(singing)* "All Woman". And consequently, she has this like, basic instinct to shop. Like it's in her DNA and you know what I mean guys? Just like we're 'hunter-gatherers' when it comes to food, they, women are, when it comes to clothes, well, 'hunter wearer-ers'… . Made up word I know, but hey, language is an expression of the moment and of the people, get where I'm coming from? What was I saying? Oh yeah. I can see from your faces. You are so with me guys on this one. Yeah, we must respect and honour the hunter in our women. Not 'our' of course because that speaks volumes of ownership and possession which as a culture we are way down, I say, way down the road from. And let's be clear guys, this isn't about emasculation, is it? Oh no. It's about empowerment. All men together. One nation under the groove. High five Ron, high five Eric … *(neither respond so he continues unabated)* … it's cool guys, we're cool. Some guys don't

	get any type of male bonding, association. Threatening. You get me? I get it. It's cool. We're cool. What was I saying?
Eric	Bollocks
Way	No. Don't think I was deep into metaphors by that stage Eric, but anyhow what I say is …
Ron	Who fancies a coffee?
Eric	Me. I'll go
Ron	No, I'll go
Eric	I said it first
Ron	My idea
Eric	Sit down Ron
Ron	No you sit down Eric
Eric	Please let me go
Ron	I'll pay
Eric	I'll pay to actually go and pay for the coffees as well
Ron	I'll pay for cake
Eric	I'll get us lunch
Way	I'll go guys

Silence

Both	YES!
Eric	God yes
Ron	Fantastic idea
Way	Tea or coffee?
Both	Coffee
Way	Now let's see. Espresso, Double Espresso, Short Macchiato, Long Macchiato, Ristretto, Americano, Long Black, Café Latte, Cappuccino, Flat White, Piccolo Latte, Mocha, Affogato, and then we need to think about how many shots, fat or skinny, hot or cold milk …
Both	TEA!
Way	Cool. The most consumed beverage in the world guys. Over 3000 types …
Ron	… please god no …
Way	… but the popular ones might be considered as English Breakfast, Earl Grey, Lady Grey, Darjeeling, Green tea, White tea, Oolong,
Both	Just water!
Ron	Please
Eric	God yes
Way	Cool. Sparkling, Still, Tap …
Both	Any!
Way	You decide
Ron	No, you decide
Eric	Please
Ron	Before one of us dies
Eric	Absolutely
Ron	Please

Eric	Any
Ron	Is fine
Way	Cool. Back in a minute
Eric	Feel free to browse
Ron	Take as long as you want. Really
Eric	Really
Way	Cheers guys. Respect. Appreciate the trust. Cool. High five

Neither respond and just stare at him

Way	No. Cool. Not your scene. I'll nip to the loo first, so I guess I should say "back in two shakes!"

He snorts laughing. Silence.

Way	Laters

He exits. Silence. Eric twitches.

Eric	Could today get any worse?
Ron	Yes. If he comes back
Eric	We need a diversion. Something small.
Ron	So he can't find us again?
Eric	Yes!
Ron	A fire?
Eric	A heart attack?
Ron	An ambulance could help us escape?
Eric	It's a plan
Ron	Cool *(Eric glares at him)* Sorry.

Wayne bounds back in

Way	Did we say…
Both	WATER!
Way	Cool

He stands there

Eric	What?
Way	Cool
Ron	And?
Way	Cool
Eric	Why do you keep telling me that everything is cool?
Way	I'm not. Water. Cool, cold, room temperature?
Ron	Cool. Is cool

Wayne laughs/snorts

Way   Saw what you did there. Amazeballs. Laters

He exits

Ron   Is it so wrong that I hope he has an accident
Eric   That stops him coming back?
Ron   Indeed
Eric   Small
Ron   But significant
Eric   Short term maiming
Ron   Not too short
Eric   An hour?
Ron   Maybe a week
Eric   To make sure
Both   Hmm
Ron   High fi ... *(he puts his palm out to Eric)*
Eric   Don't you dare
Ron   Shit. What's he done to me?
Eric   Nothing compared to what I'll do to him if he comes back
Ron   Somehow, this makes shopping with the wives not too bad
Eric   Steady Ron. Remember the formula. Remember how long we've been here and all that we must still endure. Think of this as a training session. Like what the Special Forces have to do to prepare them for going behind enemy lines.
Ron   This is a war zone?
Eric   Sort of Ron. Look out there. Enemy troops in waves. They're consolidating a beach head at the moment near handbags. But they're on the move. Snipers near evening wear are taking aim at the sale rail and I anticipate a full-frontal attack on shoes at any moment. And oh no. Look. Reinforcements
Ron   Reinforcements?
Eric   A fifty-two-seater coach of octogenarian storm troopers has just broken through the perimeter and landed near fancy goods. Ruthless bastards. Killers. Elbows like razors. Attitudes like Germans. Manners like, like
Ron   Pensioners
Eric   Yep. Cold blooded bargaineers who take no prisoners and hidden within their number and heading towards us at speed ... oh no ... the last thing we need
Ron   What?
Eric   Wayne
Ron   Bugger. So, if this is a war zone, can I just kill him then?
Eric   Well, I don't think the Geneva convention applies when seated next to the lingerie section, so, fill your boots
Ron   Where's he gone?
Eric   He was there a minute ago

They sit in silence. Battle weary. Then, Wayne bounds suddenly into the scene without warning

Way   Ta da!

Both jump

Ron   I'm going to kill him
Eric   Me first
Way   So guys, here you go. Two bottles of cool water. "Shaken, not stirred"

He snorts/laughs. They just stare at him. They then all sit in silence. Wayne is twitchy. Hyper. Can't seem to keep still

Eric   Have you had too much coffee today?
Ron   Maybe eaten funny coloured sweets?
Way   Me? No guys. This is me all the time. Full guys, full. Energy. Expectation. Wired. Drunk on life and all that it has in store for me
Eric   (*sardonically*) Me too
Way   Really?
Eric   Coiled spring
Way   Really?
Eric   No Wayne
Way   Right. Got you. Humour. Cool
Eric   Why does everything have to be 'cool' Wayne?
Way   What else can it be when everything's, well, cool?
Eric   How about fine?
Ron   Great?
Way   Sweet?
Eric   Sweet? Why would you say something was sweet? What does sweet mean?
Way   Cool
Eric   Let's just leave it
Way   Coo...fine
Ron   So Wayne, how did you meet your wife?
Way   Partner
Ron   Sorry, I assumed you were married
Way   We are
Eric   So she is your wife?
Way   Technically
Eric   Eh?
Way   We prefer the term 'partner'. She never took my family name when we became joined.
Ron   Joined?
Way   Yeah. We love that term. It sums us up on all levels. Spiritually, physically, emotionally...
Eric   Mentally

Way	Indeed Eric. My union with Wave is modelled on a psycho-symbiotic cooperative relationship reinforcing equality and banishing stereotypes to the sorry history of humanity
Eric	Union?
Ron	Right
Eric	And 'Wave' you say?
Ron	So your wif … sorry, partner, is called 'Wave'?
Eric	Was she christened that?
Way	Christened Eric? Christened? Oh no. I'm afraid we do not acquiesce to such conventional religious shackles and neither, thankfully, did her parents
Eric	Parents? How passé.
Ron	Not a term I subscribe to Eric
Eric	Indeed Ron. Speaks volumes of ownership if you ask me Ron
Ron	I thought more of controlling, conforming if you ask me Eric
Eric	I can almost hear the sound of the shackles, chains of repression, echoing down through history
Ron	Agreed brother
Way	Wow. A-Maze-Balls. And you're brothers?
Eric	In a deep and bonded way, not by a 'helix' if you know what I mean Wayne. Brothers from another Mother but connected emotionally by a spiritual birth canal

Ron chokes on his water as he takes a drink

Way	Wow. That is so cool guys. Huge, huge respect. High, I say high five guys (*he holds his hand up again*)
Eric	Passé.
Ron	So Passé Wayne
Way	Wow. You guys. So, in the moment. Grounded and in tune. I can't wait to include you in my daily blog
Eric	Blog?
Way	Indeed Eric. My running account of my life in a day-to-day, blow-by-blow contemporaneous résumé, posted online as a transparent snapshot of who and what I am. A baring of the soul to the masses who can become part of my journey. A personal and absorbing insight to those subscribers fascinated about one man's evolution
Eric	Right
Ron	So how many people follow your blog?
Way	Last count Ron, it was pretty humbling. I'd say … between six, seven …
Ron	Hundred?
Eric	Thousand?
Way	No, six or seven. Not including my mother. Or Wave.
Ron	Six or seven people?
Way	Followers Ron. They are more than individuals. We are a common socio-embryonic movement with colossal potential to influence and shape the world
Eric	So. These six
Ron	Or seven

Eric   ... 'Followers' are spread across England?

Wayne shakes his head

Ron   Europe?
Eric   The world?
Way   Doncaster. Mostly
Ron   Mostly?
Way   All
Ron   'The winds they are changing' then Wayne
Way   Right on
Eric   In Doncaster at least
Ron   Well Wayne, you're certainly courting popular opinion
Eric   In Doncaster
Way   I'm trying guys. It's a slow process, building up a head of public steam
Eric   In Doncaster
Ron   How long have you been blogging then?
Way   Six, seven ...
Eric   Days?
Ron   Weeks?
Way   Years. Was one of the first. Had a blog long before many of the big stars of stage and screen
Ron   And you've certainly shown them how it's done
Eric   In Doncaster
Way   Dedication Eric, dedication
Ron   So, why doesn't your mother or Wave read it? Have they not got the internet?
Way   No, they say they've both got better things to do with their lives
Eric   I like them already
Ron   So Wayne, you didn't say how you met your wif...partner
Way   I've got to be honest you guys, now that we've become so close, I think I can make a very, very personal disclosure to you, this being a safe and confidential bond we have developed. I've always been drawn to women in uniform and, well, when I saw her, it was genuine lust at first sight
Ron   Uniform?
Eric   Army?
Ron   Police?
Way   Greggs. That and the smell of pasties. Like a pheromone guys. The smell of freshly baked puff pastry sends me wild
Eric   Fascinating. And I take it this would probably be Greggs in...
All   Doncaster
Way   Yeah
Ron   And the smell of pasties you say ...?
Way   Yep. Wild. That and the uniform.
Ron   You're turned on by the uniform your partner wore at Greggs?
Way   Oh yes. The colours and the texture of the fabric. A sexual statement. If you saw Wave, at work, you would probably ...

243

Eric   Wave?
Way   … see a slightly overweight and perspiring woman, encased in poorly fitting cheap manmade fabrics. Through my eyes I see the subject for a Titian masterpiece
Eric   Did Titian paint women wearing polyester clothes, stained with sausage roll grease?
Way   Not in the 16th century
Ron   Maybe if there had been a Greggs in Italy
Eric   Aye. 'Gregorio's Sausage Rollios'
Ron   Selling 'Cheese Pastie-loni'!
Way   Do you both speak Italian?

They stare at him

Way   Oh. I get it. Cool. Humour
Eric   So, just getting back to polyester. What is it about it that makes you so, you know?
Way   Wild? Unfettered? Lustful? Wanton? Emasculated?
Ron   Steady on. Don't want anybody emasculating next to me
Way   Don't you feel the same about polyester?
Eric   Never thought about it
Ron   Me neither
Way   Guys. You're saying to me you have never appreciated the benefits of manmade fabrics draped wantonly across your torso
Ron   I'm warning you, if we get thrown out because of him emasculating on this couch …
Way   Hang on a minute

He leaves briefly

Ron   Where's he going now?
Eric   God knows
Eric   I preferred him when he was boring us silly about coffee
Ron   I preferred it when I didn't know him

He enters with something in his hand

Way   (*to Eric*) Grab a hold of this

He throws something to him. Eric catches them and in a beat, realises what it is: a thong. He responds as if he has been thrown something hot which he juggles and then drops to the floor, then shouting out.

Eric   Argh! Knickers!

Ron stands up and then apologetically to out front

Ron   Sorry love, he's not speaking to you

Way	Well, go on, get hold of 'em
Ron	I will bloody well not
Way	Eric, go on
Eric	Sod. Off. I never touch the wife's and I'm certainly not touching those ... and anyhow, they're not knickers! They look like off cuts

All three study them on the floor

Way	Well, to be precise, they're not either. It's a thong
Ron	Not much to them is there?
Eric	Exactly. Knickers are, well, they're they're

Wayne and Ron are staring at him

Eric	...bigger
Way	Bigger?
Eric	They are in our house
Ron	But when you've washed them, how do you peg them out to dry? Where would the peg go?
Eric	Never mind that. Where does the arse go?
Ron	Well ... *(he picks them up, hold them up and turns them around. All three are now studying them)* it goes, well it's sort of. Sod it. I don't know
Eric	When you think about it they are a feat of engineering design. Amazing
Ron	Ingenious
Way	Gorgeous
Ron	You worry me
Eric	But you've got to wonder: what is the point? There's that little there to practically do anything. I mean. They don't hold anything up, back or in
Ron	You might as well just 'go Marine'
Eric	Commando Ron. The term is 'Go Commando'
Ron	Right. But why Commando? Can imagine a Marine wearing them, but not a Commando
Eric	No Ron. It means you don't wear anything. 'Go Commando'?
Ron	Oh. Right. So, Commandos don't wear thongs?
Eric	Ron. This isn't difficult

They study them again

Ron	Saves on washing I guess
Eric	I guess. But how many pairs would you have to wash to make it worthwhile, cost effective? You'd be saving up them knickers for six months to fill one machine load
Ron	What do you know about washing knickers?
Way	What do you know about washing?
Eric	I don't
Ron	I don't

Way I do
Eric Why am I not surprised?
Way When Wave and I come shopping, we spend just as much time looking at the washing instructions as we do fondling the fabrics?
Eric Fondling fabrics?
Way That's why I love polyester
Eric The fondling?
Way And then the static (he shudders)
Ron I'm sorry to interrupt your fascinating discussion, but don't you think they look like some type of fancy-dress mask?
Eric What?
Ron Yeah. Look. The big holes are for your eyes and the string goes down your nose and the material at the back, well, fancy dress mask. No, a surgical mask if you have them the other way
Eric Don't be daft
Way He's right

Wayne puts them on his head as described. Then,

Ron/ Oh yeah
Eric

All three then look out front as if they are being observed. Wayne slowly takes them off his head

Ron Sorry mate. Just trying them for size.
Eric For his wife
Ron Birthday present
Eric Surprise
Ron His heads the same size as her arse

They look front and 'watch' as the unseen purpose walks away

Eric Bloody hell. We nearly got thrown out then
Way Security in here have no sense of humour
Ron Thank god you weren't emasculating

Silence

Eric I still don't get it though. How they, y'know, work
Ron Proper woman's knickers, well. They're functional, traditional. Not scary
Eric That's a matter of opinion
Way Hang on. We need to conduct an experiment
Ron Oh shit, he's going to emasculate
Way Hang on a mo

Wayne quickly gets up, exits and comes straight back on with a larger pair of knickers and holds

246

them up

Way   Like these you mean?

Ron and Eric cower and move away

Ron   What are you doing with those? Put them back!
Eric   Get back Satan!
Way   Keep your hair on. Scientific research

Wayne places them on the floor next to the thong. Then all three sit forward and start to study them. Then,

Eric   *(He picks up the thong)* So that's a thong and those are the real thing. Seen more material in a pair of shoelaces
Ron   *(He picks up the knickers)* And I've seen less material in a ship's sails
Way   That's the idea guys. A thong is, well, more comfortable; no VPL
Ron   VPL?
Way   'Visible Panty Line'. Means they can go with any wardrobe, more attractive, sensual ... and I feel as free as the wind when wearing them

Silence. They stare at him

Eric   I?
Ron   Wearing?
Eric   As in ...
Way   Oh yes guys, I wear a thong
Eric   You mean, there are thongs for men
Way   Probably
Ron   Probably? What do you mean?
Eric   But you said you wear one
Way   Yes. Just never worn a man's

Eric and Ron slowly slide a short distance away from him

Way   Guys. This is the 21st century. We are, underneath these trappings of social stereotypes, of conformance, Metrosexual individuals. Secretly yearning to push our boundaries
Eric   Wearing knickers?
Way   Exploring our innermost fantasies Eric
Ron   Wearing thongs?
Way   Ronnie Babes, get with the time. Don't knock what you've never tried. It's not challenging your masculinity, it's just about feeling masculine enough to embrace other forms of expression, enjoyment. It's not all about men or women, gender. It's just about enjoying

Ron	Enjoying? How do you enjoy something which looks like you need the services of a qualified Vet to take them off
Way	No Ron. That's the fun bit. You get someone else to take them off for you

They both slide away a little further

Eric	And you can sod right off!
Way	No, not me!
Eric	Oh, right. Good
Way	Anyway, you don't know until you try it
Ron	Double sod off
Eric	Right on (both high five each other across Wayne)
Both	Shit!
Ron	This is what half an hour with him has done to us

Silence

Way	Come on guys. Why not give it a go? What have you got to lose?
Both	No
Way	Look. You've come here today to allow your wives an opportunity to try on, but more importantly, to change; their wardrobe but also their image. Is us changing, interchanging with them such a big deal guys?
Eric	Oh no. I've just had a real bad picture in my mind
Ron	What?
Eric	Joyce wearing my underpants
Ron	No. Julia wearing my briefs
Eric	Briefs?!
Ron	Mens!
Eric	Good job
Way	Hang on. I need to go

Wayne again leaves

Ron	Thank god for that. We got shut of him
Eric	That was close
Ron	The people you meet in these places
Eric	Weird
Ron	Not normal like us
Eric	But are we though?
Ron	What do you mean?
Eric	I've never sat in a department store discussing the merits of women's underwear with other men. Maybe we are changing and we didn't realise
Ron	Maybe it's us that are odd and he's the normal one. What if all men go around thinking like that, acting like that? What if we're the weird ones?
Eric	Wearing knickers?
Ron	You're right. Could today get any odder?

Eric   Yes. He's on his way back

Wayne comes back in with two paper bags

Way   As this has been so much fun guys, the least I could do is get you a little something. To thank you for your company. It's been cool. Well cool. Loved it. We should meet up again. We've got so much in common
Eric   Y'reckon?
Way   Absolutely. I think you'll love the gifts I've got you. I think it will help you in finding the real you
Eric   Gifts? For us?
Ron   You shouldn't have done Wayne really. There was no …

Wayne and Ron put their hands in the respective paper bags and their expressions change

Both   Oh shit

They both pull a thong out of the bags

Way   I had to guess your sizes. Might be a bit snug

They hurriedly put them back in the bags and look around

Ron   What the bloody hell were you thinking of?
Eric   I'm not wearing them!
Way   Give them your wives
Both   Sod off!
Way   This could be the beginning of something guys
Eric   Yes, divorce
Way   No. I mean it. Give them a go
Ron   No bloody way
Way   Listen guys. I was like you once
Eric   What, normal?
Ron   Sane?
Way   No. Inhibited, repressed, frustrated. When I was given my first pair by my Wave
Both   What?!
Way   … I was vulnerable, confused. I needed supporting
Eric   You needed sectioning
Way   She knew it would be good for me, for us. So I took the money and tried it
Ron   Money?
Way   Oh yes. She bet me I wouldn't try them
Eric   How much?
Way   Fifty quid
Ron   Bloody hell!
Way   So, I guess, the money is on the table guys
Eric   What?

Ron	You mean?
Eric	You'd actually pay us to put these on? Now? Bloody pervert.
Way	Look guys. I want to share with you the joy, the freedom, the journey. It's karma. What goes around comes around. I was given a gift from Wave and it changed me for ever. It liberated me in a way no one could see, but only I knew. What's a hundred quid if it changes the life of someone who needs it?
Eric	I need a drink. And not a bloody coffee-frappe-chino-mocco-shite-o
Way	What have you got to lose?
Eric	My home and pension?
Way	Well?

Ron is silent throughout

Eric	You can bugger off. Can't he Ron. Ron?
Ron	So. Just say, for instance, hypothetically.
Eric	Dear Lord no
Ron	If I was to put these on, you'd give me fifty quid?
Way	Absolutely
Eric	Please tell me you're having him on
Ron	Let's just think about this
Eric	Are you mad?
Way	Listen Eric, just listen to him
Ron	And that's it? I go in the changing room, put them on and you give me fifty quid
Eric	Lunacy
Way	Yes
Eric	No!
Ron	Yes
Eric	No!
Ron	Yes!
Way	I'm not stupid Ron. I get it. It's all about the money at the moment. But trust me. Changing your underwear will change your life. Women figured it out years ago. Frilly is the future. Why do you think they take so long in there? It's all about changing; the new you beckons Ron
Eric	Ron, please tell me you're having him on?

Wayne gets his wallet out and holds fifty pounds in front of both of them

Ron	Well I'm game. Eric?

Eric looks at them both, looks at the money

Eric	This is ridiculous. Insanity. Perverse. Immoral. Probably illegal its, its, ... sod it, where's the changing rooms?
Way	Changing rooms are over there guys. Money is yours when you come back.

They go to exit, then

Ron   Which one do we use?
Eric   Best stick with the men's Ron. I don't think we're changing that much

They exit

Wayne smiles. Takes out his mobile phone and dials a number. He then speaks in a totally different accent, rather educated, precise.

Way   Hello, is that Joyce? Hello, Justin here, oops, sorry, 'Wayne' here. Are you having a lovely day? Delightful. All fine here. Is Julia with you? Super. Just to let you know that your husbands are just changing into their thongs now. All has gone as you planned it. I'm sitting outside your changing room now. Oh yes, they soaked it up like sponges as you said they would. And yes, you were right. They are both utterly, utterly thick. They'll be back shortly. No, they haven't rumbled it. They have no idea you two know each other or about your bet. Funniest acting job I've ever had. What do you want me to do when they come back? I see. So, give you two minutes, I text you when they're about to show me they have them on and you'll both come out and surprise them, take the photos and post them on Facebook. Lovely. Strange, but lovely. See you shortly. Goodbye.

Eric re-enters first walking very gingerly. He keeps making noises as if in discomfort. He then tries to sit down but yelps and stands back up very quickly.

Way   Are you alright Eric?
Eric   I'm in pain
Way   How's Ron?
Eric   Ron? Ron is, well, Ron is …

Ron then enters, bounds on. He is completely different. He flounces in, confident, smiling, elaborate in his deportment, OTT

Ron   I'm in ecstasy!
Eric   I can't sit down
Ron   I never want to sit down again! I'm free, glorious! It feels, it feels … amazing
Eric   It feels like I'm wearing a piece of cheese wire
Ron   Wayne, you were right. God you were right. The fabric, the form, the fun, the frills! Fantabulous darling! I'm, I'm…
Way   Changed?
Ron   Changed! Yes! God yes. I've got this burning feeling to be in a musical
Eric   I've just got a burning feeling. I feel like that thread thing's gone where the sun doesn't shine

Eric goes to sit down again. He yelps and winces in pain. Ron sits in a flamboyant manner and crosses/re-crosses his legs, making a meal of it

Ron   This feels like a road to Damascus moment!

Eric	This feels like a road to A&E moment
Ron	Wayne. I have been, in a brief moment – pardon the pun – liberated. I am ecstatic, emotionally fulfilled. One small change has changed me forever. I'm, I'm ... (*singing*) "The hills are alive, with the sound of music ..." I can't feel embarrassed
Eric	I can't feel my bits. Why can't a feel my bits? Has it changed me that much already?
Way	Eric. Stupid question. But, you have got them on the right way around?
Eric	Course I have. I'm not stupid
Way	You do know they only go on one way around don't you?
Eric	What?
Way	The cord is at the back isn't it?
Eric	Bugger
Ron	(*Stands up*) I'm free, I'm changed!
Eric	I'm numb from the waist down
Way	Are you sure you're OK Eric?
Eric	Is this thong made by Playtex?
Way	Why?
Eric	Because at this exact moment, it is doing a very efficient job of lifting and separating.
Way	Do you need to change them?
Eric	No. I just need to move. Things. Let me just move. Bed them in and, and

He gets up and moves gingerly and turns his back to the audience to adjust. As he does so, he then moves further away from the couch wincing and whimpering. We hear a sound, like an electronic alarm activating.
It makes Eric jump which makes him yelp/cry out

Eric	Ow! I think something's been severed. Get a first aid kit!
Ron	Bloody hell! What is that noise?
Way	Sounds like the security alarm has been set off. Shoplifters I guess.
Ron	Where?

Ron moves next to Eric and a second alarm starts to sound.

Ron	There must be a shoplifting team out, there's goes another one. Probably those pensioners and ... hang on, why is everyone looking at us? Have we set the alarms off?
Eric	It can't be us

Ron and Eric look at each other

Eric	Wayne. You did take the tags off the thongs didn't you?
Ron	You mean ...?
Way	I haven't bought them yet. Why should I have done that?

Eric and Ron look at each other again. Horrified

Both	Oh shit!
Eric	Quick! Coming this way! Store Detectives
Ron	Store Detectives? Run!
Eric	Run? I'll sever me bits!
Ron	Mince quick then!
Way	Where are you going?

Silence, both look at each other and then

Both	Doncaster!

They dash off stage. Eric does his best with his knees together. Ron suddenly bounds back to Wayne

Ron	Wayne. Running in a thong. Amazeballs

He bounces off stage. Once he has exited, Wayne takes his mobile 'phone out again and dials.

Way	Hello Joyce? Wayne here. Sorry love. You can come out of the changing room now. Alteration to your plan I'm afraid love. No, not how, more a matter of where. Now, about this photograph. How well do you know the police station in Doncaster?

Music from opening resumes. BO

THE END

'Changing #3'
(One act play)

Synopsis

One doctor's surgery.
One appointment.
One patient.
What could possibly be simpler?
Keith has an appointment but Lisa can't find the appointment so there isn't an appointment. That's pretty straightforward then.
But life isn't always organised and about being at the appointed place at the appointed time. And when someone walks into your life and ordered work regime, they can change a life of order to chaos; but sometimes that change is needed to find order again and importantly, the life you really need.
Confused?
Not as much as Keith and Lisa.

Characters

Lisa: Clinical, organised, officious, uptight, easily flustered when her ordered world is upset. She cannot cope when her 'ying has been yanged' ... and Keith well and truly bowls her a curved yang.
She can be any age but it is envisaged she should be much younger than Keith.
Keith: Laid back, slightly sardonic (look it up, I had to) and completely the opposite in personality to Lisa. It would work better if he was old enough to be a father figure. Oh, and dry, dreadfully dry.
Ages of the characters are not set, but Keith needs to be much older than Lisa.

Running time approx 20 minutes.

Music track commences.

The stage is set with a desk with a sign on it which simply reads 'Reception'.
Sat behind the desk is Lisa.
There is a second chair on the opposite side of the desk.
Lisa is wearing a uniform top which gives the clear impression that this is a Doctors.
She is on the telephone and answering calls. There is paperwork and a laptop on the desk which she works on as she speaks.
Music fades.
The telephone rings.

Lisa Hello, Greenbank surgery. Just hold the line and let me get on the appointments system. Yes, may I have your date of birth please? Thank you. And your surname please? Thank you. Yes, I've found you Mr Reed. And is it for a check-up concerning your medication? Fine. Are you able to make 10.00am tomorrow?

That's great. You'll receive a text confirming the time and if for any reason you can't make it, just give me a call. See you then Mrs Reed. Goodbye.

The telephone immediately rings again.

Lisa   Hello, Greenbank surgery. Just hold the line and let me get on the appointments system. Yes, may I have your date of birth please? Thank you. And your surname please? Thank you. Yes, I've found you Mrs Bowen, what may I do for you? Oh dear, I am sorry to hear that. Yes, well, we have an emergency slot at 4pm today if you can make it. Concerning your procedure next Wednesday, you will be sedated for it so you will need a responsible adult with you for the 24 hours afterwards. Yes, it's not ideal, but I suppose your husband will have to suffice. Great, we'll see you then. You'll receive a text confirming the time and if for any reason you can't make it, just give me a call. See you then Mrs Bowen. Goodbye.

The telephone immediately rings again.

Lisa   Hello, doctors' surgery. Yes, I'll put you through to him now.

The telephone immediately rings again.

Lisa   Hello, Greenbank surgery. Just hold the line and let me get on the appointments system. Yes, may I have your date of birth please? Thank you. And your surname please. Thank you. Yes, I've found you Mrs Sherrington, what may I do for you today? Well, the doctor is quite busy this morning, could you let me know what the problem is and … no, I'm not a qualified doctor, but I'm a qualified … I think I'm more than … If you could just tell me what … yes, I can see from the screen how old you are and … no, I'm not being obstreper-whatever you just said, I'm just trying to establish how we can … hello, hello?

She puts the 'phone down

Lisa   … and she's gone. Lovely

She picks up the 'phone to make a call

Keith enters. He is an older man with a stick to help him walk. He moves very slowly and is breathing in a very controlled way, blowing out through pursed lips like many people with breathing/respiratory conditions do. He is moving towards the desk. He is squinting giving the impression he does not see very well either. He takes out a glasses case and goes for the contents, finding it empty. She puts the telephone down.

Keith   I've got an …

It immediately rings again. She holds her hand up to him.

Lisa   Hello? Yes, will you just hold the line for me please (and then to Keith) Just bear with me a moment

Keith   I've got an ...

She holds her hand up to him.

Lisa   Just bear with me a moment

Silence

Keith   All I was ...

She holds her hand up to him.

Lisa   Just bear with me a moment

Silence. Then,

Keith   Is that your ten-pound note on the floor?
Lisa   (*standing and looking over the desk*) Where?
Keith   (*He holds her hand up to her*) Found a moment then?
Lisa   Funny. Bear with me. Sir

She resumes her seat. He sits in an adjacent chair. During this he is fiddling with a hearing aid which he puts back in at the end of what now follows

Lisa   I'm afraid we have no appointments left today. Yes, I know who it is. I recognise your voice Ms Taylor. We do speak quite a lot don't we? Well you are aware Ms Taylor, especially as we've had this conversation on many occasions, that our well-publicised policy for emergency appointments is that you must telephone at 9.00am prompt. Prompt. When the surgery opens. Well, yes, I appreciate it will have been engaged because everyone else is trying to get through as well with their own earth-shattering medical needs. I'm sorry Ms Taylor, but contrary to popular opinion, the world does not revolve around your irritable bowel. No, I'm not being facetious, I'm just stating a fact. Yes, I know it is now only five past nine. Well, Ms Taylor, that window of opportunity to secure an emergency appointment may only seem like five fleeting minutes to you. But in the primary care world of vital frontline staff supporting health care professionals, it is, indeed, an eternity. No, the doctor is not available to speak to you at present. Yes, I will get him to call you. Yes, I do promise. I've just said that I promise, you heard me promise then, didn't you Ms Taylor? Twice? I said the words, "I promise" distinctly. Very well then, yes, if it makes my promise more legally binding, I do cross my heart but sincerely hope not to die. Has that assisted in adding weight to the veracity of my assurance? Well, if I do die because of breaching the blood oath you've just made me take Ms Taylor, you'll probably be the first to realise. Why? Well, because the doctor won't have called you back as I will have expired due to divine retribution for having reneged on my sacred pledge of not telling him to call you. He will then be otherwise engaged trying to give me emergency medical treatment and therefore, still unable to make a call to you about your irritable bowel. Yes, it is a long-winded version of saying 'yes', but with the greatest of respects Ms Taylor, you started it. Always a pleasure. Good morning. And you.

She puts the phone down and stares at Keith

Lisa	Sorry you had to sit through that
Keith	Through what?
Lisa	That little conversation. Ms Taylor. I have a love-hate relationship which sadly this morning, only explored one facet of the joy she regularly brings to my day
Keith	I wasn't listening. Only just turned my hearing aid back on. Save the battery you see. Pointless wasting it listening to things that are nothing to do with me
Lisa	That's very logical
Keith	Not really. You've obviously not had to buy batteries for these things. Be cheaper to buy a pair of new ears
Lisa	So. How may I assist you?
Keith	I telephoned yesterday and made an appointment
Lisa	I see
Keith	It's about ...

She holds her hand up

Keith   I just ...

And again

Keith	Can I just ...
Lisa	Please. No talking just now. I will ask you for the information I need, but not as part of a conversation. This requires structure. I must do this in the sequence it appears on my screen otherwise, vital information might be missed, and this exchange will become overly time consuming and therefore, inefficient
Keith	Inefficient. Well, we can't have that can we? I guess it's a bit like going to McDonalds and asking for a hot apple pie before you've told them which burger you want. Throws them and their finely tuned systems into total disarray
Lisa	I don't eat processed meat
Keith	There's a surprise. Vegetarian?
Lisa	Vegan. Now I need your ...
Keith	(interrupting her) It's just that ...
Lisa	(interrupting and holding her hand up) I think I was still speaking? Thank you

Silence

Lisa   Date of birth

Keith   Date of birth?
Lisa   Yes
Keith   Why do you want that?
Lisa   It's a requirement
Keith   Of?
Lisa   Our appointments system
Keith   Can you not just find me against today's date?
Lisa   No. In sequence. Efficiency. Date of birth?
Keith   Don't you want my name?
Lisa   No, your date of birth
Keith   Why?
Lisa   So I can find you on our appointments system
Keith   Why can't you do it by my name?
Lisa   Because. That's our system. In any case, someone might have the same name as you
Keith   Someone might have the same date of birth
Lisa   Highly unlikely
Keith   Not if you're a twin. Or it could just be a coincidence. I went to school with a lad who had the same name as me. But you could easily tell us apart. He had a pronounced limp and a very large ...
Lisa   Date. Of. Birth
Keith   *(gives a date)* Oh, and a large fries please. Sorry. There I go again. Speaking

She glares at him. Silence

Lisa   That can't be. That's impossible. This system is infallible. You're not here
Keith   I think I am
Lisa   No you are not
Keith   What am I then? Bloody Marley's Ghost?
Lisa   You are not on my system. Everyone is on my system. Everyone
Keith   Do you want my name then?
Lisa   No. That is not the correct initial defined search parameter.
Keith   Well, I've been called worse
Lisa   Did you give the correct date of birth when you rang yesterday?
Keith   I can't remember giving one
Lisa   But if you did, would you give the correct one??
Keith   It's not something I tend to get wrong
Lisa   And was it the same one you have just given me now?
Keith   Well, I don't know. Let me see. I do have a habit of shaving a few years off but that's usually on dating websites or if I think I'm going to get lucky
Lisa   Get lucky?

He winks at her

Lisa   I see. I'm afraid I haven't got time for joking

Keith	Who says I was joking? I might not look like god's gift to women, *(he pats his belly)* but all the best sweet shops have a small canopy
Lisa	That's vulgar. Anyhow, I don't have time for humour
Keith	Everyone has time for humour
Lisa	Not when you are in a high-pressure role supporting frontline professionals
Keith	Especially then, I would have thought
Lisa	Look. Efficiency. I haven't got time for idle chat
Keith	Why?
Lisa	This is a very busy place
Keith	There's only me and you here
Lisa	That's not the point
Keith	It is when there's only me and you here
Lisa	I don't understand. You must be in my system. When did you ring?
Keith	Yesterday
Lisa	Time?
Keith	Don't know
Lisa	You don't know what time you called? I remember the time I have done everything
Keith	Fascinating life you must lead
Lisa	Yes. And a punctual, efficient one
Keith	Hang on. I could have made a note of it in my daily journal
Lisa	You keep a daily journal?

He looks at her

Lisa	I see. You're doing that humour thing again aren't you?
Keith	Yes. I know. It's plagued me throughout my life. Might start making a mental note of every time I make a joke. If only I did keep a journal. I could start being humorous in a far more efficient and productive way
Lisa	If you're not here then something has gone seriously wrong. I need to call the helpdesk
Keith	If I could just …

She dials a number as she holds her hand up to him

Lisa	This is Lisa at Greenbank. We have a serious systems failure. We have an invalid date of birth and a man that doesn't exist
Keith	Shit. I really have got problems
Lisa	Would you like permission to remotely enter my system?
Keith	Now that is a chat up line
Lisa	But I just need to … if I could just … the fact is that … I need to say that … they've put me on hold and …
Keith	What?
Lisa	I don't believe it
Keith	What?
Lisa	The Sugar Plum Fairy
Keith	You really know how to curse

Lisa	The help desk. Their 'on hold music'. The Sugar Plum Bastard Fairy
Keith	'Sugar Plum Bastard Fairy'. Whatever next? 'Swan Fucking Lake?'
Lisa	They've put me on hold
Keith	Well fancy. Who would have thought? The help desk can only have a conversation with a structure. A sequence as it appears on a screen otherwise, vital information might be missed, and the exchange would become overly time consuming and therefore, inefficient. Don't you just hate it when that happens?
Lisa	I don't know what to do. How can I work without my systems?
Keith	You could just ask me what it is I want and perhaps, you know
Lisa	What?
Keith	Talk?
Lisa	How?

Keith takes the phone from her and disconnects the call

Keith	Just like that

Silence

Lisa	What now?
Keith	Ask me my name
Lisa	What's your name?
Keith	Keith
Lisa	Now what?
Keith	Ask me what's the matter
Lisa	What's the matter
Keith	See? Isn't this fun
Lisa	See, isn't this fun?
Keith	No, that wasn't part of our conversation
Lisa	Then what was it?
Keith	Polite. Chat. Small talk. Friendliness
Lisa	This is hard
Keith	Not for long. Go on. Give it a go. For me

He flutters his eyelashes at her. Silence

Lisa	So, I guess, I should now ask, how I might help you?
Keith	Well done
Lisa	Thanks. Well?
Keith	I've had a replacement valve and I think it's leaking. I didn't have it done around here, so that's why I rang you up
Lisa	Shit. A leaking valve. That's serious
Keith	Only if I crash
Lisa	My god. We don't have a crash team here!
Keith	Well I'll have to make sure I don't crash then, won't I?
Lisa	I don't think you can control things like that

Keith	Well, well. Something you don't think you can control. What a day, eh?
Lisa	This isn't funny. Do you feel OK? I mean, do you want me to get a doctor now?
Keith	Why the chuff would I want a doctor?
Lisa	To check your heart is OK
Keith	Why, how much are you going to charge me?
Lisa	Charge you? This is the NHS
Keith	The NHS?
Lisa	The NHS
Keith	Not ATS?
Lisa	ATS?
Keith	Is there a bloody echo in here?
Lisa	You shouldn't joke about this. Your heart valve is leaking
Keith	No. My near side front tyre valve on my Ford Fiesta is leaking
Lisa	You've lost me
Keith	I think that happened a while back love
Lisa	So, why have you come to see the doctor?
Keith	I haven't. This is, this is … this isn't ATS tyres and exhausts?
Lisa	No. This is Greenbank Medical practice
Keith	I guess you're not going to repair a slow puncture in a 185SR R14 radial then?
Lisa	No. Not unless you've got the weirdest physiology I've ever heard of

Keith bursts out laughing, which trails off. Lisa just stares at him

Keith	So as well as having a dodgy tyre and a crap hearing aid, I guess I should have worn my glasses today?
Lisa	So, you've got nothing wrong with your heart?
Keith	Oh yes, but nothing which is leaking today. I also need two new knees, cataract surgery, I've got a dodgy hip, I'm deaf as a post and I've got a prostate that's had more probes than the planet Venus. Apart from that, tip top thanks for asking

She looks at him and then she suddenly bursts out laughing. He then joins in and it trails off

Lisa	I'm not used to this
Keith	What
Lisa	Laughing
Keith	Laughing?
Lisa	Is there an echo in here?
Keith	See, you can do it
Lisa	It?
Keith	Laughter. Fun. Enjoying work
Lisa	Enjoying work?
Keith	It's a short life if you don't
Lisa	It's my life and that's the way it is, always been.
Keith	Then do something about it?
Lisa	I don't know how. I don't know you
Keith	I don't know you, but by the sounds of it, neither do you

She stares at him

Keith   Go on love. Drop the parachute, the safety net and the façade. Take chatting out for a spin. What have you got to lose?

Silence, then

Lisa   You spend your life convincing yourself that this isn't the life you want for yourself – your 'option one'. And then you decide one day, you might, just might want to go live the life you think you've always wanted – your 'option two'. Then, you panic thinking about what might have been, if you'd stayed who you were. Were you being true to yourself thinking of being a new you or would you be cheating the old you who you'd invested so much time, so much hope in? Which one of 'you' was the truth and which one was a lie?
Keith   So is this the truth or the lie?
Lisa   I don't know any longer
Keith   Do you want to know what I think?
Lisa   I'm not sure
Keith   Our lives revolve around changing. Changing your socks, your TV channel, your diet, your car, your job, your partner; but those changes never change the things that really matter
Lisa   What matters?
Keith   You decide that. And with that comes change
Lisa   Then what do I change?
Keith   Cop for this: what if the old you and the new you are not the real you?
Lisa   You mean?
Keith   What if, after all these years, you haven't found you yet?
Lisa   Meaning?
Keith   'Option three'
Lisa   Shit. But I didn't have a third option on my list
Keith   Then perhaps you have the wrong list
Lisa   Then what do I do?
Keith   Are you sure you want to know?
Lisa   You mean, you know?
Keith   Sure do
Lisa   Well?
Keith   Sod it
Lisa   Pardon?
Keith   Your third option. The non-list one. Sod it
Lisa   I don't understand
Keith   Forget lists. Forget systems. Forget menus and help desks. Forget the silence you need to think. Perhaps, the truth is in the noise?
Lisa   What noise?
Keith   The noise of life. Of chaos. Of uncertainty and spontaneity. Of following your nose instead of someone else's. Hopes and dreams that you own, not, the ones the

	'list people' tell you that you need. Forget the people who made post-it notes an imperative for sustainable life to exist. Just sod it. Go with the flow
Lisa	Which flow?
Keith	Jump into the first one you find
Lisa	What if it's the wrong one?
Keith	What if it's the one which needs you?
Lisa	Needs me?
Keith	Now, that's made your head hurt
Lisa	What if I sink?
Keith	What if you float? Think of where it might take you to, the people you might meet?
Lisa	But what if I drown?
Keith	What if you teach others how to swim?
Lisa	This is scary
Keith	This is life
Lisa	But what about the one I have?
Keith	What about the one you might have, which you have never even considered? The questions you didn't even know to ask because you didn't realise they existed?
Lisa	But this is too much
Keith	No it isn't
Lisa	You make it sound easy
Keith	It is
Lisa	But how?
Keith	Walk out of the door
Lisa	When?
Keith	Now
Lisa	But what about my job?
Keith	What about it?
Lisa	Who'll do it?
Keith	Who cares?
Lisa	What about the people who need me?
Keith	The people need the person doing your job, they don't need you. Like they don't need that desk or that pencil. They care about what they want. They don't care about what you want. So, go, walk out the door
Lisa	"Don't turn around now?"
Keith	My god! Humour?
Lisa	Did I really just do that?
Keith	Walk out of that door and find a life, a world and people that do care; for probably the first time in your life, care to care about yourself
Lisa	Is it really that simple?
Keith	It is if you allow it to be

She picks up the phone and dials

| Lisa | Hello, Doctor Taylor? It's Lisa. Sod off |

She puts the phone down and puts her jacket on. She goes to leave, pauses and turns to him

Keith	Where's a fanfare trumpeter when you need one! And now?
Lisa	Where is the start of the stream?
Keith	Wherever you want it to be. But if you really want to know, it's in a little town called…
Both	'Sod it'
Keith	Bingo
Lisa	Bye Keith
Keith	Bye Lisa
Lisa	How do you know my name?
Keith	It's on your badge

She takes it off and drops it on the floor. She exits. He sits in silence. She comes back, looks at him and bursts out laughing

Keith	What?
Lisa	"Your prostate has had more probes than Venus"!
Keith	You've only just got it?
Lisa	I got it ten minutes ago but didn't know what to, how to ..
Keith	Laugh
Lisa	I guess
Keith	Well, you can't leave now
Lisa	Why
Keith	It's taken a lifetime, but I've eventually found one
Lisa	One what?
Keith	A woman who finds me funny
Lisa	You need to meet more women then
Keith	Halle-bloody-lujah. But we won't tell the wife that, eh?
Lisa	Funny
Keith	I'll stick with being how I am then, eh?
Lisa	Changing is a two-way street you know
Keith	Touché
Lisa	Bye then. I've got a stream to catch

Then

Lisa	Oh, and Keith
Keith	Yes?
Lisa	The tyre place is just around the corner. Thought I best tell you, you know, you not knowing which stream it was in you blind bugger
Keith	Thanks
Lisa	I think I'm gonna like this humour thing

She exits. The phone on the desk rings. Keith sits at the desk and answers it

Keith	Hello, Greenbank surgery. No, this is Lisa. I have a cold. Just hold the line and let me get on the appointments system. (he just bangs away randomly on the keyboard making a noise) Yes, may I have your date of birth please? Thank you. And your surname please? Thank you. A heavy cold is it, you too? Oh dear. Just so you know, I don't know how this computer works, what to do or say. I don't actually work here. I thought they did tyres and exhausts, but that's another story. I guess you want a doctor and I can tell that you're used to there being two options. But there is a third which I need to explain to you. No matter how you feel, there's someone more worse off than you and a lot of the time, things are never as bad as they first appear. Who'd have thought it eh? So, having what you have, I'll get you a prescription prepared for the medication which has helped me. It's changed my life. Certainly, you take it whenever you feel you can't cope. Yes, it's a new wonder drug. It's free and the only side effect is prolonged euphoria. It's called Sodittol. How do you spell it? However, you like my love. You're welcome.

'Phone rings again

Keith	Hello, Greenbank surgery. How may I assist you? You want to discuss your impending valve replacement? Well, this is your lucky day my friend. You've just been put through to the consultant…

BO.

THE END

'Last Bus to Whitby'
(One act monologue)

Synopsis
'Big Al' is taking a bus journey to Whitby.
It is a journey he has waited his whole life to take.
He is an innocent abroad and clearly, an innocent to so much more.
During his trip he speaks to an unseen fellow passenger about his journey and unsurprisingly, as is the case with so many passengers, he talks about more than the view.
As his journey twists and turns, so do his disclosures and eventually, the reason for it is laid bare, as is his life and his plans for it.
Last Bus to Whitby is a play about resonance and honesty with oneself; about finding peace. It explores in a gentle, innocent and bygone way, how happiness and self-fulfilment, do not, for some, require other people or wealth to make them a reality. All it sometimes needs is a stranger to listen and the opportunity to talk. But life's journey sometimes hands us the most unexpected of opportunities to find our own perfect moment and within it, much needed clarity and peace of mind. And clarity of mind can be found in the most surprising of places. Even the 840 bus to Whitby.

Character Description
Big Al is 50+ and this is evident in the nature and structure of the language, the references he uses. The dialogue gives a flavour of his (almost) closed world and upbringing, cosseted by the traditional values of his parents. He has a strong Yorkshire accent. He is 'old fashioned' in manner and bearing, almost innocent and with a painfully simple and upbeat disposition. He is uncomplicated, gentle, naïve, warm, sincere, sensitive and unreservedly honest; losing himself at times in the moment, in the view, in the journey, in himself: of what was and what could have been. And clearly, 'Big Al' could be 'Little Al' depending on the actor!

Notes
There is no reason, with the appropriate minor adjustment to references in the script, why the gender of the actor could not be changed. Indeed, two other versions are available, both for a female actor with one version set in Eire. If necessary, the only set required is a suitable seat. Certain lighting cues are simply suggested to allow for the actor to change position or posture, remove a hat or jacket, take out his phone etc. The journey in real time is over three hours and the writer feels that this will assist in dramatically facilitating a passage of time for the audience.

Although present day, wardrobe is dated, older than he actually is. In consideration of the actors true age, some periods and dates i.e. '1950' may need altering.

Running time approx 40 minutes.

The piece is dedicated to the actor, Graham Martin. He read the piece and was so taken with it that he wanted to take it to Edinburgh. Sadly, he died in 2020 before we could progress the idea of him performing it.

We commence in darkness.
Music: Anton Dvorak 'Largo' from his New World Symphony, played by brass band.
The stage is set with (ideally) a bus seat or a bench seat
SFX of a bus.
He enters and remains standing.
He is moving, swaying as if being affected by the motion of a bus.

Big Al   Excuse me? I say excuse me? This is the 840 bus to Whitby isn't it? The 840? Thanks. Had to run you see. Me, run. Nearly killed me. As you can see, I'm not built for speed. Not built for comfort either; or anything else come to think of it. Sorry to interrupt you listening to your music, but do you mind if I sit here? Thanks ever so. Don't mind me. You just carry on listening to your music. Won't get a peep out of me now. Not a word. Zip. I said 'zip'. No not your zip. Sorry. Just an expression, not an observation. I'm surprised you heard me. I say, I'm surprised you heard me. You've got them earphone things in and I can still hear it. Has a heavy beat, doesn't it? Beat. Not much of a tune. But the beat, well. Funny tune. None really. Very clear though. And regular. And loud. I say it's very … no don't stop listening on my account. Sorry. No, your zip is fine.

He looks out of the window (off to the side) but keeps being drawn back to his fellow passenger.

That'll be one of those new things won't it? That what your listening to your music on. One of them 'new generation' fancy mobile-things. Well, not new, just new to me. Never owned a mobile phone until this week. Never used one until then either. I recognise that one from the adverts in the paper. That one of yours. It's a banana isn't it? Oh, an Apple? Knew it was a type of fruit. I don't do fruit. Acid. And five a day? Don't think I have five a year. But I've not got one of them. An Apple. Too clever for me. And expensive. I'm happy with me Adenoid. What? Android? Is that what it's called? Explains the odd conversation I had at Carphone Warehouse. Went in yesterday and told him I was having trouble with my Adenoids. He said "does it affect your speech? I said "Yes, I can't get a signal when I'm in the vault at the Legion." We did laugh. Well, I did. He just stared at me. For quite a while actually. Nervous type. He sorted it for me though. Nice lad. Not much of a conversationalist. Ended up there was nothing wrong with it. I was holding it the wrong way around. I was listening to the bit you speak into. I must have been speaking like we are. I say, I was speaking like we … never mind. Sorry.

Phew. Good to get the weight off the feet, especially in this temperature. But why sitting down should make you think you're going to be any cooler is a bit daft isn't it? 'Psychosomatic' my mother would say that was.

Not sure it's the right word for that, but neither did she, she used it that much. Didn't stop her using it though. I remember that she read it in a Reader's Digest and we got it then at least once a day for forty years. 'Psychobloodysomatic' my father would mutter every time she said it. By, she did like her favourite sayings and words my mother. Generation thing I think. If I ever got caught out she always said to me "Your promises are like biscuits; easily broken." And if I didn't do as I was told she'd say, 'It's like banging my head against a brick wall." I'd laugh. Father would sigh. Did a lot of sighing, did father.

Silence. Mops his forehead with a handkerchief.
LX: BO and then lights to full. SFX to cover if required.

Lovely day. I can't believe all the papers are full of folk complaining about how hot the weather is. But I don't. Older I've got the more tolerant I think I've become. Just with the temperature, nothing else. I'm a nowty bugger with everything else. When I was younger, I had no tolerance at all to the heat. Not a bit. Always whining about the heat. I knew it used to anger my father. I could tell from the way he spoke to me. His tone. The way he'd look at me and sigh heavily. Great sigher was father. It was a giveaway. That and calling me an annoying little shit. "Leave him alone father" my mother would say. "Don't you stick up for him mother" he'd say. "Why must you find fault in him?" she'd say. "He's an annoying little shit mother" he'd say; "Gets that from your side" he'd say. But she never rose to him, never argued. Not an argumentative bone in my mother's body. A living saint. She'd never retaliate either. Or be baited, or goaded by him. No. She'd just look at him, square in the eye, all kindly like and whisper "Keith?", that was father, and he'd reply, with an equally gentle tenor "What mother?" And she'd smile at him and say again gently to him, "Stick it up your arse." And we'd all laugh. Except him. He'd be sighing.
That was a marriage. The old-fashioned type. Built on mutual respect. Theirs was marriage not built on faddy fashions, like love. Practicality, knowing your place and realising when to keep your gob shut. Kept us together as a family and meant that father never spoke.
We're stopping. It's hot still, isn't it? Can't think we'll be stopped long.
I've downloaded the app you know. For the local buses. On my new phone. You'll be used to things like that but it's all Blackmagic to me. Bloody clever aren't they? Phones, apps. Did you know that this bus has 36 stops before it gets to Whitby? 36. It tells me that on the app. And it takes 3½ hours from Leeds.
That's a long journey for some. But not for me. Not today. I don't mind it one bit. The countryside, the places, the views. Nice being out in the fresh air. Smelling the air rushing through the open window. Giving you a sense of the scent of where you're passing through. The trees, the flowers, the villages, the lives. Not right now, clearly. Being stopped. All you can smell is diesel. Not exactly the nasal snapshot of life's rich rural tapestry I was after.
Oh, off we go again. I said, of we go a… never mind.
Smells are funny things though aren't they? You can look at an old photo and not remember a thing. But a smell can transport you scores of years, thousands of miles; unlock a draw on the mind and recover a memory as if it had just been put there. A memory you didn't even know you had. You know, I passed a lady the other day on the market and caught the scent of her perfume. And suddenly, I wasn't in the market hall anymore. No, I was in my parents old terraced house, sat on my mother's lap, what, fifty year ago. Can't have been more than two years old. Looking up at her I was and she, looking down at me, smiling. She was a

beautiful young woman again. I recalled her as clear as you are, sitting there right now. And I could smell it, her. That perfume she wore; surrounding me, invading my senses, my memories. 'Goya Black Rose' it was called. By she wore a lot. Made her feel chic she said. Chic. In bloody Pickering. It could wilt flowers at 20 feet. And I remembered hearing the coal on the open fire crack and then hiss as the vapour came out. The clock on the mantlepiece ticking and through it all, the smell of 'tater ash drifting in from the kitchen. And y'know what? Then, I remembered that we always had a maiden standing in the corner and a mangle in the yard. I'd completely forgotten that. Why would I remember that at the same time? The brain, the memory. All from a smell. An amazing thing. I read a book about it in the library. Mind, I can't remember what I had this morning for my bloody breakfast. But fifty years ago; it's as close by as my last heartbeat, as if I could reach out and touch her. Not anymore.

Silence. Mops forehead with a handkerchief. LX: BO, then lights to full. SFX to cover if required.

Now. No laughing at this. Look at it. My phone. Bloody gas powered compared to yours I bet. Look at that beauty. Alexander Graham Bell will be turning in his grave. Now then, according to me and this timetable on my phone, we should be just arriving at, by eck, we're here! 11:44 hours dead. Thornton-le-dale. Bloody good, don't you think? Less than an hour we'll be at Whitby. I say, bloody good, an hour to Whitby, don't you think? Never mind, stick listening to your beat son. The efficiency of the … never mind. Sorry. I will shut up. Eventually. I don't get out a lot you see so it overwhelms me a bit when I do. Especially now. Especially knowing, well, knowing.

I'm Big Al by the way. Daft name, I know. I've always been called Big Al. Since school. No one ever used my name, or even knew it I guess. Friends didn't really feature in my life at school. Or since. Loner you see. Spent every spare minute in the local library. What we used to term a 'book worm' I was. I loved that place. Still love reading. Don't have a telly. Pointless. I don't need someone else's pictures, films to show me the world. A good book paints those pictures for you. In your mind. And them are the type of pictures that don't fleetingly pass by your eyes, disappear in a second to obscurity like the ones on the box. With books, the words make the pictures and you imagine from them, the detail, the beauty of another's words; you paint in the magic. Magic. Books were my friends you see. My only friends. Mother once said to me "Friends are an anathema to you son." I had no idea what anathema meant, what it was. So, as you would imagine, I went to the library to look it up. The dictionary said: "…a procedure in which liquid or gas is injected into the rectum." I'd looked up enema. Ironic really, with father always calling me a little shit. We did laugh. Me and the Librarian. Briefly.

Anyhow, the name Big Al has stayed with me through work and life. That's all folk know me as still. If you go anywhere in Pickering and ask if they know Big Al, I can guarantee they'd say "Oh, I know who you mean. You'll be meaning Big Al. From Pickering." Apparently, I'm known for being talkative. Don't know why. I don't even know why I got the name Big Al. What it stood for. You see, I've never been fat, and my names Derek. Crazy. But it stuck. I felt more of a pillock telling them my real name, so I just never bothered. Bit like my mother. Mother was called Joyce, but everyone knew her as Olive. Took me years before I got it. The joke. Olive Hoyle. I had to look that one up too. Another occasion the Librarian laughed. Spent a lot of time in the library. Being laughed at. Father once commented on it. "You might be an annoying little shit, but you do try and better yourself."

Silence. Mops his forehead with a handkerchief.
LX: BO and then lights to full. SFX to cover if required.

    They don't hang about at these stops do they? If you're not here waiting, you're buggered. But I can understand that. Can't be waiting just in case someone turns up or has the times wrong. I nearly missed this one. I was that busy looking at the app on my phone to see when it would be arriving, I didn't notice that it had stopped right in front of me. I had to be in Leeds first thing this morning for an appointment, rushed all the way. Good job I didn't miss it. I've only ever gone the one way on this bus. Pickering to Leeds. Never thought about what world was in the other direction. I did look it up on a map in the library though. Whitby. I became fascinated with it when I was young, reading about it; obsessed you might say. Dreaming of one day having the time to see it, to visit. Life, circumstances never allowed me to go. Until now. Couldn't go anywhere really. Working in father's greengrocers' shop was enough for me. Took up all my time running it on my own. That and reading was enough for me.
It's a Tesco Express now.
I'm not very good with big towns, cities. They make me nervous. And the folk are odd. You know. Loud. Not quiet like me. Quiet and reserved. Not like in Pickering. I remember the day I left Pickering for the first time and that was only by accident. I only got on the bus to help a lady. Said she couldn't manage with her shopping. But it set off and I ended up in Leeds. Had to be the bloody express one didn't it? That hospital in Leeds is big though. Have you been in it? Like a city within a city. Folk are nice there though. Helpful. Understanding.
Mother never liked the big towns, well the folk in them. I remember her getting home one day having been shopping and saying to father "Father, if I never leave Pickering I will be content until they carry me out of here. I will never set foot in another upmarket metropolis as long as I live." So, father said "Do you fancy Bradford tomorrow then?" He laughed. She didn't. He sighed. And she said to father, "Father, this is not a laughing matter. I consider townsfolk the most egregious of types."
Egregious. Now, she got that word from when she was at the dentists and read a copy of Family Circle. I had to go to the library and look it up for her. 'Obstreperous' was another word she liked to use. Usually when referring to father. And she had a field day when she learnt 'verisimilitude' in a word puzzle book.
Much better now with the internet though isn't it? The lad in the 'phone shop showed me how to look things up. Amazing. Told me about my free minutes. Don't see how they can be free when you're paying for the buggers. Anyhow.

when he got to explaining 'data allowance' to me I lost the plot. I thought he was trying to sell me women's hosiery. "You get a couple of bigger tights with this model" he said. "You'll need them if you are Roaming." "Why the bloody hell would I want to wear any tights when I go out for a walk?" I said. "Rambling in tights? Do you all do that in Leeds?" And then he says, "No. it means you can surf as much as you want." "Surf, in bloody Pickering? We haven't even got a pond" I said. Took me a while to figure he'd actually said 'Gigabytes' not 'Bigger Tights'. Caused much jocularity in the shop. Then a young girl comes over laughing and gives me a hug and kisses my cheek and says. "You're just lovely. I'd love it if you were my dad." What a funny thing to say. A complete stranger. To think that even in this world, today, innocence can still be endearing, understood, permitted. Even in Leeds.

Anyhow, earlier today, I tried it. My 'data allowance'. 'Surfing the net.' Get me. But it's an amazing thing, the information, the knowledge at your fingertips. Finding out things you want to know. Answers. Not so good when it isn't the answer you wanted or expected. Better off not knowing sometimes, don't you think? Can't un-forget things can you?

Eh, now, look at those houses. By, they look just like ours. Must have been built around the same time. The detail and make of bricks, the tiles and window frames. Looks just like our house. 1952 I'd say they were built. I remember mother telling me about when they went to see our house for the first time. They didn't have sales staff, show homes then you see. Certainly not for council houses. Site Foreman showed them around. Mother told them what he said when she got back to her parents. She says to gran "And he says to me and father "This is the premier design on the whole site. Going like hot cakes they are. Get your name down quick. Well I said to him ..." that's mother now "...I said to him, what's so special about them? "Well" he says, "These are our 'Sunshine Houses'." "Sunshine Houses?" asks mother "Aye" says he "Because the sun shines on them all day. Front in the morning and back at night." Well, apparently, father sighed, which was never a good sign. Then father says to him "What's that again?" and he says again "Sunshine Houses." And father does no more than walks to the window, opens the curtains and looked outside and says to him "Then you best rename 'em lad. By the looks of the weather, they should be called 'Pissin' down Houses." Aye. That was the only occasion I recall that father laughed and mother sighed.

By god we were happy then. Not a worry in the world. Too young and carefree to be thinking of the future and what it had in store. Our 'Sunshine House' had no space for clouds; either in our little bit of sky or in the lives they looked down on. Childhood felt like summer could never end. Like you could never end. That time didn't pass, and clocks ticked just to make you attend to how lucky that perfect moment was, that we were.

And I had such great plans back then.

Go to college. Get qualifications. Perhaps even university. And read. So much reading.

A world of books that a little boy on his own in a library could not conceive in his wildest dreams. So many libraries. So many dreams. And travel. See the peoples of the world. Put faces and experiences to the pictures I pored over, the lives I'd read of, the cultures and peoples I had wondered about. The smells and sounds; more than was found through an open bus window. A world beyond Pickering.

Then one morning, all those grand ideas of mine changed in an instant. That ticking clock on the mantlepiece remembered it had a job. I must have been 16, no more and I recall mother came downstairs. She did the same thing every day of her life, but I could sense this day was different. She made herself a cup of tea, sat down and just looked at me. "What is it mother?" I said. "Father's dead" she replied. "He's in bed." Simple as that. Nothing more. Then she stood up and said "Doctor's on his way. I told them he's dead, but they apparently know better." She then got right indignant and says "As if I don't know when someone's dead. I told him on the phone: "I know what death looks like. We've kept chickens for thirty years" she said. She got her hat out and put it on in the mirror. Always wore a hat outdoors. Like it was then just another day. "Let him in when he arrives. I'm off out" She told me. "I'm going to buy some Finney Haddock for tea." And then she stopped at the door and turned and looked at me and said "No more books now lad. Shop's yours now." So, I just sat there. Doctor came. Doctor says to me "What's happened lad?" I said "Father's died doctor. Mother's gone for some haddock." And he looked at me and said, "Well lad, it is Friday."

They took father away. Mother came home. Went in what we called 'the front parlour' and I didn't see her until morning. The worst of it all was, the waiting. Because I bloody hated haddock.

I got up the following day, went to the shop and never left it until the day I handed the keys over last week to the man from Tesco. I pointed out all the oak drawers in the cupboards in the shop to him. Handmade by father they were. The spotless cold room in the basement, the beautiful marble tops and glass cabinets, the wooden boxes for loose veg. "The locals like it all presented naturally" I said. "Is there anything you want to take out?" he asked. Well there wasn't really. "Pity" he says "… as it's all going in a skip." And for a moment, I could swear I could hear our mantlepiece clock ticking.

Anyhow, mother never said a word about father that day. Never said much ever again come to think of it. Never bought haddock again. And I never thought about Whitby again.

LX: BO and then lights to full. SFX to cover if required.

So, college never happened. Neither did university. Or travel, or books, or peoples. "Ah well" I said to mother years later. "It could be worse. They might have closed the library." Then the worst thing that could have happened, happened.

The bastards did.

The world is a very small place when all you know is Pickering and a greengrocer's shop. They always say 'small is beautiful' don't they? But I guess them that say it never spent their lives stood behind a counter selling vegetables, did they?

Mind, when I had to start going to Leeds to see mother in hospital, I made a day of it.

And I always used to think to myself: if I crossed the road and got on a bus going the other way, where might I end up? But I knew, of course I did; it was Whitby. Every time the bus passed the shop with the destination on the front, it reminded me what could have been and might, just might be: Whitby was at the end of my rainbow. Although, I can't conceive why any folk would want Leeds at the opposite end of a rainbow.

Mother's gone now. Last week actually. The last thing she said took me back years.

She beckoned me over to the bed she was in, at the hospice by then, and speaks in a low voice, gentle, like she did when I was a child. She says to me "Son" she says to me "No matter what, I never thought you were a little shit." And she cried. First time I ever saw mother cry. And she took my hand and kissed it and then she said, "Never forget son" and I said, "I'll never forget you mother." And she smiled, and do you know what she said? She says "I know lad. But never forget Whitby either. You deserve it. It's waiting for you. Just like I will be."

Not like her at all that. Nice to know though.

Life is a bit like a bus journey, don't you think? I decided that this morning when I was setting off for Leeds. When I made up my mind about today. I thought to myself "Well Big Al. You can choose life's bus journey and let it run its course, if that is what you fancy. Or you can pick your own route and see if it's all you hoped it would be."

I think that early on in my journey, my life, some bugger must have been bought a ticket on a circular because I just seem to have gone around and around the same place and never got anywhere. Never seen anything really, except veg'. Never found life. Or me. But now, well. I can't change the destination, but I can change the route.

I know a lot about Whitby. Did you know that the earliest mentioned English poet lived in the Abbey? Captain Cook learned his trade there, in Whitby. And not forgetting Bram Stoker and Dracula. Fascinating.

I found some more stuff on my phone you know. On the internet. But it's not the same as the library; at least no one laughs at you when you look for the wrong thing, ask a daft question on the internet.

Silence. Then,

I know you've got your music turned up on purpose. I get that. You turned it up seven stops ago. I noticed. I could tell from the look in your eyes that when I was talking about – well, when I was just talking – it was of no interest to you. So, I know you haven't heard a word I've said or what I'm even saying now. Can't even lip read can you I bet? You're not interested in me. I don't blame you. You have your own journey, possibly your own things you are saying to yourself right now about your life. What was and what might have been; rehearsing more than a journey, more than anything this bus holds in store. It's just a bus journey to you. But not to me.

You see, I don't need you to hear me or be interested. In a way, I'm glad you're not. I think I'm imagining right now that you're agreeing and smiling, telling me I'm right.

You know the way people do? Them that smile and nod and haven't even listened because in their mind, they're having the conversation they wish was happening; with someone else. But I'm also hearing you telling me that I'm doing the right thing even though you don't know what that is. I just need the chance to say my piece to me. 'Say my piece.' Funny. That's what this journey is all about.

I'm saying my piece and discovering that peace I need to find. Different spellings, same journey. Same realisation. No need for a library this time to explain it. No need for a Librarian to smile. No one laughing now. Tick tock, tick tock.

And you know what? I'm not interested in pity or sympathy either. Odd. I thought I would be after all these years. But the passage of time doesn't give you peace does it? And pity and sympathy are the reserve of people who have time to wallow in it. This morning when I was at the hospital in Leeds, I didn't need the doctor to tell me I was dying. I already knew that before I got there. Symptoms. And the code they use in the wording of the letters they send to you. "Please make an appointment to come in as soon as possible" and "You may wish to bring someone with you." Says it all really. He confirmed this morning what I knew, what I was expecting. I just needed to know when. I'm not interested in why because, it is what it is. My phone told me the 'what' and the 'why' when I looked it up when I was stood in the bus station on my own crying.

For the first time, he becomes emotional and loses control and then suddenly regains it again as quickly as he was overwhelmed.

I'm OK, you're alright lad. Just sneezed that was all. You get on with your music. Silly bugger. When I did that in the bus station, I pretended I was on the phone talking to someone, so they'd stop staring at me. And then I remembered that I didn't have any numbers in my phone. Just my home number. And there's only me there now. Why the bloody hell would I be ringing myself? And why had I bought a phone?

Made me laugh, stopped me skriking. Anyhow, that's when I saw the app for the bus again, on my phone. This bus. And I thought, why not? I've just been told I'm going on a journey beyond my control, but the 840 to Whitby; well, my opportunity to control a journey I want to be on, the last one. The one I've always wanted.

The doctor wanted to give me the ins and outs of a cat's bum before I left. What it was and why. "Anytime now" was what he told me when I asked him when.

No warning, no pain. Just gone. "So, an unexpected end to my journey then?" I said. He looked at me all puzzled like. "Yes" he said. "But I want to end the journey on my terms. I want to control my journey." I said. "How will you do that" he said. "I've got an app on my phone" I said. And I left. "I don't want to leave Pickering without having seen what happens at the end" I said as I walked out of his room; and then I was running, running all the way to the bus station. And I just went up to the kiosk there and the words I waited a lifetime to say, just came tumbling out: "a ticket for the 840 to Whitby please."

Silence. Mops his forehead with a handkerchief.
LX: BO and then lights to full. SFX to cover if required.

So. Two journeys in one really today. Not an exotic island, not swimming with dolphins, not a sun-kissed beach as a destination. They're unattainable to me. Always have been. Just like Whitby has been all my life. Well. Not now.
I'm realising a dream, so why is that so wrong? Why can't Whitby be my paradise? Why shouldn't I find the end of my rainbow? Does it really matter how I find my own little paradise, how I make it? I realised that when I was waiting in the bus station in Leeds: for an extra few pounds, I can travel to what has been a world beyond Pickering, what felt like a thousand miles away in my world, for me. Funny. After all those years waiting. Fulfilling my dreams has taken an extra hour and an extra £2.50. A journey of a lifetime at the end of a lifetime. That's what dreams are made of, aren't they, what they're for?
And in my mind, I have it all figured out that when you get up to leave, you'll slap me on the back and say, "Good on you Big Al. Good on you." And then I'd say "Cheerio young man" like some actor in Brief Encounter. And you'd get off the 840 and we never meet again.
Not used to talking about anything bad; not the done thing. Just the good stuff. Big tales of big lives. "Big hopes for a short journey." That could be the headline if the local paper puts something in about my death.
And when I'm gone, if they ask anyone in Pickering who Big Al was they'll be told, "Everyone knows Big Al" they'll say. "Stick that in your death notice." And some reporter from the local rag might come up with some play on words about what finished me off all sudden like, y'know "Death of a local vegetable legend". And folk who I knew from the library days will say "Good old Big Al. He did like to read. I wonder if he got that dream he always used to tell us about before he..." before he, y'know.
You know what my 'piece of peace' is going to be when I get to Whitby? It's going to be fish and chips, mushy peas, two rounds of buttered bread and a large pot of tea. Sitting in a café at a table with a red check tablecloth; freshly cut wildflowers in a small porcelain vase in the centre of it, and a crystal bowl with sugar in with a fine bone china cup and saucer. And a spoon. The shiniest of silver ones, glinting in the sun. Bone china and a silver spoon: a brew fit for royalty.
And sat in the window of that café will be Big Al having the best meal ever that a man could wish for. In God's own county and best of all, in Whitby. And you know what else? Why not, why not indeed: an iced finger. Sod it. Two - to take out. Walking around town then, eating iced fingers. Luxury. My idea of heaven.
I've drawn all my money out of the Post Office you know. And written a cheque out for the lot. In my pocket it is. And I'm going to put it in the collecting tin of the Salvation Army chap who I'm told is always on the front. Only folk father would ever give money to, the Sally Army. I can just picture the chap's face when

he opens his tin up and finds a cheque in it for £415,287.26p. By gum. I hope he's on a bonus.

Then a walk along the front and up to the Abbey; I've downloaded an app on my phone about that too. A strong breeze from the sea, blowing away the cobwebs and any regrets attached to them. Then candy floss and slot machines. I've dreamed about candy floss and slot machines. I've got £30 in 50 pence pieces that I've brought with me. With the weight of it in my pocket, I can't feel my left leg. But that probably isn't the 50p's causing that. I'm not daft. But it's my way. Making light of things. No use being glum for nowt. Glass half full kind of person. That's me. That's Big Al.

And then after a face full of candy floss and gambling my money away, and just as the sun is beginning to set, I'll find a quiet bench on the tops, with a cracking view. I can see it in my mind even now, have done all my life. Sunlight bathing the Abbey and streaming through the ruins; dancing on the water and punctuated by the sound of seagulls crying. But that's the only crying there'll be today. No more tears. No more ticking clocks.

I knew it was going to be bad news today. So, I've got a hip flask with me that belonged to father with what was left of father's sherry in it. Can't think it will have gone off. Always kept it in for Christmas day he did. "Just a tot for me mother" he would say after we'd finished Christmas dinner "just a tot". Must be nearly half a bottle of it left in the flask in my pocket. Just enough, I thought. Just enough to remember father and to wash the tablets down. The last of mother's morphine. Knew they'd come in handy.

Nice having something of both of them to send me on my way, don't you think? And then, I will just fall asleep watching the sun go down and never wake up. Champion.

Got a note in my pocket for whoever comes across me, to explain things and all. Saying sorry for any inconvenience like. But I'm sure they'll understand. After all, I've got rid of the shop, cleaned the house and cancelled the milk. Don't like being a trouble.

So here we are. The end of a journey that I have chosen. No one else.

Now you tell me, why that isn't the most perfect peace a chap could ask for?

Not sure why I bought a return ticket though. Habit I guess. But I think I'll leave it in the bus stop when I get off, in a prominent place so folk can see it. Just in case. You never know, some poor soul might need to get home who's got nothing. Always someone more worse off than you.

Not like me.

I've got, I've had, everything I could ever need or want for. And at this precise moment, I am the happiest man alive; more alive than I've ever been in my whole life.

And who wouldn't be, eh? On't last bus to Whitby.

BO.

THE END

'Gymnopédies'

Synopsis

Los Angeles and an empty stage in a 'dark' theatre. An unexpected invitation to attend a read through for a play reunites three actresses for the first time in thirty years; thirty years since they rehearsed together, what was then a 'new' play, *Gymnopédies*. Thirty years of three very different lives which now converge for one brief day. One day to reacquaint, to rehearse, to reconcile, to remember. But what else might happen when you are forced to remember, not just the make-believe of theatre, but also the reality of the past? The past is a big place when you need a somewhere to hide. But not when you're trying to hide from yourself.

Cast

3f: Joan Dupre, Diane Sangster and Katherine Lamar
Accents: American
Period: Present day, with the action spanning one day (mid-morning until late afternoon)

Joan: Cool, sophisticated, smart, elegant, composed, controlled and controlling; well-dressed, she speaks 'money'. She is sharp, cutting, aloof, the Queen of put-downs. Successful in her career, hungry for success at all costs. She is difficult to know, understand, devoid of true friends, relationships, love, existing behind a façade. Although she is suspicious of intentions, blinkered, in resolution she is vulnerable, damaged, complex, craving of warmth, of friendship, of hope. You could imagine that her back story is of one of a person who would wish to be, at times, a million miles away from this world and the profession. But in resolution, she has a genuine assuredness and composure, determination, confidence, sincerity and pride; she is finally at home in her skin.

Diane: She never made it as an actress or as anything. She exists. Tired, angry, downbeat in presentation. Suspicious, questioning. She is bitter about the life she feels she could have had, the money and material value she feels should have been hers. Joan is her nemesis. Her sarcasm rises to match her, but never trumps that of Joan, with whom there is no love lost. She is a little unkempt, unfashionable, dated, not 'showbiz'. Joan smokes out of style. Diane smokes out of desperation and necessity. A heavy drinker which flavours her character, neediness, habits, mannerisms, but not a drunk. Nervy but not nervous. She has an existence but wants a life. Her history has made her bitter, dismissive, cold. A loner in a self-made world of black and white.

Katherine: Genuine, sincere, warm, haphazard and initially, the nearest to whatever 'normal' might be perceived to be. She is 'mumsy' in appearance, like she has just dropped her brood off at school and is on route to a coffee morning with the other moms. She lives in a bubble of family, faith, abstracted somewhat from the real world of city life and its complexities; she is content, yet not. She lives her life through her family and their lives, their successes and aspirations. She wants something she has never had but does not know what that is. Her poor health has been a wake-up call, albeit an unacknowledged one, to discover something of herself which is for her and not for the satisfaction of others. We also see a side of her which she did not know existed, but which is darker, unexpected, shocking – even to her.

The play represents one day, a brief window through which we see the three women revealed, warts and all. Their journey is not finalised by the end; the end of their day back together is, in effect, a new beginning for all of them. And reconnecting with each other affords them an opportunity to embrace their dreams and the lives which they realise are still within their reach. To finally put to bed their respective demons and rediscover hope, contentment, self-worth, fulfilment, friendship, and vitally, themselves.
Directions are only included to give a picture of one take on how it might be conceived, presented, interpreted.

Set/Staging
We are in Los Angeles in the present day.
The action takes place over a couple of hours during one day and is pretty much 'real time.' It is a theatre stage, empty with no lighting whatsoever to begin with. It is devoid of set or staging, no cloths, just bare walls, untidy, not swept, with stacked scenery flats, disregarded prop's, litter etc. If the actual rigging, structure of the stage/theatre is therefore exposed as a consequence, then all the better to set the scene of what/where we are: ill-maintained, unloved, unprepared. In effect, it could be presented on any stage, any space. It is suggested that there is a door up/centre stage, but it is simply that, a suggestion.
Furnishing/props are referenced within the text but are minimal: coat/hat stand, two table, three chairs, a pot of pencils, a telephone, a record player, coffee pot and cups and a bundle of scripts.

With reference to the Sarabande, see: https://www.youtube.com/watch?v=judV76gLib0

The total running time is just over 90 minutes. With a 7.30pm start time and an interval of 20 minutes, the anticipated curtain would be at approximately 9.30pm.

Act 1

A bright white light casts down the stage from centre/off as the door opens up centre stage leading into the black, empty space. It is filled by Joan, in silhouette. She pauses. She is smoking and the smoke curls up from her as she stands, silent. She walks slowly into the stage to centre. She is expensively, immaculately dressed in a suit and overcoat; handbag, hat, jewellery, sunglasses. For what follows and subsequently, 'George' is unseen in the lighting box (say) at the back of the auditorium.

Joan   George? They told me you're up there. George? (*mutters to herself*) For Christ's sake (*again*) George? Does this theatre still have the same lighting as thirty years ago or does it actually work now? Geo …

A stark bright light now comes on from the wings and we catch her side-on/cross-lit

Joan   Is this a stage or a firing squad? Don't answer, I know; no difference.

The stage lighting then comes up, harsh, bright

Joan   Hey, careful with those lights tiger. A Fresnel can be a very unforgiving light on a complexion of a certain age

The lighting changes, warmer, although the light from the wings is still up

Joan   My, my. You do know how to win a woman 'round

She takes off her glasses and looks around, surveys the scene. She takes off her coat and hangs it up during the following

Joan   Well, I gotta hand it to you George. You kept the place just as I remember it. Thirty years and nothing has changed. Chic. They do say in Bel Air this season, that black is the new black. The cobwebs are a nice touch. And the layers of dust on everything add a certain 'je ne c'est quoi' ... ambience? Hey, remind me to suggest to the Management that they consider 'Great Expectations' for next season. They won't need a set. And God knows, I'm getting to an age where Miss Havisham might not take that much make-up. (*Then*) Can I smell fresh ... (*she sees it*) coffee. Thank you, Lord. It's alright George, you're safe now. Once I've absorbed my first gallon of the morning, I do mellow; after that, I don't chew when I bite.

She pours herself a coffee and takes a large drink of it

Joan   Ahhh. You know what George, with coffee this good, you could open a diner. And between 7 and 9 Monday to Friday, you would have scores of middle-aged women, prostrated at your door, begging for this coffee to keep them sane and not under arrest for domestic homicide. For whatever you may have done wrong, I absolve you of your sins (*she makes the Sign of the Cross*). And from a Jewish woman, that's some compliment. Oh, and before you go, could you please knock off that goddamn...

The light from the wings goes off

Joan   Thanks

She walks down stage with her coffee. The up-stage door opens, and Diane enters. She is in profile/semi lit and stops in her tracks, silent. She is plainly dressed contrasting greatly to Joan

Joan   (*to herself*) Thirty years. In my worst nightmares I never thought I'd be stood here again
Di   Now there's a voice from the past
Joan   "By the pricking of my thumbs, something wicked this way comes."

Di	Macbeth. Classy. How out of character
Joan	I guess one of us has to be
Di	Touché
Joan	What? No classical retort?
Di	How's about: "In all the bars in all the world?"
Joan	So passé. So you

They contemplate each other

Di	Well, lookie here: Joan Dupré
Joan	In the flesh
Di	And here was me recalling you only provided that service for men
Joan	Just yours Diane
Di	'Dupré.' Is that still what you go by? Or did you rename several husbands back?
Joan	And with her first few phrases, she insults me like thirty years ago was thirty minutes
Di	What did you expect honey? That we kiss and play nice?
Joan	I have a long memory
Di	Ditto
Joan	You stole my part, *Diane*
Di	You stole my husband, *Joan*
Joan	Trust me dear. You won hands down with that prize
Di	Like you won pants down?
Joan	Oo. Saucer of milk, *kitty*?
Di	Oo. Modicum of decency, *baby*?

Diane walks down stage. There is distance between them; and more than just on the stage. They consider each other. Like cats. Diane sees the coffee, pours one and then turns to her.

Di	Can't beat coffee of a morning. Sets the world right
Joan	Any 'setting right' going on now do you think?
Di	Well, let me see
Joan	What? No 'bygones' calling around today?
Di	What do you think?
Joan	I guess not

They still consider each other

Di	I see you still like to dress up
Joan	I see you still like to dress down
Di	(*laughs*) Me. Ow. See? You still make me laugh
Joan	That's me. Always been a giver
Di	No shit. Well, rumour always was that you had more beaus than the string section of the New York Philharmonic
Joan	'*Sangster the Gangster*'. Still firing those bullets

Di   My, My. I haven't heard that delightful epithet in years. And what was it they used to say about you? Oh, I remember: Joan *Dupré* … as in *'do pray that she leaves your husband alone'*
Joan So, tell me Diane. How is the career? But no. You *still* don't have one, do you? Unless you count the time you spend volunteering down at the liquor store
Di   You bitch
Joan She pitches the ball and it's a home run! See I haven't lost my touch
Di   Or your aim
Joan You bet honey pie

Diane knocks back the coffee then go pours herself another

Di   Look Joan. Let's be straight. Nothing has changed. We don't like each other
Joan No shit
Di   Or ever will
Joan Your point?
Di   I need this job. I haven't had good fortune with my career like you
Joan Let you into a secret, baby. My career has had nothing to do with luck; just like getting this part won't be
Di   Whatever it is, I need this part. But we both know we can't be in it together
Joan So?
Di   You're rich
Joan So?
Di   You don't need the job or the money
Joan Well. I do now
Di   You bastard

The door at the back opens suddenly and interrupts the moment. A woman appears, again in silhouette. It is Katherine Lamar. She is also very different in appearance. Untidy, casual, every inch the homemaker who has just dropped the kids off at school

Kath Hi. I'm here for the audition, the reading? I'm sorry I'm late. It was one long drive to get here. I'm …
All   Katherine Lamar
Kath I'm sorry, who is that?

They both turn up stage and she moves towards them

Kath Joan? Diane? My god. Is that really you?

She walks to centre between them. They look at each other for a moment. The triangle still appears eternal for them. As do the cats

Kath I just can't believe it. We haven't been together, since … when were we last together? Wasn't it here, for Gymnopédies?
Di   Wow

Joan	Now there's a name I thought I would never hear again
Di	The play that never was
Kath	But it *was* that play, the last time, wasn't it? I recall that last rehearsal after they told us it was pulled. I came back into the dressing room and you had both gone. I never got the chance to even say goodbye
Joan	Nothing personal honey. Some things don't need to be savoured
Di	Like people
Kath	But, what are you both doing here?
Joan	One of us has come for an audition. The other has come to see how it's done
Di	Ignore her. Same thing as you I guess
Kath	What are the chances of the three of us, again, after all these years? Turning up back here, at this theatre, now, together?
Joan	Whatever the chances, looks like the house has paid out. Ain't we just lucky bitches

Katherine drops her bag and goes over and hugs Diane. She receives it uncomfortably, stiffly. She goes to do the same to Joan who instead, holds her hand out. Katherine instinctively 'gets the message' as she approaches her and accepts the handshake

Kath	Well, well. Thirty years and here we are
Joan	And here we are
Di	Ain't we just
Kath	Thirty years
Di	You said
Kath	Sorry. I just can't believe it
Joan	Oh, believe it honey. The joy just keeps overwhelming me in waves
Kath	But, don't you think that this is just swell?
Jo/Di	Swell?
Di	Do people still say that?
Kath	Gee, I do
Jo/Di	Gee?
Kath	Golly gosh, are you two gonna keep repeating everything I say?
Jo/Di	Golly gosh?
Joan	Christ, this is like being in a remake of a Mickey Rooney film
Kath	Please don't blaspheme
Joan	Pardon me?
Kath	Blaspheme. I don't think people should take the Lord's name in vain
Di	Jesus. Sorry. Coffee? *(She goes to get her a cup. The next line stops her in her tracks)*
Kath	That'd be just dandy
Di	Dandy?
Kath	You're doing it again
Di	Well, I'll give you something Katherine. If I don't go away from here with a part, I'll certainly leave here cursing like Mother Theresa

Kath Oh, I know. Sorry. It's my husband's family. They're old fashioned. Innocent. After all these years, they have me talking like them. They come from a different world
Di   Mars?
Kath Kansas
Joan I know it. Turn left at Venus
Kath I can't help it. Living in the middle of nowhere with just the folk from the other farms as company, you do tend to adapt to their ways
Joan Farms?
Kath U-huh. The children are worse than me
Di   Children?
Kath Six
Di   Children?
Joan On purpose?
Kath My kids are my world. Aren't yours?
Joan I don't have any
Kath Oh, I'm sorry?
Joan Sorry?
Kath Well, you know
Joan No
Kath Is it medical?
Joan Is what medical?
Kath The reason you don't have children?
Joan Oh. It's a brain condition
Kath I'm so sorry. You poor thing. Can it be treated?
Joan I don't want treatment
Kath Why?
Joan I've learned to live with it
Kath That is so brave
Joan I bear it
Kath Will it be something I've heard of?
Joan No. Apparently, it's rare
Kath What's it called?
Joan 'Common Sense'
Kath Right. I see
Di   Here honey. Have some 'swell coffee'. So, how do you come to be here?
Kath I got an email. It just invited me here, today at 11 it said, and that a production company were looking for an actress. They'd been told about me and would I come along. I haven't worked, well, since I was last here with the both of you for Gymnopédies, so I thought, why not?
Di   You haven't worked in all these years?
Kath Not in theatre. I met Horace just after the play closed, well, didn't open. Literally walked out the door here and bumped into him in the street. He knocked me over onto the sidewalk
Joan Old fashioned type

Kath	We were married six months later. Our pearl wedding next month. I moved out to Kansas and I've been tied up with family things ever since. Oh, and church
Di	Fascinating
Kath	Horace is the Minister at our church. I help out with Sunday School, Bible Class. I find it really …
Joan	Dandy?
Kath	Rewarding
Joan	Sounds it
Kath	How about you both?
Joan	Oh, you know. We've been that busy catching up on old times before you arrived, we haven't had a chance to figure anything. In fact, I think when you walked in, Diane was just about to invite me over to hers for a pyjama party so that we could, you know, braid each other's hair and toast marshmallows
Di	(*oblivious, ignoring her*) I got a call from my agent
Joan	You mean he still had your number?
Di	(*shouting, unexpected*) Why don't you get off my back!

Silence. Uncomfortable. Thirty years really were like thirty minutes

Kath	Well. This is nice. Like old times
Joan	Perfect
Di	Unforgettable
Kath	So. What about you Joan?
Joan	I got an email, I guess the same one you did, asking me to be here for a play. Nothing more. I was intrigued so I thought, 'why not?' It might be a blast
Di	And up to now, it hasn't disappointed
Joan	You bet
Di	But if you haven't worked since all those years back, how did they track you down?
Kath	You know, I never thought about it
Di	Weird
Kath	I guess. I was just flattered that someone, somewhere, remembered me
Joan	That's what Diane was hoping
Di	Cute. But why the three of us? Now, after all these years?
Kath	Perhaps they heard about Gymnopédies and thought, well, whatever the play is they're looking at now, we were right for it; you know, kept our names on file
Joan	The play that never was, remember?
Di	Ten weeks of my life I'll never get back
Joan	You got paid
Di	For rehearsing. Peanuts
Kath	I did call the number on the email, but the lady just said they were acting for a producer and it would all be explained when I got here
Joan	Well, I can't wait to hear that explanation

Silence

Di	How long they gonna keep us waiting?
Joan	Settle down honey. You're amongst old friends, remember?
Di	No shit
Kath	The place hasn't changed much that I can recall
Joan	Well, you know, once a dump
Kath	What do you mean? I loved it here. It was so welcoming, warm, y'know?
Joan	Seriously?
Di	Oh yeah. Welcoming and warm. I mustn't have been in that day
Kath	Well, it was for me. Everyone here was so friendly, so kind
Joan	Yeah. I remember that. It was Diane's day off
Kath	I remember Mr Tracey who sat at the side of the stage handing us props. And those two sisters who looked after the wardrobe, you know
Di	Gladys and Rosie
Kath	Gladys and Rosie. Of course. And what was he called? George? The lighting guy?
Joan	The everything guy. Ran this place single handed and still does. Was paid peanuts to do it
Di	Perhaps he did it for love?
Joan	Love? He did it for the money, just like we did; just like some of us still do
Kath	Oh, I don't know. Not everything is always about money: family, friends, faith, happiness and there's no place like home
Joan	Don't you forget to keep clicking those heels Dorothy. This is a world away from Kansas, and the monkeys here do more than fly
Kath	I had forgotten how cynical you were
Joan	And how gullible you still are. Still seeing the world through that rose tint? I'm a realist Katherine. It kept me in work and it will keep me there. It will keep those pay cheques rolling on in and the big bad wolf from the door
Di	Do you mean there are two?
Joan	That's right Diane. And this one doesn't give a shit about Grandma. I'm going out on the parking lot for a cigarette. Now don't you go enjoying yourselves too much whilst I'm gone. I'll even get more coffee. See Diane? I can be giving in more ways than you choose to remember
Di	Don't poison it
Joan	Well, you'll just have to try it, won't you?

She exits

Kath	What is it with you two? You tolerated each other years back but I don't ever recall it being this bad; that's some history
Di	It's how you might say, 'complicated'
Kath	No kidding
Di	We always seemed in the early days to be pitching up at the same auditions. I'd get a part; she'd get the next. It was amicable-ish. We were both competitive, wanting to succeed. But there was this one role. A new play. Every woman with a pulse was going for it. And she knew that I had the edge and more chance than her of getting that dream part
Kath	So you gave the better audition?

Di	No. I married the writer
Kath	And she didn't like that you would probably get the part?
Di	No Katherine. Joan is far more complicated than that. She couldn't accept it, even the chance of it. So, she set out to improve the odds by preparing
Kath	She took lessons?
Di	She took my husband
Kath	Lordy
Di	Indeedy
Kath	And she got the part as well?
Di	No. And it was that which screwed her up even more. I never forgave her, and she never forgave me
Kath	But she took your husband. How could you getting a part in a play be worse than that?
Di	It is in Joan's eyes. Add a dash of 'rivalry' to a large shot of 'being looked over' and it's a cocktail which is hard to swallow. So, we've spent the last thirty years like cats in the yard at midnight: hissing and circling the few times we've crossed paths
Kath	But she's done OK? I see her all the time in TV shows and read about her on stage. And you, well, you've done, OK
Di	Don't be polite Katherine. You haven't seen me because I've not been there. The truth is the truth. She's never been out of work and I've hardly been in it. I care for my mother. I get by. She's worked hard, married hard. There's a whole load of dislike, distrust, disingenuous stuff all flying around inside me when I think of Joan Dupré. She got what I wanted. She got it all. And it kills me to say it
Kath	Say what?
Di	She's good
Kath	Wow. And what happened to the wandering writer?
Di	He wandered off. Permanently. From me and her
Kath	The lure of the bright lights?
Di	The lure of a combination of things: but mostly, a woman with bigger titties, higher hems and lower morals. A dream woman for the likes of him. Whoever she was, she grabbed that bastard's attention quicker than you could say "Last Orders at the Altar"; after that, Joan had a string of marriages and I had a string of losers
Kath	Wow
Di	Please don't think I'm painting myself as a professional victim. I'm not. I know that life on this spinning rock is a series of choices and consequences. In the end, many of us – including me – have made our own choices; I'm pretty good at making my bed and lying in it. I'm just shit at deciding who to share it with. And I'm not a people-hater. One of those people who give you great reasons why you should hate men, women, the world? Well, I want to start living off good times, not relying on good memories to keep me sane. Y'know? The type you keep in a box and retreat to when you need to touch who, what you once were? We all have one. Under a bed, in a loft. Far enough away not to distract, but close enough to reassure. You can feel the warmth inside it, waiting to flood out the moment you peel back the lid. You pore over your mementoes, your keepsakes, those little pieces of your happy history, the happy you. The more I look in mine, the more I

	realise that I've been relying on my past to get me through today. Like a drug. That my past will be enough to sustain my soul and my sanity. But then, deep down, when I close the lid, I know that I don't want to be 20 again. I just want what it felt like. And every audition is another chance to find that feeling, find myself, find the old me: rediscover hope. Funny isn't it? Life? That the old you is someone younger, yet the new you is someone older?
Kath	You poor thing
Di	As a church mouse. I'm rambling. Anyways, what little money I make goes on Mom's medical bills and my bottles of JD: one keeps her alive and the other keeps me sane
Kath	(*sincerely*) Lucky that you got that volunteering job at the liquor store then
Di	That ain't a job honey, more a vocation. But look at you. Six kids. A Farm. Horace! I think by anybody's standards you've done OK
Kath	I'm happy enough
Di	Odd answer
Kath	I don't think so
Di	"Happy enough." Can you have too much happiness?
Kath	I don't think so
Di	There you go again
Kath	I've got everything I need
Di	Then I'd say you've got it all. So why bother with this crock?
Kath	Oh, you know. It was always there, back of my mind. Gnawing away at me. College gave me such big dreams about the stage. I guess those dreams never really went away because I never took them out for a spin. And when the email landed, Horace said that I should try it. "Get it out of your system" he said
Di	There you go again
Kath	You've said that already. Twice
Di	Then stop giving me reason to. It was an odd thing to say
Kath	Odd? Why?
Di	"Get it out of your system." Not exactly a glowing affirmation of support from a husband
Kath	Oh, he just wants me to do this and get home, that's all
Di	And that glow just keeps dimming honey
Kath	It's just what he wants
Di	And what do you want?
Kath	What do you mean?
Di	Exactly that. Whatever this thing is we're here for, what happens if you get it?
Kath	Oh, I won't
Di	Then why are you here?
Kath	Well, you know
Di	Not at the moment. Do you love him?
Kath	What?
Di	Do you love him?
Kath	What has that got to do with it?
Di	Everything from where I'm standing
Kath	Yes. Of Course. Yes. I do. Yes

Di	Are you telling me or convincing yourself?
Kath	What is this? Therapy?
Di	No Katherine. I think I'm asking the question you won't ask yourself
Kath	And you get all of that from simply asking me if I love my husband?
Di	No, I get all that from what the question generated. You haven't been on a stage in thirty years, it takes you, what, two days to drive here to audition for something you know nothing about, no intention of doing and it's to 'get it out of your system'?
Kath	I needed a break
Di	From him?
Kath	No. My health hasn't been good
Di	I'd have thought all that fresh air, enough energy to make six kids, you'd have been …
Kath	I had breast cancer
Di	Shit. I'm sorry. And I was rambling on about my life and you've had to deal with …
Kath	No. No need to be. It's fine, I'm fine. I've had one removed and everything seems OK now. But don't say anything to Joan. I don't want to complicate today
Di	Sure, I won't. But, how can you be so, so …
Kath	… matter of fact about it?
Di	Well, yeah
Kath	How else am I supposed to be? I'm here ain't I? There's plenty of women who aren't. I'm blessed I guess
Di	Blessed for getting cancer?
Kath	Blessed for being alive. That was another reason for coming here. Makes me focus on the things I haven't done, the corners I never turned. What have I got to lose?
Di	I don't think I could be that brave
Kath	I'm not brave. I can take you countless hospital waiting rooms and show you what 'brave' really looks like. I locked myself in my room for days on end, cried for longer. Still do now and again. For absolutely no rhyme or reason that I can see. Horace tried to help but there was nothing he could say or do that could, would, help. I wanted to be angry, to feel at least something which would give me a chance to let it out; like that was how I thought I should be. Confusion. So much confusion. Unanswered questions. Smiling doctors and nurses, who'd hold my hand and tell me I was doing well, but not saying at what. I'd spend hours just staring at my children, watching their lives happen and be overwhelmed by this empty desperation. Trying to be practical made it worse. Pretending for others. Made me realise that the world would keep on spinning without me, the kids would still carry on, grow up, smile without me. And my faith took a beating. Still does. But I keep that a secret. And despite it all, here I am. I did a lot of 'taking stock' after the surgery. You don't know what you are capable of until you decide to actually do it. But, hey. I have a lot to be thankful for. We have a fine life and great friends. I support my husband and the church and his work; we have a busy, busy life full of people and laughter
Di	But is any of it yours?
Kath	I beg your pardon?

Di   I'm not trying to be shitty and with what you've been through I don't want to offend
Kath   Go on
Di   You must have one crazy bucket list if coming here today was on it
Kath   But I had to come
Di   What for?
Kath   The audition of course
Di   And what else?
Kath   I'm not sure what you're …
Di   You've gotta admit, none of this stacks up
Kath   Who are you? J Edgar Hoover?
Di   It just doesn't make sense, that's all
Kath   What part of me are you accusing of something?
Di   I'm not
Kath   Look Diane ...

Joan enters with another coffee pot

Joan   Here we are, fresh coffee

She turns and immediately realises she has interrupted something due to the abrupt silence

Joan   Looks like the fun just isn't letting up
Kath   Do you have a cigarette Joan?
Joan   Sure, here.
Kath   I'll get a light outside
Joan   When did you take up smoking?
Kath   Just now

Katherine exits

Joan   *(slowly clapping)* Nicely done Diane. Looks like I'm not the only person who doesn't 'do' people
Di   Oh, I do people. I just don't offend all of them all of the time
Joan   Except now?
Di   For just this one afternoon, could we please tolerate each other? Is it too much to ask?

Joan pours a coffee and unexpectedly, pauses, pours a second and walks over to Diane with it. Hesitance, dumbfounded

Di   Well lookie here at us. Just need a porch, two rocking chairs and a mouth organ
Joan   Is it a 'Glory, Glory Hallelujah' moment?
Di   Don't push it

They both smile, unsure

Di	You surprise me
Joan	I surprise myself
Di	And the day is yet young
Joan	What do you think this is all about, today?
Di	Are you setting me up now?
Joan	No, just talking. You want to play at normal, well, I'm game
Di	Alright then. I'll give normality a shot with you. I have no idea. We rehearsed a play a lifetime ago that hasn't seen the light of day since, haven't spoken – civilly anyhow – in as long; one of us has never actually acted on stage and the three of us end up mysteriously here, invited to audition for, hell knows what
Joan	Do you think it's a scam?
Di	If it is, they've got a theatre fooled
Joan	Yeah, I guess. But still
Di	Weird
Joan	So we just wait here for the big reveal then?
Di	I'm more interested in someone paying me the expenses we were promised
Joan	That bad?
Di	That bad

Silence

Joan	Do you think it could ever have been different?
Di	Sorry?
Joan	Us
Di	Seriously?
Joan	Yes
Di	How exactly?
Joan	Friends

Diane walks away, picks up her handbag, takes out a small bottle of Jack Daniels and walks back to Joan with it. She pours a large slug into her own coffee and then offers it up to Joan. She hesitates and then accepts. They eye each other as Joan takes a sip. Diane knocks her coffee back in one. Joan then follows suit

Joan	Shit. Do you make a habit of this?
Di	Just on bad days
Joan	And when are they?
Di	They only usually last Monday through to Sunday. You didn't laugh
Joan	No
Di	Feeling sorry for me?
Joan	No
Di	So we're still where we were then?
Joan	Not sure

She moves away

Joan Do you remember this place from last time? I mean, really remember it?
Di I don't know. Sort of
Joan I do. Like I only stepped out of the door last night. Like I've been here every day for thirty years. You know what I mean?
Di Maybe. But I don't wear your shoes. We're different. Everything about us. Being on this stage is all that connects. Our lives bear no resemblance. When I go home every night, I stare at the apartment, at my mother and her medication, the bills and think, what if I'd just took off those thirty years ago? Left the people and the shit they create and just took off. Bought a car and found a soulmate and a sunrise to chase. So, I guess, not the same set or same play, but this final scene seems to resonate
Joan I'll let you in on a secret Diane. From where I'm stood, the only difference between me and you is that I don't have a mother any longer
Di And where's a second-hand car lot when you need it, huh?

They laugh(ish). Joan walks to her, takes the bottle from her and takes a huge gulp. Diane follows suit

Di Welcome to my world. We're navigating deep waters here
Joan And without a map
Di Where's this goin'?
Joan I have no idea. But I'm thinking it's …
Di Long overdue?
Joan Yeah
Di Does this scare you? Us? Now? Here?
Joan You bet your shit it does. And for reasons you could never understand. But I've thought of this moment though. A lot
Di Dream or nightmare?
Joan Is there any difference?
Di That's heavy
Joan That's us
Di Is this when I say that I want to apologise, but you say "No, me first" and we find those elusive bygones, put history behind us and hug?
Joan No
Di Thought not. You had me worried for a minute
Joan Why?
Di I think I'd feel cheated, y'know? After all we've said and done to each other – even today – just to walk away from it all
Joan Doesn't seem right
Di Or fair
Joan Or easy
Di I guess
Joan So what happens now?
Di We audition. We get cast, we don't. We do the piece, or we don't. We stay or we go

Joan	And we just walk away, like thirty years ago?
Di	We did it then
Joan	Could it be that simple?
Di	Sounds it when I say it out loud
Joan	We've said a lot out loud to each other for over thirty years
Di	And thought worse
Joan	Oh yeah
Di	Does that mean we have a lot in common?
Joan	Wow. And now this screws with my head. Listen. I didn't travel here today down the Road to Damascus. I don't think we can fix anything right now, even if we wanted to
Di	OK. Then I'll go into the deep water first and without that map: at some point, some time, would you want to?
Joan	Woah there Ahab, I see sharks here and not just whales; and they're beginning to circle
Di	Joan, the only sharks here are you and me. Pointy nosed, spiky toothed, bad-ass, judgemental ole sharks. Always have been. Always will be. Unless they unexpectedly swim their little ass's over to the waters where common sense, decency and respect live, nothing in shark-world is ever gonna change for us. You know that and so do I
Joan	I'm not, it's just. I can't do this now. There's stuff you don't know, couldn't. I'm not ready to do, to be, this. Not here. Especially here
Di	What does that mean?
Joan	Please. Leave it
Di	What is it? What's going on here?

Silence. Then, suddenly

Joan	You know what? I don't think this play, whatever it is, will be right for me after all
Di	Where the hell did that come from? Were we not just having a conversation?
Joan	Yes, but it's made me realise something. I'm thinking that, if their choosing actresses for whatever this play is, based on what we three *didn't* do back then, well, it might benefit from a different actress
Di	Meaning?
Joan	Not me
Di	What? Welcome to Confusedville, Arizona. Honey, I'm lost. You mean it? Seriously?
Joan	Yes Diane. I do. And for genuine reasons that I'm not going into, but which you've made me recall. You're a good actress
Di	I'll get my mother on the telephone and you can tell her
Joan	I mean it. If they are auditioning more women then you can bet your bottom dollar that the best will turn up. And you're one of the best. You need an equal. That ain't me. Not today and not here
Di	Whoa there. Wait just a minute. You don't get away with this sermon so easily. Why?

Joan	Look. This ain't church and this Jewish lady ain't lookin' for a confessional. Let's just say, it's complicated
Di	We wrote the book on complicated
Joan	Maybe. But I think I need to check out from this one
Di	You're messing with me, aren't you? Our little love-in just then was a ruse, wasn't it? Any minute you're gonna surface again, that bitch of all bitches, slam my face in the mud, throw your head back laughing and destroy me like you always do. Come on. Even I don't deserve these mind games
Joan	No games Diane. I'm tired of all this. We both need space, air, distance to do our thing without the other in our shadow. I don't need this work, but you do. And I'll tell you something else girl, neither of us can do with the shit any more
Di	I'm shocked, I'll give you that. But I'm not gonna say no to it. Thanks
Joan	I'm not doing it for your bank manager, I'm doing it for our sanity
Di	Then my therapist thanks you
Joan	You have a therapist?
Di	Don't we all?

Silence. Joan moves away

Joan	You know what? When I went out before, I stood in the kitchen getting the coffee and stared in the mirror and you know what I saw?
Di	I can't wait to hear
Joan	Nothing. Zilch. I saw the same person who looked in the same mirror on the same wall thirty years ago. The same ambition, the same determination, the same hard-faced bitch. I've added money to the bank and added nothing to me. I've existed, I haven't lived. And like you said, it's complicated
Di	Well I never noticed
Joan	I'm being serious
Di	Sorry, I'm just confused at what is going on here and, well, ...
Joan	Not used to seeing this?
Di	Not used to seeing you. Ever. I don't think I know you. I don't think you know you. You should slug back JD more often
Joan	And you know what else? What really made me feel it? Being here and then seeing Katherine. Hearing about her perfect life and her perfect family. Existing on nothing but fresh air and being happier than I could ever dream of; she's got all that I ever wanted and got it by walking out of here and falling into the arms of a stranger. Why has that always been a role for me but never my life? Why do some people get it so easy?
Di	She hasn't had it easy
Joan	Yeah, sure. I bet she can tell stories of those real bad days, y'know, when the bread didn't rise, the washing didn't dry, her kids didn't tell her enough how much they loved her
Di	She's had issues
Joan	I bet
Di	She had breast cancer
Joan	What?

Di	She's had a mastectomy
Joan	She told you that? When?
Di	Just now when you went out. I think it was in confidence
Joan	In confidence? How convenient
Di	I beg your pardon?
Joan	Convenient. Don't you think?
Di	What the hell are you taking about? She said she's only here because she wants to get acting out of her system
Joan	Really? Let's step back and look at the bigger picture here. We all get an email from, god knows who. And the three of us get invited here for an audition by an unknown producer for an unknown play. The three of us who were together for ten weeks, thirty years ago. We don't know who they want, what they're looking for. And then, conveniently, little ole' Saint Dorothy from Kansas gets you on your own with a sob story which will either give her the edge or have us walk away and leave her with it; and us walking out that door with nothing more than a warm feeling and an empty purse. Jesus. I thought I was devious. Tell reception I'm not checking out after all. No one pushes over Joan Dupré

Silence. Diane has been staring at her. Still is

Joan	What?
Di	I don't know what to say, to think
Joan	I know, she's twisted
Di	She's twisted?
Joan	Oh, I get it? Has the brutal truth of what people are capable of, kicked you in your delicate sensibilities?
Di	And here was I, for the briefest of moments, thinking we had gotten somewhere. That I had seen the genuine, albeit bat-shit crazy you. That you had …
Joan	What? Changed? I have Diane. I want to be a different person. But I'm not dumb or naïve and I'm not being taken for a fool by little Miss Perfect. Don't you see it? I've just told you I was gonna leave you with this. Her plan has worked, yet you can't see it
Di	I didn't think even you could stoop this low
Joan	Oh, come off it
Di	You think a woman, any woman, would lie about something like that?
Joan	Show me the scar and …
Di	What Doubting Thomas? That you'll believe? So, in one breath you want to forgive and forget and in the next you want to accuse and insult? Shit, I had you all wrong lady. You are one complex sonofabitch. You know what, keep this play, and whatever it brings you. I'm sure you and good fortune will remain the best of friends. I am so glad that I have stuck around today to hear this. I think I must've caught my own reflection in that same mirror today but only now, just realised what I was seeing: that my life just isn't as shit as yours
Joan	How dare you judge me
Di	You judge yourself Joan. With every drop of venom you spit, the sentence you impose on yourself gets harsher

Joan	I'm being lectured at by a washed up drunk who can't even care for her own family? You best have another long, hard stare in that magic mirror over there honey
Di	I'm so glad that today has happened. You know why?
Joan	Enlighten me
Di	Because I've realised that the thirty years of being worried by you have been wasted years. You don't frighten me any longer. In a way, I did have some perverse respect for you
Joan	And now?
Di	Pity. Just that. All along it should have been pity
Joan	*(Claps slowly)* Bravo. That was some performance. Keep that up Diane, the job's as good as yours. The pay cheque for this play will keep you and mommy dear in booze and tablets for months
Di	No. I'm not rising to this any longer. Goodbye Joan. The job's yours. Enjoy unpacking your emotional baggage for someone else

Silence. Diane goes to leave

Joan	Well, I guess I'll just have to ask her myself
Di	Who?
Joan	Little Mary Sunshine
Di	You wouldn't dare
Joan	Dare what? Find out the truth?
Di	She told me that in confidence
Joan	She lied to you in confidence
Di	The woman has survived cancer
Joan	Well if that's true, let's see if she can survive me
Di	You bastard, you wouldn't dare
Joan	You said that thirty years ago Joan. And here we are

Katherine suddenly enters, carrying a package

Kath	After five minutes of coughing, that cigarette actually felt good. I think. I'm sorry Diane. Must've got out of bed the wrong side. That drive I guess didn't help. You were right to ask me. I wish I'd have asked myself too! And I'm sorry Joan. I snapped at you when I went out. No need for that. Anyhow, you'll never guess who I've just seen? They have the same fella on the stage door that they had when we were here. How about that. He gave me this. Said the Producers left it last night. He should've left it out for us this morning with the coffee but forgot. There's a note from the producers and the scripts for us to read apparently. What's going on?
Joan	Nothing, I was just ...
Di	Joan has something to ask you, don't you Joan?
Joan	Not just now
Di	Sure you do Joan. I'm sure Katherine would love to hear it
Kath	What is it Joan?

Joan	(*Pause*) It can wait
Di	But ...
Joan	It. Can. Wait ... for now
Kath	OK. Shall I open this?
Di	Why not?
Joan	You sticking around?
Di	Like you said. For now

She does so

Kath	There's a sealed envelope in here addressed to the three of us and three scripts
Di	So what are we reading for?
Kath	Gymnopédies
Joan	Are they fucking serious? Who in their right minds dreamt this joke up?
Di	Who in their right minds kept the script?

Katherine tentatively puts her hand up and they stare at her

Kath	What?
Joan	But they pulled it. They pulled it knowing that the public – never mind the critics – were going to pan it
Kath	That was thirty years ago. Times have changed. Tastes have changed. And maybe the play has now come of age
Di	Like we have? Honey, I don't know about you but thirty years ago I would have only got naked on stage with a very, very bright light behind me. Now, the only way I'm going native is if the audience are in a different room
Kath	Horace says I should be proud of my body. It has borne us children and he says it is a testament to growing older
Di	Then honey, you get Horace from Kansas up here to bare his butt for all the world to see. Me? I'm out of here
Joan	Just let's wait a minute. We're asking the wrong questions here, worrying about the wrong things.
Kath	How do you mean?
Joan	Didn't you say there was a letter?
Kath	Sure (*She gets it*)
Joan	I say before we do anything else, we open it and read it. We still don't know why us, why now or who brought us here, so what's the harm?
Kath	Fine by me
Di	OK. Read it. After all, this can't get any worse

Katherine opens the letter and begins to read it

Kath	"My dear ladies. I trust this letter finds you all well. Thank you for accepting the mysterious invitation to attend today and I hope that, now you are here, you will read together, *Gymnopédies*." It's from Hamer.

Joan stands suddenly. Katherine continues.

"All I ask is that you read, remember and consider the possibilities of the great opportunity which I feel this piece presents. I genuinely believe the time is now right to present the play and the response – public and critical – will leave us with a great triumph. When you have read and considered, please call my office and let me know your decision. I have also left a copy of Erik Satie's LP on the record player if it helps. I look forward to seeing you all soon, and in the flesh. As ever, Johnson B Hamer."

Diane   Johnson B Hamer?!

Joan is by now breathing heavily; unexpectedly and uncharacteristically anxious, affected

Joan   I feel … I gotta … excuse me

Joan dashes out without a further word or glance

Kath   (*stands, calls to her*) Joan? Joan!

They both look at each other then slowly sit in silence, staring front. BO.

End Act 1
Interval

Act 2

Scene continues from where we left it, with Joan exiting

Kath   (*calls her*) Joan? Joan! (*then*)

They both look at each other then slowly sit in silence, staring front. Then,

Kath   What was that about?
Di   I have no idea. Joan has never liked surprises and I guess this was one too many. With Joan, it's hard to figure when the make believe disappears and reality emerges. She is an actress, remember
Kath   Is she that difficult to figure?
Di   Put it this way. She makes a Jackson Pollock painting seem obvious
Kath   Should I go after her?
Di   No. She's a big girl. She'll be back
Kath   So? Gymnopédies. Wow! What do you think?

Di	I have no idea. But Johnson B Hamer? Or as they call him in the business, 'Johnson *Bastard* Hamer.' I never thought I'd be asked to be in a play by him again. How old must he be now?
Kath	I'm not sure. He must be in his late seventies? So, he was probably, what, late forties back in the day?
Di	He's come far since then. And what was that last line in the letter? "…see you all soon - and in the flesh." Creep. I don't think the Hollywood Press Corp are sufficiently prepared *and* medicated to see my saggy ass on here
Kath	Well, I'm up for it
Di	What? Are you serious? Just like that?
Kath	Sure. It's theatre. It's what we trained for. It's a good play and I think we should at least read it through again and then decide, like he says. And there's the money
Di	So the farm girl has a business nose?
Kath	I manage
Di	Yeah, I bet you do. But Hamer. We're playing with the big boys now
Kath	I can't remember that much about him. I recall he was very overweight; constantly sweating. Is he a name now?
Di	Are you kidding me? He is THE name. Worth a fortune. Back then he was just a writer/producer, pushing his wares and hoping for a break like all of us. One of the most influential men in theatre now. He has that Midas touch. Even an average play is gold when he applies his magic. He's clearly sat on this script like a Realtor sits on a piece of land, waiting for the right time and opportunity to sell. He knows something. And he no longer needs a backer. And now I'm talking it through Katherine, this could be the big time. For all of us. He has money. A shitload
Kath	You have quickly changed your tune. So, what about baring your body on stage?
Di	I find that money in sufficient quantities can appease any fears. We all have our price Katherine. I think I just figured what mine is. This couldn't have come at a better time. This one play might set me up. For life. Get the treatment mom needs, open doors for me. Kick start my career. I have no strings and nothing to stop me. But forget me, you've gotta start thinking about that difficult conversation you need to have
Kath	Difficult conversation? About what?
Di	Not about what, but with whom. Horace? Remember him? And that little cosy Christian community you live in? This will be one helluva introduction to your hidden acting talents when they realise on opening night, that the most elaborate costume you wear at one point, is a smile
Kath	The place I live in is a very free and forward thinking community
Di	Shit. I can't wait for a sleepover
Kath	Do you think he might have arranged to see other actresses on different days? You know, to read it? Why just go with trying us out again? He could've had people here all week doing what we're doing. It can't be just us. There could be competition
Di	That's an odd thing to say? Anybody would think you were trying to put me off staying
Kath	No. I'm just being a realist
Di	I'll be sticking around. This isn't a bucket list choice for me. This is life

Kath	So, it sounds like that's you and me who are in. But what about Joan?
Di	What about her?
Kath	From that response, I get the feeling that no price is going to be high enough
Di	Trust me. This is just all part of what makes Joan tick. She's complicated and there's always been a drama just like back then. But when it comes to money, she's as ruthless as they come. And she looks good. Damn good. One thing Joan Dupré doesn't suffer from is inhibitions so with her name, reputation, looks and tight naked ass, I smell dollars. BIG dollars – for all of us
Kath	Well, the church does need money
Di	Honey, with the money we're gonna make, forget Pastor Horace, I'm thinking Bishop Horace, Pope Horace

Joan has appeared again

Joan	How about Rabbi Horace?
Kath	We're not Jewish
Joan	Honey, you go back far enough, everyone is Jewish
Di	So then Joan, looks like you're sticking around?
Joan	As I said, for now
Kath	Is everything OK Joan?
Joan	Sure. It was just that when you opened that envelope, you opened a closet and a skeleton fell out. Caught me off guard, that's all. For a second, the last thirty years hadn't happened
Di	My saggy ass wishes the same

She wanders away looking at the script, consumed in herself and the possibilities. Katherine is staring at Joan

Joan	I'm fine. Really. I'm an actress, remember?
Kath	You can't spend your whole life acting
Joan	Wanna bet? Life is an act. This is an act. We're all pretending to be something we're not; quoting good times and memories which have been embroidered for the sake of our sanity. If your own life doesn't make you happy, then you remember the life you wish you'd had. We all do it. We just don't like to admit it
Kath	Real or not, the past is no place to hide forever. At some point, the truth always catches up with you
Joan	Not if you run fast enough

Diane breaks it

Di	You know what? I'm thinking I might need to catch up with Sam, my Editor friend
Joan	That sleaze ball? I haven't heard of him in years. Does he still run that that trashy showbiz magazine?
Di	He sure does. I'm thinking he might need the low down on an exclusive on Hamer's big new hush-hush project; I see interviews, photo shoots, up-front payments

Joan   Nudity?
Kath   I don't think Horace would like to see me naked in a magazine
Di   I'd do it. Think I'd look good as a centrefold with a little something to cover my modesty
Joan   Do they make staples that big? Sorry, the truce still stands, but some opportunities can't be ignored
Kath   I thought neither of you would really be that interested in this. You know. With your history and the baggage. I thought you might want to walk away from it
Joan   And leave it all with you Katherine? Now that is an interesting thing to say right at this exact moment. Wouldn't you say so Diane? An interesting thing for Katherine to say? Why would she say something like that Diane? Why do you think?
Kath   I am here you know
Joan   Oh, I know that. But the thing is Katherine, why are you here? And why would you want us not to be?
Kath   I said why
Joan   Really? Because I'm beginning to wonder what is really going on here. Remember at college in our drama lessons Diane? They used to talk about finding what the motivation was, the true intent of a character? So, I'm just wondering, what Katherine's true intentions are in this little act she's putting on for us
Di   Joan
Kath   I'm not acting
Joan   Saint Katherine of Kansas, who's graced us with her presence and is "… just here to get things out of her system"
Kath   What is this?
Joan   Who apparently doesn't want anything but is so keen on suggesting we should walk away
Kath   Diane?
Joan   Why is that Diane? You know, that we both should just walk away from this? Leave Katherine and her magnanimous gestures, her kind heart and her issues to get on with it without us?
Kath   I don't have issues
Di   Joan, leave this alone
Joan   Hear that Diane? Katherine doesn't have any issues. Are you sure about that? Really sure? Because that's not what I hear from Diane
Kath   What have you told her?
Di   I'm sorry Katherine
Joan   The truth honey. The truth. Tell me. How is recovery going?
Kath   You told her?
Joan   Sure she told me. Me and Diane are reformed characters now ain't we Diane? We've agreed to bury the hatchet and better still, not in each other
Di   Joan, stop this
Joan   Stop what? "The truth must out" – I said that in a film once I think. And now life imitates art. Never known so much acting happen on a stage outside of rehearsals. I got to hand it to you Katherine, you keep this up after we've conveniently left, I see award nominations in this for you

Kath	But I don't want you to go
Joan	Bull – shit! You've played us like a whore on a sidewalk
Kath	I told Diane about my cancer in confidence
Joan	And it arrives! She deals her ace right on cue. You can't beat a little bit of the good ol' Big C sob story to get people on side. Do I see a bit of that 'embroidering of history' goin' on here?
Kath	(*she is getting upset*) Why are you two doing this?
Di	Katherine, this is nothing to do with me
Joan	Really? But it has everything to do with Saint Katie of Kansas, doesn't it?
Kath	Please (*she now gets more – and quickly – worked up*)
Joan	Shit, this is better than the actual play
Kath	Please stop
Joan	Listen to her Diane
Diane	Enough now
Joan	Watch the actress at work! Milk that sympathy kid
Kath	I nearly died
Joan	Sure you did honey
Kath	Stop (*she stands and paces*)
Joan	And now she works the space for added effect
Kath	Why are you doing this?
Diane	Enough!
Joan	Three actresses perfectly cast and ain't we just a pretty bunch
Kath	Stop
Joan	Lookie here at how pathetic each of us are: no life, no career … and no titty
Kath	Stop!

Katherine erupts, slaps her hard across the cheek, shaking with anger, then, incandescent

Kath	What are you? What are you?! I thought it was all just some superior act, your arrogance, your … insecurity
Joan	I …
Kath	Shut the fuck up! You despicable, inhuman, conceited … monster. I gave you every chance, all those years ago. Every chance, now, to be what I thought you really were, what I hoped you might just be. But this is you, isn't it?
Diane	Katie
Kath	Get off me! There's nothing to strip away, nothing to discover, to hope for, other than this, is there Joan? You are incapable of being what I honestly thought you might really be; nothing more than an empty, soulless caricature. There is no beauty within you, no capacity to emit the slightest, tiniest ounce of warmth, of affection, of empathy. You wretched woman. That we are even the same sex disgusts me

She moves quickly, suddenly, sits down and reads the script, leaving Joan and Diane stood, looking at each other. Diane slowly sits. Diane and Katherine are sat in silence. Forced. Unnatural. Uncomfortable to watch. Joan, remains standing, isolated, alone; then, as if nothing had happened, Katherine resets to Katie from Kansas

Kath   Diane? Will you listen to me read this? I'd like your opinion

The lights go down and the soundtrack comes in and underscores. Throughout what follows, they reset, they are rehearsing, reading. They reset as the lights fade in and out to show the passage of time. Katherine is 'speaking' a piece to audience. Diane is watching, on the book. Joan is isolated. At one point, Joan approaches Katherine, to speak, connect with her. She blanks her, purposely moves away, abandoning her. Each time, the lights go down and we reset again. Another sequence of them rehearsing, another rebuttal; another, Joan bringing coffee to them, Katherine blanking her. Then a dance, a Sarabande with Katherine and Diane which they slowly perform for a brief sequence, remembering, recalling. Intimate, personal. Lights eventually come up and Joan is sat apart with her back to them and the audience.
Finally, we find them reading their scripts. Silent for their own reasons. Then,

Kath   How did you remember that dance we had to do? The Sarabande? I remember going to the library back then which was an interesting experience as I didn't even know how to spell 'Sarabande'. The old lady in their ended up getting a book out and trying to show me how to do it!
Di   One thing I could never do at college was dance so I can tell you, it was fear that etched it in my brain, not ability; not that I can remember that much of anything now

Silence, then,

Kath   Do you really think he'll have changed much?
Di   Who?
Kath   Hamer. I would have thought he'd have come. I just wondered if we'd recognise him when he eventually does
Di   Well, I've never met a man who'd aged well. And let's face it, he wasn't exactly god's gift to woman kind. He was old enough to be my father

Joan is silent. Alone within it all

Kath   Do you remember much of this play? The words?
Di   Bizarrely, now I'm reading it, I do. What about you?
Kath   You know what? I think I could do the play now
Di   You're shitting me
Kath   Nope. I think I could probably even act it out, exactly as we rehearsed it thirty years ago
Di   Even though we never performed it? You said you kept a copy, but have you been reading it now and then?
Kath   Yeah, sometimes. But with it being the only professional part I ever got, I just kept thinking about it a lot down the years and I guess it's kept it in my mind, my memory
Di   For thirty years? So, what do you remember?
Kath   All the words
Di   And do you remember everything else?

Kath   Like?
Di   Being here. The first time. I remember some stuff, but it's all a bit hazy
Kath   It was hot. That's my overriding memory. That summer and those weeks. No let up. And humid
Di   Wasn't it though
Kath   And all there was to cool us down was a huge fan on the stage, over there
Di   You're right. It just blew hot air around the place. And the noise!
Kath   The noise! That humming, constant
Di   And that clicking it made as it pivoted around
Kath   Annoying wasn't the half of it
Di   And they had to keep turning the stage lights off because they were overheating
Kath   And the water in the cold taps were hotter than the hot!
Di   Wow. The things you do remember when you're back in a place
Kath   With the people
Di   Like time doesn't matter
Kath   Like stuff never happened
Di   Yeah. Like stuff never happened

Silence as they read, then

Kath   Do you remember going out to buy towels?
Di   Do I! To cool down; soaking them in a bucket over there. That reminds me, you owe me four dollars for them! With interest!
Kath   When I got them here, I soaked them first in cold water in that dirty sink in the scene dock
Di   And you got blue paint on one, didn't realise and wiped it all over my face

They laugh

Di   I was livid!
Kath   And I had to go out and buy soap because you were afraid what your mother would say
Di   She's 90 and I still am!

They laugh. Joan has been silent throughout. Looking, more staring at the script. Diane, rescuing,

Di   Do you remember that Joan? Joan?
Joan   (*Nothing. Still with her back to them/the audience. Then, as if answering a different question, detached*) I'm sorry
Di   I said, do you remember that Joan?
Joan   I heard. I'm sorry
Kath   (*as if she is not there, interrupting*) And what was that old guy called?
Joan   I said I'm …
Kath   Joe! It was Joe. Every stage door had a Joe didn't they? He was the stereotype, the first one you saw going in and the last one when you left at the end of the night. Painfully helpful, always happy

303

Joan (*quietly, turning*) I'm sorry
Kath He always appeared warm, caring. Always wanted to know about you, how you really were; a listener. The epitome of caring. But the sad thing was, I don't think I really knew about him. He was so concerned how I was all of the time.
Joan I once asked him ...
Kath (*talking over her, still ignoring her*) I gabbled away telling him about my life and never took the time to discover his, to listen. But ain't that just life? People come into your life, and out. You think you know them, and them you. But we're all strangers Diane. The saddest part is that you're best keeping some people as strangers. Sad, like I said. That you have to be like that. Be something less than you are to protect who you are from ending up like them: damaged goods, cheap, shop soiled trash

Silence. They are reading, then, from nowhere, in her own world, a past moment, recollection

Joan Joe came from a family of people who were involved in theatre. Went all the way back to the vaudeville Showboats on the Mississippi when they got big again after the Civil War. The folk on it, it was actually the ingenue in the troop, taught his great granddaddy how to dance when he was eighteen and it just got passed down through the men in the family. He told me about his great granddaddy's family who had been cotton slaves and were freed by their Master because one of them saved his life in a boat accident on the river. Joe was the youngest one of fifteen children. Was so proud of every single one of his siblings. Had miniatures of them mounted in a frame which he kept hidden away in his tiny office because he didn't want to seem too proud as people might think it was a sign of arrogance. The kindest and gentlest man I ever knew. Such a ...
Kath Diane, can we look at page 49. My monologue. I'm sure I recall it but let's see anyhow
Joan His greatest regret was that he never had children. Never had a small piece of himself to share himself with
Kath Gosh I forgot how many words were in this one piece. And there's that dance we need to try and nail
Joan I'd forgotten how fascinated I was by him. He adored mint tea and sponge cake. I'd never known anybody who drank mint tea. An ordinary man who had lived through so much, but had no possessions, no wealth but his family. He said they made him the richest man alive; had so much to be grateful for, to be thankful for
Kath Did he never do a rewrite on this do you think? I'm sure they always do one, don't they? I'll be destroyed if I've kept all those words in my head for thirty years and they end up being changed
Joan So many deep lines on his face. Like grooves on a record. I used to think if I could run my fingers across them, I would feel, hear the story of his life, of what was and what it had done for him, made him
Kath So many words
Joan I was the only one who went to his funeral
Kath (*she erupts*) Well, praise the Lord! Diane, I was wrong, she <u>did</u> do one decent thing in her life. Wash away those iniquities Lord, cleanse her of those sins; the girl is a

	living saint. And here was me thinking she was lost. Well, the lost lamb was never lost Diane. She just hid it so well under that wolf outfit. Make way world for the repentant sinner, because everything is just dandy now
Di	Kathy …
Kath	Oh, I'm sorry Diane. I'm sorry. Listen to me. Looks like you ended up stuck with the bad Christian. The one who didn't sign up to the 'turn the other cheek' part. Well you know what Diane? I think I'm preferring the 'eye for an eye part' after all. Got a real taste for it now I know how good it makes you feel. Can't wait to get back and teach the Sunday School gang what I've picked up from my trip back to civilisation. Being a bitch makes you rich: being nice comes at a price.
Joan	I'm sorry
Kath	(*snapping*) So am I sister. So am I. Sorry that I put up with all your shit back then. Sorry I have children. Sorry that I'm happy. Sorry that my cancer offends you. Sorry that I'm answering back after all these years. Sorry that Jesus no longer wants me for a sunbeam. I'd like to say you're getting on my titties, but that would be hard, wouldn't it Joan?

Silence. Diane is visibly shocked. Joan puts her head down and starts to quietly cry. There is an air of even Katherine shocking herself. Diane stands but does not know what to do, how to respond.

Kath	Leave her
Di	I can't
Kath	Why not?
Di	Because this isn't you
Kath	Well maybe it is

Diane moves behind Joan, uncomfortably. Puts a hand on her shoulder as a token gesture. Joan without warning, turns in her seat and hugs her, crying

Joan	I'm sorry, I'm sorry …

*Katherine has been watching, initially unmoved, she can't maintain it
She moves slowly towards them, Joan breaks and rushes to her*

Joan	I'm sorry. Forgive me. Please forgive me. I don't know why I said that, why I'm like this
Kath	It's OK. I know, I know. So am I Joan. So am I. None of us are who we were any longer. And I guess that we're never what we think we are either. If we're lucky, our past lights the way. Other times, it casts shadows which, no matter what, are always just behind you. Tapping you on the shoulder. Daring you to turn around and face them. Travelling back to here, and now, opens up memories of, memories of what could have been, lives that should've been; friendships which might've been. Memories of a life that, now I'm here, I'm not sure that I want to remember the truth of. Looks like the grass isn't always greener. It's just another field

Joan eventually breaks and Diane sits her down. Silence, then

Di   Well. Golly gosh, ain't we all just dandy

They all laugh and then all three stand and hug as one

Kath Look girls. It's been thirty years. Can we just start afresh? Cut the history, the histrionics and the getting even and just do this? See if it's what we want? If it's right for all of us; and I do mean, all of us? And if not, then we walk out that door, together
Di   You want us to stick around? Really?
Kath Of course I do. I want all of us to stick around. We started with this together and if it's happening, we eventually perform it, finish it together. Let's just do this, we're here now. Can we just try and be normal and cut the crap?
Di   Did you just use a profanity?
Kath No, I used an idiom

They laugh

Di   You OK Joan?
Joan OK. Katherine?
Kath I'm fine. Really, I'm fine
Joan If it's any consolation Diane, he was lousy in bed
Di   And here was me thinking he was a slow learner. And anyhow, that part you didn't get? Was awful. You were better without it
Joan Wow. Should we all just sing Kumbaya now?
Kath I can start it
Jo/Di No!

Diane and Katherine laugh

Kath OK girls. Therapy over. We all love each other
Di   Let's not be too overly optimistic here
Kath Let's drop it now
Di   I know. Start at the top. Should we do that opening scene? Read it through and just see what we think?
Kath Sure Diane
Di   "Sure Diane?" You mean, if you'd slapped her thirty years ago, we could all have been lifelong friends?
Kath Don't push it

Diane and Katherine laugh. Silence as they begin to read, prepare themselves. Joan has been silent. Katherine stands as if about to speak, then

Joan Girls, before we do any more with this, before we get into this. You asked me something earlier
Di   What?

306

Joan	You asked me if I remember
Di	Sure I did, but haven't we had enough for now? I know what. Let's get us a coffee and go outside, get a cigarette and some fresh, polluted, downtown air in our lungs before we get into this
Kath	Good idea
Joan	I'd rather get an answer to the question
Kath	Will it do us any good?
Joan	It will me. There are sharks circling me here that you could never know about Diane. And they've been doing it for thirty years
Di	Shit. Then shoot

Joan stands, moves away

Joan	What do you remember? Both of you, of when we were here in the early days, rehearsing
Di	Like what?
Joan	Just that
Di	Not much if I'm honest. Bits
Joan	What's the thing that sticks in your mind most of all?
Kath	Well, just like I said, the heat, the fan, some of the people, all of the words!
Di	Mine's not great, my memory. It was thirty years ago
Kath	Was it something particular you wanted us to remember, to talk about?
Joan	I'm not sure. This is crazy
Di	No it's not. You wanna talk, we talk
Kath	What is it Joan?
Di	Is something the matter?

Silence

Di	Joan?
Joan	I don't know when, how to start
Kath	Just start
Joan	OK. Do you remember all the chats we had about clothes?
Di	Clothes? Are you serious? I can't recall what I wore yesterday
Kath	You mean your clothes?
Di	Gosh, your clothes, of course. Those outfits you always used to wear. You must remember Katherine?
Kath	How could I forget?! The Queen of Colour Coordination
Di	Wasn't she though
Kath	A set of accoutrements for every outfit
Joan	I need to know if you remember one in particular, one you both fell in love with and I only wore the once. A particular day. You both never stopped talking about it and Katherine said it was too nice to rehearse in and Diane said …
Di	The red one
Kath	White polka dots
Di	Fitted at the waist

307

Kath	And those matching patent shoes and bag
Di	And the sunglasses that were to die for
Kath	Golly, I had forgotten all about that. You sure knew how to dress
Di	Still does
Joan	So I need you to remember more. More than you ever have before
Di	Sure Joan
Kath	Yeah, if you need us to
Di	Like what?
Joan	OK. It was the only time I ever wore it here for a rehearsal for the play. It was during that really hot spell and that morning, I was late. I burst through those doors and
Di	Bagels!
Kath	Of course!
Di	You came in with coffee and bagels
Kath	And we laughed at you because we'd asked for doughnuts. Always doughnuts in the morning
Di	And you joked that we had to humour you because
K/B	… "what else would a good Jewish girl bring for breakfast"

The two of them laugh. Joan isn't

Di	Can you believe that? Fancy after all the years …
Joan	What else do you remember of that moment?
Kath	Well, I'm not sure I …
Joan	Think!
Di	Joan, what is this, what's the matter?
Joan	I'm sorry. I just need you to help me. It's important. Just trust me
Kath	OK. Well. OK, so we admired your outfit and, and I joked about it having to be in other sizes because it wouldn't fit me
Di	Yeah. And the rehearsal. There was something that happened that day, that moment. An arrival.
Kath	Hamer. You don't mean … was that the morning he …?
Di	Oh dear Lord. I'd forgotten. How could I, we, have forgotten that
Kath	What?
Di	Kathy, the final dance?
Kath	The dance? THE dance! We were that busy earlier remembering the steps, I plain forgot
Di	He stood for ages looking at you in that dress, remember? And that was when he first mentioned it, told us of that painting he had seen by an artist; his inspiration for the play
Joan	It was by, Chavannes? It was entitled
All	'Young Girls by the Seaside.'
Kath	Of course. He used odd words, that he was, what, "Intoxicated" by the setting and the idea of using a dance?
Di	The Sarabande
Joan	The Sarabande. Yes. But the one at the end

Di	He said that it spoke to him, mesmerised him. An image which projected to him, a story of three young women, meeting by chance on a beach. Sharing a moment, an afternoon together. The basis for the play
Joan	A simple picnic
Kath	Discovering each other
Joan	Discovering themselves
Kath	In one brief afternoon
Di	And then, leaving never to meet again
Joan	He envisioned the centre piece of the stage being a rock pool in which the women bathed by the sea, and danced
Kath	A woman came along that afternoon and taught us the moves. But he wanted it to be
Di	More
Joan	Different
Di	Yes. Less formal than the original dance. He wanted us to be dancing together
Kath	To unheard music. Music only we could hear in our minds
Joan	And not just naked
Kath	My gosh. How could this have slipped my mind? I recalled the naked but not, y'know, not …
Di	And how
Kath	Eating food, drinking wine
Di	They would be dancing with each other and with the idea of themselves and their, and their, how did he describe it?
Joan	'Promiscuity'
Di	Yeah. He'd spent hours locked in that office, thinking of how to present a relationship between three women, strangers, of where it might go, what it could be
Kath	What was it he said he wanted it to be? "Something secret"
Di	"Sensual"
Joan	"Forbidden"
Kath	He'd read about it in the library. And a suggestion that the painting had inspired the music of
Joan	Satie
Kath	When he listened to his music, he said that he wrote, solid, for 48 hours
Di	He dramatised the painting and the music – the music we would dance to
Kath	Gymnopédies was born
Di	And it was then, that day, that moment and staring at your dress, he told us what he wanted
Kath	Not just a nude scene
Joan	It was what he wanted us to do
Kath	To each other
Di	Shit. That bit had completely gone out of my head. I crapped myself when he said it
Kath	What would my friends say?
Di	What would my mother say?
Joan	But what happened then, that afternoon? Think

Kath	He made us stand and walk around him. 'Round and around. Like we were in a fashion show
Di	In a cattle show
Kath	And he stared at us. Through us. Orchestrated us. Sat on a chair in the middle, smiling and staring, undressing us with his gaze
Di	I felt like I was already naked
Kath	"That's it girls. "Round and 'round for Mr Hamer."
Di	The heat, the smell of his sweat
Kath	I can still see it; smell it. The sweat was pouring down his face and he was wiping it with a dirty handkerchief that he held to his mouth as he watched us
Di	And he kept asking you to twirl around
Kath	"Keep twirling Joanie.
K/D	"Keep twirling for Daddy"
Di	Made me feel, feel
Kath	Dirty
Joan	Then what, please, then what
Di	I can't remember
Joan	Try
Di	I'm not sure
Kath	You just tell us
Joan	No. You need to remember this
Kath	Well, whatever we then did that afternoon, I recall it was only Diane and me on here
Di	Of course. Your monologue. That was it. Page 49. We ran through it for what seemed like ages. We rehearsed together and Joan, Joan was …
Kath	Wasn't here
Di	Joan was …
Kath	Joan was …
Di	You rehearsed with him
Kath	Alone
Di	In there

And the world stops for a moment. Joan slumps to her chair

Joan	You remember. Thank God. I've been going insane. All these years. Thought it was all in my mind. Thirty years of anger, fear, disgust. But it wasn't me. It was never me

Katherine moves away; a dawning

Kath	Dear Lord
Di	Shit
Kath	How could I, we, have forgotten?
Di	Where has that memory been?
Joan	It's been with me: hiding in the past

Silence, then,

Kath   Diane. The record player. Remember? Remember? You put the record on

Diane goes to it, lifts the lid and plays the LP: Gymnopédies. Joan puts her hands to her face

Di   We heard you in the office, through the closed door. We heard it Katherine
Kath   "Please don't Mr Hamer. Please stop"
Di   "Relax baby. Dance for Daddy"
Kath   God forgive me
Joan   No. Not now. Not yet. You need to remember it all. Everything. You need to say it. I need to hear this
Kath   I picked up the script, tried to reconcile the words, the sounds from the office from the fragments of sentences in the script; I thought you were rehearsing
Di   No. No, we didn't. That's what we want to remember. That's the history that we rewrote. That we've all embroidered. That was no rehearsal and I knew it. We knew it. I remember Joan
Kath   And I walked back over to the record player and ...

Kath moves to it, turns the volume up full. Joan turns away. After a moment,

Joan   Turn it off!

Diane does so. Silence

Kath   I turned it up. Cleaned, blanked out the sounds of the real world, filtered it all with the music; drowned out you. Drowned out the truth. I remember Joan. I remember too. What did we do Diane?
Di   Nothing, that's what. That's why we didn't remember. Because we did nothing
Kath   I made an excuse that I needed a cigarette – but I didn't smoke. I flew out of that door, got on a bus and just rode around the city for hours. I got back and, well. Eventually, I went to Kansas. I convinced myself it was to get married, be happy. But it was also to forget all of you; to forget my silence. New memories for old
Di   I went to a bar. Drank, then drank some more. I woke up the following morning in my apartment. And I've been drinking ever since. You hid in another world, I hid in a bottle
Joan   And I hid in the past
Kath   When we all came back the following morning
Di   We never spoke of it
Kath   Not a word
Di   Not ever
Kath   We ran away Joan
Di   We left you and we ran away
Kath   And worse of all. We pretended like nothing had happened
Di   For the next few weeks he put us through hell
Kath   I went home every night and cried

Di	You never said
Kath	How could I?
Di	How could any of us? And then that final rehearsal before we opened, when we performed for the backers
Kath	Shit
Di	And that was the end of the play, the end of us
Kath	They all stormed out
Di	And they kept shouting, screaming
Kath	"Shame on you Hamer"
Di	"Shame on you all"
Kath	"What would your families say?"
Di	"Not in my theatre"
Kath	"Not in my name"
Di	"Not with my money"
Kath	And they dropped him
Di	And he dropped us
Kath	And remember? He blamed it on asking for help from the wrong backers, from the 'Conservative Dollar'
Di	The office. What actually happened Joan?
Kath	In there
Joan	What happened? Really? Seriously? Did Kansas change you that much? You've got six kids. Use your imagination honey. I've lived with this for thirty years; what he did and what he said. "Ever mention a word of this Miss Dupré and the next job, only job you will ever have is as a cocktail waitress; a cocktail joke shared by studio executives for years to come"
Kath	He said that?
Joan	He's been saying it in my mind every day ever since. And that music. That goddamn music
Kath	Why didn't you ever …
Joan	Say? Tell? Speak up?
Kath	Well, yes
Joan	And what was I going to say Katherine? One of the most powerful men in the theatre abused me. This was our first job, our big break
Kath	It was wrong
Joan	It was life. It still is
Di	Then what the hell are we doing back here? Why has he brought us here again?
Joan	Power. Control. This isn't a stage, it's a prison. His pages are the cells and his words are the bars. They've kept me trapped in this place for years. Screwed me and screwed up my life. He controlled us then and he's still doing it now. We were nothing to him. Back then, I was a digression an afterthought; I was merely his 'in parenthesis.' When does art and real life begin and end girls? Well? Because I'm struggling to figure at the moment
Di	Then let's just get the hell out of here. Screw him and his play
Kath	Is that it then? We just walk away?
Di	Well honey, we've done it once before
Kath	But we need to fix this. Fix him. We can't let him get away with it

Di   With what? Who do we tell? Who will be interested? We're a commodity to men like him. It would all be shown as our fault
Kath But we were young
Di   We were stupid
Joan We were innocent
Kath What about the police?
Joan The police? Are you serious? He owns the cops. They work overtime doing security at his events. Can you imagine even trying to tell them? "Well officer, we were nearly in a play thirty years ago about a painting and a poem and some music. And in one part we took our clothes off and boy, did that cause a shitload of trouble because of what we had to do to each other on stage. And by the way, the guy who wrote it and directed it is a rapist."

Silence

Kath It's not fair
Di   It's life
Joan It's this business. That's it I guess
Di   That's it? So, what the hell have I been through just now with you, huh? A therapy session? Do you feel better now? That you've made us all remember and that we all now feel shit? Look. I'm sorry. I'm sorry that I didn't go through that door and punch the sonofabitch. I'm sorry that I hid inside a bottle of booze. I'm sorry that I was a coward
Kath Stop it!
Di   What?
Kath Stop being sorry! We've done nothing wrong. There is only one person in all of this who has done wrong and walking away, blaming ourselves means, well it means
Joan It means that he's still making us
Kath And worse, we're accepting that blame, that guilt. You know what? What the hell, let's get even
Di   Screw him and screw his play?
Kath Too right
Di   You really have changed in a couple of hours sister
Joan Well, I'm game – but not for revenge. This is so much more. And I'll tell you something for nothing: if we do this right, it'll last a lot longer and be a damn sight more satisfying than a statement to the cops
Di   How?
Joan Katherine's right. We don't walk away. We don't take the blame
Di   So what do we do?
Joan He knows. He's always known. In his smug little world, he thinks this has been forgotten and we'll play nice with him again. Let him carry on being Mr Big with impunity. But leaving here leaves an unanswered question. So, I say let that bastard start living with it, the doubt; of who or what might come knocking on his door after we leave. Losing your reputation takes a moment. The fear of it can last a lifetime

Di   So come on, how?
Joan   I think this has to be done by me

She goes to the phone and dials a call. They follow her

Joan   Hello is that Mr Hamer's office? Hello, this is Joan Dupré. I, we, have a brief message for Mr Hamer. Could you let him know that Katherine Lamar, Diane Sangster and I have met as per his generous invitation and considered very carefully the offer to reprieve his piece, Gymnopédies. We have re-read it, rehearsed it this afternoon. Tell him not to bother coming over as we have come to the conclusion …
Di   He can stick it up his ass!
Joan   … that having considered the proposition with great care …
Kath   He can go fuck himself!
Joan   … we would like to politely decline his offer to audition. Why? Well, where do I start? The play is like him: vacuous, unimaginative, banal, obsequious, controlling, sleazy…
Di   A crock of shit!
Joan   … over-inflated, pretentious, insipid …
Kath   A crock of shit!
Di   I said that already
Joan   How do I spell vacuous? Well, honey, as my two best friends in the whole world have just so beautifully commented, and I quote, he can stick it up his ass and then …
Kath   Go fuck himself!
Joan   Yes, I think that sums it up. Have a nice day

Joan puts the phone down. She and Katherine burst out laughing and hug each other. Joan stands and then hugs her

Kath   Boy, that felt good
Joan   "Go fuck himself?" I need to take up religion
Kath   Did I really say those things?
Joan   You sure did sister
Kath   I've never used language like that in my life before
Joan   You're a natural. How did it feel?
Kath   Fucking amazing
Joan   Well, at least you weren't too profane
Kath   Indeed. But I'm sure that Our Lord must have used at least some profanities with all that he faced. After all, King Herod was one sonofabitch
Joan   Honey, from now on, your bible study classes will be the toast of Kansas
Di   *(who has been quiet)* But it still all counts for nothing
Kath   Why?
Di   He's still got away with it. With everything. What he did to us. Where's the real consequence? I can guarantee that he is still doing this to the women he meets, controls. We've just come out the other side, but that's all. I bet there are plenty

314

	more suffering and will again in the future. From him and men like him. From their culture of contempt, control. Of treating women like commodities, playthings to use how they like. And what if all we're doing is creating a space for three more women, three more victims – and a haven for men like Hamer
Kath	God you're right

Silence, then

Joan	Oh my dear ladies. Hearing us all taking the blame, being sorry. Remember who and what we are. All good plays resolve themselves, don't they? Well, I think there is another scene which needs to be written to achieve just that. And I have an idea how and by whom
Kath	Meaning?
Joan	I think it is time for the final blocking in this rehearsal and this last scene can only be devised and performed by one actress
Kath	Who?
Joan	Why my dear, enter stage left, the greatest character actress I have ever known - Sangster the Gangster *(who had moved away and is mid-gulp from her bottle of JD)*
Di	Me? How?
Joan	This part was written for you sweetie
Di	I don't get it
Joan	Well, let's see. Perhaps, a certain actress considering a certain part in a certain play might need that overdue catch up with a certain Editor of a certain sleezy magazine
Kath	*(cottoning on)* And do you think, maybe, innocently mention certain things to him?
Joan	<u>Allude</u> to certain things
Kath	Oh yeah. And might he want to take a certain actress to a restaurant?
Joan	An <u>expensive</u> restaurant
Kath	An <u>exclusive</u> restaurant
Di	Oh my darlings, my sweet innocents; the best friends a girl never knew she had. Step aside and watch a true artiste at work

She composes herself, cat-walks, works it to the table. They cheer, whoop, whistle as she milks the moment. She composes herself, sits, picks up the phone and dials a number. She owns every second and word of this. Mae West lives again.

Di	Good afternoon. Could you put me through to the Editor please? Why thank you my child. Sam? Is that you? My goodness you sound so young, so virile. I thought it was an intern. This is, oh how sweet, you recognise my voice. What's that, how could you forget it after all these years? Oh, stop it you old rogue. Well yes, I am in town, how did you guess? And would you believe, hearing your voice, it's now slipped my mind why I called you. You were always able to blind a girl. Am I available for dinner? You still don't stand on occasion I see. Oh, you are a sweet man. I couldn't. What, you insist? Well, if you're insisting. Just let me check my schedule *(puts her hand over the phone and yawns)* You know, I am free this evening. And it would be so nice to see you again. And maybe, we could catch up

on what's been going on in theatre-world and you could fill me in on the gossip. What gossip? You know, the stories and stuff that has been going on. But you know everything, surely? You have the ear of the industry *and* the grapevine. Y'know, what they choose to talk about. What they choose to ignore. The things they want to hide to protect their little expensive applecart from tipping over. Yes, it is an intriguing metaphor. What did I mean by it? Well, as I've always said "Only wine will tell." Be fun to chat it over though, don't you think? Chew the fat. The people we know. What's in the headlines. What's kept out of them. The angle from an award winning, leading industry professional and highly respected journalist of the people, like you. What? You never won an award? Well, personally, I am appalled. But who knows? That elusive exclusive may be just around the corner. Poised to 'put right' that wrong. To set the record straight. Separate fact from fiction. And as a <u>very</u> dear friend of mine said to me only today "When does art and real life begin and end", huh? Yes. A little chat and dinner will be divine. I'm so lucky to have a friend like you. A trusted confidante. Who appreciates what 'off the record' means. Friends who respect discretion. If needed. Seven at San Rocco's? That is just too expensive you disgraceful, wicked, delightful man. Oh well if I must. Seven it is. Goodbye you dear thing.

She hangs up. They stare at her

Di   What?
Joan   How the hell have you been out of work?
Kath   What will you say to him at dinner?
Di   Not a word
Kath   I don't get it
Joan   She doesn't need to. And he won't ask either. Directly, anyhow
Kath   I still don't get it. Surely, you're gonna tell him everything? Isn't that what this was all about?
Di   The last thing a gossip magazine is interested in is facts
Joan   And the only thing that this Editor is interested in is sales
Di   This business employs a very capable, professional executioner. And his name is 'Doubt.' In the entertainment world, worse than being accused, is being alluded to; and the possibilities it presents are endless and priceless
Joan   I'd bet my last dollar he's got his reporters ringing everybody in their address books right now trying to figure out your riddles and metaphors and an hour after your dinner date, it'll go viral
Kath   So. We're gonna hit him in the only place that matters
Di   His wallet?
Kath   His reputation
Joan   Praise the Lord, the girl has seen the light!
Kath   Why didn't we do this thirty years ago?
Joan   Because it was thirty years ago, and <u>we</u> needed to figure it out
Di   Figure ourselves out
Kath   I guess so. But I'll tell you something. It's been worth the wait
Di   Absolutely

Kath	To find the friends I never knew I had
Joan	And girls? Remember. This isn't about revenge. We're bigger than that. This is bigger than us. We've shone a light and maybe, others will now be caught in it and hopefully...
Kath	Know they're not alone?
Joan	Have the strength, the courage to speak about it. That's how it begins
Di	Come on. There's a bottle of bourbon out there with our names on
Kath	But I haven't drunk alcohol in years!
Di	I hear your pain sister, but a man called Saint Jack of Daniels will help you though it
Kath	Hallefuckinlujah!
Joan	Man, Horace is gonna be in for one hell of a shock when Dorothy gets back to Kansas
Di	Hold on one minute. I've got dinner at seven and ... shit. What am I going to wear?
Joan	Settle down girls. I have plenty of bourbon at my apartment on Seventh. While we're at it, we'll raid my wardrobe and pick an outfit for Cinderella to go meet her Prince Charming. You know. Something elasticated

They all laugh. Diane suddenly stops, realising

Di	Did you just bury that hatchet in me again?
Joan	I guess I tickled you with it. A sort of, side-ways compliment
Di	I think I preferred it when we hated each other

They laugh

Kath	Is this for real?
Joan	It sure is. And it's just the beginning; for us and for, well, who knows?
Di	Then, let's start how we mean to go on. I'm not turning this into an AA meeting – and Lord knows I stood at the door of so many over the years, too scared to go in – but I want to make a pledge to myself, here and now. I don't want this job to be a job that just pays bills any longer. I don't want to exist. I want to live. I want to be able to add more to me, as an actress and as a woman. I'm gonna start caring about self; not be put off by the demons which weren't of my making and the people who conjured them up. I'm not gonna sit around waiting to find a box of memories to remind me what happiness felt like. Standing here, now, I can taste life. I can almost touch it. For the first time in a long time, it's time to make memories worth having ... and make those consequences good ones. Fuck everyone else's baggage. And fuck mine

Katherine and Joan start clapping

Joan	Go girl!
Kath	Diane for President!
Di	Be careful what you wish for. What about you Katherine?
Kath	Seriously?

Di   Why not? You've driven a long way to get here. Travelled further in one afternoon than I bet you have in years. So, why not take them hopes out for a spin?

Kath OK. Well. You know, I think pretty much the same - but without the need for the profanities. I think I realise now that 'wife' and 'career' can be two chapters of the same book. It's down to me to write the chapters that come next – and the ending. I've allowed myself to be dogged by comfort and ease and making everyone else happy – and fooling myself into believing that's what made me happy. Y'know? Whether it's revolution or evolution, I think today hasn't so much, taught me about what I've missed, but made me figure what I could have, and could be. So, thank you. I've found my friends again … and found me in the past hiding with them

Joan and Di start clapping

Kath   And what about you Joan?
Joan   I'm good
Di   Is that it? We pour out our souls and all we get is "I'm good"?!
Kath   I think with what you've been through, it's enough. It's a beginning
Di   You're dead right. And beginnings are good too
Kath   What will happen with Gymnopédies now do you think?

Joan picks up her copy and drops it in the bin.

Joan   Beginnings

The other two follow suit

Di/Ka Beginnings

They get their coats and go to leave

Kath   Was that true what you said on the 'phone earlier?
Joan   What?
Kath   That we are your two best friends in the whole world?
Joan   Well, you know, I was just saying that … well, what I was trying to get across was
Di   Yes, we are. This evil, this demon, this succubus, this scourge on humanity and all that is decent is, it would appear, actually a nice person
Joan   Let's just keep this one between us girls. I have a professional reputation to protect
Di   You have a reputation to protect? Now this is a conversation for more than one bottle
Kath   Don't start. Come on, let's go find Saint Jack of Daniels

Diane and Katherine get ready to leave

Di   And Saint Jack has so many friends who I'm gonna love introducing you to
Kath   Really?
Di   Oh yeah. Saint Bacardi, Saint Vodka, Saint Gin of Tonic …

Kath   Saints? But shouldn't they perform miracles?
Di   Honey, in my world, every day of my fucking life

They are laughing as they exit

Joan   Wait for me out front girls, I forgot my bag

She walks down stage and picks up it up. As she then goes to leave, she speaks to herself

Joan   Dammit. The lights

As she hits her mark c/s, the lighting suddenly changes to the harsh plot from the beginning.

Joan   George? Are you still up there? So. You've been there all along, huh?

She bursts out laughing and then trails off

Joan   I'll tell you kid, that was one complimentary ticket you've had today; from the best seat in the house. Funny. That you were here for this. After all, on this stage, I guess you have shone a light on the best and worst examples of my career. Strange. I don't see any shadows in this place any longer. Anywhere any longer. Who'd have thought this morning that a single Fresnel could throw a light that could reach back thirty years? Thirty years of shadows, of history, fear, self-loathing. All dispelled by the glare of truth, honesty, friendship; hope. That's one powerful light. Y'know what I've learnt today George? Jerry Herman got the lyric wrong. Time doesn't heal everything. Time isn't a healer. Time is just somewhere we wait until we find the strength to heal ourselves. And that's good. I'm good. But I think there's one more thing I need to do – for me – before I leave.

She walks across to the record player

Joan   George, if you wouldn't mind?

The general lighting goes out and the light from the wings comes up and catches her cross lit. She kicks off her shoes starts the record player. It crackles and the music begins again. Slowly, subtly, she performs part of the dance from the play. At the conclusion, the sound of a needle clicking as the track comes to an end. She bows towards the light. She looks around, picks up her shoes and goes to leave. But instead, addresses the stage, her surroundings, as she recalls a line of dialogue: the woman alone with her epiphany. Proud, confident, resolved, at ease; the consummate actress.

Joan*   "If we shadows have offended,
Think but this, and all is mended:
That you have but slumber'd here
While these visions did appear.
And this weak and idle theme,
No more yielding but a dream,
Gentles do not reprehend.

If you pardon, we will mend."

(* from Puck's soliloquy in 'A Midsummer Night's Dream')

Again, goes to leave. Stops and without turning back,

We <u>will</u> mend.

Lights snap to black. A loud crack of a main power switch being knocked off.

THE END

'Ancient & Modern'
(One act monologue)

Synopsis
Stella is now of an age whereby she realises she is from a different age. Opinionated, unforgiving, exacting, even gently and unwittingly xenophobic. She is a woman of routines, of rituals, of expectations, of standards. Her likes and dislikes have become entrenched and easily supported by evidence of life experience which she relies upon to self-justify. Because of this she is a watcher of people, an observer, an interpreter of life and how she thinks people should live theirs; equally, she is a reflector, painfully sensitive and whilst not searching for something, has chosen to avoid the painful truth which is the most painful truth of all: the home truth. Until now. And now, on Christmas Eve, forced by circumstances, surrounded by recollections and shadows and conditioned by expectations, the extremes of her ancient and modern worlds gently collide with humour, sincerity and a wholly unexpected personal revelation.

Cast
1f, 'Stella.'
Playing age of 65+
'Katherine' at the end is a pre-recorded voice played as part of the final SFX.

STELLA is seated in a wing-back armchair.
To her left, set back is a 'standard lamp' which is switched on. In front of the armchair is a low coffee table with a box of Christmas cards and a 'house' telephone.
To her right is a 'side table' with various photographs/picture frames which are made of silver, all of varying sizes and which are angled towards her.
The whole of her small playing area is situated on a large patterned rug.
She is dressed in smart, outdoor wear including an overcoat and hat, clutching her handbag and is ready to leave to attend a Christmas Eve service at church.
She has a mobile phone in her hand which she alternates between looking at and looking towards a window which is stage right of her. SFX of a Christmas carol which fades out as the lights come up.
A silence, then

Stella   'Speedy Taxi Cabs.' Well. Not at this precise moment in time they're not. The text message says that " ... Stuart, your driver, is on route to you. Click on the link to check his progress." I don't think I need to "click on a link" to know he's not bloody here. I can see he's not bloody here. I wouldn't be bloody here if he was bloody here, because I'd be at bloody church by now. And now they've got me bloody swearing. On Christmas Eve of all days. And worst still, it's Sunday.
And if 'Stuart' thinks he's getting a tip, he is very much mistaken. The only tip he'll get from me is to go ask Father Christmas for a new watch. I don't know. It didn't take Mary and Joseph this long to get to Bethlehem. And the roads in Galilee two thousand years ago were dreadful apparently. Well, according to that programme on BBC4 about The Holy Land you know, last week. They were

horrendous! And Dan Snow is always very accurate in his historical assessments. Not one to exaggerate. I'm surprised anybody in Galilee got anywhere on time for an appointment. They'd probably have to set off the day before just to get to the Dentist. If you don't turn up at my Dentists on time, three strikes and you're out. I bet you'd know about it if you missed your appointment in Galilee. You'd probably be crucified.
Or worse.

She looks at her watch, then the phone and then the window again

I know I'm early for church. Three hours early to be precise. But this is the very reason. And to get a decent seat. Packed it will be as it's the Christmas Eve Service. And as always is the case, it'll be full of people who arrive late and go home early. Dreadful. They've nowhere to sit or stand so the adorn the place like it's a bus station. No respect. I've always needed an aisle seat. Preferably, on the second row, left hand side so I have a very clear and uninterrupted view of the pulpit and the Vicar. Always. And woe betide if anybody is sat in my place in my pew. Forty-four years I've sat there. Had to wait for Mrs Ormiston to die before I could sit there. It has a plaque on the seat of the pew dedicated to the memory of her husband. Mind you, you have to be careful as the nails holding it on stand a little bit too proud. I ruined a good overcoat on them. I told the last Vicar, but he wasn't the slightest bit interested. I said to him, I said "That pew is lethal. Any gyration of one's bottom on Mr Ormiston's memory and you get a pull on your posterior." But I don't expect to have a problem getting to sit in my seat tonight. People know that I have Mrs Ormiston's place. Even the 'once a year-ers.' People sometimes call me the "New Mrs Ormiston" as a consequence. Not that I look in any way like her. Rather bland she was. Not much clue about style. Nothing ever matched. Brown, black and green; stripes and spots. The girls at church would say: "Here she comes. Mrs Bon Marche Pick and Mix." Funny woman. Could be very insulting. Once, quite vocal in her disparagement of M&S lingerie. Unthinkable. Yes. People know that Stella Blackford has always sat on Mrs Ormiston's husband. I did think of asking the Vicar if I could add my name to the plaque, you know, engraved underneath what was already there. Like they do with headstones. An appropriate acknowledgement of my service and standing within the parish I thought. Deserved. But not even my name would fit. If she'd not included all that guff about "loving husband, devoted father and conscientious Justice of the Peace" the Church Warden said I could have been squeezed in at the bottom. But I said to him, I said "I refuse to be underneath Mr Ormiston." On top of him, well, that's a wholly different matter. He said it would work if the lettering was smaller. I think not. I said to him, I said "I refuse to be memorialised in an inferior sized font." And then - the cheek he says "I think you would look very refined in a Times New Roman" and I replied "How dare you. How old do you think I am?" I did ask if he could just take the plaque off, turn it over and engrave my name on the blank side, you know, ensuring that he screwed me quite firmly on the pew. But the Church Warden - who clearly knows better than me - said it "wasn't appropriate." As if Mr or Mrs Ormiston are going to complain. Nobody's bothered. She only had a daughter and she's a Baptist. Very accommodating I find them. Baptists. Not sure why. Just a very agreeable congregation on the whole. Very smiley.

Silence, then

I thought the Vicar might have called around this week after I made it known at the WI that I'd been under the weather. But no. Didn't even telephone. Shocking really. Not like the old days. Almost lived here, the last one. Or was that the one before? I forget now. They all merge into one when they all look the same. You know. Black with a bit of white. Like Magpies but not as annoying. Anyhow, there's no way the current Vicar would call without telephoning first. And not on a day when I haven't polished the house plants. He knows that's a Monday task and it's more than his life is worth for him to see me with a dusty Aspidistra. Callers are received, expected or otherwise, Tuesday through until Thursday; 10am until 3pm. People know my exacting expectations. It's a well-known fact in the advanced baking fraternity that Victoria Sponge will not keep past Thursday. Nothing worse than your seeping juices creating a soggy bottom.

I had expected that Katherine, my goddaughter, would have called to arrange her annual visitation by now. But I do appreciate that she is very busy with her career. All over the world. High-power meetings, lectures, 'symposiums', whatever they are; just posh conferences with a lot of fresh fruit probably. She has her own website. That can't be cheap. She's on a good screw. And the cars she drives. I thought the Prime Minister was arriving last Christmas. Big long black thing pulls up outside. Out she floats in a very smart business suit. 'Givenchy' or 'Gucci' or something else expensive beginning with 'G.' Breezes in and drapes herself on the couch. "Do tell me you have Earl Grey and a slice of your Victoria for me Aunty Stell'." That's what she calls me. "Aunty Stell'." Nobody else would dream of doing that but I do allow her to as she lives in the Home Counties. She offered to make tea one time. Oh dear Lord. "You? Make tea? You don't infuse the teabag you either baptise it or drown it" I said. She uses a teaspoon like a weapon of torture. I took one taste and said "Never again. That is not a cup of tea dear. It tastes more of fluoride than Earl Grey." She brought some Green Tea last time she came around. Green Tea. I ask you. Took one sip. Pond water. Even a Garibaldi did nothing to help it.

Silence, then

I'm amazed she's amounted to anything considering how she was as a child. Very reserved. Never spoke. We never heard her mention a boyfriend. Or any friends really. Not that we ever thought she was, you know, one of, well, a "you know what." I haven't a problem with that type of thing. But she does know a lot of women with short hair who don't eat meat. Less said. Anyhow, they're tripping over themselves now to be with her. 'The Jet Set.' Such a gang she goes skiing with every season to 'Courchevel' or 'Courmayeur' or somewhere else dreadfully exclusive beginning with 'C.' Always sends me a card and photographs of everywhere she travels to. How the other half live. Thoughtful to a fault. She's worked hard. She deserves it. And the jewellery! Goodness me. Dripping off her like Midas or Croesus or some other rich foreigner.

But proper relationships? Oh, I don't know. She hasn't had what I would call a proper friend since infant school. And that was a doll. I said to her last Christmas, I said "Do you remember? You would never come out of the Wendy House unless everyone had left the nursery first?" It was like hostage training for toddlers. It took her mother ages to convince the teacher that there was nothing to worry about. But she blossomed as she got older and eventually became attractive. Such an ugly child until she was 12. I think it was helped by her head growing to accommodate her front teeth. Apparently, very intelligent people are like that. Physically awkward when younger. Look at Princess Anne. But such a loner then. Dreadful. Her mother tried. Got her in the Brownies. A fortnight she lasted. A fortnight. She said she didn't like wearing a uniform. Her mother said on the second weekend she let her go camping. She stripped naked and peed on Brown Owls foot. I remember her coming around here afterwards, flouncing onto the couch and saying "Aunty Stell, Brown Owl is a fascist." I said "Katherine, Brown Owl is the Vicar." She's says to me "So. The black uniform is no coincidence then?" Even at that age, very historically and culturally aware.

Silence, then

I don't particularly like going to church in my own parish any longer. Changed so much. Not the same. God isn't what he used to be. Anyhow, I have no option though. I do it for them actually. They'd be lost without me. I give it and them a sense of occasion, dignity, class. Chavs, tramps and swingers the lot of them. And that's just the clergy. Give me a good old-fashioned High Church service any day of the week. That's why I often nip over the border to Saint Margaret's now and again. They always give you your collections worth. They make sinning worthwhile. Not like our lot. The 'born again' bunch who've invaded us. Their sense of contrition is to clap your sins away. And why they hold their hands in the air for so long whilst singing hymns - which I've never heard before - is beyond me. Like a workshop for trainee Popes. I'm telling you, if it's not in Ancient and Modern, it should not be in the service. But that's life really, isn't it? You know. Extremes. Opposites. One thing or the other. Ancient and Modern. Have or have not. Young or old. You're in or your out. Remembered or ... Being alive or, or ...

A beat. Distant, then

Anyhow, our parish isn't a bit like High Church in the one next door. Their afterproceedings always have an air of quality about them. Decent cakes, nice china, clean lace. Ours is a war zone. Smells of stale biscuits and pets. Do you know, the last Edwardian themed 'Bric a Brac Bonanza' they had at St Margaret's' could have easily been graced by dear Fiona Bruce and Antiques Roadshow. And ours? Ours had a 'jumble sale'. Dear lord. It was like a remake of Lord of the Flies filmed in Primark. People with dyed clothes, dyed hair and fair number who looked like they had actually died. So many body piercings, you could have weighed them in for scrap. And enough plot ideas for a new Tolkien trilogy. And those types always seem to be crying for some reason. Like being in an episode of that TV programme they always used to broadcast on Christmas Day. You know. The one when the BBC made Christmas nice for sad people. And they spend all the time waving their hands at their faces whilst they're talking. Quite bizarre. And did you ever notice that none of them ever have proper a handkerchief? Always an old piece of kitchen roll stuck up their sleeve. They can't talk. They all shout. It's like I've always said. Emotional impropriety is the disease of the working classes. But I rise above it. As I say many a time down at the WI, "Girls, try to be like me. Understanding and accepting."

She stands suddenly, to the window

I can hear an engine. Could it be 'Speedy Stuart' perchance, or is he still stuck at the lights near the Red Sea? Oh, it's next door's daughter on her annual guilt trip. Look at all those presents. They can't all be for her mother, surely? Oh that's far too extravagant. A woman her age will never get the use out of all of them. They've seen me. "Hello love. Yes and you. I'm fine thank you for asking." Dreadful woman. And those children. Pretentious brood. She's given them the most ridiculous names. The poor things will spend their lives spelling them out. Shania, Cindy-Lou and Tinker-bell. Should have set them up for life with proper names. Edna, Edith and Ethel would have been more than adequate. Oh Lord, she's coming up the path. "Oh that's so kind of you. Just leave it on the step and I'll come and get it. You get inside you'll catch your death." She's brought me something. A gift.

She exits and returns carrying a cactus which she places disdainfully on the table.

Well. What might one say? Not a poinsettia then. Dreadful. I suppose I'll have to put it here next to my collection of very expensive family heirlooms. My precious pictures of my relatives, my ancestors; my heritage. Bit insulting but it can't be helped. Oh and the price is still on it. Tacky. Well, at least it proves that she bought it and that it's not an unwanted gift. I think that's appalling when people do that.

Y'know, when someone goes to the trouble as to be so thoughtful and buy you a small something and then, folk insult the sentiment of the season by disposing of it by giving it away. Anyhow, I suppose it'll be fine as a raffle prize at the WI.

She sits

Well. If 'Speedy Stuart' isn't here soon, I may as well hang on at church for Easter Sunday. I suppose I should expect delays on this of all nights. Busy. Parties. Dinners. People with places to go. Seeing family. Friends. Family. Some of my girlfriends are inundated with invitations. Others drown in expectation. I could walk really. To church. It's not that far and the snow has melted so the paths are clear. Always been a strong walker. "A formidable constitution" the Practice nurse said when I went in for my flu jab. Mr Waters who lives next door always comments on how much walking I do. He doesn't miss a thing. He's an obsessive ornithologist you see, so he's painfully observant even without the advantage of his Swiss binoculars. We have a lot of nature in our gardens you see. Teeming. And he's always there in the window. Obsessive. He said to me once "If you're lucky enough to have Great Tits, nothing better than watching them resting on some fat balls." So, when Joan from the WI - that's Joan M, not Joan F - called a while ago with a rather small jar of her home-made chutney, he was out like a shot. I was talking to him in the side garden by the pergola as she arrived, and he was just commenting on the cut of my clematis when he said to her "I see you've driven here" and she said "Yes" and he says, "Stella" I don't mind him being over familiar despite the fact we've only been neighbours for 18 years, "Stella" he says, "Stella walks everywhere. Very virile woman is Stella." I knew that he meant 'agile.' But at my age, there's very little difference. Well, it soon got around the WI that the young man next door - he's only 78 - referred to me as 'virile.' Since then, well, the number of them that now come to me for marital advice is quite extraordinary. Make your toes curl some of the problems that they have. It's too big, it's too small, I'm not wearing that, I'm not doing that. I'm allergic to rubber. I had to Google 'Gimp Mask.' Well' it doesn't feature in my Betterware catalogue. But then it all took on a life of its own when Barbara T started talking to me. Apparently, she started having affairs because he couldn't, you know, 'perform'. Fascinating. So she started having ... 'parties.' Very popular. At one point, she was advertising them with a card she put in the Co-op window. Purely by accident, she told the milkman about them. Oh yes. It was all because of him that it really took off. She was having a chat with him one morning about her problems with her husband which went a bit too far and, well, she invited him in. He soon became a regular thing once she found out it wasn't just his milk that was sterilised. Anyhow, one thing led to another and he brought a friend. Who brought his wife. Dressing up. Sex games. Toys. Bondage. Body Paint. Problem was, ends up that the neighbours could hear everything they got up to through the walls. Their antics. She was mortified when she found out. So, they moved house. She vowed never to live in a block of houses again because of her shame. So they bought an end terrace. She said that it's the nearest her husband ever got to having a proper semi. But it wasn't long before they started their parties again. Once a week. The new neighbours heard all the goings-on. They nicknamed her husband 'Mr Meringue'. "Vigorously whip until stiff." But she knows I'm the soul of discretion. That I'd never breathe a word of it. Only yesterday, my hairdresser commented on my discretion when I was telling her about Mrs Warburton's husband's 'dysfunction.'

A beat, then

The world has changed so much. "People, have changed." We say that, hear it so much, don't we? But have I changed? I don't know. Have lives always been so colourful, so varied, but it's only now that we dare to talk about them? Is it just that I never realised? Did I never have a life that was, well, a life? Perhaps I'm odd and it's the rest of the world that's 'normal' - whatever that means. "It wasn't like that in my day." That's another one. Well. Perhaps it was. Perhaps the 'olden days' happened without me being there. What have I missed? Was I missed? Missed! Oh, I'll forget my head next. Christmas cards.

There is a box on the table from which she recovers several cards in sealed envelopes.

Here we are. Can't be wasting money on stamps. Joan F. Joan M. Mary from the Bridge Club. Doris from the Bridge Club. Phyllis from the Bridge Club. Oh. All at the Bridge Club. The Vicar, the Warden, the Organist. Not forgetting my special catch-all card for anybody I've missed: "To the Congregation." May as well check my list whilst I'm waiting. Now. I've had one from 'All at the Bridge Club.' That's all well and good, but I still expect one back from everyone I've sent one to otherwise, next year, they're out. Since Katherine has shown me 'spreadsheets' - get me - and colour coded, I have transferred my extensive Christmas card list along with my weekly cycle of dusting and cleaning onto them. She bought me a laptop last Christmas. I Googled it, naturally, after she had left. Quite expensive actually when I checked the make and model. Anyhow, I do monitor who returns my cards quite fastidiously. Kathleen added a formula to my spreadsheet so that on the 26th of December, unless I've received a card back, it automatically deletes the person from my list for the following year. Ingenious really. And then, if anybody gets touchy about not having received one of my handcrafted creations, which this year are entitled 'A Bethlehem Tableau', I can just blame Excel. Took me ages to make them. A feat of engineering and origami. When you open this years card, the baby Jesus tastefully rises up out of the manger and this little gadget stuck inside does farmyard animal sounds. I tell people one of them is a camel noise, but my friends don't know what one sounds like so it's purely academic. Mr Hussain at the corner shop loved his and the 'camel' sounds. Asked me if it was a Bactrian or a Dromedary and I said, "No. Definitely a Christian."

She opens the card which came with the cactus.

Oh dear. Glitter. Dreadful. 'Happy X-Mas.' Appalling. At least she has had the good taste to send a card with a nativity scene. Oh, apart from the fact that Mary and Joseph are bears. Oh and the baby Jesus is a kitten. Lovely. Puts a new spin on the birth of our Lord and Saviour. Surprised they've not got him scratching on the stable door to go out. Wonder if there's another scene with The Three Kings bearing gifts of Gold, Frankincense and Whiskers.

She takes her mobile phone out and dials a number

Still engaged. Looks like 'Speedy Taxi Cabs' are just as timely in picking the bloody phone up as they are picking me up. There I go again. Have to pray for myself when I eventually get there. Assisted of course by 'Stuart of Galilee' and his trusty chariot.

Silence, then

I hope it is our own Vicar tonight and not that new one they're trying out on us. Dreadful. I had to speak to the new one last Sunday. Jason he's called. I mean. Who names a Vicar 'Jason?' Dear Lord, can he drone on. I told him "If the rest of the world can deliver sound-bytes, you should try God-bytes." You know. Give us a parable if you must but make the point and move on; two minutes for each and no more. I mean, we don't need preaching to, do we? And make it humorous. If he's going to pick a letter from the Thessalonians, pick an interesting one. In a book that big, they must have written at least one. You know, lighten the mood with one about, well, where they'd been on holiday perhaps. Doesn't have to be theologically factual. If they'd been that desperate about being believed when they wrote The Bible, they'd have set the Great Flood somewhere genuinely wet like Manchester. I said to him that maybe, he could pretend to read postcards from famous biblical figures. "Lovely weather, great scenery. Wildlife a bit dangerous. Not much fresh fruit. Brought too many outfits. Speak soon, Adam & Eve." Or, "Done loads of walking. Can't believe how many people from back home are here. Eventually found the beach. The tides are a bit lethal though. Love, Moses." Nobody minds a bit of poetic licence do they? I mean, we're not stupid. But if it helps foreigners understand the power of God, then yes, tell them he made the world in seven days. But don't expect English people to believe that included the Cotswolds. I could see it in his face. Grateful. And I gave him some feedback concerning his delivery the week before that as well. Told him he could do with being a little less staid. I mean. There's only so much in a church service one can absorb about God. He needs to make it interesting. It's nearly Christmas for god's sake. "Saviour this, salvation that." I said to him, I said "If we're stuck with you at Christmas it will somewhat take the fun out of the day when all you talk about is Jesus." I said to him, "It would be a very different Christmas Service if we were in a Synagogue." Very happy, joyous people. The Jews. But then again, they do like a drink. Like the French but with a personality. I said to him, I said, "Give them a different perspective." I gave him a number of suggestions to link the Christmas Story into; practical, modern-day issues. He could talk about Mary and Joseph in the stable. And The Three Kings arriving bearing gifts. And then move on to, well, the modern age and the need to bring useful gifts when one visits friends. I mean, myrrh? Where's the message in that? It's as odd as turning up with a cactus. Then there's the impact of unexpected visitors when one is making dinner. And who in the right mind would invite a shepherd to anything? Hardly interesting people. You only need to watch Springwatch on the BBC to realise that they're all dull as dish water. And poor Mary is trying to prepare dinner - in a stable - and uninvited guests turn up with their pets. Who owns a camel for god's sake? Then shepherds arriving in work clothes. Treading sand in everywhere. Three Kings completely overdressed for the occasion in silk, jewellery and hats? I said to him, "Only gays go out dressed like that." But Jesus was very inclusive apparently. And then the final straw. The poor woman having to endure such a distasteful discussion over dinner. Just think. It's Christmas Day. Our Lord and Saviour has just been born and she has the insult of three camp royals and a boring farmer turning up telling all and sundry that she's had someone else's baby. And then the bit they conveniently gloss over in the book: she was a married woman! Like the Springer Show with tinsel. I could tell in his expression he was most grateful. As I walked away, I heard him say "Bless you." Something like that. But he is difficult to understand is Jason. It's not his fault though. He's from Bradford and his mother never had his adenoids done.

A beat, then

Got a new jigsaw for tomorrow. For after The Queen and before the 1976 Morecambe and Wise Christmas Special. 500 pieces. 'A Festive Robin Redbreast.' I'll give it away in the New Year. To the local sheltered accommodation. You know. Help the old folk. Got my Harvey's Bristol Cream to have with it. My, that bottle has lasted. Another few Christmases still left in it yet. Fourteen years now since I bought it. Never goes off. One small schooner to mark the day is more than enough for me. But it isn't my first choice. Warninks Advocaat. Nectar of the Gods. Haven't seen Warninks Advocaat in Waitrose for years. I know you can still buy it. But I refuse to shop around and go into a shop specifically to buy alcohol. Gives altogether the wrong impression of one. We always used to have Blue Nun with dinner. Every Christmas since 1973. And Mateus Rose in reserve. It's been the foundation of Christmas in this house. Highly recommended still by the girls at the WI. And according to Woman's Realm, very popular down the years with celebrities. They all drank it you know: The Beatles,

Rod Stewart, David Bowie, Mr Presley. Father said, "If it's good enough for the nouveau riche, I'm sure it'll be good enough for us.

We hear the sound of a car horn. She prepares herself as she speaks

It appears that my chariot awaits. Another Christmas Eve calls. Another service of Lessons and Carols. Nothing better. Tradition. A blessed relief from the modern world. Best make sure the answering machine is on. Just in case. Don't want to miss a call, a message from, well, anybody.

She does so

Now then. Bag, keys, purse, scarf, mobile phone, cards, mints, gloves, handkerchief, Dentafix ...

Car horn sounds again

Well, well Stuart. We are an impatient little Galilean. Welcome to my world. "Once more unto the breach." Time to enter my festive time machine. Next stop, Bethlehem.

She turns off the standard lamp. BO. SFX of a Christmas carol as she exits and which covers her change.
Stella re-enters during BO, now in a dressing gown and slippers and with a mug and sits. SFX of a Christmas carol which fades out as the lights come up.

If heaven doesn't have Ovaltine then I will refuse to remain there. That and Bovril. Oh, and Seville Marmalade. Thin cut, naturally. But not Marmite. Food of Satan that stuff. And anchovies? Perverts. Well. Must check the TV guide and then set my alarm before bed. Not much of a sleep tonight. Alistair Sim is on at 6am in Scrooge. I don't know what I'll do if they ever miss putting it on. No matter what the time of the day or night. I'm there. The start of the Festive Season for me. Every year. You know, the proper version from 1951. Gloomy, but now and again, uplifting. Bit like Rochdale. I said to Mary P at the WI "I'm not surprised that people died early in those days. The sanitation was dreadful. And they all appeared to have bad teeth." And she says "Yes, but they're just actors Stella." And I said, "But that's the point Mary. Actors have dreadful dental health. Have you never watched Eastenders?" I always feel that Black and White films have something about them. Traditional. Appropriate. A remembrance of ones roots. Of who we are. Of what was. Of good times and who we shared them with. I taped the wrong one last year. Dreadful. Settled down to watch it and was faced with 'A Muppet Christmas Carol.' Ruined the whole day for me. Pigs in blankets accompanied by Miss Piggy was an altogether unholy juxtaposition. That being said, I can't face large meals these days. The volume. All too rich for an older palate. Just enough gravy to bring the turkey to life is more than adequate. It doesn't need to be swimming to an island of mashed potato for refuge. Festive Fowl is not everyone's fancy, but it's a must for me. And thank the Lord for Aunty Bessie and her croquettes is what I say. And her Yorkshires. Not worth buying fresh. Can't abide waste. I plate one up for Katherine. Just in case. Just in case, you know, she's passing on her way to Switzerland. But she never is. I never waste it. Saves cooking on Boxing Day. Oh reminds me, I haven't checked.

She picks up the phone handset and looks at it.

No. Looks like I haven't missed any calls, messages. I always check. You know. For calls. Every half hour sometimes. Looks like there haven't been any. Not that I trust these things. Number of times Katherine says she has called and it hasn't connected. I've queried it with the GPO or whatever they call themselves these days. Had them out so many times. They swear blind the line is in order. Never been the same since they became a PLC. I had shares in them for a while but I got rid. I refuse to profit out of the inefficiency of others.

A beat, then

Packed in church tonight as I anticipated. When I got there, the only spare seat in the place was mine. And the one next to it. But it was lovely. So festive. The manger, all the candles, the tree, tastefully decorated; the organ, the carols, the lessons. The smell of food from 'The Rose of Lahore' restaurant across the road. And then, faintly in the background, drifting in on the night air, the sound of the folk in 'The Bull's Head' joining in with Cliff Richard and 'Mistletoe and Wine.' But my word, some of the congregation. No shame. Christmas jumpers - in church. Flashing reindeers, elf hats. And I saw less lycra when we went to see the musical Cats; and the makeup was on a par. There was a young woman sat next to me who had lips like a guppy fish. I swear, if you'd licked her face you could have stuck her on a window. Children with toys – electronic ones which made noises. Buzz Lightyear accompanied us down the aisle for communion. People using their mobile telephones. And a young girl did a selfie with the Vicar – during the service. But I guess we should just be thankful they were there. All with their families. Their loved ones. Some probably didn't know why they went, but somehow, felt the need to; compelled by tradition perhaps. A need to respect something in their past, honouring the memory and ritual of relatives. Funny. Doing something others of always done, just because of that and yet, clearly finding a comfort, a completeness in a thing that they don't entirely understand or believe in. And after all I thought about it, said about him, complained about him, you know, Jason the young Vicar. He was ... amazing. Because as he spoke I noticed something. Silence. Worshippers who'd spent a lifetime there, whispering and chatting in the background throughout, were quiet too. Not because they were indoctrinated to be. I guess, because they found a connection with a man young enough to be their grandchild, talking about the past with the wisdom of today. The regulars came out of some odd obligation but were silent because they wanted to be. I looked at them, looked around. And you know, they weren't just quiet because of the moment, the service. They were listening. His words, his manner, his age. The language he used was theirs. Not of some dusty old book. He spoke of real things, real problems, real hopes - their hopes. My hopes. He took the Bethlehem of my imagination and all that it stood for and placed it in front of me. He painted a picture in that church which was as real as I am now. And I didn't feel old, I didn't feel young, ancient or modern. I felt something more. I felt I belonged. I felt alive. I wasn't alone. And when I got back here, I sat on my own in the dark. Never done that before. And it dawned on me that I still didn't feel on my own. Something about that evening had got me thinking. Still am. About me, all of this. I sat here like I do, for ages, staring at these bloody photographs. All these years I told myself, fooled myself that I'd bought them because I liked antique silver frames. That I was a 'collector'. Rubbish. I hadn't bought any of them for the frames. It was the old pictures in them. Other peoples pictures. That's the real reason I bought them. I'd bought someone else's memories, relatives, because I didn't have any of my own. I didn't know these people. But I told people who came to visit that they were my family. I sat here many a night and made up lives for them, names for them. Put me in them. I'd spent a lifetime listening to my girlfriends as they pored over their own pictures, their own memories. I was embarrassed. And it all came to a head, tonight. In a beautiful way. Surrounded by people making real memories. Jason, making those lives, those new memories mean so much for them all. You know, when I left church tonight, young Jason came up to me and thanked me for taking the time to tell him what I thought. He thanked me. And then he hugged me. And it suddenly made me think. I couldn't remember the last time someone had done that. Is this what making memories actually feels like? And I turned around and Mr Waters from next door was stood there. And he smiled and said "Stella, may I hug you?" And I looked at him and said "No, bugger off." And I laughed like I can't remember that I have done in years. And so did he. So did Jason. Then he told me I shouldn't swear in church. So I told him to bugger off. And we all laughed again. Jason said "I won't forget tonight in a hurry. You've made it special for me." Me. And I said "Neither will I. Ditto." He brought me home. Mr Waters. Well, he shared my taxi and Stuart brought us home. And going by the cost of the return trip, he again went via bloody Galilee. I've asked Mr Waters if he's got any copies of photos I can have that he's taken of the birds in the garden. He said he's got lots so I've asked him to pick the best, his favourite ones. You see, I want to replace all of these pictures. About time I think. Pictures of my life, my world.

And I've telephoned and left a message for Katherine too. Asked her to send me a photo of herself. Said I've got just the frame for it now.

She stands, preparing to leave.

Best get to bed. Scrooge is on telly in five hours. Just enough time I think to get to Christmas Day service afterwards. I never miss. Even though I've been the night before. It's my routine, not church, but what I do afterwards. You see, I make a point of walking around the graveyard. Do it every Sunday. I've discovered fifty-two graves there that have no headstone, or writing you can read any longer that says anything about them. There's even one with just a home-made cross. Looks like it's been made with old metal tubing from thrown out furniture. No name. It would be easy to think it's insulting. I found it quite touching. The effort. That someone would want to do that. Fifty-two forgotten lives. That's one for every Sunday for me to visit. Just for a moment. To let them, you know, know that, well, you know. Like being in church really. Same people in the same places. I've been sat in that place, in that pew, longer than some of those people have been buried. And I'm none the better off for it either. And that suddenly hit me last night at church. And then I got home and sat here, staring at photos of more dead people that I don't know. So I've decided. It's time to 'find time' to spend with the living; make genuine memories. "Never too late." That's what Jason said last night. "Never too late to find your story in the Christmas story - and make it happen." Stuart says he's working today so he'll come and get me for the 11 o'clock service. I told him to get me at 10.50am and not a minute sooner. He looked at me like I'd gone mad. He said "But that's only 10 minutes before kick off! What's up with you?" I said "Nothing. We'll be there on time. Traffic around Galilee is usually fine in late morning." I laughed and he looked at me right queer he did. He asked me if I was feeling OK. Cheeky bugger. I said I felt great. Champion, actually. And I gave him £20 for Christmas and told him to put it towards a new watch. And I've also decided that when I get to church this morning, I'll sit somewhere else. Let someone else park themselves on Mr Ormiston's memory. I've kept him warm for forty-four years. Maybe give the back pew a go. I might even stand yet. Give that famed constitution a run for its money. Bloody rebel. And on the way home, I'm going to get Stuart to stop off and I'll call in and see Mr Hussain at the corner shop. I'll extend the greetings of the season to him, then take advantage of him being open on Christmas Day - and to check if he sells Warninks Advocaat. Sole of discretion Mr Hussain. Just like ... well, perhaps not. And I think I'll take the opportunity to stock up on Blue Nun ... now as I've decided I'm going to invite the neighbours in for New Year's Eve. Get me. You never know. Might even put a card in the Co-op window...

She goes to leave but then pauses, returns and picks up the cactus. She considers it, smiles then drops it unceremoniously in the bin directly below where she is stood.
She goes to leave. SFX: we hear the telephone ring. She turns and hesitates, listens.
The answering machine clicks on. We then hear the answering machine greeting and then and we hear a voice. Katherine.

Kath "Hello Aunty Stell. Are you there? Thought you'd still be up. Sorry. We do keep missing each other don't we? And sorry to call back so late. Got your message. And surprise! I'll see you tomorrow afternoon, for Christmas dinner, if the invitation still stands? Get me. I sound like Ebenezer Scrooge speaking to his nephew, don't I? I thought that instead of me bringing a picture, let's take some shall we? I'm sure we can do better than those old ones you have. I know this is unexpected, but it's just, I'm just … Aunty Stell', I'm just fed up of being on my own. I miss you. I'm sorry. Can't say this on here, now. But, just to say, I love you. I really do. Sorry I don't say it enough. Or ever. Anyhow, see you later. Oh, and please, PLEASE say you'll give me an update on Mr Meringue!"

She bursts out laughing. Stella joins in.
Slow fade to black.
SFX of a Christmas carol which also covers the bow.

THE END